"The Sailing of the Griffon"
Wall Panel in the Historical Building, Buffalo.
Painted by H. T. Koerner

AN OLD FRONTIER OF FRANCE

Volume I

An Old Frontier of France

The Niagara Region and Adjacent Lakes under French Control

Volume I

—ILLUSTRATED—

Frank H. Severance

Author of *Old Trails on the Niagara Frontier*,
Studies of the Niagara Frontier,
The Story of Joncaire, etc.

HERITAGE BOOKS
2009

HERITAGE BOOKS
AN IMPRINT OF HERITAGE BOOKS, INC.

Books, CDs, and more—Worldwide

For our listing of thousands of titles see our website
at
www.HeritageBooks.com

A Facsimile Reprint
Published 2015 by
HERITAGE BOOKS, INC.
Publishing Division
5810 Ruatan Street
Berwyn Heights, Md. 20740

Copyright © 1917 Frank H. Severance

— Publisher's Notice —
In reprints such as this, it is often not possible to remove blemishes from the original. We feel the contents of this book warrant its reissue despite these blemishes and hope you will agree and read it with pleasure.

International Standard Book Numbers
Paperbound: 978-0-7884-4947-5
Clothbound: 978-0-7884-8180-2

TO
ANDREW DICKSON WHITE
EDUCATOR, DIPLOMAT

MY TEACHER IN YOUTH, MY
FRIEND THROUGH MANY YEARS

These volumes are inscribed as a testimonial
of personal regard and in appreciation
of his distinguished services to
his fellow men

ACKNOWLEDGMENT

Acknowledgment is due, for help received, to many persons. My inquiries led me to the Canadian Archives when that office was under the charge of the late Douglas Brymner, whose cordial assistance and friendly interest in my undertaking it is pleasant to recall. I am no less under obligations to the present Dominion Archivist, Dr. A. C. Doughty, and to his librarian, Miss Magdalen Casey. In Paris, in that ancient portion of the Louvre known as the *Pavillon du Flores*, which the Government has used in recent years as a depository of maps and documents, the late M. Victor Tantet first showed to me the original drawings of Chaussegros de Léry the elder, according to which Fort Niagara was built; and since I might not carry off the originals, assisted me in procuring copies of these and other useful material. It was a friend, resident at Grenoble, who searched the parish records of St. Hugues church in that old town to discover the baptismal name of Captain François Pouchot. The Rev. J. J. Aboulin of St. Ann's church, Detroit, has obligingly supplied data from the records of that ancient parish, relating to Chabert-Joncaire and family. From Mrs. John P. Bronson of Monroe, Mich., a great-great-granddaughter of Chabert-Joncaire, and from Mr. F. H. Maisonville, Detroit, also of the same family, I have received welcome assistance. Mr. Lewis Johnstone of Tompkinsville, N. Y., very kindly supplied the letters written from Niagara during and after the siege by the Rev. John Ogilvie. Mr. Benjamin Sulte of Ottawa, to whom I have more than once appealed, with unstinted courtesy and patience has given me the benefit of his great knowledge of French Canadian families and institutions. I have also been the beneficiary of many librarians and officers of institutions; among others Mr. George Parker Winship, late of the Carter Brown library, Providence, R. I.; Mr. Clarence S. Brigham, American An-

ACKNOWLEDGMENT

tiquarian Society, Worcester, Mass.; Mr. Wilberforce Eames, formerly of the Lenox, now of the New York Public Library; Mr. Victor H. Paltsits, New York Public Library; Messrs. A. J. F. Van Laer and Peter Nelson, New York State Library, Albany; Mr. W. H. Cathcart, Western Reserve Historical Society, Cleveland, O.; Mr. Clarence M. Burton, the Burton Library, Detroit.

To this list it is a pleasure to add the names of my longtime friends, Mr. John Miller of Erie, Pa., and Mr. Brayton L. Nichols, of Westfield and Buffalo, with whom, on sundry pleasant occasions, I have traversed the old portage roads, from Presqu' Isle (Erie) to Le Bœuf, and from Westfield to Chautauqua Lake, and gained some familiarity with conditions of old.

It may not be out of place to add that during the preparation of this work I have passed over every portage route touching these lakes, and have visited every place of historic import on the lakes and the portages mentioned in the narrative. As for the Niagara, with its wealth of scenic and historic sites and associations, its picturesque portage and its gray old fort, it has been my pleasure-ground, from lake to lake, for more than thirty years.

F. H. S.

Buffalo, N. Y.

PREFACE

My purpose in the following study has been to record, with all useful detail, the events of French occupancy in the region of the Niagara and adjoining lakes; and I would here anticipate a possible criticism — that my pages are overladen with details — by stating that it was a desire to know what had happened in the region during the time it was dominated by France, a desire to make the facts available for others, and an inability to find many of them in existing works, that induced me to write the narrative that follows.

If I have seldom turned aside from the mere recording of events, to remark on the policies of the Powers which were rivals in the region, or on the consequences of their conduct, it is because I have felt that the truest exposition of these ambitions of courts, these failures or achievements of Ministries, lay in setting forth as simply and clearly as possible, the things that were done. The student of history, like the scientist, is on safest ground when he draws his conclusions from an assemblage of facts. Such a contribution to historical study, this work is designed to be; and those most familiar with the subject will perhaps be first to note that the narrative here offered supplements rather than duplicates existing works of wider scope. An especial aim has been, to present new matter; minimizing, so far as consistent, the narration of episodes elsewhere adequately recorded.

The customary claim of those who have engaged at all in research work, may fairly be made here: The work is based on original sources. Events relating to Franciscan and Jesuit missions are necessarily drawn from the published Relations of those Orders. For La Salle and his times, I have trusted to the documents collected by Pierre Margry, and have made more ample use of them, it is believed, than has heretofore been done, in relation to the particular region here under study.

PREFACE

The narrative of La Hontan, written by a participant in the events described, is assuredly a source, and a useful one, for our history. To the journals of De Baugy, Perrot, Malartic, Captain Pouchot, Bonnefons, Captain La Force and others existing only in French editions, I am also much indebted.

Chapters Ten to Fifteen, printed in the Publications of the Buffalo Historical Society, Vol. IX., under the title, "The Story of Joncaire," have been revised and are here given their proper place. In writing them much that was useful was found in the London and Paris documents which constitute respectively volumes five and nine of the "Documents relative to the Colonial History of the State of New York." Other sources drawn on for this portion of the narrative are, the Provincial Records of Pennsylvania and the unprinted "Correspondance Générale" of the Paris Archives. Considerable use has been made of the collection known as the Moreau St. Méry papers. There is also some slight indebtedness to the short but precious "Histoire du Canada" of the Abbé de Belmont; the "Histoire de l'Amerique septentrionale" of De Bacqueville de La Potherie (Paris, 1722); the works of Charlevoix and one or two other chroniclers who were contemporary with the events of which they wrote. Very slight use has been made of Hennepin, who gives us little not found in more trustworthy form elsewhere.

The Messrs. Joncaire, father and sons, in this work receive for the first time, I venture to claim, something of the attention to which their services entitle them. Much that I give regarding Chabert Joncaire 2d, and his brother officers hereabouts, during the last years of the French control, especially Hugh Péan and Duverger de St. Blin, is drawn from their own memoirs and depositions. These were printed in Paris in 1763 but appear to have remained unused by if not unknown to most students of the subject. Mr. Parkman knew them, and possessed some of the reports of the "Affaire du Canada"; and in the library of Harvard University, the present repository of many of his books, I have found it a pleasure to study his own copies of these very rare volumes. But Mr. Parkman had no occasion to draw from them, what they have so richly afforded me: that is, a wealth of details regarding the operations of the French on the Niagara and the Lakes in the last few years of their domination.

More important than even the rarest printed source here drawn upon, are the unpublished manuscripts without study of which this story could not be told. These include the journals of Chaussegros de Léry, the originals of which are owned by Laval University, at Quebec; the Sir William Johnson papers at Albany, most of which I was so fortunate as to have studied before their partial destruction in the fire of March 29, 1911; the orderly-book of Joseph Bull, and another preserved by John McKenzie of the 44th Royal Scots, kept during the Niagara campaign of 1759; the diary of Lieut. Christopher Yates; numerous letters and documents from many sources, which are acknowledged in the following pages; and above all, the great collections of manuscript material, some study of which I have made in the library of the British Museum, the Public Record Office, London, and various depositories in France; but which are now in large measure accessible, by means of trustworthy copies, in the Archives Office at Ottawa.

CONTENTS

VOLUME I

	PAGE
ACKNOWLEDGMENT	vii
PREFACE	ix

CHAPTER I
EARLY KNOWLEDGE OF THE NIAGARA

SCOPE AND CHARACTER OF THIS STUDY — PROGRESS OF KNOWLEDGE OF THE LAKE REGION, AS SHOWN BY EARLY MAPS — HOW THE WORLD LEARNED OF THE GREAT CATARACT . . 1

CHAPTER II
BEGINNINGS

FIRST WHITE MAN IN THE NIAGARA REGION — PROBABILITIES REGARDING BRULÉ AND GRENOLLE — FRANCISCAN AND JESUIT MISSIONS — DAILLON, BRÉBEUF AND CHAUMONOT . 13

CHAPTER III
FRANCE TAKES POSSESSION

DOMINION OF FRANCE OVER LAKE ERIE FORMALLY PROCLAIMED — DE CASSON AND GALINÉE — JOLIET AND PÉRÉ — THE UNCERTAIN ADVENTURES OF LA SALLE — FRENCH ENTRY UPON LAKE ONTARIO 23

CHAPTER IV
A FAMOUS EPISODE

LA SALLE AND HIS LIEUTENANTS OF 1678 — FORT DE CONTY — BUILDING AND VOYAGE OF THE GRIFFON — AN ADVENTURE ON LAKE ERIE AS RELATED BY LA SALLE 36

CHAPTER V
A DRAMA OF DISASTER

STORY OF THE RASCALS WHO ROBBED LA SALLE — TONTY THE FAITHFUL — JACQUES BOURDON, A FINE FIGURE IN NIAGARA HISTORY — LA SALLE'S ACCOUNT OF A LAKE ONTARIO TRAGEDY 54

CONTENTS

CHAPTER VI
FOLLOWERS OF LA SALLE

Return of Accault and Hennepin — La Salle's Last Visit to the Niagara Region — The Achievements of Tonty — Grim Comedies of the Wilderness 72

CHAPTER VII
LA BARRE'S FIASCO

Perrot Brings "The Army of the South" to Niagara — Awakening of English Interest in the Region — Trade Rivalry Develops a Tragedy — Misadventures of Johannes Rooseboom 86

CHAPTER VIII
DENONVILLE'S CAMPAIGN

The Expedition of 1687 — The Case of Marion La Fontaine — The Building and Abandonment of Fort Denonville — Father Lamberville's Narration — Conflicting Records 103

CHAPTER IX
WILDERNESS STRIFE

English Claims Reasserted — Adventures of the Baron La Hontan, Explorer of the South Shore of Lake Erie — The Revenge of Dubeau — Frontenac's Raid of 1696 130

CHAPTER X
JONCAIRE THE ELDER

The Dominant Figure of His Time on the Niagara — The Embassy of Clerambaut d'Aigremont — Two Nations Strive for Trade Control — Raudot Pictures Joncaire 146

CHAPTER XI
ACTIVITIES OF JONCAIRE

The Murder of Montour — Joncaire Wins English Enmity — A Trade Episode of 1717 — The House by the Niagara Rapids — A Stormy Visit from Lawrence Claessen 171

CONTENTS

CHAPTER XII
NIAGARA AND THE WEST

EARLY TRAVEL BY THE NIAGARA ROUTE — FIRST WHITE WOMEN OF THE WEST — THE BRITISH COVET THE NIAGARA TRADE — THE HUGUENOT SPY OF THE NIAGARA . . 197

CHAPTER XIII
"A HOUSE OF PEACE"

THE BUILDING OF FORT NIAGARA — SERVICES OF JONCAIRE, LONGUEUIL AND DE LÉRY — JONCAIRE'S LETTERS FROM THE FORT — AN IMPORTANT OUTPOST FOR FRANCE IN AMERICA 225

CHAPTER XIV
A TROUBLESOME TREATY

POLITICAL ASPECT OF THE STRIFE ON THE NIAGARA — THE TACTFUL COURSE OF GOVERNOR BURNET — FORT NIAGARA AND THE FUR TRADE — INCIDENTS OF A PICTURESQUE TRAFFIC 251

CHAPTER XV
ANNALS OF THE WILDERNESS

THE VENTURES OF JOSEPH LA FRANCE — THE NIAGARA MUTINY OF 1729 — FATHER CRESPEL AT NIAGARA — DEATH OF JONCAIRE THE ELDER — THE MYSTERIOUS RIVER CONDÉ 277

CHAPTER XVI
SONS OF THE ELDER JONCAIRE

THE VARIED SERVICES OF PHILIPPE THOMAS, DANIEL AND FRANCOIS DE JONCAIRE — THE VALUABLE MEMOIR OF DANIEL — EXPEDITION OF 1739 AND DISCOVERY OF LAKE CHAUTAUQUA — A NIAGARA INCIDENT 303

CHAPTER XVII
IRONDEQUOIT AND OSWEGO

CLAIMS AND CONTESTS FOR STRATEGIC HARBORS — PROJECTS OF GOVERNOR CLARKE AND HIS SUCCESSORS — FEATURES OF THE FUR TRADE AT OSWEGO — FORT NIAGARA THREATENED 333

CONTENTS

CHAPTER XVIII
THE NIAGARA-OHIO ROUTE

INSEPARABLE IN TRACING THE STORY OF TRADE AND WAR — TRAGIC EPISODES IN THE DEVELOPMENT OF THE GREAT CONTEST — THE BROTHERS JONCAIRE ON THE OHIO — THE NIAGARA PORTAGE FORT 358

CHAPTER XIX
THE FUR TRADE IN THE '40'S

PERPLEXITIES OF A CONTRACTOR — EFFECT OF THE WAR OF 1744 — FOUNDING OF TORONTO — THE CONVOY SYSTEM — CÉLORON'S EXPEDITION OF 1748 386

CHAPTER XX
TWO FAMOUS EXPEDITIONS

CÉLORON'S UNDERTAKING OF 1749 — ADVENTURES OF THE BROTHERS JONCAIRE — THE CHAUTAUQUA PORTAGE — GREAT BRITAIN WARNED FROM THE OHIO — THE ABBÉ PICQUET COMES TO NIAGARA 407

ILLUSTRATIONS

VOLUME I

VIEWS

"The Sailing of the *Griffon*"		Frontispiece
(From the painting by Herman T. Koerner.)		
"The Building of the *Griffon*" (Hennepin) . .	Op. Page	46
The Shipyard of the *Griffon*, modern view . .	" "	48
An imagined *Griffon*	" "	50
A Lake Ontario brig of 1757	" "	50
The Niagara at Lewiston	" "	186
The Niagara Gorge	" "	214
"A House of Peace ": The Castle, Fort Niagara	" "	226
Kalm's "Niagara," 1751	" "	330
Old Fort Oswego	" "	348
One of Céloron's lead plates	" "	418

PORTRAITS

Two alleged portraits of La Salle	" "	70
The Marquis de Denonville	" "	70
De Beaujeu	" "	372

MAPS AND PLANS

"An old Frontier of France"	" "	1
Long Point Bay, Lake Erie	Page	52
Signatures attached to the Five Nations' deed of July 19, 1701	"	190
De Léry's map of Lake Ontario, 1728	"	236
The great house, Fort Niagara, plans, 1727 . . .	"	240
Second story, the great house, Fort Niagara . . .	"	241
Map of 1745, with Chautauqua Lake and portage	Op. Page	320

xvii

AN OLD FRONTIER OF FRANCE

Volume I

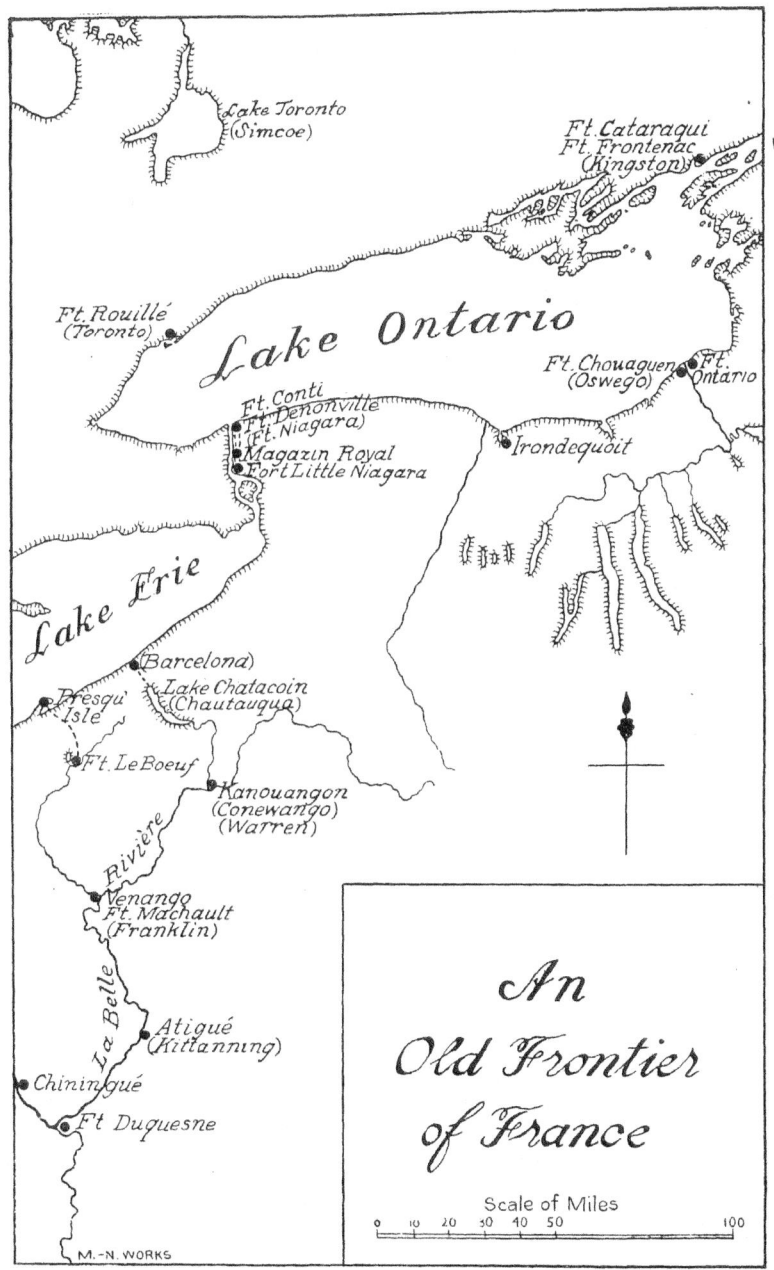

AN OLD FRONTIER OF FRANCE

CHAPTER I

EARLY KNOWLEDGE OF THE NIAGARA

SCOPE AND CHARACTER OF THIS STUDY — PROGRESS OF KNOWLEDGE OF THE LAKE REGION, AS SHOWN BY EARLY MAPS — HOW THE WORLD LEARNED OF THE GREAT CATARACT.

I INVITE the reader to a survey of events in the region of the Niagara and the Lower Lakes while it was under French control, and of events elsewhere which had a direct bearing thereon. The picturesqueness and variety which make the scenic features of this region world-famed pertain also in no slight degree to its history. Our chronicle is perforce a tale of adventure.

Erie and Ontario, styled the Lower Lakes, were part of the highway by which France gained the interior of the continent. Their story begins later than that of the St. Lawrence, later indeed than that of the Ottawa and the Upper Lakes, by which the West was first reached. Forming part of the story of both East and West, the region also has a concrete history of its own.

By "the Niagara region," to which much of our narrative will relate, is meant not merely the borders of the river from Lake Erie to Ontario, but more or less broadly the country contiguous to both lakes and river. It is a region especially linked with the old routes southward into the Ohio Valley, by portages from the eastern end of Lake Erie, which with the Niagara formed for many years a continuous and important highway into the heart of the continent. No study of the Niagara region in the days of the French is anything but fragmentary and inadequate if it fails to view the Niagara as a portion of a great thoroughfare which crossed the divide south of Lake Erie and had as its main objective the posts of the Ohio Valley, the Illinois country and communication with Louisiana.

For many years the Niagara was of less value to the French as a gateway to the Western Lakes than as part of a road, difficult, but practicable, to the Ohio. It must be borne in mind that when the French spoke of the Ohio, they meant also the Allegheny; so that Le Boeuf Creek, down which they voyaged from present Waterford in Pennsylvania, and the Conewango, fed by Chautauqua Lake, brought the Ohio within a very few miles of Lake Erie. In lack of better roads, the expeditions of the French followed these usually inadequate waterways until, below Warren and Franklin, they found a deeper and more reliable current.

With this delimitation of field, the study here entered upon is seen to be chiefly that of a highway; of coming and going. We do not enter upon the story of Detroit. Of the present settlements on Lake Erie the city of Erie is the only one which has any considerable ties with the French period. On Lake Ontario numerous communities do have, notably Kingston and Oswego; and in less degree, Toronto. Of the cities and towns on the Niagara River, those that are now least were, in French days, greatest. Our tale must largely relate to old Fort Niagara on the Lake Ontario shore at the mouth of the river, to the Fort Little Niagara above the falls, its site now included in that of the city of Niagara Falls, New York, and to the fourteen miles of road between, forming in old days the arduous Niagara portage. In particular, the story to be told is of that portion of the Niagara River below, or north, of the great cataract. Speaking generally, one may say of this portion of the river, since the advent of the white man, that its annals are longer by a century and a half than are those of Buffalo and its populous vicinity at the other end of the river. The most populous portion of the Niagara frontier to-day will figure least in our story of it under French domination. The most stirring, the most dramatic, the most significant, events will be found centering around the old fort at the mouth of the river, the sole remaining habitation which testifies to the period of French control on the Niagara.

That period ended with the surrender of Fort Niagara in July, 1759. It is less easy to fix the date of its beginning.

One might say, with little fear of competent contradiction, that the course of history hereabouts was modified by French influence as soon as the tribes dwelling by these lakes had news of the advent of Jacques Cartier on the lower St. Lawrence in 1535. The same could be said of most of the American continent as far west as the Mississippi. Yet for well nigh a century after that arrival we find only scant tradition, too vague, too little related to the present purpose, to make it worthy further consideration.

Not even the exploits of Samuel de Champlain can be said to have materially modified the course of Indian events in the region under notice, except as they may have deepened into hostility the natural antipathy which the occupants of a land feel toward a murderous invader. It was Champlain who in 1609, on the lake that bears his name, first showed the Iroquois the death-dealing magic of the musket, and kindled a fire of hatred toward the French, on the part of the Iroquois tribes, which that nation was never able to overcome, and had abundant reason to rue. We do not know the exact date of the formation of the Iroquois League; but there is no question that from Lake Champlain to Lake Erie the news of that baptism of gun-fire was quickly spread and dramatically told; so that even among the Neuters on the Niagara and to the north of Lake Erie, and among the Eries to the south, Champlain's rash act made the conception of Frenchman synonymous with that of foe. His sojourn among the Hurons to the north of Lake Simcoe, 1615–16, and subsequent passage across Lake Ontario and into Central New York, could have had no more direct effect upon the tribes of the Niagara region than to give them a keener apprehension than before of a new element to be treated with, and, inferentially, a new enemy. Champlain's interpreter, Etienne Brulé, the hero of adventures and a narrow escape from death among the Andastes, supposedly on the headwaters of the Susquehanna, is conjectured to have been at or in the vicinity of the Niagara, between September, 1615, and the summer of 1618; but conjecture is not history.

Before entering further upon a narrative of events in the region we propose to study, it is well to consider briefly the spread of knowledge regarding it. This is best accomplished by an examination of a few early maps.

The slow acquisition of knowledge respecting the Great Lakes is realized when one studies the early maps. The Sixteenth century maps, while they show a gradually increasing accuracy in the Atlantic coast line of the American continent, and in the location of the West Indies, are grotesque and conjectural regarding the interior. The early voyagers received some information of the interior from the aborigines whom they met near the sea. It was some such vague report carried over-seas that led the Venetian map-maker, Zalterii,[1] to put on his map of 1566 a large unnamed river which crudely stands for the St. Lawrence, and then to show, south of it, a large "*lago*," emptying into the sea by a short river "S. Lorenzo." Several later maps, long intervals apart, gradually straighten out the St. Lawrence, but the region of the Great Lakes is left a blank, or filled in with the imaginings of the engraver.

From the time of Cartier, maps of the northeast part of America indicate the St. Lawrence River.

Mercator's great world-map of 1569 vaguely indicates lakes as sources of the St. Lawrence. So does a map of Ortelius, 1570. Many other Sixteenth century maps practically copied the suggestions of Mercator and Ortelius, with little approach to greater accuracy. The globe of Emeric Molineaux, made in 1592, and still preserved in London, shows a small lake, inland in America beyond the St. Lawrence. His map of 1600 shows this lake, very large, communicating with the sea to the north and the St. Lawrence to the east. This is the prototype of the Great Lakes.

The map of Marc Lescarbot, 1609, shows a "*saut*," or fall, at the extreme west of his great river; no doubt indicated because of Indian report of Niagara.

The fact that there was a great cataract far up the sources of the St. Lawrence was known to the early navigators and settlers, and to map-makers in Europe, before any accurate information of the Great Lakes was ascertained.

Champlain's map of 1612 gives us, in a fashion, the St.

[1] Harrisse, No. 295.

Lawrence, and, for the first time, Lake Champlain. The St. Lawrence flows from a large unnamed lake (Ontario) into the western end of which empties a stream, the outlet of a " great lake 300 leagues long." Near the mouth of the connecting stream is marked: " Waterfall." This is the Niagara cataract. A stream corresponding to the Genesee River, flows into the unnamed lake from the south; and also from the south, corresponding to the Oswego River, another stream enters the lake. It has its source in a large "*lac des irocois,*" which stands for all the small lakes of Central New York.

The "America" of Henrico Hondio, 1631, delineates a singularly swollen St. Lawrence, with several tributaries each having its source in a lake. None of these lakes bears a name, but the southwestern branch or tributary shows two lakes, and above the stream which joins them are the words "*Premier sault.*"[2] That this "first fall" among the sources of the St. Lawrence, is a hearsay record of Niagara, there can be little doubt. This map of 1631, though made so many years after Champlain discovered the lake that bears his name, and after Hudson sailed up the river that bears his name, shows neither the river nor the lake, but does show, though far from right, the southern extremity of Hudson's Bay.

Champlain's map of 1632 records information gained by him from 1614 to 1618. He had visited Georgian Bay in 1615, crossing thence by Lake Simcoe and the River Trent to Lake Ontario. He crossed that lake near its eastern end, and advanced into Central New York, probably to Onondaga Lake. In view of this personal knowledge, one would expect greater accuracy than his map of 1632 shows. It is in fact exceedingly crude. Lake Ontario, styled *Lac S. Louis*, is shown with some approximation to its true shape and position. Lake Huron ("*Mer Douce*") is shown as a vast body of water, extending as far east as the middle of Lake Ontario; south of it, reaching like a river west of Ontario, is an island-dotted stretch of water, receiving two large rivers from the south. At the western end of Ontario is marked a fall, of which an accompanying explanation says: "Waterfall, very high, at the end of St.

[2] "*America noviter delineata, auct. Henrico Hondio*," 1631.

Louis fall [*sic:* lake], where several sorts of fish are stunned in their descent." This is Niagara. The residence of native tribes is indicated, but nothing on this famous map has the accuracy that shows personal knowledge. Its distortions are negative proof that Champlain did not visit Lake Erie or the Niagara region.

The Hudson and Lake Champlain both appear on De Laet's map of 1633. The same map shows the "*Lac des Yroquois,*" or Ontario, as a small body of water, while to the westward lies a "*grand lac,*" in which are merged all the other of the Great Lakes group. But here is no hint of any fall in the connecting river.

Bearing date 1650, the "North America" of N. Sanson d'Abbeville, a royal geographer, shows the St. Lawrence River somewhat more correctly than its predecessors. Ontario, bearing also the name "*L. de St. Loys*" [St. Louis], is to the northeast of an unnamed lake, though the lands to the north of it are marked "*N. Neutre*" (Neuter nation) and those to the south "*N. du Chat*" (Nation of the Cat). The two lakes are joined by a river, but no indication of a fall is given. The Detroit, Lake Ste. Clair and Lake Huron are sketched, without names; Superior and Michigan are very erroneously indicated, their western bounds not being drawn in at all.

Sanson's map of "Canada or New France," dated 1656, shows a marked advance. Connecting Ontario, or "*Lac de St. Louys*" with the lower lake, now for the first time marked "*L. Erie, ou de Chat,*" is a river much too long, but broken by a fall marked "*Ongiara sault*"— a spelling shortened from the earlier "*Onguiaahra.*" Here then is a map published in Paris by the official map-maker of the kingdom, 13 years before La Salle came into our region, which located and named the great fall he is sometimes said to have discovered. The same map shows the Genesee River, the small lakes of Central New York, and many other details not set down on earlier maps. The modern spelling of "Niagara" is first noted in a memoir of La Chesnaye, 1676; and in printed books, in Hennepin's "*Louisiane*" of 1683.

The detail of the Lower Lakes and Niagara region is for

the first time shown with approximate accuracy in Galinée's map of 1670. It gives the St. Lawrence and Ottawa River routes and the lake shores along which Galinée and his companions passed in 1669-70. It is a sketch map, and such reproductions as have been made are in facsimile,[3] without the usual niceties and adornments of the engraver. It has the singular feature of presenting the region mapped as though viewed from the north, so that, to read most of its many inscriptions, it must be laid before the student with the south at the top. The outlines of the lakes, distances, etc., lack the accuracy of the surveyor, although Galinée had some repute as a geographer. But its inaccuracies are more than offset by its fullness of record. Numerous data are given along the south shore of Ontario. The Genesee River is indicated, though carried inland but a short distance. Several villages in the Seneca country are located, and a "*fontaine de bitume*"— the earliest indication, on a map, of the oil and gas phenomena. The Niagara, much too long, has the cataract marked: "Fall which descends, by report of the natives, more than 200 feet." Galinée does not claim to have seen it, and the drawing of the upper river, in which no islands are shown, and of the eastern end of Lake Erie, which is wholly without description, is further proof, were any needed, that he did not explore the region. His route into Lake Erie, by the Grand River, is shown. Long Point, vastly exaggerated, is called "*Presqu' Isle de Lac D'Erié*," and its bay is the "*Petit lac d'erié.*" In the middle of the lake he very honestly writes: "I show only what I have seen until I see the rest." The south shore is not drawn at all.

Another great advance is found in Coronelli's map of the western part of Canada or New France, published at Paris in 1688. Here we have the whole Great Lakes system, shown with considerable accuracy and much notation. Evidently all the known designations of all the lakes are here recorded. One is entitled: "*Lac Frontenac, ou Ontario et Skaniadorio ou St. Louis.*" Our more southerly lake appears as "*Lac Erié ou Teiocharontiong et Lac de Conty et du Chat.*" A note

[3] Except in Faillon, which has a redrawn and engraved reproduction.

adds: "It empties into Lake Frontenac." Niagara Fall is shown, "100 *tois en perpendiculaires*," i.e., 640 feet — which somewhat excuses the subsequent exaggerations of La Salle, Hennepin and La Hontan. Forts Frontenac and Conty are shown, the latter where Fort Niagara stands to-day. On the south shore of Lake Ontario, say 40 miles east of the Niagara, is "*Cap Enragé*." A small unnamed stream enters Lake Erie at about the confluence of Eighteen Mile Creek.

Coronelli's "*L'Amerique septentrionale*," etc., Paris, 1689, shows the Great Lakes on a smaller scale and with less detail than in the preceding. The lower Ohio is shown, its conjectured middle course by dotted lines; but nothing is indicated of its head waters or the Chautauqua or Presqu' Ile portages.

Coronelli's "*Partie orientale du Canada*" (eastern part of Canada), etc., Paris, 1689, includes the eastern end of Lake Erie, and the Niagara. The fall is shown; and the river above mentioned (map of 1688), flowing from the southeast, is shown somewhat longer than on the earlier map, but still unnamed. All of the Coronelli maps give many Indian locations in the region around Lake Ontario.

Most of the maps of Guillaume Delisle, though of later date than Coronelli's, do not show our region so well as do the Italian's. Delisle's "North America," published at Paris in 1700, locates Forts Niagara and Frontenac, but lacks, in our region, numerous details of the earlier maps.

A Delisle map of 1703 ("*Mexique*," etc.) shows the lower portion of the lakes, with "*F. Denonville*" for Fort Niagara; and skirting the south shore of Lake Erie runs an extension of the Wabash "otherwise named Ohio or beautiful river." Chautauqua Lake is not shown, or any correct delineation of the two great sources of the Ohio. Another Delisle map of 1703, the "*Canada*," has the Ohio system wrong, as in the foregoing; marks a town of Niagara on the west side of the Niagara River opposite Fort Denonville, and indicates the falls. In Lake Erie the present Long Point is named East Point ("*Pte. de l'Est*"). The Central New York lakes are shown, and several Indian villages in the region are located, one of them, Tegarondies, on the south shore of Lake Ontario. On the north shore are Fort Frontenac, " Kinté," Gandaraeque, Gandastiago, and Teiaiagon, the latter approximating the present Toronto.

De Fer's map of Canada, published in Paris in 1702, indicates Fort Niagara as on the west side of the river; marks the falls " of a half league "— in width; and on the south shore of the lower lake, which is blunderingly named " *Lac Frié*," is an unnamed fort. At so early a date no white man's construction had been made there.

Delisle's " Map of Louisiana and of the course of the Mississippi," published at Paris in 1718, shows nothing essentially new for the Lower Lakes region. Fort Denonville is shown, although it had not existed for 30 years. The falls are marked " 600 feet high "; and in Lake Erie " *La Grand Pointe* " indicates Long Point. No data are given for the east and south shores of Lake Erie except the western end where a deep bay with three islands is marked " *Lac Sandouské*." The Ohio is still made a tributary of the Wabash, with its sources to the east of Lake Erie.

In 1719, Herman Moll's map, " A new and correct map of the whole world," shows the Great Lakes, one named " Errie," another " Frontignac," and between them " the great Fall of Niagara." His " North America " of the same date, puts Fort Denonville on the west side of the Niagara River; and into the southeast corner of Lake Erie — truly enough a " corner," as engraved — runs the considerable river Condé, rising in a lake far to the southeast, in Virginia. This mysterious Condé figures on many maps, but not on those of the French geographers. Moll's " America " of 1720 shows this river; has " Fort Deonville " (*sic*) misplaced as before, and lakes " Frontenac " and " Irrie " extremely ill drawn.

The maps of the French engineer Jacques Nicolas Bellin mark further progress towards a correct showing of our region. His " Louisiana, course of the Mississippi and neighboring countries," dated Paris, 1744, shows the fort and fall of Niagara; east of the fort " *le grand marais* " or great swamp; and among other small streams emptying into Ontario from the south, is " *R. aux Beufs* " or Oak Orchard Creek. The Genesee River is fairly well shown, but not named. Long

Point in Lake Erie is for the first time so named. Also, for the first time, the Ohio is drawn with something like accuracy, receiving the Wabash as a tributary; and having one of its sources in " *Lac Hiatackonn*," near Lake Erie — a clear indication of Lake Chautauqua, which appears to have been first made known by the expedition of 1739.

A year later, Bellin's map of " The Western part of New France " shows Chautauqua Lake without any name, but marks the portage between it and Lake Erie. Three small streams empty into the eastern end of this lake, the most northerly one being perhaps the first delineation which may be regarded as Buffalo Creek. Along the unnamed Genesee River is printed: " River unknown to the geographers, full of falls and cascades." East of this river in the country of the Senecas, is marked " *Fontaine Brulante*," or burning spring, probably the first cartographical indication of our gas wells since Galinée in 1670. Numerous Indian towns are designated on the Upper Allegheny; and Le Boeuf River and Lake are shown.

Ten years later, another of Bellin's maps shows the increased knowledge that had come from French incursions into and occupancy of this region. The Niagara portage is indicated. The Genesee is marked with its early name, Casconchiagon, and " *Lac Tjadakoin* " is an approach to our " Chautauqua." The valley of the Upper Allegheny is full of data. On Lake Erie, the contour of which is considerably corrected, now appear Presqu' Isle peninsula and fort; but across the lake Long Point has once more become " *Grande Pointe*."

Numerous other maps there are that show the Lower Lakes and upper Ohio regions under the French. One of them, published in the year of the Conquest at Augsburg (with French text) by Matthieu Albert Lotter, presents some features of interest; but for the student who would know this region as it was known by the French in the last years of their control, there is nothing better than the later maps of Bellin, save one, and that the very useful, epoch-making, one may quite say famous map, published in Philadelphia in 1755 by Lewis Evans.

In 1755 there was printed and published by Benjamin Frank-

EARLY KNOWLEDGE OF THE NIAGARA 11

lin and D. Hall, in Philadelphia, a quarto pamphlet entitled, "Geographical, Historical, Philosophical, and Mechanical Essays. The first, containing an analysis of a general Map of the Middle British Colonies in America," etc. The map accompanying, about 26 by 19 inches, shows the Middle British Colonies and a part of New France. The work — map and pamphlet — was by Lewis Evans, the first American who won distinction as a map-maker. Ten different editions of this famous map were published between 1755 and 1807, with none of which Evans had anything to do. He died, poor, in 1756; but his map, although criticised, had such great excellencies that it was appropriated, re-engraved and piratically copied, by numerous British publishers. Evans' work is the basis of Kitchin's map of 1756 ("The Middle British Colonies in America," etc.); of the Jefferys map of 1758; and of others issued before, during and after the Revolution, notably that by Thomas Pownall, in 1776.[4]

It shows the Lower Lakes and Niagara region better than any other map, up to that time. Correctly located, on the east side of the Niagara, are Fort Niagara, and the swamp to the east of it, the lower rapids, and the "Portage, 8 M." around the Falls. Near the upper end of the portage is marked: "Fishing battery." The current of the Niagara opposite the present city of Buffalo is indicated as "swift." On the west side of the river, near Lake Ontario, it is marked: "Gentle." "The great rock" which Hennepin mentions, is indicated on the west side at present Queenston; and the cataract is named Oxniagara, the "x" being a character to represent the guttural "gh" or "ch," often shown in early printed books by a device somewhat like the figure 8. Chautauqua Lake and portage are marked "Jadaxque," but the distance is erroneously given as 20 miles. Presqu' Isle portage, shown with approximate accuracy, is indicated as 15 miles. Western New York and the territory north and south of Lake Erie abound in data not so well given on earlier maps; but the

[4] For an account of the fortunes of the Evans map see "Lewis Evans His Map," etc., by Henry N. Stevens, London, 1905.

region between the Genesee River — here called "Kaskuxse or L. Seneca "— and Lake Erie is a blank, with only a suggestion of Buffalo River.

Many other maps might be mentioned which present some feature of interest in our region. For instance, the map of Lake Ontario and the Iroquois country which accompanies the Jesuit Relation of 1664–65, has for "Niagara" the unusual form "Ondiara." The map which accompanies Hennepin's "*Louisiane*," 1683, styles our Fort Niagara as "*Fort du Conty*," and carries Lake Erie or "*Lac du Conty*," as far south as Virginia. The map in La Hontan's "*Nouveaux Voyages*," printed at The Hague in 1709, shows on the present site of Buffalo, a "*Fort Supposé*." It also shows the large River Condé, entering the eastern end of Lake Erie from the southeast. Herman Moll, in his map above noted, may have borrowed this mysterious river from La Hontan.

The exaggeration of the height of Niagara Falls did not begin with La Salle or Hennepin, but as stated above, is to be found on maps antedating the latter's work. Long after the true altitude was ascertained and published, careless or ignorant map-makers continued to give the cataract excessive height. Even as late as 1740, or about that date, George Willdey's large folio map of North America, made and published in London, has the legend: "Niagara cataract, it falls 600 feet." [5]

[5] The Evans' map has "Oxniagara," "Jadáxque," etc., the "x" being a modification of a character used by early writers to represent an Indian guttural. Similarly, a character like a figure "8" open at the top was employed. In the few cases in which this occurs in the following pages, the "8" is used.

CHAPTER II

BEGINNINGS

FIRST WHITE MAN IN THE NIAGARA REGION — PROBABILITIES RE-
GARDING BRULÉ AND GRENOLLE — FRANCISCAN AND JESUIT
MISSIONS — DALLION, BRÉBEUF AND CHAUMONOT.

THE first white man known to have voyaged on any of the Great Lakes was Champlain, who skirted the shore of Georgian Bay, and crossed Lake Ontario. There is strong probability, but no proof, that he was preceded on Lake Ontario by his young interpreter, Etienne Brulé. The meager records which tell of this man, warrant the inference that Brulé crossed Ontario, or coasted its western shores before Champlain was on its waters; and that he saw the mouth of the Niagara, if not the falls, which Champlain never saw nor clearly learned of.

No adventurer in our region had a more remarkable career than Brulé. But little of it is known. He was with Champlain on his journey to the Huron country. He left that explorer in September, 1615, at the outlet of Lake Simcoe and went on a most perilous mission into the country of the Andastes, allies of the Hurons, to enlist them against the Iroquois. The Andastes lived on the headwaters of the Susquehanna and along the south shore of Lake Erie, the present site of Buffalo being generally included within the bounds of their territory.

Brulé appears to have come down the valley of the Humber, early in September of the year named. If that was his route, he stood on the shore of Lake Ontario before any other white man had looked upon its waters, and he made his discovery at the mouth of the Humber, the present site of Toronto. Later that same month Champlain crossed the lake near the eastern end, his exact route being matter of disagreement among those who seek to make clear his writings. Champlain is also our principal source of information regarding Brulé, who appears to have crossed Ontario, or skirted its western shores, to the vicinity of the Niagara. From this point he gained the Susquehanna, but by what route is conjectural. He was taken captive by Indians, and tortured, but survived, escaped, and rejoined Champlain. As the knowledge of the country gained in his wanderings would naturally have been communicated to Champlain, and as that explorer, on his map of 1632, does not show Lake Erie or indicate Niagara Falls, the inference is warranted that Brulé did not see either the lake or the cataract.[1]

Resting the matter wholly upon our best authority — the writings of Champlain — we find two striking facts, which give to the somewhat uncertain figure of this French interpreter a sure and shining place in the annals of our region:

First. Brulé's exploration which led him across or around the western end of Lake Ontario, and through Western New York more than five years before the Pilgrims set foot on American soil, was not the idea of his great employer, but Brulé's own. He was not ordered, but had sought the privilege of the expedition. Parkman's phrase, "Pioneer of pioneers," in no sense applies more truly to him than in connection with the history of the region here under study.

Second. It was Brulé who took back to the Huron mission word of the Neuter nation in the Niagara peninsula, which led to the first visit to these wilds of a Christian missionary — the Franciscan, Joseph de la Roche Dallion.[2]

It was in October, 1626, that this priest set out from the

[1] Original sources which afford some knowledge of Brulé are Champlain and Sagard, from whom Parkman has drawn. The reader is also referred to Benjamin Sulte's paper, "Etienne Brulé," in Trans. Roy. Soc. Can., 3d ser. 1908; and to Consul W. Butterfield's work, "History of Brulé's Discoveries and Explorations," Cleveland, 1898. Obed Edson (*Mag. of Hist.*, Mch-Apr., 1915) concludes that Brulé's route is shown by the dotted line on Champlain's map, 1632. See Shafter's "Champlain," III, p. 208; Winsor's "Cartier," p. 117.

[2] Spelled also "Daillon" or "d'Allion," the latter form suggesting origin from the name of a place, as is common in the French. Charlevoix sometimes wrongly has it, "de Dallion." I have followed the spelling as given in the priest's own signature to a letter to a friend in Paris, dated at "Tonachin [Toanchain], Huron village, this 18th July, 1627," and signed " Joseph de la Roche Dallion." This letter is the chief source of our knowledge regarding the visit to the Neuter nation in 1626-27.

Franciscan mission in the Huron country, with two French companions, Grenolle and Lavallée, and journeyed by Indian paths six days through the forest, apparently skirting the western end of Lake Ontario and coming to the Niagara at or near its mouth. Brulé had " told wonders " of the Neuters — a statement (in Dallion's narrative) which somewhat indicates the route of the interpreter. If he had personal experience with the Neuters, on his journey to the Susquehanna, he undoubtedly saw something of the Niagara and mid-lake region which was their abode.

Dallion remained among the Neuters for three months, making sojourn at several of their villages. He was back at the Toanchain mission station in the Huron country by July, and there he wrote at some length the story of his missionary visit to the Neuters. His account, in a letter to a friend in Paris, is the earliest document known relating to a personal experience in the Niagara region. He tells of his kind reception at one village after another. At the sixth village a council was held, at which the priest told the assemblage, " that I came on behalf of the French, to contract alliance and friendship with them, and to invite them to come to trade. . . . They accepted all my offers, and showed me that they were very agreeable. . . . I made them a present of what little I had, as little knives and other trifles. . . . In return, they adopted me, as they say — that is, they declared me a citizen and child of the country, and gave me in trust — mark of great affection — to Souharissen, who was my father and host." This name, or title, of the worthy savage, is the first designation in history of any individual resident in our region; and the simple barter between his people and the priest was for this region the beginning of recorded trade.

Under Souharissen's sway were 28 " towns, cities and villages," besides " several little hamlets of seven or eight cabins." Careful students of the episode are of opinion that Dallion crossed the Niagara and visited Neuter towns east of the river, apparently resting that conclusion on the following passages in his letter above quoted from:

After this cordial welcome our Frenchmen returned, and I remained, the happiest man in the world, hoping to do something there to advance God's glory, or at least to discover the means, which would be no small thing, and to endeavor to discover the mouth of the river of the Hiroquois, in order to bring them to trade. . . .

I have always seen them constant in their resolution to go with at least four canoes to the trade, if I would guide them, the whole difficulty being that we did not know the way. Yroquet, an Indian known in those countries, who had come there with 20 of his men hunting for beaver, and who took fully 500, would never give us any mark to know the mouth of the river. He and several Hurons assured us well that it was only 10 days' journey to the trading-place; but we were afraid of taking one river for another and losing our way or dying of hunger on the land.[3]

It is a perplexing passage. By "river of the Hiroquois," or Iroquois, was usually meant the St. Lawrence; but Dallion here appears to allude to the mouth of the Niagara, as a place of trade; yet, if he had crossed that river, one is at a loss to understand his statement that "Yroquet [which may or may not mean, an Iroquois] would never give us any mark to know the mouth of the river."

Disregarding all commentators, who are sometimes prone to make deductions to support theories, and taking for guide Dallion's own story — the only known original "source" in the matter — one is warranted in saying that his missionary journey of 1626-27 apparently brought him into the Niagara region. It is idle to attempt to be more explicit.

If he was in the region, one may say, as of Brulé a dozen years before, that he probably saw Niagara Falls; but if so, it is more remarkable in the case of an educated priest, than of an unlettered forest ranger, that he did not mention them.

[3] Dallion's letter is to be found in Sagard's "*Histoire du Canada*," Paris, 1636, and in Le Clercq's "*Premier Etablissement de la Foy dans la Nouvelle France*," Paris, 1691; but Le Clercq omits the passages relating to trade. One modern investigator, Dr. John Gilmary Shea, concludes that the above allusion is to Niagara River and the route through Lake Ontario; and in this the Very Rev. W. R. Harris evidently coincides; the reader is referred to his "History of Early Missions in Western Canada," Toronto, 1893.

The mention of Grenolle and Lavallée again brings the student to the borderland of the unknown. Since they were sent with the priest as guides, it is clear they were not merely *engagés* at the mission, but *voyageurs* who had some knowledge of the land into which they were going. It is to be wished more light could be focused on Grenolle, who plainly was a man of uncommon resolution and energy. According to Sagard, it was he who had accompanied Brulé to Lake Superior, and brought back the first " lingot " of red copper. Such hardy, half-savage forest rangers as he no doubt made up the vanguard of white man's advance into the Niagara peninsula, the land of the Neuters. A few names we know; of many others we have no trace. " Many of our Frenchmen," says the Jesuit *Relation* of 1640–41, " have in the past made journeys in this country of the Neuter nation for the sake of reaping profit and advantage from furs and other little wares that one might look for. But we have no knowledge of any one who has gone there for the purpose of preaching the Gospel, except the Rev. Father Joseph de la Roche Dallion, a Recollect."

The priest recites many acts of ill-usage to which he was subjected. In the spring of 1627, Grenolle, and probably others, came to him, and escorted him back to the Huron village, which was their haven in the wilderness. Much of Dallion's difficulty in the region was due to his ignorance of the language. He himself records that " being the greater part of the time without an interpreter, he was constrained to instruct those whom he could, rather by signs than by word of mouth." That such efforts, amidst savage conditions, should have been well nigh barren of result, calls for no comment here.

The historian Sagard, writing prior to 1636, urged that French traders be sent to winter among the Neuter villages; but we find no record, after Dallion, of any white man's presence on Lakes Erie or Ontario, or on the Niagara, until November, 1640, when two Jesuit fathers from the Huron mission came into the territory where Dallion had so devotedly labored, 14 years before. These were the missionaries Jean de Brébeuf and Joseph Marie Chaumonot. With their visit the Niagara region first emerges from the hazy uncertainty of Brulé's wanderings and even of Dallion's mission, and its chronicles become definite.

It is possible that, after Champlain, white men had entered or passed through Lake Ontario, earlier than we know. The Jesuit Brébeuf, in his Relation of 1635, explaining why he went to the Huron mission by the Ottawa River, says: "It is true the way is shorter by the Saut de St. Louys and the Lake of the Hiroquois [Ontario], but the fear of enemies, and the few conveniences to be met with, cause that route to be unfrequented."[4] It could not have been unfrequented or deserted, had it never been frequented, or used.

The mission of Brébeuf and Chaumonot to the Niagara in 1640 has been much and beautifully written of by those who have emphasized the spiritual and psychological aspects of the experience. Stripped of these, it still remains a considerable adventure.

Setting out on November 2d, from the Huron mission, which has been determined as in the present town of Medonte, Ontario (near Penetanguishene, on Georgian Bay), the Jesuits made their way to the banks of the Niagara. Their probable path has been determined, as through the present towns of Beeton, Orangeville, Georgetown, Hamilton and St. Catherines. They passed the winter in the Neuter villages, the victims of much cruel usage, insult and even bodily harm. In February, 1641, they returned to Huronia.

Of this experience Brébeuf himself wrote but little. In a letter to the Rev. Mutius Vitelleschi of Rome, he summed it up with singular brevity: "This last mission [to the Neutrals] fell to the portion of Father Calmonotus [Chaumonot] and me. We spent five months therein, and in truth we suffered much."[5] Father Chaumonot does not appear to have written of it at all; self-effacement characterized them both; but Jerome Lallement, completing Le Jeune's Relation of 1640–41, gives details of which we must take note.

Having told of the desire which had long been felt, at the Huron mission, to carry Christian truths into the villages of

---

[4] In the original, "*en rēd le passage desert.*"
[5] The original is in Latin.

BEGINNINGS 19

the Neutral nation, and of the choice, for that mission, of Fathers Brébeuf and Chaumonot, Father Lallement writes of the journey, four days south or southeast, " to the entrance of the so celebrated river of that nation, into the Ontario or lake of St. Louys." The Niagara was " celebrated " in 1640! " On this side of that river," he continues, meaning the west side, " are the greater part of the villages of the Neuter nation. There are three or four beyond, ranging from east to west towards the nation of the Cat, or Erieehronons." The easternmost village of the Neutrals is supposed to have been in the vicinity of Lockport. Somewhere near the eastern end of Lake Erie their territory was joined by that of the Eries (The Cat nation), most of whose people dwelt to the south of Lake Erie, as the Neutrals did to the north. Of the Niagara, Father Lallement continues:

> This stream or river is that through which our great lake of the Hurons, or fresh-water sea, empties; it flows first into the lake of Erié, or of the nation of the Cat, and at the end of that lake, it enters into the territory of the Neutral nation, and takes the name of Onguiaahra, until it empties into the Ontario or lake of Saint Louys, whence finally emerges the river that passes by Quebek, called the St. Lawrence. So that, if once we were masters of the coast of the sea nearest to the dwelling of the Iroquois, we could ascend by the river St. Lawrence without danger, as far as the Neutral nation, and far beyond, with considerable saving of time and trouble.[6]

Here we have, in this Relation of Lallement to his Superior, the first recognition and statement of the desirability of French control over the region of the Niagara and the Lower Lakes. All unconsciously, a gentle priest, consecrated to the service of the Prince of Peace, had struck the keynote of a call to strife which was to be waged for more than a century to come.

There is no known earlier reference to the Niagara, by name, than the passage above quoted. Champlain, as early as 1604,

---

[6] Lallement to the Rev. Father Jacques Dinet, Provincial, S. J., etc.; the narrative is dated at the mission of St. Mary's in the Huron country, May 19, 1641.

in his very rare book, " *Des Sauvages*," had alluded to the Great Lakes and a cataract, his statements being based on reports made to him by the Indians in 1603. These statements were virtually repeated in Lescarbot's " *Histoire de la Nouvelle France*," published in 1609; but neither in those works, nor in the narratives of the Franciscan missions which had preceded the Jesuits in the region, does the name of Niagara occur. Lallement's spelling of " Onguiaahra " was an attempt to represent the Neuter — or possibly the Huron — pronunciation of the river's name. A simpler spelling of approximately the same sounds is " Ongiara." The river and fall were known by this name until La Salle's day. Father Hennepin's " *Louisiane* " of 1683 is the earliest work in which we have the modern spelling of " Niagara," though it occurs in that form in documents at least as early as 1676.

Half a dozen years after Lallement another Jesuit makes interesting allusion to the cataract without using the name. This is Father Paul Ragueneau, who writes in the Relation of 1647-48:

Almost due south from the country of the same Neutral nation, we find a great lake nearly 200 leagues in circumference, called Erie; it is formed by the discharge of the Fresh water Sea [Huron], and throws itself over a waterfall of frightful height, into a third lake, named Ontario, which we call Lake Saint Louys.

Father Lallement wrote at graphic length of the Neuters, into whose vaguely-known history it is unnecessary to enter in the present narrative. It may be noted, however, that the name of Neuter, or Neutrals, was given them by the French, and represents, not so much their actual relationship towards neighboring nations, as the French conception of their attitude towards the irreconcilable Iroquois and Hurons.

And here it may be noted that throughout the period of our narrative, chiefly in the earlier years, there were feuds and raids, hostile expeditions, or friendly alliances, between the tribes, especially between the Iroquois and the less warlike peoples to the westward, into the story of which we do not enter. Often these friendships or enmities among the aborigines

BEGINNINGS

affected their attitude towards the whites. History, always a palimpsest, is never more so than in its annals of our region, where, beneath the records of our race, are dimly seen those of alien early folk, whose story in its last days is involved with that of the white man, and in its more ancient periods recedes through imperfect records, through legend and myth, until it grows illegible on the parchment of time, lost in the realm of the unknowable.

Nearly 40 years elapsed after Champlain before we have clear proof of a white man on Lake Ontario. It was July 30, 1654, when Father Simon Le Moine, bound for the land of the Onondagas, reached in his canoe " the entrance of a great lake, called Ontario." Keeping close to its eastern shore, crossing, when the water was quiet enough, from headland to headland of its great bays, skirting the shore to the mouth of a river — perhaps the Salmon, possibly the Oswego — he gained no personal knowledge of the vast expanse to the westward. On August 20th, he would again embark for the return journey, but the lake, he says, was in a fury. The next day, he and his companions did venture forth and followed the coast until, on the 23d, they " arrived at the place which is fixed on for our house and a French settlement. Beautiful prairies, good fishing, a resort of all nations." I find nothing by which to determine this place, nor did any French settlement result from his journey.

Something of the eastern end of the lake was seen by the priests Joseph Chaumonot and Claude Dablon, in 1655; and by the Jesuit Father Paul Ragueneau, who, leaving the Onondaga mission in March, 1658, found so much ice on the Lake Ontario shore that his men had to cut it away with axes, to make a passage for their canoes. Ragueneau's actual experience with the lake was even less than Le Moine's.

In the Relations of these and other early missionaries, bits of information about Ontario and Erie, usually based on Indian report, were year by year recorded. In a Relation for 1664–65 is given with some detail, an account of the Thousand Islands. " After leaving this melancholy abode," as the writer oddly designates it, " the Lake is discovered appearing like unto a sea without islands or bounds, where barks and ships can sail in all safety."

Governor De Courcelles, in 1671, with a view to lessening Iroquois hostility, came with a flotilla of canoes to the entrance of our lake, paddled up to the Sulpician mission at Kenté, where he summoned the chieftains to a council, then hastened back to the securer precincts of Quebec. It was a brave enough show of power and dominion, with something of display and ceremony to impress the red man; but he did in fact merely peep into Lake Ontario; the splendid panorama of its far shores he never saw.

CHAPTER III

FRANCE TAKES POSSESSION

DOMINION OF FRANCE OVER LAKE ERIE FORMALLY PROCLAIMED — DE CASSON AND GALINÉE — JOLIET AND PÉRÉ — THE UNCERTAIN ADVENTURES OF LA SALLE — FRENCH ENTRY UPON LAKE ONTARIO.

THE first formal effort made by France to take possession of the Niagara and Lake Erie region was in 1669. The course of earlier exploration, as of earlier missionary effort, had lain more to the north. In the 54 years that had elapsed since Champlain reached Lake Huron by the Ottawa River route, many had followed that highway: Nicolet in 1634; Jogues and Raymbault in 1641; Radisson and Grosseilliers apparently in 1654 — certainly in 1656; Father René Ménard in 1660; Father Allouez in 1665; Marquette in 1668; and Joliet in 1669. These had all reached the Lakes by the Ottawa and Lake Nipissing route. It was an arduous journey, but the Algonquin Indians of that region were counted as friends of the French; the Iroquois to the south were enemies, at least until 1667.

Knowledge had come of still other routes to the Great Lakes, as yet but vaguely known. One route skirted the north shore of Lake Ontario to Toronto, thence by portages, and the waters of Lake Simcoe and convenient streams, gained the shore of Georgian Bay at Penetanguishene. Still another was by portage from the head of Burlington Bay, at the extreme west of Lake Ontario, to the Grand River, down which canoes readily made their way to Lake Erie. But prior to 1669, neither trader nor priest is known to have attempted to reach the West or Southwest by the Niagara route.

In the summer of this year, the Sulpicians of Montreal determined to send a small expedition to the westward. The preceding year they had planted a mission on the Bay of Quinté, where Trouvé and Fénelon (half-brother of the distinguished

abbé of that name) had now labored for a year among the
"Iroquois of the North," a fugitive band of Cayugas, who,
when hard pressed by their ancient foes, the Andastes, had
crossed Lake Ontario and settled on what is now called Weller's Bay.

The activity of the Jesuits may have spurred the Sulpicians
to extend their missionary work. The Government found it an
auspicious time for exploration, and not only dispatched its
own emissaries to learn of the reputed copper deposits of Lake
Superior, but gave permit to an exploring project supported
by private means. This and an expedition organized by the
Sulpicians of Montreal were induced to join forces; and when
the consolidated company at length set out it was under the
command and guidance of three men destined to play a very
important part in our regional history.

Three more striking figures were not to be found in all
Canada. One of them, François Dollier de Casson, had been,
in his native France, a trained soldier. As cavalry captain
under the great Marshal Turenne, he had won a reputation
for bravery. Tales are told of his physical strength: with
arms extended, he could hold a man, seated, in each hand.
Like the saintly Brébeuf, he comes into our history with almost
the qualities of a demi-god; and though the lapse of centuries
and the admiration of the devout may have magnified these
attributes, clear it is that he was in fact an extraordinary man.
Active and capable as a soldier, he leaves the camp for the altar,
and becomes a priest of the Sulpician order in the Diocese of
Nantes. In 1666 he is sent to Canada, where he naturally
seeks and shares in the most adventurous and arduous service
open to him. He attends Governor de Tracy in his momentous
expedition against the Mohawks — momentous, in that it gives
to Canada, for nearly 20 years, the respite of some measure
of peace with the Iroquois. We next find Dollier sent as chaplain to Fort Ste. Anne, a new outpost of France and of the
church, on Isle la Motte, near the outlet of Lake Champlain.
He found the garrison at death's door with disease, and by
his ministrations, physical and spiritual, brought them new
life. He passed the winter of 1668–69 among the Nipissings,

preaching, baptising, and studying the language. When Queylus, the Sulpician Superior at Montreal, conceived the project of establishing a mission somewhere in the Far West, among tribes that never yet had received the gospel, his choice naturally fell on the stalwart soldier-priest, Dollier de Casson.

With him was René de Brehant de Galinée, of a noble Breton family; a man of mathematical and astronomical training, with skill in map-making; qualities useful in an exploring expedition.

And with these two, René Robert Cavelier, de La Salle, the young adventurer of Rouen, who, after a brief service with the Jesuits, had come to Canada, and acquired the seignory on Montreal Island which he called St. Sulpice, but which the world will always know as La Chine. Eager for western exploration, he sold his establishment, put the proceeds into canoes and equipment, and was about setting out by himself, when he was induced to join forces with the Sulpicians. Who was the acknowledged leader, seems to be nowhere a matter of record. Dollier de Casson was 49 [1] years old, Galinée's age is unknown, that of La Salle 26. The elder man may have been given precedence; but La Salle had not the temperament for service under any one.

It is foreign to the present purpose to enter into the detail of their expedition except as relates to our immediate neighborhood; the rest, elsewhere amply recorded, may here be briefly summarized.

Leaving Montreal on July 6th, with nine canoes and 21 men, two of the canoes being those of attendant Senecas, they skirted the eastern and southern shores of Lake Ontario, as far as Irondequoit Bay. Thence, pushing southward into the Seneca country of Central New York, they reached the village of Boughton Hill, near present Victor. They hoped here to get guides who should conduct them to the Ohio, but were disappointed. The Indians dwelt on the dangers of such an undertaking. More than a month the Frenchmen lingered here

[1] According to Thwaites, Jesuit Relations, L, 320, where he is said to have been born "about 1620." Dr. Coyne, editor and translator of Galinée's Journal, says Dollier de Casson was 33 years old at the date of the journey.

— an interval long enough for the restless La Salle to have made considerable journeys, but if he did we have no record of them. A captive was burned at the stake, to the abhorrence of the more humane of the whites; and finally, despairing of further progress to the southward, they returned to Irondequoit and continued westward.

It is to Galinée's journal that we turn for the story of the journey. Although few exact dates are given, it was about the middle of September that the expedition reached the mouth of the Niagara. "We discovered a river," says Galinée, "one eighth of a league wide and extremely rapid, which is the outlet or communication from Lake Erie to Lake Ontario. The depth of this stream (for it is properly the river St. Lawrence) is prodigious at this spot; for at the very shore there are 15 or 16 fathoms of water, which fact we proved by dropping our line."

They were the first Europeans known to have reached the Niagara by Lake Ontario; and this is the first description pertaining to the river by any one known to have reached it. It is the first of which we can say, "This man saw what he wrote of." The earlier accounts by the Jesuits might have been written from hearsay; but Galinée, Dollier de Casson and La Salle crossed the river at its mouth, and Galinée clearly recorded it.

He is equally clear about what he did not see. The Indians told them of the great cataract, which was "higher than the tallest pine trees; that is, about 200 feet. In fact, we heard it from where we were." But, he adds, "our desire to go on to our little village called Ganastogué Sonontoua Outinaoutoua prevented our going to see that wonder." He adds other descriptive statements, but leaves it plain that the expedition continued westward along the lake shore, with no detour whatever up the Niagara.

They passed up Burlington Bay, and leaving it near the present city of Hamilton pushed on by Indian path towards the Grand River. On September 24th, plodding through swamp and forest, they were greatly surprised to meet Joliet, Péré and their men, coming eastward. Joliet had been sent

FRANCE TAKES POSSESSION

by Governor Courcelles to learn the truth about reported copper deposits on Lake Superior. Going thither by the Ottawa route, he had failed to find the copper, and now, under Indian guidance, was following a route no white man had ever taken. He had come down Lake Huron, through the rivers then unnamed, which we know as St. Clair and Detroit, and had skirted the north shore of Erie to the mouth of the Grand River, up which he had traveled.

Joliet is the first white man known to have passed through any part of Lake Erie. That lake, unlike all the others, was "discovered" from the westward. Had he continued a day or so longer on its waters he would have reached the Niagara and would have had the glory of adding the great cataract to the possessions of his King. His own name, too, would have belonged to the region even more certainly than it does to the Mississippi. Fame coquettes with the adventurer, whom she may crown, or forget. Never was the uncertainty of her favor more strikingly shown than in the case of these two young men, Joliet and La Salle, who meet in the Beverley swamp of Canada.

The result of that meeting was that La Salle parted company with the Sulpicians. Galinée gives details, most of which we must pass over. "M. de la Salle, having gone hunting, brought back a high fever which pulled him down a great deal in a few days. Some say it was at the sight of three large rattlesnakes he found in his path whilst climbing a rock that the fever seized him," and the writer indulges in a dissertation on the frightful nature of rattlesnakes, leaving the reader with a suspicion that he did not wholly attribute La Salle's course to this cause.[2] At any rate, on September 30th, they parted, apparently in friendly fashion, and after Mass was said, Father Dollier administering the Sacraments, La Salle,

[2] Brodhead, in his usually accurate "History of the State of New York," says that "after observing the Falls of Niagara, La Salle was seized with a violent fever, which obliged him to return to Montreal" (II, 163), a statement not substantiated by any known authority. Galinée's Journal clearly states that the party of which La Salle was a member in 1669 crossed the Niagara at its mouth but did not go to view the falls. Jared Sparks' life of La Salle makes no mention of this expedition of 1669.

Joliet and their retinue took the path to Burlington Bay; Dollier with seven other Frenchmen, one Dutchman and de Casson, Galinée and several Indians, passed down the Grand River, and embarked on Lake Erie. In the meeting with Joliet they had learned things which upset their plans. The original purpose would have carried them to tribes already reached by Jesuit missionaries; but Joliet had told them of the Pottawatamies, to whom no missionary had yet gone. Their zeal kindled for this work and they now undertook to reach these people, following such directions as Joliet had given. The lateness of the season compelling them to go into winter quarters, they built a shelter that served as dwelling, as chapel, and as storehouse, the site of which may be seen to this day;[3] and they erected a cross, placed the royal arms at its foot, and took formal possession of the Lake Erie country in the name of Louis the Magnificent. The Act of taking possession, dated October, 1669, is signed by François Dollier and De Galinée, respectively priest and deacon, the former for the Diocese of Nantes, the latter of the Diocese of Rennes. Joliet in his passage is not known to have tarried for any ceremony. To these two stalwart sons of Brittany, therefore, belongs precedence in asserting the sway of the white man over this region. The document runs as follows:

We the undersigned, certify that we have seen, on the lands of the lake named Erie, the arms of the King of France attached to the foot of a cross, with this inscription: "The year of salvation 1669, Clement IX. being seated in the chair of St. Peter, Louis XIV. reigning in France, Monsieur de Courcelles being Governor of New France, and Monsieur Talon being Intendent therein for the King, there arrived in this place two missionaries of the Seminary of Montreal, accompanied by seven other Frenchmen, who the first of all European people have wintered on this lake, of which they have taken possession in the name of their King, as of an unoccupied territory, by affixing his arms which they have attached here to the foot of this cross. In testimony whereof we have signed the present certificate.

[3] The exact spot was identified in August, 1900, at a meeting of the Norfolk (Ont.) Historical Society. See Ontario Historical Society "Papers and Records," IV, XXV.

Here they abode until March. On the 23rd of that month, 1670, being Passion Sunday, says Galinée, " we all went to the lake shore to make and plant a cross in memory of so long a sojourn of Frenchmen as ours had been." [4]

With Joliet, when he set out from Montreal, was the Sieur Jean Péré; and he was apparently with him in the return journey; for Galinée, describing the meeting of the two expeditions west of Lake Ontario, speaks of " two Frenchmen . . . who were on their way from the Ottawas." If Péré was Joliet's companion through Lake Erie to the Grand River, he should have place in our narrative, no less than Joliet; but he is at best a shadowy figure. Even the name, sometimes Peré, sometimes Péré, and sometimes Perray, is, in a measure, conjectural, and has led to confusion with Nicholas Perrot, and even François Marie Perrot, both well defined figures. This Péré, who is credited with the discovery of a copper mine on Lake Superior, apparently returned to Montreal in 1670. The next trace of him is in 1677, when he is with La Salle at Fort Frontenac. In November, 1679, Frontenac wrote to the King that Governor Andros at New York " has retained there, and even well treated, a man named Péré, and others who have been alienated from Sieur de la Salle, with the design to employ and send them among the Outawas, to open a trade with them." The Intendant, Duchesneau, wrote to Seignelay that " a man named Péré, having resolved to range the woods, went to Orange to confer with the English, and to carry his beavers there, in order to obtain some wampum beads to return and trade with the Outawacs; that he was arrested by the governor of that place, and sent to Major Andros, Governor General, whose residence is at Manhatte; that his plan was to propose to bring to him all the *coureurs de bois* with their peltries." So bold a plan of diverting the fur trade evidently failed, for Péré was sent to London and held a prisoner for eighteen months.[5] One suspects him to have been the " Mons. La

[4] The scene of this ceremony was near the harbor entrance of Port Dover. Some memorial stone or tablet should be set up in the vicinity, and the site of the priests' lodging also marked.

[5] N. Y. Col. Docs., III, 479.

Parre" whom Dongan sent to Canada, September 8, 1687, "with an answer to the French Governor's angry letter."

On Franquelin's map of 1688 the present Moose River of Hudson's Bay is named Péré. The geographer Bellin says it was so named for its discoverer. While these scattered facts indicate a man of varied adventures and exceptional activities, they do not clearly establish his place in our history; but that he is entitled to some place in it, is probable, from his apparent association with Joliet and La Salle in 1669. He and Joliet may indeed have accompanied La Salle back to the Niagara after parting with the Sulpicians; and these three worthies may have entered the Niagara and visited the Falls, making then and there the actual "discovery" of the cataract. If they took the south shore route through Lake Ontario, with which La Salle was familiar, they all saw the Niagara. It was not Joliet's fear of the Iroquois, but his Indian guide's fear of the Andastes, the tribe at the east and south of Lake Erie, which had kept him from coming on through the lake.

If, on the other hand, Joliet and Péré followed the north shore, what became of La Salle? His movements, from the time when he parted from Dollier de Casson and Galinée, have not been clearly followed, and probably never will be. Gabriel Gravier, in an elaborate work [6] published in 1870, explicitly states that after the visit of La Salle and his companions to the Senecas in August, 1669, and after they had been denied guidance to the Ohio, La Salle "set out again on the way in the hope that chance would furnish him with guides. He did in fact meet an Iroquois who conducted him along the Niagara to Lake Erie, and in five days, to the western extremity of this lake." This statement, of the highest importance, if true, in substantiating a claim of priority in the region, is absolutely unsupported by any known documentary evidence.

Some slight indication of his whereabouts in the two years that followed his meeting with Joliet is afforded by the documents. In February, 1671, Colbert wrote to Talon of "the

[6] "Découvertes et Etablissements de Cavelier de la Salle de Rouen dans l'Amérique du Nord," Paris (also Rouen), 1870, p. 58.

resolution you have taken to send Sieur de la Salle towards the South . . . to discover the South Sea passage."[7] That La Salle was absent on such a journey in this year is a fair inference from a statement in a letter from Talon to the King, dated Quebec, November 2, 1671: "Sieur de la Salle has not yet returned from his journey to the southward of this country."

That he was back in 1673 is matter of clear record. In May of that year Frontenac sent him to Onondaga to summon the Iroquois, to a meeting at Kenté. In July La Salle wrote to Frontenac, advising the Count that 200 Indians would come to see him, the meeting-place being changed to Cataraqui.

Of many subsequent events in La Salle's career, bearing more and more upon the region we are studying, it is superfluous to enter into detail. In 1674 he petitioned for a grant on Lake Ontario; his prayer was granted by royal decree, May 13, 1675. The new establishment which he there built up, he named Fort Frontenac; and although its earlier name of Cataraqui was often applied to it, for many years thereafter, for convenience in this narrative it will be referred to as Fort Frontenac.

On this same May 13, 1675, La Salle was granted a patent of nobility; and three years later (May 12, 1678) he was licensed "to endeavor to discover the western part of New France"— an ingenuous phrase, establishing claim before discovery. For the execution of this undertaking, La Salle was authorized "to construct forts in the places you may think necessary." Armed with this authority, he fitted out his famous expedition of 1678.

Several modern writers have undertaken to show that La Salle, between 1670 and 1673, not only discovered the Ohio, and passed down its waters to present Louisville, but that he is entitled to great distinction in the annals of Western New York for having discovered Niagara Falls, voyaged on Lake Erie (prior to 1679), and having been the first white man on the site of Buffalo. Still another concludes that he was the discoverer of Chautauqua Lake, and entered the Ohio by that

[7] N. Y. Col. Docs., IX.

route. But all of these claims are unsupported by evidence from trustworthy source authorities.

It is to be noted that from La Salle's own day, the English doubted, or pretended to doubt, and denied, much that the French claimed for La Salle. In 1686, while the explorer was yet alive, Governor Dongan sent to England a map showing " a great river discovered by one Lassal a French man from Canada." Whether he referred to the Mississippi or the Ohio, or to the combined water-way which they make, it was an indiscreet admission, for presently the English set up the claim that the French had no claim to the Ohio region by discovery.

Some attempt has been made to show that La Salle was on the Niagara between 1670 and 1678. A possible basis for such a claim is found in the English translation of reports and memoirs of Denonville, one of which says that La Salle's ship above the Falls sailed in 1677. It also states that La Salle had employed canoes in trade " for several years in the rivers Oyo, [Ohio], 8abache [Wabash] and others "; this, prior to 1677. The English translation of Denonville's Act of taking possession of Niagara in 1687, says that La Salle built cabins and established settlers at Niagara in 1668, and that the lodgings were burned " 12 years ago," *i. e.*, in 1675. In 1688 Denonville mentions " two writings drawn up by Sieur La Salle for the benefit of Moyse Hilser (*sic*), dated at Fort Crèvecœur the 1st and 2d March, 1680, which afford evidence of the said Sieur de La Salle's residence and trade at Niagara in 1676." He further says that La Salle had built a store, forge and other buildings at Niagara in 1676.

Of these statements — assuming that the English translations are accurate — it need only be observed that they are palpable errors; that Denonville's dates in 1687 do not agree with his statements of 1688; and both are disproved by authentic and well-known documents. We have no proof that La Salle entered the Niagara prior to December, 1678.

Frontenac was the father of Fort Niagara. Scarcely had he completed his palisades at Cataraqui — which post hereafter becomes Fort Frontenac — than we see him projecting another establishment. November 13, 1673, he writes to the

Minister of Finance that by the aid of another fort at the mouth of the Niagara and a vessel on Lake Erie the French could command the Upper Lakes. The Minister, Colbert, replying in May, 1674, counsels the Governor against undertaking exploration of the interior. He is explicit in stating the royal will. " His Majesty's view is not," he wrote under date of May 17th, " that you undertake great voyages by ascending the River St. Lawrence, nor that the inhabitants spread themselves, for the future, further than they have already done. . . . He deems it much more agreeable to the good of this service that you apply yourself to the clearing and settlement of those tracts which are most fertile and nearest the sea-coasts and the communication with France, than to think of distant discoveries in the interior of the Country, so far off that they can never be settled or possessed by Frenchmen." Yet the cautious Colbert immediately added two exceptions to this rule. Frontenac might take possession of countries " necessary to the trade and traffic of the French " which were " open to discovery and occupation by any other Nation that may disturb French commerce and trade "; and he might seek to establish himself in any country which would afford to France a sea communication from the interior more southerly than the mouth of the St. Lawrence.

In view of the privileges allowed in the exceptions, Frontenac could not have been greatly hampered by the general rule. He was convinced that by establishing Fort Frontenac he had secured to the French the allegiance of the Iroquois, and furthered the safety of the missionaries. In the General Memoir on the state of Canada in 1674, which he sent to Colbert in November of that year, he pledges the support of Fort Frontenac without cost to the King, promises to pull it down if its abandonment were insisted on, and says: ". . . It is certain that the Country will never be thoroughly formed until it will have towns and villages. This however will never be accomplished unless by following the example the English and Dutch have set in their country; which is, to designate the place where the Indian trade will be carried on, with a prohibition to pursue it in private settlements, or to take possession of rapids and carrying places. It is thus our neighbors have built up Manatte and Orange.[8]

"Sieur Joliet, whom Monsieur Talon advised me, on my arrival from France, to dispatch for the discovery of the South Sea, has returned three months ago, and discovered some very fine countries, and a navigation so easy through the beautiful rivers he has found, that a person can go from Lake Ontario and Fort Frontenac in a bark to the Gulf of Mexico, there being only one carrying-place, half a league in length, where Lake Ontario communicates with Lake Erie. A settlement could be made at this point and another bark built on Lake Erie. These are projects which it will be possible to effect when Peace will be firmly established, and whenever it will please the king to prosecute these discoveries."

If Joliet advised Frontenac to fortify and hold the mouth of the Niagara, he must have done it on the strength of what de Casson, Galinée or La Salle had told him when they met in the wilderness. The priests were not likely to give much heed to such a matter, but La Salle was exceedingly likely to see the advantage of a post at this point. For that matter, enough information about the Niagara region had already reached Frontenac to enable him to appreciate the desirability of a post there. The passages above quoted are the first official record counseling the erection of a fort on the Niagara. The specific annals of Fort Niagara therefore date from November 13, 1673, and to Louis de Buade, "Count de Paluan and de Frontenac," belongs the credit for the inception of the enterprise.

That considerable knowledge of the Lower Lakes and Niagara region was possessed by French officials in Canada before the time of La Salle's great undertaking, is indicated by many documents. In a memoir of M. de La Chesnaye, written in 1676, occurs a statement of the size of the Lakes: "Ontario is 200 leagues in circumference, Lake Erie, above the Niagara, 250 leagues, Lakes Huron and Michigan together, 552 leagues"— a singular attempt at precision. "Communication may be had by vessel through these lakes. There

[8] New York and Albany.

is only the Niagara portage of two leagues, above Lake Ontario. All who have been in these lakes say they are an earthly paradise, full of game and fish, and with the best of lands. The way into this vast country is by the great river [St. Lawrence], and Lake Ontario and through the Niagara. It would be made easy, in time of peace, by establishing families at Niagara for the portage, and by building vessels on Lake Erie. I should find no difficulty about that."

These suggestions, it will be noted, were made three years before La Salle built the *Griffon*.

CHAPTER IV

A FAMOUS EPISODE

LA SALLE AND HIS LIEUTENANTS OF 1678 — FORT DE CONTY — BUILDING AND VOYAGE OF THE GRIFFON — AN ADVENTURE ON LAKE ERIE AS RELATED BY LA SALLE.

No episode in the history of the Great Lakes has received more attention from writers than the coming of La Salle in 1678, and his operations and adventures of the years following.

Sparks was the first to recognize the large importance and significance of La Salle as a figure in American history. Parkman was drawn to him as to one with spirit somewhat akin to his own, wrote of him with wonderful clearness and appreciation, and with a fullness and accuracy that make most subsequent studies of him superfluous. Marshall established certain facts of peculiar import in the Niagara region. Margry with his mass of documents, and followers claiming overmuch for their hero; Shea with his subtle study, granting to the hero too little; these and a host beside, French, British, Canadian, American, have now for many years been adding to the abundant literature of the subject. A detailed recital of La Salle's exploits on the inland waterways of America would be now in large degree superfluous. Yet these exploits, so far as they relate to the Niagara and adjacent lakes, belong to our story and must be chronicled. The more familiar facts may be stated briefly; while less familiar phases of the episode, if not shown in new light, may at least be viewed from a new angle.

Frontenac wrote to Colbert (November 11, 1674) that Joliet, who had returned three months before, had discovered splendid countries " and a navigation so easy by the fine rivers that he had found, that from Fort Frontenac on Lake Ontario, one could go by boat even to the Gulf of Mexico with but one unlading to make in the strait where the Lake Ontario

A FAMOUS EPISODE

falls into Erie"— a most strange slip for Frontenac to make —" which is perhaps a half league in length, and where a house should be built and another barque on Lake Erie. These are Projects," he adds, " which can be attended to when peace is well established and it shall please the King to push on these discoveries."

In May, 1675, the French Government granted certain privileges to La Salle. The mature Frontenac and the young and ardent La Salle were not unlike in temperament. The latter's activity and ambition commended themselves to the former's judgment and policy. La Salle was willing to assume the responsibility of Fort Frontenac, and to give up his estates in France for it; and on May, 1675, it was granted to him as a seigniory and he was ennobled. This first fortified spot on Lake Ontario now became the base of operations, from which the occupation of the Niagara was conducted. At St. Germain, May 12, 1678, the King and the Councilor Colbert signed the license giving La Salle permission to pursue his explorations, or, in the words of the precious document, " to discover the Western part of New France." " There is nothing," said Louis, " We have more at heart than the discovery of that country, where there is a prospect of finding a way to penetrate as far as Mexico. . . . These and other causes Us moving hereunto, We have permitted, and by these Presents, signed by Our hand, do permit you to labor in the Discovery of the Western part of New France, and for the execution of this undertaking, to construct forts in the places you may think necessary, where of We will that you enjoy the same clauses and conditions as of Fort Frontenac . . . on condition, nevertheless, that you complete this enterprise within five years, in default whereof, these presents shall be null and void; and that you do not carry on any trade with the Savages called Outaouacs [1] and others who carry their beavers and peltries to Montreal; that you perform the whole at your expense and that of your associates, to whom we have granted, as a privilege, the trade in Cibola [2] skins."

La Salle lost no time. He sailed from Rochelle — that his-

---
[1] Ottawas.   [2] Buffalo, i. e., bison.

toric old port which was the point of departure for many an American undertaking — July 14th; he was at Quebec September 15th — an average voyage for those days; and was soon after fitting out his expedition.

From Fort Frontenac he planned an exploration to the west and south, and for the prosecution of the fur trade. Late in 1678 he sent 14 or 15 men to the Upper Lakes, with goods for trade. They traveled by canoe, but which route they took, whether by the Ottawa River, the Simcoe portage or the Niagara and Lake Erie, is nowhere stated; but that they went by the Niagara portage and Lake Erie is evident from Tonty's statement that La Salle " sent me with five men to the strait and separation of Lake Huron from that of Erie, to join 14 Frenchmen to whom he had given rendezvous in that place." Had they gone by a more northern route La Salle would not have made the Detroit the place of meeting. Tonty's statement practically establishes the fact that 14 Frenchmen passed up the Niagara before La Salle is known to have done so; and that they, Tonty and the five men with him, preceded La Salle in voyaging through Lake Erie.

Having sent off this advance party of traders, La Salle sent another company of 16 men, ship-carpenters, blacksmiths, and other artisans, to the Niagara, to build a vessel above the falls, in which to continue his explorations. Under command of the Sieur de la Motte, and accompanied by the missionary Louis Hennepin, they sailed from Frontenac November 18th, in a brigantine of 10 tons.

On December 6th they entered the Niagara River. The next day Hennepin and five companions, in a canoe, ascended the river until stopped by the rapids; then proceeded on foot, on the Canada side, to Chippewa creek. Returning to the brigantine they reported that they had not found a suitable place for the proposed ship-building. December 15th, they sailed and towed the brigantine up the river to the foot of the rapids, moored her on the American side — present Lewiston — and devoted the next three days to building a storehouse, which they surrounded with palisades. It was the first white man's structure on the Niagara.

A FAMOUS EPISODE

The Senecas showing signs of hostility, it was thought advisable to visit their village, some 80 miles to the eastward, to placate them with gifts and speeches. La Motte, Hennepin and four French companions, one of whom was Anthony Brassart, interpreter, left the cabin at Lewiston, upon this mission, on Christmas Day, 1678, returning January 14, 1679. They had met with but a dubious success.

In the meantime La Salle and his chief lieutenant, Henri de Tonty, who had remained at Frontenac to procure supplies and materials for the vessel which was to be built, sailed on a brigantine of 20 tons, bound for Niagara. On the way they landed near the mouth of the Genesee River and went inland to the Seneca village Tagarondies, to treat with the natives. La Salle had been there in 1669 with Dollier de Casson and Galinée. Now, the Senecas granted to him — what they had not granted to La Motte and Hennepin — the sought-for permission to build on the Niagara. Returning to the brigantine, La Salle sailed for the Niagara, but becoming impatient with her slow progress, he and Tonty were set ashore, apparently in the vicinity of Oak Orchard Creek. Setting out to walk thence along the high bank to the mouth of the Niagara, La Salle ordered the pilot to steer for the Niagara, if the wind came from the northwest, to run into shelter at the river of the Senecas — that is, the Genesee — until it changed. The pilot and crew left to themselves, did as they pleased. On January 8, 1679, they left the little vessel at anchor, and went to sleep on shore. The wind rising, they were unable to regain the vessel, which dragged her anchor, struck and was wrecked. It was a grievous loss, for she was loaded with everything needed in the enterprise. Several canoes, also laden with goods, were lost.[3]

La Salle and Tonty followed the shore westward, no doubt walking for the most part along the edge of the high bank which for much of the distance commands an extended view.

[3] "*Relation des descouvertes et des voyages du Sieur de La Salle,*" etc., Margry I, 442. According to this document the place of shipwreck was ten leagues from the Niagara. Tonty says nine leagues. (*Relation,* Quebec, Nov. 14, 1684.) Marshall locates it near Thirty Mile Point.

Reaching the Niagara on the evening after they had left the brigantine, they were taken across the mouth of the river by friendly Indians, and given a supper of white-fish and corn soup.

The way in which La Salle divided and scattered his force is at times striking. For instance, at this juncture, when the two leaders are at the mouth of the Niagara, a part of his men are supposed to be making their way westward in Lake Ontario in the brigantine. Of the men under La Motte, some are at Lewiston, others with La Motte, and far in the Seneca country; and fifteen, as we have noted, under an unknown leader, with their canoes filled with trading goods, have vanished up the Lakes. This scattering of forces, as we study the career of La Salle, is constantly to be remarked. Often, it was no doubt necessary. At other times, it told against safety and success.

With his usual impatience La Salle, accompanied by Tonty, set out at midnight, "by moonlight," to join La Motte and his company; but when the cabin under Lewiston heights was reached, they found La Motte and those who had gone with him to the Seneca town still absent.

It is recorded that the next day, leaving Tonty at Lewiston, La Salle went up the river — whether wholly unaccompanied or not is not told — and located the spot where he would build his boat. Undoubtedly, he followed an Indian path through the forest, which afterwards became the old portage road, coming out on the river above the upper rapids. He found a favorable place for constructing his vessel on the east bank of the Niagara just south of the mouth of Cayuga Creek. A narrow but deep channel was separated by an island from the main river.

La Salle returned to Lewiston; then, with increasing impatience at the prolonged absence of La Motte and Hennepin, to the mouth of the river, where he learned of the loss of his vessel on Lake Ontario. At once he set out along shore to the scene of the disaster. What ensued, between him and the unfaithful pilot, is not recorded. One readily perceives, however, that it was an anxious time, with the success of the whole

A FAMOUS EPISODE   41

great adventure in jeopardy. It was the sort of crisis that tests leadership; and the outcome shows that whatever qualities of leadership La Salle lacked, he was not easily discouraged.

There was much coming and going. On January 22d we find La Salle with Tonty and Hennepin at the shipyard above the falls. On the way there, La Salle visited the great cataract, which he is not known to have seen before. Carpenters and blacksmiths were set to work, cabins were built and a chapel, all of logs and bark. Who that knows the climate of the Niagara region in January can conceive the degree of comfort afforded by these hasty and inadequate structures. Indian hunters helped out the supply of food. The keel of the boat was laid, January 26th; and with the work seemingly well under way, La Salle returned to Fort Frontenac, to appease his creditors and obtain more supplies. The journey was made on foot, with two companions. They wore snowshoes, and a sledge drawn by a dog carried their luggage. Their only food was a bag of parched corn, which gave out before the journey over the ice and through the forests was accomplished.

La Salle was accompanied as far as the mouth of the Niagara by Tonty; and on February 1st, before starting on his long tramp over the ice, "he traced at the outlet of the river a fort which he named Fort Conty."[4] This is the first white man's construction on the site of Fort Niagara.

The first building erected on the Niagara by civilized men was the palisaded house at Lewiston, built by La Motte and his men, December 16 to 18, 1678. In January various constructions were made at the shipyard above the falls; but it was not until February 1, 1679, that ground was broken on the present site of Fort Niagara.

The question is often asked, "Did La Salle really fortify the present site of Fort Niagara?" Let two of our ancient authorities answer. Hennepin, in his most trustworthy narrative, ("*La Louisiane*") puts the matter thus: "It is at the mouth of Lake Frontenac [Ontario] that a fort was be-

[4] Tonty's *Relation* in Margry, I, 577.

gun, which might have been able to keep the Iroquois in check and especially the Tsounontouans [Senecas], the most numerous and most powerful of all, and prevent the trade which they carry on with the English and Dutch, for quantities of furs which they are obliged to seek in the western countries, and pass by Niagara going and coming, where they might be stopped in a friendly way in time of peace, and by force in time of war; but the Iroquois, excited by some persons envious of the Sieur de la Salle, took umbrage so that as they were not in a position to resist them, they contented themselves with building there a house defended by palisades which is called Fort de Conty and the place is naturally defensive, and beside it there is a very fine harbor for barks to retire to in security."

La Salle's own account, written at Fort Frontenac August 22, 1682, is more edifying yet: "The Iroquois did not oppose the construction of the fort commenced at the discharge of Lake Erie;[5] but the loss of the first bark having obliged me to use most of my men, during the whole winter, for the transport of what I had saved from it, I contented myself with making there two redoubts 40 feet square, upon a point easy of defense, made of great timbers, one upon another, musket-proof, and joined by a palisade, where I put a sergeant and several men, who during my absence[6] allowed all this work to burn, through negligence; and not being in condition to reëstablish it, there remains there only a magazine."

In his memoir of 1684 La Salle wrote: "There is a house at the mouth of the Niagara River, the most important on the whole lake, to cut off the trade of the English, and which the barques of the Fort [Frontenac] can reach in two days; it cost about 2000 livres. It is all that remains from the fire which happened at the little fort which had been built there."[7]

[5] He alludes to the entire Niagara as "the discharge."

[6] His word is "*voyage,*" referring to his journeys of 1679-80.

[7] Denonville, writing to Seignelay, Oct. 27, 1687, said: "The post I have fortified at Niagara is not a novelty since Sieur de la Salle had a house there which is in ruins since a year when Serjeant La Fleur, whom I placed at Cataracouy, abandoned it through the intrigues of the English who so-

A FAMOUS EPISODE

Here then is the history of the first fort on or near the site of the present Fort Niagara, told by the man who caused it to be built. Who superintended the work? Not La Salle, for he presently returned to Fort Frontenac; not Tonty, for he was busy at the shipyard above the falls. The man chosen by La Salle for this work was Dominique de la Motte-Lussière, who had come to Canada with him the preceding year. He should not be confused with a far more distinguished soldier, Pierre de Saint Paul, Sieur de la Motte-Lussière, a captain of the Carignan regiment and the builder of Fort Ste. Anne on Isle La Motte, named for him, in Lake Champlain. Several other soldiers of France serving in America bore the name La Motte, and more than one writer has confused them. One was Jean Deleau, Sieur de la Motte, who commanded at Chambly in 1677. Another was Claude de la Motte, Marquis de Jourdis (or Jordis), killed by the Iroquois in 1687. Still another was Louis de la Rue, Chevalier de la Motte, a lieutenant, who was killed by the Iroquois at St. François-du-lac, in 1690.

To Dominique de la Motte-Lussière was entrusted the actual construction of La Salle's proposed fort. But he very soon took a final departure from the Niagara.

There is preserved [8] a letter in which La Motte described his relations with La Salle. "In March, 1678," he writes, "I had the good fortune to meet M. de La Salle, who engaged me for his company in the discovery which he has made in the Illinois, promising me a share in his fortune. I resolved to follow him everywhere, with no guarantee except his promises."

He joined La Salle at Rochelle and embarked with him. Who can doubt that during the tedious voyage much talk was

licited the Senecas to expel him by threats." We know but little of La Fleur. In 1679 he was at Fort Orange (Albany) and narrowly escaped being sent a prisoner to New York. Through him news reached Quebec in November, 1679, of war between England and France. In 1684 he was stationed at Frontenac. A letter of 1709 (Ramezay to Vaudreuil) speaks of a fort on the Hudson "where La Fleur lived," apparently in British interest.

[8] Margry, II, 7–9.

had of this marvelous region into which they hoped to come! La Motte continues:

"We arrived at Katarouqui November 8th, after a very fatiguing journey; and a few days later, complying with La Salle's orders, that I should go to Niagara and choose a spot for a fort, to protect the building of a barque, I set out on Christmas Day from Niagara with presents and went on foot through the woods to the Senecas, at least 80 leagues going and coming." The barque was to be built above the Falls; and one may well question how a fort near Lake Ontario could protect it. The storehouse which was built there, was a convenience when supplies from Fort Frontenac were to be landed and forwarded over the portage. The documents nowhere mention the construction by La Salle of a fortified building above the falls, either at the head of the portage or at the shipyard.

La Motte gives some particulars of the visit to the Senecas, by which, he says, a quantity of corn was secured in trade, nineteen minots of which he sent to Frontenac "by Gastaret and the Gascon," and 22 minots were sent to Tonty, "who I found at the cape where the first barque was wrecked; and 18 minots of which I brought in in the said brigantine after having fished up an anchor which M. de Tonty had lost in the lake. I set out the next day to return to Frontenac, to take command there, under orders of the Sieur de La Salle, endorsed by the Count de Frontenac. All these exposures brought about such a severe inflammation of the eyes that I had to go down to Montreal, in the fear of losing my sight." He adds a complaint because La Salle had never reimbursed him for services rendered.

The relations of La Motte and La Salle at the last are curious. In the earlier part of this Niagara episode, there is nothing to show that La Motte was not worthy of the trust imposed upon him. Perhaps his rough experience among the Senecas soured him against the expedition. He lacked physical endurance, and snow-blindness or some other affection nearly robbed him of his sight. He was sent to Fort Frontenac, but seems immediately to have gone on down to

Montreal, though still, apparently, in La Salle's service. There is a letter dated Niagara, January 27, 1679, in which La Salle writes to La Motte as follows: "Sir, I will say no more concerning the sentiments I hold as to your zeal and your courage. It only remains for me to beg you to have as much firmness with respect to our people, and to beg that their discontent shall cause no change in what you shall once have resolved upon, and what I shall have asked of you."

The letter — the first one on record as having been written from the Niagara — concludes with a postscript admonition for La Motte to "be careful of the new hatchet." "That wonderful instrument the Ax" was a precious thing in the wilderness in those days.

In the letter above quoted from, La Motte virtually says that La Salle used him in the Niagara wilderness all winter — in fact, nearly a year, for he joined La Salle's party in France, March, 1678 — and then sent him back to Montreal with nothing but promises. La Salle, on the other hand, complained bitterly of La Motte's treachery, and his attempts to estrange the men from the expedition.

Bidding adieu to his chief, Tonty returned to the shipyard. On the way thither he turned aside to view the great fall. "I may say," he afterwards wrote, "that it is the most beautiful fall in all the world. According to our reckoning, it descends perpendicularly 500 feet and is at least 200 toises [9] in width. It throws up vapors which can be seen 16 leagues away, and it can be heard a like distance when the weather is calm. When swans and bustards [10] become caught in the current, they are unable to take flight, and are dead before reaching the bottom of the fall."

La Motte's letter [11] gives him the credit of recovering the wrecked brigantine. He also says that it was he who had the

[9] Equal to 1279 feet, the toise being 6.39459 feet. The actual width of the gorge opposite the American fall is 1250 feet; but the width of the American and Horseshoe falls together is more than 4,000 feet.

[10] Tonty's word is *outarde*. What he mistook for the Old World bustard, might have been any of our large aquatic fowl. Charlevoix uses *outarde,* which Shea renders as Canadian goose. (*Bernicla Canadensis.*)

[11] In Margry, II, 7-9, where it appears without date or address.

brigantine hauled up "into a ravine between two mountains, by means of a capstan, so that it would be safe from the ice which in great quantity came from Lake Erie and over the Falls." The ravine is still to be seen in the river bank above Lewiston. Hennepin gives the credit for the preservation of the craft to Thomas Charpentier of Artois, of whom we hear no more in all the adventure; he was apparently among those who returned to Fort Frontenac.

Not the least interesting phase of this episode is the part taken in it by the missionary priests of the Franciscan order. Father Hennepin, whose association with La Salle began in France, is the principal historian of that part of it relating to the Great Lakes. It is unnecessary here to recite the familiar failings which discredit his books for the use of the student. It is enough to bear them in mind as one turns to his often valuable narrative. It was Hennepin who signalized the entry of their brigantine into the Niagara, December 6, 1678, by leading in the chant of *Te Deum*, and by offering prayers. Although La Motte, who commanded the vessel, had little regard for priests or the faith they professed, many of his men were no doubt devout, and shared in a service which dignified what Hennepin regarded as a discovery. He it was, too, who on December 11th, celebrated the first Mass ever said in the region. The records afford no hint as to which side of the river may claim this service; or whether indeed it were not held on board the boat; but it was on the eastern side of the river, at present Lewiston, that the first altar for Christian worship in this region was set up.

By his own accounts, Hennepin bore an important part in much of the work that went forward. By the accounts of others, he was at any rate busied with secular as well as religious duties. He shared in the unproductive embassy to the Senecas, and he passed many times up and down the river, carrying burdens or messages. One of the bark cabins built for the workmen at the shipyard was set aside for his use as chapel, in which he held service on Sundays and other occasions. When the *Griffon* was launched, he blessed it, and sang *Te Deum*. His miscellaneous activities included the keeping of

The Building of the "Griffon," as Pictured in Hennepin's "Nouvelle Découverte," Amsterdam, 1704

a journal, at which, he tells us, Tonty took umbrage. Whether so trifling a thing made him think of leaving the expedition, it is not worth while to inquire. Hennepin set out to return to Frontenac, accompanied by one Charon, who also cherished resentment, for some cause unknown, against Tonty. Charon we hear no more of; Hennepin came back, and when La Salle presently returned to the Niagara, he brought three other priests. One of them was Gabriel de la Ribourde, 64 years old, but capable and zealous; one was Zenobe Membré; and the third was Melithon Watteau. Among all the picturesque incidents of these eventful months on the Niagara, nothing is more striking than the picture of the aged Father Ribourde, willingly shouldering whatever burden needed to be carried, and toiling cheerfully up and down the Lewiston heights, those "three mountains" which figure so impressively in the early narratives.

When the *Griffon* finally sailed, Hennepin, Membré and Ribourde sailed with her; but Father Watteau stayed behind, with a clerk and a few soldiers and laborers, to care for the goods left at the head of the portage. What his experiences were, during the months that followed, are unrecorded; but he may fairly take his place as the first resident priest, ministering to white men, in what we know as Western New York.

Through the winter and spring of 1679 the construction of the boat went forward. Tonty was in command, but not a practical boat-builder. Hillaret appears as chief of the skilled artisans. There was little disturbance from the Senecas, most of the warriors being absent on an expedition south of Lake Erie. A few lurked about ready to plunder or do any possible harm. One, pretending drunkenness, tried to kill the blacksmith, "but," says Hennepin, "was vigorously repulsed by him with a red-hot Iron-barr, which, together with the Reprimand he received from me, oblig'd him to be gone." As the boat took shape on the stocks the Senecas planned to burn it, but the plot was revealed by a Seneca woman who was friendly with one of the workmen. La Salle was sternly intolerant of loose relations between his men and the native women. In this case, however, the evident devotion of the daughter of the forest to a white admirer saved the ship, and introduces into the chronicle, somewhat hazily it is true, the only woman who figures in the seventeenth century history of the Niagara region.[12]

From this time on, the work was hurried, under guard, and in May the hull was launched, to the amazement of the Indians, who had never seen anything like it. Anchored in the stream, greater security was felt, and the workmen hung their hammocks under the deck and slept there, in preference to the huts on shore. What with fear of the savages, dread of starvation, resentment because wages were overdue, and an utter lack of zeal for the enterprise, the workmen had been in unhappy humor from the outset. One of them deserted, through the wilderness, towards the distant English settlements.

Stress is laid, by Hennepin, on the greater security which the men enjoyed on board the vessel, than in their huts on shore. If the *Griffon* were built and launched, as supposed, in the eastern arm of the Niagara just south of the mouth of Cayuga Creek, she floated, between the east bank and Cayuga Island, in a very narrow channel. The Senecas, if in any force, could readily have gained and boarded her; but they were a good deal in awe of " the floating fort."

That news of La Salle's work on the Niagara soon reached the English is shown by a letter of Governor Andros to Mr. Blathwayt, dated " N. Yorck ye 25th of March 1679." [13] in which we read:

An indian Sachem reports that ye frensh of Canada intend this year to send a Garrison or setlem^t into one of their towns where these Xtian captiues were a this ye lake wch being of import ile endeauor to preuent but if Efected will not only endanger all ye indian trade, but expose all ye King's plantations upon this continent where they please they pretending no bounds that way.

[12] The incident recalls one of like character, in the early history of Detroit, when the garrison was saved from probable massacre by the disclosures of an Indian woman to one of the soldiers.

[13] N. Y. Col. Docs., III., 278.

Present Appearance of Site where the "Griffon" is Supposed to Have Been Built

Same Site as Preceding View. Across the Little Niagara is Cayuga Island ; the Main River beyond

La Salle had personally little to do with the building of the *Griffon*. He drove the first bolt, January 26; but after that he was most of the time absent, trying to procure supplies and to adjust his involved finances with merciless creditors. It was Tonty who met the problems of the shipyard; and at one time it was La Salle's plan to have Tonty sail the *Griffon* to the westward. " May 20th," says the Tonty relation, " the Sieur de La Forest, major of Fort Frontenac, sent to me orders from M. de La Salle to go with the barque which was of 40 tons, through the lakes, to notify the Illinois that he was about coming to live with them, by the King's order. I took the barque as far as the entrance to the lake, and finding there a great rapid, it was impossible to ascend, because of a strong head-wind." [14] Tonty sailed her to an anchorage under the shelter of Squaw Island.

La Salle did not return to the Niagara until August. " He found his barque ready to sail," says the official relation, " but his men told him they were unable to get it up to the entrance to Lake Erie, not being able to sail against the Niagara River current. La Salle made them all embark. Thirty persons with three Recollet missionaries, arms, provisions, merchandise and eight little cannon of cast-iron or brass.[15] Finally, against the opinion of his people, he managed to ascend the river. He set sail when the wind was very strong, and they towed [16] it in the most difficult places, and so came happily to the entrance of Lake Erie."

Hennepin says: " Most of our Men went ashoar to lighten our ships [*sic*], the better to sail up the Lake. The wind veering to the North-East, and the Ship being well provided, we made all the Sail we could, and with the help of Twelve Men who hall'd from the shoar, overcame the rapidity of the

[14] His words are: "*un foudre de vent.*"
[15] The original is *canon de fonte*, which may be either iron or brass.
[16] In the original this word is *fouir*, which means only, to dig. Margry comments on it, and questions whether it should signify *aller à la perche*, that is, was poled up the stream; or whether it should be regarded as a copyist's error for *touer*, to tow. Hennepin's account, and the conditions of the river, as known, are satisfactory evidence that the Griffon was towed, along shore, past the upper rapids.

Current, and got up into the Lake." [17] While they were waiting for a favorable wind, La Salle had his men " grub up some land, and sow several sorts of pot-herbs and pulse," says Hennepin, " for the conveniency of those who should settle themselves there, to maintain our Correspondence with Fort Frontenac." The site of this first tilled land on the Niagara is of some interest. Hennepin says it was on the west side of the river; inconvenient, one would suppose, if the men were all lodged on the east side.

No one knows how the *Griffon* looked. In his first book Hennepin wrote: " This vessel was only of about 45 tons and which we might call an ambulant fort." In his second work, 14 years later, he spoke of her as of " but 60 tons." We learn from Hennepin that she was a boat with a keel, and a deck under which the men " hang'd their hammocks." She was a sailing craft, but how she was rigged we are nowhere told, nor whether she had one mast or more — though we may infer two, from an allusion to " topmasts." Hennepin styles her " ship," while he calls the smaller craft on Lake Ontario " brigantine "; but one would hardly be warranted in inferring from this that the *Griffon* was full ship-rigged. " She carry'd five small Guns, two whereof were Brass, and three Harquebuze a-crock.[18] The Beakhead was adorned with a flying Griffin, and an Eagle above it; and the rest of the Ship had the same Ornaments as Men of War use to have "— whatever that may mean.

This is all the description we have of the first vessel on the Lakes above the Falls; nothing of dimensions, length, beam or draft, nothing definite as to her tonnage or rig — but she had ornaments like a man-of-war! Writers and artists, giving rein to fancy, have constructed various *Griffons*, some of them elaborate enough to tax the resources of the best shipyards of old France. Reason and reflection cannot accept these

---

[17] " New Discovery," Eng. ed., 1698. Garneau (Bell's trans., I, 261) has the singular statement of La Salle: " He has the honor of founding the town of Niagara. The vessel he built there he called the *Griffin*." He elsewhere says the *Griffin* was built " some six miles above the Falls."

[18] Fr. *à croc*, with a prop or support.

An Imagined "Griffon"
The Commonest Picture of the Pioneer Vessel on Lake Erie

A Lake Ontario Brig of 1757
From a Sketch by Captain Pouchot, in the British Museum

A FAMOUS EPISODE 51

works of the imagination. We know that the boat was built in a hurry, at the Niagara River side by a few workmen, hampered by lack of supplies, lack of tools, of iron, of food even, and with none too much zeal for their task. Crude beyond question she must have been. That she was seaworthy at all is greatly to the credit of the men who built her. Some of them could evidently build better than Hennepin could describe.[19]

More than one writer, beguiled by the undoubted charm and picturesqueness of this great adventure, has pictured La Salle and his companions as sailing prosperously and serenely through a summer sea to the delectable regions of the Detroit. They have perhaps overlooked La Salle's own account of difficulties into which they soon run. Lake Erie, all untried though it was by any craft larger than the red man's canoe, was reputed not only to lack harbors, but to be full of shoals and sand-bars. However ready his reckless men may have been, to press on and take chances, or how rebellious, the leader himself showed caution and some knowledge of conditions. It was, apparently, the first night out from the Niagara that the *Griffon* narrowly escaped shipwreck. La Salle himself tells of it:

[19] In August, 1879, there was celebrated at Grosse Pointe, Michigan, the 200th anniversary of the passage of the *Griffon:* In the historical address of Mr. Bela Hubbard, on that occasion, it is stated that the *Griffon* "was a two-masted schooner, but of a fashion peculiar to that day, having double decks, and a high poop projected over the stern, where was the main cabin, and over this rose another and smaller cabin, doubtless for the use of the commander. The stern was thus carried up, broad and straight, to considerable height. Bulwarks protected the quarter deck." (Mich. Pioneer Coll. III, 650.)

The printed program of the day's exercises bore a picture of the craft that admirably conformed to the orator's description; but whether the artist got his design from the speaker's description, or the speaker merely described the picture as the artist drew it, is not specified. Certain it is, that neither of them gave any authority for the data so confidently presented. As conceived by Mr. Herman T. Koerner, an artist who painted a wall panel in the Historical Building at Buffalo, the *Griffon* was not schooner-rigged, but a brig of the hermaphrodite type, with yards and square-sails, even on the jib. Numerous other designs attest by their variety to the utter absence of authenticity, beyond deductions of probabilities — and some of these are highly improbable.

52 AN OLD FRONTIER OF FRANCE

Night came on, and a thick fog concealed the shore, from which we supposed ourselves some ten leagues distant. I heard breakers about a league ahead of us. Everyone thought it was but the ordinary sound on the lakes when the wind changes, which is always heard from the side it comes from, and the pilot wished to crowd on sail to gain an anchorage before we stranded ahead; but as I knew that these two sand banks extended out very far, and as I was of opinion we were near the one which was in fact just ahead of us, I

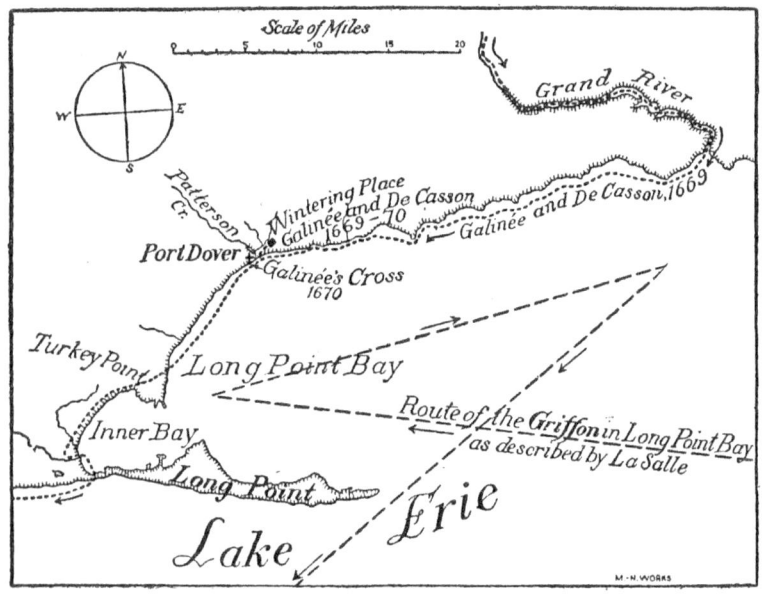

Long Point Bay, Lake Erie.
Showing Galinée's route, 1669-70, and the course of the *Griffon*, 1679.

ordered, notwithstanding everybody, that we change the course and bear east northeast, instead of as we were going, west northwest with a light wind from the southeast. We sailed two or three hours, sounding constantly, without finding bottom; and still we heard the same noise ahead of us. They all insisted that it was only the wind, and I, that it was the sand-bar which made a circle and surrounded us on the north side, from west to east. In fact, an hour later, we suddenly found only three fathoms. Everyone worked ship, I tacked and bore to the southwest, always sounding without finding bottom.

A FAMOUS EPISODE

At length the fog lifted, my conviction proved true, and they all saw that they owed their escape from danger to me.[20]

Following the general trend of the north shore the *Griffon* had blundered into Long Point Bay and narrowly escaped wreck on Long Point. This experience is in a measure proof that Tonty was not on board. Having canoed through these waters he would have known the danger and told of it.

La Salle's avowed purpose on this voyage was the exploration to its mouth of the great river to the westward of the Lakes. If, half a dozen years before, he had already found his way down the Ohio, one may naturally inquire, why did he not follow that route, instead of incurring the labor and expense of building a vessel on Lake Erie. Two answers may be made. He contemplated not only a voyage to the Gulf, but an exploration of the upper Mississippi — though, as the sequel shows, he never attempted this himself, but sent others.

A more impressive answer is, that he sought to profit by the fur trade of the lake region. It offered him a revenue for the prosecution of his exploration, but it involved him in difficulties and in a measure undermined his success.

[20] Letter of La Salle, Fort Frontenac, Aug. 22, 1682. Margry, II, 230. Parkman does not mention the incident.

CHAPTER V

A DRAMA OF DISASTER

STORY OF THE RASCALS WHO ROBBED LA SALLE — TONTY THE FAITHFUL — JACQUES BOURDON, A FINE FIGURE IN NIAGARA HISTORY — LA SALLE'S ACCOUNT OF A LAKE ONTARIO TRAGEDY.

THE story of the men who stole La Salle's goods, destroyed his buildings and deserted from his service, if it could be truly and fully recorded, would be the rarest narrative of adventure the history of the Great Lakes affords. Much of it belongs to the region we are studying, and something of it should have place in these pages.

The loss of the brigantine on Lake Ontario, which La Salle ascribed to treachery, forewarned him of what he had to expect from his men. From the outset, there were discord and discontent among them. Some were Normans, some were Canadians — and even at that early day many sharp discriminations were made against the *habitant*. The man whom they had to obey, for more than eight months on the Niagara, was an Italian soldier. The priests were Flemings — natives of the Spanish Netherlands. Such worthy men as Dautray and Boisrondet no doubt comprehended, in a measure, the aims and ambitions of their great leader, and were zealous for exploration and discovery. Most of the others thought more of the opportunity to profit by trade with the Indians, lawful or otherwise; and some had no soul above getting food and their promised wage.

When the *Griffon* sailed, she had on board, according to one account,[1] 23 men; according to another,[2] 34, this perhaps taking into account Indian hunters and servants. Some of the company were, naturally, men whom it is not worth the

---
[1] Margry, II, 31, where the paper entitled "*Préliminaires de l'exploration*" states that La Salle "*s'embarqua avec vingt-deux hommes pour traverser le lac erié.*"
[2] Hennepin.

A DRAMA OF DISASTER

student's thought to consider, yet others of the baser sort were destined to such evil activities in our region that record should be made of them. As for the rest, among them were several of ability and character, whose part in our history has been overshadowed, if not lost, by the deeds of their leader.

Who were they? From the imperfect and contradictory records, it is not easy to be conclusive. We know that La Salle himself sailed on the *Griffon*. As the breeze filled her sails, and she cut her cautious course through the waves of Lake Erie, he must have experienced a moment of exultation, rare in his baffled career, over a long-cherished purpose accomplished.

Was Tonty with him? He had gone on in advance by canoe, with five men; but Tonty himself is made to say, in the account of La Salle's journeys attributed to him, that after having gone the length of Lake Erie by canoe in two days — no slight achievement — he returned to Niagara and sailed with La Salle on August 7th. Other and better authorities indicate that he did not sail on the *Griffon* from Niagara, but joined it in the Detroit.

Tonty was in the service of La Salle; yet in many respects his actual achievements surpass those of his leader, while his steadfast and trustworthy character commends him to our esteem and admiration. It was Tonty, far more than La Salle, who gave personal attention to the operations on the Niagara in 1678–79. He it was who built the *Griffon*. He voyaged the length of Lake Erie before La Salle had ventured upon its waters — unless one accepts the claims of eulogists who profess to find certain evidence of La Salle's travels in those hazy years of 1669–72. When the *Griffon* sailed, if Tonty were aboard, La Salle and her pilot would have profited by information of the lake which Tonty picked up in his swift canoe journey; that they had need of more we have already seen. It was to be Tonty who made the establishment on the Illinois, of which La Salle hoped for so much. When, harassed and impatient, he was exhausting himself in unfruitful journeys back and forth, Tonty held on. And when most of their men turned thieves and traitors, and deserted, Tonty still held on, sturdy, resourceful and discreet. When La Salle vanished down the Mississippi and nothing was heard of him for months, it was Tonty who went far down the unknown river in quest of him. When Governor Denonville undertook to discipline the Iroquois of Central New York, in 1687, it was Tonty who came again to the Niagara, leading a great war party of Illinois. He shared in the campaign, and returning to the Niagara, saw Denonville begin a fort on the scene of his own activities of eight years before. We have no record of his presence on our river, after that; but from what we know of his career, here and elsewhere, the statement is warranted that of all the men who shared in the varied drama enacted in America by the soldiers and servitors of France, none played his part with greater sincerity and credit, none is more entitled to the respect and admiration of posterity, than the Italian knight, Henri de Tonty.

Three Franciscan missionaries there were on board: Fathers Louis Hennepin, Zenobe Membré and Gabriel de la Ribourde. The first named was to have his share of adventures and to assert himself in years to come as the historian of the expedition, but with such conceit, exaggerations and mendacities that the student is now amused, now exasperated and at all times perplexed by the uncertainty of pages which should give us a clear record. Father Ribourde, aged 64, was to die a few months later in an Illinois wilderness by the hand of a Kickapoo savage. Father Membré's destiny it was to share in La Salle's unhappy fortunes to the very end and to become the most trustworthy historian of his later years.

Father Watteau and Sergeant La Fleur, with a few soldiers, remained on the Niagara. The Canadian, Charon, returned to Fort Frontenac, and so, apparently, did Anthony Brassart, the interpreter.

Fifteen of La Salle's men had gone west by canoe before he began operations on the Niagara. Five others had accompanied Tonty to the Detroit, also by canoe. The names of the men in these advance parties are not recorded except when, as deserters, they reappear at Mackinac, on the Niagara and Lake Ontario. Some, therefore, whose names are known, may

A DRAMA OF DISASTER 57

have been in the advance parties, or may have sailed on the *Griffon*.

There was the pilot, Luc, fated to perish with ship and crew of five among the islands of Lake Michigan, in trying to navigate the *Griffon* back to the Niagara.

Among the more trusty who stood with La Salle as he sailed into Lake Erie was Jacques Bourdon, the Sieur Dautray, son of Jean Bourdon, first procurer-general of Quebec; "always very faithful," La Salle said of him. Dautray is to be righthand man, and serve him well, on many occasions. Here too, were André Henault; Collin; Michael Accault and Antoine Auguel, otherwise known as Du Gay, and because he was from Picardy called " Le Picard "; these two, with Father Hennepin, were to explore the upper Mississippi. In La Salle's service were also the Parisian, the Sieur de Boisrondet; La Chapelle; Noël Le Blanc; Pierre You; L'Esperance, La Salle's servant; and one or more Indian hunters.

It was a strangely mixed lot: a few gentlemen, soldiers who had proved themselves in service, missionary priests, craftsmen, mechanics and dubious *habitants* who only needed opportunity to turn villain. By no means least in evidence in the motley crew was Moyse Hillaret, ship carpenter. Another carpenter, François Sauvin, was called La Roze;[3] a blacksmith, Le Meilleur, is oftener mentioned as La Forge; others were La Violette; Martin Chartier; Duplessis, Jacques Monjault; La Rousselière; Baribault; Lacroix. Highly poetic, some of the names, but a more rascally and unfaithful crew never sailed.

Moyse Hillaret, ship carpenter, was a ring-leader for mischief from the first. He and his fellow workmen were afraid of the Indians, and when the brigantine bringing previsions was wrecked on Lake Ontario, they were greatly depressed by fear of starvation. One can readily picture them loudly discussing the situation and caring less for exploration than for their dinner. They were in fit mood to listen to the proposals of " a villian amongst us," as Hennepin has it: " That pitiful Fellow has several times attempted to run away from us into

[3] So spelled in the documents. Margry, II.

New York, and would have been likely to pervert our Carpenters, had I not confirm'd them in their good resolution, by the Exhortations I us'd to make every Holy-day after Divine Service; in which I represented to them, that the Glory of God was concern'd in our Undertaking, besides the Good and Advantage of our Christian Colonies; and therefore exhorted them to redouble their diligence, in order to free ourselves from all those Inconveniences and Apprehensions we then lay under." Hennepin never underestimates his own importance and influence; but as, to this day, the French-Canadian priest has a great hold and restraining influence on even the most lawless and perverse young men of his parish, so Father Hennepin undoubtedly did help to keep the faint-hearted and false-hearted to their task on the banks of the Niagara. More potent yet was the wilderness itself. Only a brave and resourceful man dared run away.

As for "the villian amongst us" of whom he writes, he may have meant Noël Le Blanc, who, according to Tonty, made great trouble. Whoever he was, he takes his unenviable place in history as the first labor agitator of the Lower Lakes.

The fortunes of the 15 who had gone up the Lakes in the autumn, with a rich quantity of La Salle's goods, must often have been discussed in the shanties by the Niagara. Men who lightly regarded the rights of ownership, may well have envied these adventurers their opportunity, and have been disposed to act for themselves, whenever they could do so with profit or safety. Of loyalty to La Salle among the workmen there was none.

When Tonty rejoined La Salle on board the *Griffon*, in the Detroit, he brought the unhappy news that most of the advance party of 15 had deserted, taking La Salle's goods for their own use; and when La Salle set foot ashore at Mackinac he was surprised to find some of his men there, whom he supposed had gone on long before to the Illinois. They told him that they had been kept back by reports which had reached them since their departure from Frontenac. "They had been told that his undertaking was chimerical, that his barque would never reach Mackinac, that they had been sent to certain ruin,

A DRAMA OF DISASTER

and several other like reports, which had discouraged and debauched most of their comrades, whom they had been unable to persuade to continue the journey, and that six of them, Saint Croix, Minime, Le Barbier, Poupart, Hunaut [or Henault] and Roussel (called La Rousselière), had deserted, stolen and carried off nearly 4000 livres of merchandize; and that the others had wasted or used for their own subsistance at Mackinac, where provisions were very dear, more than 1300 livres." [4]

Four of these men La Salle arrested at Mackinac. Tonty captured two at Sault Ste. Marie — Henault and Roussel; but was delayed so long by adverse winds that La Salle went on without him. Some of the advance party of 15 appear to have been taken along, a new source of treachery and danger. Others escaped and vanished in the wilderness; possibly making their way to the English, as many renegade Frenchmen did; wandering to distant tribes, or meeting the early death which is usually the fate of the violent and the outlaw.

La Salle and his uncertain following, good and bad, made their way to the Illinois River, where a fort was built and a boat begun for exploration of the great river. With these undertakings, elsewhere so fully and ably recorded, the present work is not concerned. From Green Bay, in September, the *Griffon* had been dispatched for Niagara, but she only reached the Port of Missing Ships. Loaded with furs and still having on board a large amount of the goods and material which had been put into her before she sailed from the Niagara, her loss was a staggering blow to La Salle.

In March, 1680, not knowing of his loss, he set out with four French companions and an Indian hunter for Fort Frontenac. He needed supplies for his men, material for the new boat, and was anxious to know the fate of the *Griffon*. The story of the Lakes, rich as it is in adventure, has no episode surpassing this in hardihood.

By canoe and on foot, they came across Southern Michigan, but not without grave experiences. Reaching the Detroit, La Salle dispatched two of his men, by canoe, to Mackinac, to

[4] "*Relation officiale.*" Margry, I, 449.

learn if possible, the fate of the *Griffon*. With his faithful hunter and two white companions, he crossed the Detroit on a raft. Let his own narrative [5] tell what ensued:

We followed on foot the shore of Lake Erie until, the continued rains and the great thaw having flooded all the woods, the Indian and one of my men succumbed to exhaustion due to constant walking through water, so that, at 30 leagues from the fall of Conty [6] they were taken with a very violent fever, inflammation of the chest and a vomiting of blood, which obliged me, with the man who remained well, to build a canoe for carrying them. This we did in two days; and the day after Easter I arrived at the fall of Conty, where I found still other causes for anxiety, learning, from two of my men who had wintered there, of the loss of the ship in which were the goods which you and M. Plet were sending here, at least the great part of them; the return to France of the men who were to come for the Illinois establishment, the disturbance which my brother had caused in my affairs, and the urgency of those from whom I had borrowed a quantity of goods payment for which I could easily have arranged, if those to whom I entrusted them had not stolen them.

But that which gave me the greatest grief, was, to have no news of my barque, by the arrival of which I would have remedied everything; and the loss of which was not only considerable because of the value of its contents, which with the hull and rigging of the boat amounted to more than 10,000 crowns,[7] but because it made impossible the execution of my enterprise by reason of the distance and the cost of transport by canoe to places so distant; besides the rigging and ship fittings, and quantity of provisions, arms, ammunition, tools, iron, goods and utensils which were cared for by seven or eight men in a cabin above the fall of Conty, where they had been carried with great cost, and where they were cared for during the winter, running risk of being stolen, as indeed a part of them were, and not being able to care for them, while they were in shipment, except at great expense.

[5] Letter of La Salle, in Margry, II, 63–64.

[6] That is, Niagara. La Salle had called his fort at the mouth of the river Fort de Conty; and the name of this prince was for a long time applied to Lake Erie; but so far as observed, the letter here quoted from is the only record in which the great cataract is also styled "Conty."

[7] La Salle's word is *escus* (modern spelling, *écu*). Reckoning the crown at three francs, he estimated his loss on the *Griffon* at more than $6,000; but the purchasing power of the franc was probably greater in La Salle's day than in ours.

A DRAMA OF DISASTER

This was the consolation which I found on my arrival after a journey of 450 leagues. There still remained 70 before reaching Fort Frontenac. The men who had attended me not being able to go on, I took three fresh men from the fall of Conty; and, the rain being incessant until May 10th, I did not reach Frontenac until the 6th.

At the worst season of the year for such an undertaking, La Salle had journeyed, in part by canoe, but mostly on foot, more than a thousand miles in 65 days, including numerous detentions. It was a wonderful thing to do. He was in his 37th year — at the zenith of physical vigor. If we knew nothing of him save this achievement, we could picture him as of exceptional determination and physical endurance.

As he was first to sail into the West, from the Niagara, so was he the first white man to arrive at the Niagara, from the West.

On his way, at the mouth of the Miami, he had hoped for news of the *Griffon*. Later, on the Detroit, he still cherished a hope of finding her. It was not until he stood once more on the bank of the Niagara where she had been built, and found no trace of her or her men, but only news of loss and misfortune crowned by misfortune, that he abandoned all hope of this venture, on which he had staked so much. No wonder that he writes in irony of the "consolation" that awaited him there. We have seen him in what may well have been a moment of exultation, as he sailed out of the Niagara into the untried lake. Now, eight months later, again on the Niagara, with his ventures gone wrong, a victim of knavery, he would appear a pathetic figure, but for the fact that there is nothing in word or act to indicate that his spirit was broken. However some of his deeds in later years may be construed, there is nothing throughout the time of his activities on the Niagara and adjoining lakes, that does not breathe of fine resolution and undaunted courage.

La Salle's companions, in this hard journey, were Dautray, Henault, La Violette, Collin, and his Indian hunter. On his way, at the little post at the mouth of the St. Joseph, he found Chapelle and Le Blanc, whom he had sent to Mackinac in search of the *Griffon*. They were now returning. That they had not deserted, speaks well for their loyalty, up to this time.

Which were the two men dispatched from the Detroit to Mackinac, is not known, but Dautray was one who came through to the Niagara, enduring the fatigues of the journey better than any one save La Salle himself. Taking three of the men who had spent the winter at Niagara, to go on with him to Frontenac, La Salle sent Dautray back with four men, to Tonty.

Much has been written of the hardihood of La Salle; yet here is his faithful follower, Jacques Bourdon, the Sieur Dautray, who had shared in his leader's most adventurous exploit, setting out at once from the Niagara to retrace all those wilderness leagues until he shall rejoin Tonty on the distant Illinois. His name appears in the documents sometimes as Jean, sometimes as Jacques. There were two brothers bearing these names, sons of Jean Bourdon, Sieur de St. Francis. The father was a man of standing in the Quebec colony, and was a public prosecutor at the time his son Jacques joined La Salle. The son Jean was styled Sieur de Dombourg, and Jacques the Sieur D'Autray (or Dautray), from seigniories which they received from their father. In September, 1672, Count Frontenac granted a passport to Father Crépieul, Jesuit, the Sieur Dautray and others, to trade with the Indians and to winter at Lake St. John, " about 70 leagues above Tadousac.[8] Jacques is said to have been born at Quebec in 1637. He joined La Salle in 1675; shared in the preparatory work on the Niagara, and sailed on the *Griffon* in 1679. He was to have many grim adventures in the West; was to be one of four who accompanied La Salle in his search for Tonty in November, 1680 [9] and one of three who first discovered and passed through the mouths of the Mississippi. When in April, 1682, La Salle found himself at the delta of the great river, he followed the channel to the west, Tonty took the middle channel, and Dautray explored the eastern pass. In the culmination of the great adventure, the Canadian Jacques Bourdon, Sieur Dau-

[8] Paris Docs., IX, 995.
[9] The others were Henault, Pierre You and an Indian hunter.

A DRAMA OF DISASTER

tray, shared equally with La Salle and Tonty. Little is recorded of him, but that little is all good. His deeds and his fidelity entitle him to remembrance in the annals of the Lakes and the Niagara. His rank prior to engaging with La Salle was that of lieutenant, and his service was in the first company of troops maintained in Canada by the Minister of Marine and Colonies. In 1687 he accompanied Tonty in Denonville's campaign against the Iroquois, a service that brought him again to the Niagara. After that affair he went down to Quebec, then returned to Montreal, planning to return to Fort St. Louis of the Illinois, where he had "house and seigniory"; but he passed the winter in Montreal. In the spring of 1688, having escorted a party to Frontenac, he was returning when he was killed by the Iroquois. Such, in brief, was the career and the fate of the man who, after Tonty, stood closest to La Salle; a man who shared, and merited, the confidence and affection of his leader.

Dautray was the first man, after La Salle, to leave the Niagara for the West. He filled two canoes with arms and provisions, and with three soldiers who had spent the winter on the Niagara — La Violette, Dulignon and Pierre You, and a servant of La Salle called La Brie, paddled up the river and followed the north shore of Erie to the Detroit. He was directed by La Salle to pick up and take along with him two soldiers, Nicolas Crevel and André Henault, who with Jacques Messier had been sent to Mackinac. At Niagara La Salle and Dautray had learned that an Iroquois war party was about setting out for the Illinois and it was desired to forewarn Tonty. Dautray pressed on and joined Tonty at Fort Crèvecœur; while Crevel and Messier, with Laurent, bearing a message from Tonty to La Salle, telling of the thefts and desertions from Fort Crèvecœur, did not return to that point with Dautray, but hastened eastward until, at Fort Frontenac, they found La Salle loading his brigantine with new supplies for the Illinois.

At Niagara, La Salle had become convinced of the loss of the *Griffon*. At Frontenac, more heart-breaking news was to reach him. On July 22d, three of his men arrived with a message from Tonty. They had evidently followed the route of La Salle, Dautray and others, across Michigan, down Lake Erie to Niagara. How many of these intrepid and wonderfully quick "voyages" those old days saw! Tonty had dispatched four men, but on the way one had either got lost or deserted. On the day named, as La Salle was busy loading his brigantine with goods for Tonty's relief, Jacques Messier, Nicolas Crevel and Nicolas Laurent (who is also called La Chapelle) appeared and gave him a letter from Tonty. It told him that Moyse Hillaret and others, who were supposed to be building the vessel in which he planned to proceed with his exploration, had stolen what goods they could lay hands on, and run off.

All those months of toil on the Niagara, all those years of planning and outlay, had gone for naught. The great undertaking was a failure.

On a day in the early summer of 1680 several canoes made their unaccustomed way out of Lake Erie and down the swift Niagara. They were beached above the fall, on the American side. Of the men who stepped ashore, a number were French. Ragged and unshorn, foul and half starved, they had made their way back from the ruined Fort Crèvecœur on the Illinois. The leader of the disreputable band was Moyse Hillaret, La Salle's master ship-builder. With him were Noël Le Blanc and François Sauvin ("La Roze"), ship carpenters, and the blacksmith Jean Le Meilleur ("La Forge"), hero of the episode of the murderous Seneca and the red-hot iron. They were a quartette of precious rascals, who seem to have hung together in acts of villainy from the outset, and who might very well have been hanged together, with wholesome justice. With them, or joining them soon were other renegades: Jacques Richon, Jean La Croix, Petit-Bled, Martin Chartier, Boisdardenne, Jacques Monjault, Pierre Poupart, Jean Roussel, Nicolas Duplessis, Baribault, all deserters from La Salle's service; and the outlaw Turcot, a fugitive from justice, a thief and assassin, who ten years before had fled into the wilderness. Just where the men from the West picked him up is not clear, but they were together on Lake Ontario, if not on the Niagara.

Led on by Hillaret, they broke into La Salle's little storehouse above the falls, where, finding a cask of wine, they broached and drank it — not a surprising act, under the circumstances. Hillaret helped himself to a quantity of cloth and other articles. Everything that had been stored there, of any value, was appropriated. Then the canoes were portaged to the lower river and the thieves took their way into Lake Ontario, where they separated into two parties, eight of them, including Richon and Lemire, carrying a quantity of La Salle's furs, following the south shore in the hope of reaching Albany; the others, numbering about a dozen, crossing to the north shore, by which they hoped to gain the St. Lawrence and Montreal.

Messier and Laurent reached La Salle, at Frontenac, July 22nd and gave him Tonty's letter, with the news of the destruction of Crèvecœur, and the desertion of all the men. One questions how it happened that these messengers and the runaway thieves had not fallen in with each other on the way down the Lakes, as they probably all came by the Niagara route. La Salle may well have been stunned by this new proof of calamity, but instead, he was roused to righteous wrath. He at once took nine men aboard the barque which he had been loading with supplies for Tonty. His own account of what followed deserves place in the annals of Lake Ontario:

I sailed at once in my barque, with nine men to seek them [the deserters] and ordered 15 others to follow me, but they were unable to come on, the wind several times compelling even me to return.

Finally, on August 2nd, I anchored at the head of an island on one side of which they would have to pass, to go to New York,[10] as some few have done. About four in the afternoon I saw a canoe in which were two of my people, who, having fallen in with the deserters, hastened day and night to tell me that they were 20 in number, and that, not content with what they had done on the Illinois, they had destroyed the redoubt which I had left on the river Miami, had taken the beaver which I had deposited at Mackinac, and pillaged the store-house above the fall of Conty; that they had separated into two bands, that eight had taken the route for New York and 12 that

[10] "*A la Nouvelle-Hollande.*"

for Fort Frontenac; resolved, if they encountered me, to kill me and to fire only on me; that they could not be far away and were coming in two canoes, six in each.

I immediately sent these two *habitants* on to the fort with orders that every one there should arm and mount guard at three different passes, so that, if the marauders escaped me by night, they would be arrested by the others. I left the barque with five well-armed men, and went by the other side of the island, which is five leagues long, to discover their fire at night. I continued three leagues further, and at daybreak was at the end of a *traverse* [11] called Okoui, where I saw two canoes coming straight towards us, as the woods near us prevented them from seeing us.

When they were half a league or so from us, I took after them, and as their two canoes were separated some distance, we came up to the first, in which were five men. I had ordered my people, in giving chase to these canoes always to follow in a line (*en queue*), because that would lessen their danger; and, in case of resistance, to bring down the head man; because, the Governor being dead, as they cannot change places in these canoes, they can do no more than turn, and cannot fire accurately nor even at all without turning the canoe.

Overtaking them, I, with gun ready to fire, ordered the rascals to come with me; and when my two men raised their guns, they had to submit. I took away their arms and put every thing, with their provisions and baggage, in my canoe, and then attacked their second canoe, which yielded readily, having only two men, the five others having made another canoe, which lagged behind and which I was told should arrive the next day.

The prisoners acknowledged to me all that I have been told by the two *habitants*. I put them in prison, at the fort, and set out at once to catch the others, about four in the afternoon. At six in the evening, I saw a canoe a league away. I made for it, but as it was only half a league from land, and I a league and a half, before I could prevent, it gained a point, where they landed, but around which, for the distance of a league, it was impossible to set foot ashore because it was a steep rock at the foot of which the waves of the lake beat. I drew near, however, within gunshot and saw that there were five deserters, and thieves who waited, each behind

---

[11] Two very common words in the old French records of the Lakes are *portage*, a crossing by land, and *traverse*, a crossing by water. The voyage through Lake Ontario, from Fort Frontenac to the Niagara, is often called *la grande traverse*. Modern English has adopted the former word, but not the latter.

a tree, and as we afterwards learned, with their guns loaded with three balls. I could scarce restrain my men who wished to land, openly; but as those who paddled my canoe did not wish to go nearer, through concern for me, I on my part would not permit them to expose themselves, but remained with four, guns ready, to prevent the runaways from embarking, while I sent four others to land at a distance and circle round in the woods behind the thieves. They followed them by land, with guns ready; but the canoe going too fast for them, my people made landing a league away, but night coming on, they had to reëmbark and return along shore to land nearer the cabin of the runaways, fearing that if they came by night through the woods from a distance, the noise of rotten wood and branches snapping under their feet would make known their approach.

They had not gone far when they encountered those they sought, who had embarked without our seeing them, the night being very dark. Having ordered them two or three times to stop, and seeing that on the contrary they put themselves on the defensive, my men charged, killing two and capturing the three others whom they brought to me and whom I put in irons [at the fort], until the arrival of Count Frontenac, who was expected soon.

La Salle goes on to tell how, the next day, he set out in pursuit of those who had taken the south shore route, for the New York colony. Head winds and heavy seas delayed him so long that he gave up the chase. Leaving orders with Sergeant La Fleur to watch for them, should they reappear in the lake, La Salle completed his preparations. Undaunted by the failure and losses of the year past, he now made a new start, with plans modified by experience and the exigencies of his situation.

There are different accounts, seemingly at variance, of the route he now took. Father Membré explicitly states that La Salle left Fort Frontenac in his barque, July 23, 1680, but was so detained on Lake Ontario that he did not reach " the straits of Lake Conty [*i. e.*, the Niagara] till the close of the month of August. Everything," continues the priest, " seemed to oppose his undertaking. He embarked in the beginning of September on Lake de Conty."

Parkman, relying on a letter of La Salle, says that " he

ascended the river Humber; crossed to Lake Simcoe, and thence descended the Severn to the Georgian Bay." Had the historian made further citation from what is perhaps the most valuable of the La Salle documents, at least for this part of his career, he would have cleared up the seeming contradiction. La Salle, as usual, divided his forces; went himself with 12 men by the Simcoe route, but sent the others with the heavier freight, by Niagara and Lake Erie. The blacksmith, two sailors, two soldiers and a rope-maker, with boatmen and hunters, came through the Niagara; while La Salle, Dautray, a surgeon, three soldiers, two sawyers, two masons, and two laborers undertook the Simcoe route, which, though shorter, was more difficult for the transportation of heavy goods, because of the long portage.[12] The Niagara party soon lagged behind. They carried iron, hemp, tar, sails and tools, 300 pounds of lead, powder and guns. There were always the winds of Lake Erie to reckon with; and although they had left Frontenac before their leader,[13] yet La Salle reached Mackinac, and lingered there, and went on, before they came.

Noël Le Blanc, apparently reconciled, was again with La Salle. The explorer was too great to be vindictive — and boat-builders were hard to find. There had been, also, a reconciliation and new agreement with Moyse Hillaret.

La Salle's course towards his recalcitrant followers, was magnanimous. We find no record of attempts at punishments; there is abundant record of pardon. More than 60 men, at one time and another, deserted from his service. "It will not be found," wrote a friendly hand,[14] " that he has killed or caused to be killed one, although he has had arrested or arrested himself more than 20. It is true that two of them were killed in 1680, but it was neither in his presence nor by his order.

[12] La Salle says he arrived at Lake Simcoe the 23d Aug. (Margry, II., 115.) It was there he arrested two of his deserters, Gabriel Minime and Grandmaison.

[13] Membré says the departure from Fort Frontenac was on July 23d, which may refer to the canoes that came to Niagara. La Salle says he set out Aug. 22d. He also says he reached lake Simcoe (" *au bord du lac Toronto*") on the 23d; hardly credible.

[14] "*Mémoir pour Monseigneur le Marquis de Seignelay,*" in Margry, II, 286.

These two, with their comrades, deserted from the Illinois, stole what they could carry away, ruined the fort of the Illinois or of Crèvecœur, and that of the Miami, carried away the skins which he had at Mackinac, pillaged and ruined the house of Niagara, and determined to kill him. He himself arrested seven of them without doing them any other harm; and the other five, refusing to surrender, and wishing to fire on his people, two among them were killed. He had the right to pursue them, in quality of governor and master,— and by natural right as [they were] deserters, thieves, enemies and assassins; and he would have been blamable had he not put forth all his efforts to capture them."

"As for the bad treatment which they say I give my people," wrote La Salle,[15] "there is not the least truth in it, and there is no other proof than the complaints of those who have deserted and robbed me, to whom is given as much credence as to honest men; and the contrary justification is easy to make, as since that time not one has left me, not even those whom I have pressed into service, and who have been with me seven or eight years. Their accounts prove that I owe them nothing, and I hope they have done nothing except at the instigation of my enemies; but as the cabal is powerful here, I need a strong recommendation in order to have justice."

Of the ultimate fortunes of the deserters little precise information is afforded by the documents. While La Salle was in the West, and before he learned the fate of the *Griffon*, deserters from the party which he had sent on in advance had reappeared in the East. In November, 1679, Governor Frontenac informed his king that Governor Andros, at "Manhatte," was sending all the Frenchmen that fell into his hands to Barbadoes, but that he has retained there [New York] and even well treated a man named Péré, and others who have been debauched from Sieur de la Salle, with the design to employ and send them among the Outawas, to open a trade with them." We shall see presently how the English and Dutch were helped in their first trading ventures on the Lakes by renegade Frenchmen.

[15] La Salle, letter from Missilimackinac, Oct., 1682. Margry, II, 290.

The names of the two who were killed near Fort Frontenac are not given; nor is the treatment specified which Count Frontenac meted out to the prisoners, save in one or two cases, notably that of the turbulent ship-carpenter, Moyse Hillaret. This worthy, being taken before the Intendant, DuChesneau, made no denial of his deeds, but boldly sought to justify them. He gave his own version of the trouble on the Illinois. He testified that six of the men ran away from Fort Crèvecœur "about the time of the king's fête"; [16] that Accault, Du Gay and Father Hennepin set out on their journey to the country of the Sioux, February 28th, and that on March 2d La Salle left the camp with four men, for his forced march to Fort Frontenac. After they had gone La Chapelle and Le Blanc arrived from a fruitless journey to Lake Michigan, and told the few men left at Fort Crèvecœur that Fort Frontenac had been seized by the Sieur Guiton and La Salle's creditors, that La Salle was a ruined man and would never come back. So they took counsel as to what they should do. Le Blanc's reports were the final discouragement needed. In Hillaret and the blacksmith he found kindred spirits. They figured, according to Hillaret, that La Salle owed them nearly three years' wages, at the rate of 800 livres per year for each carpenter and 1,000 for the blacksmith. They determined to pay themselves with anything they could lay hands on, and go away. Hillaret's declaration [17] recites at length what they took: guns, powder and lead, clothing, hatchets, an old kettle, canoes and a quantity of furs. The testimony of Monjault, La Croix and Petit-Bled agreed with that of Hillaret, who also showed a note from La Salle, for the amount due.

At Mackinac, La Salle learned to a certainty of the shipwreck of the *Griffon*. A hatch, a bit of rigging, a cabin door, the end of a flagstaff and some bales of rotted furs, washed ashore, told the story. In view of these and other details stated by La Salle, there would seem to be little warrant for any longer making a mystery of the fate of the *Griffon*.

[16] "The King's fête" means the King's birthday, which in this case was on September 5th.
[17] Made at Montreal before Du Chesneau, Aug. 17, 1680.

Two Alleged Portraits of La Salle
(*See Appendix*)

Jacques-René de Brisay,
Marquis de Denonville

A DRAMA OF DISASTER 71

On this journey La Salle met and arrested two others who had deserted his service, Gabriel Minime and Grandmaison. They were thieves and scoundrels, but he appears to have added them to his force. The doctor above mentioned was Jean Michel; he accompanied the explorer to the Gulf, and he was one of the witnesses of the ceremony by which La Salle claimed the Mississippi Valley for France, April 9, 1682.

Others who went by the Simcoe route in this summer of 1680 were André Henault and Pierre You, tried and trusty men; Tamisier, who died; and one named Baron.

With La Salle's troubles and adventures of the months that followed, the present chronicle is not concerned. In May, 1681, he returned to Mackinac, where he found Tonty and Father Membré. With the latter, he continued by canoe to Fort Frontenac, but by which route seems to be nowhere specified. At Montreal, August 11, 1681, he made his will. In it he acknowledged his great obligations to his cousin, François Plet, to whom, in event of his own death, he gave Fort Frontenac and its dependencies, "as well as all my rights over the country of the Miamis, Illinois and others to the southward, with the settlement among the Miamis, in the state it may be at the time of my death; that of Niagara and all others that I may make up to that period, with all the vessels, boats, long-boats, goods, chattels and real estate, rights, privileges, rents, buildings, and other things to me belonging which may be then found thereon." So far as the Niagara was concerned, it was the emptiest of bequests. Long before his death, all traces of his fleeting occupancy of these shores had vanished.

CHAPTER VI

FOLLOWERS OF LA SALLE

Return of Accault and Hennepin — La Salle's Last Visit to the Niagara Region — The Achievements of Tonty — Grim Comedies of the Wilderness.

Michel Accault, Du Gay the Picard, and Father Hennepin, after their wanderings in the land of the Sioux, accompanied Du Lhut to Green Bay and Mackinac; at the latter place they spent the winter of 1680–81. In the spring of 1681, Accault, Du Gay and Hennepin came by canoe through Lake Huron and the Detroit, to the Niagara. Hennepin's account of their return mentions his companions but once by name, and always exhibits himself as the life and leader of the journey. That he was not, we know from La Salle's own words: "I sent a canoe up the Mississippi (*fleuve Colbert*) . . . in charge of two of my men, Michel Accault and the Picard, to whom the R. P. Hennepin attached himself," etc. And Accault was still leader of the party, when they stepped ashore above Niagara Falls. One must regret that we have only Hennepin's account of the journey or of this his last sojourn in the region. None of them appears to have been burdened by any sense of obligation to La Salle. It is not recorded that they made any effort to rejoin him, or to report to him the result of their travels since he sent them out. Hennepin tells us of their success in getting game, as they came through Lake Erie. They were " upon a large point of land which runs itself very far into the water "— probably Long Point — when they saw a bear far out in the lake. " We could not imagine how this creature got there; 'twas very improbable that he should swim from one side to t'other, that was 30 to 40 leagues over." It being calm, two of the men paddled off to poor Bruin, and after firing many shots, overcame him, attached him to the canoe and towed him ashore, " with much ado, and great hazard of their lives. We had all the leisure that was requisite," continues Hennepin, "for the dressing and ordering him, so as to make him keep; and in the mean time took out his Intrails, and having cleans'd and boil'd them, eat heartily of them. These are as good a dish as those of our Sucking-Pigs in Europe. His Flesh served us the rest of our Voyage, which we usually eat with Goats-flesh, because it is too fat to eat by itself."[1]

With his companions, Hennepin revisited the falls "and spent half a Day in considering the wonders of that prodigious Cascade." Of this, his last visit to the region, which was apparently in May, he wrote in the "*Nouvelle Découverte*" a very long account, repeatedly referring to the cataract as of more than 600 feet in height, with space behind the falling water "big enough for four Coaches to drive a breast without being wet"; and other equally edifying observations.

They carried their canoe "from the great fall of Niagara, as far as the three Mountains [Lewiston], which are two leagues below, in all which way we perceiv'd never a Snake," though he had just assured his readers that the vicinity of the falls was infested with them. At the mouth of the river he looked for La Salle's fort: "We thought we should find some Canadians at the Fort of the River which we had begun to build, at the beginning of our Discovery: but these Forts were only built for a Show, to cover the secret Hopes M. de la Salle had given to the French Court." He charges La Salle with having used the protection of the French Court for "his own private Interest," and repeatedly assails with misrepresentation and more subtle implication the leader to whom he owed everything.

"The Fort of the River of Niagara was become a deserted place," he writes, of his last glimpse. With his companions, he followed the south shore of the lake; and after a stop among the Senecas of the Genesee, crossed to Fort Frontenac, where he found Sergeant La Fleur, still commanding in La Salle's absence, and Father Luke Buisset. After a sojourn for rest

[1] "New Discovery," London, 1698, p. 214. Like other early writers, Hennepin speaks of goats as a game animal in the Lakes region. Reference is probably to the deer.

and devotion, he made his way to Quebec and soon sailed for France.

It is unnecessary here to add to the literature of Hennepin, already ample and exceedingly varied in valuation of the priest's writings. We give him due recognition for the part he bore in our regional history; and merely append the following decree of Louis XIV., addressed to Governor de Callières and the Intendant, De Champigny, in 1699:

> His Majesty has been informed that Father Hennepin, a Dutch Franciscan who has formerly been in Canada, is desirous of returning thither. As his Majesty is not satisfied with the conduct of the Friar, it is his pleasure that if he return thither, they arrest and send him to the Intendant at Rochefort, to whom his Majesty will communicate his intentions in his regard.[2]

In August, 1681, with a new company, La Salle is once more on the Niagara, on his way west. Of this visit Le Clercq says:[3]

> We have said that Lake de Conty empties into Lake Frontenac by a channel 14 or 15 leagues long and by a cataract or waterfall 100 fathoms high. The current of this channel is of extraordinary rapidity. One of the canoes, launched a little below the mouth of the lake, was carried away by the current, but the men and goods were saved. This accident caused a delay of only one day. At last the Sieur de la Salle, after sending new orders to the Sieur de la Forest, commandant at Fort Frontenac, and leaving men at Fort de Conty, embarked on Lake de Conty on the 28th of August in the year 1681, and at the beginning of November arrived at the river of the Miamis.

Now came the realization of his dreams, the accomplishment of the thing at which he had twice before failed. Down the great river he went; and when on April 9, 1682, at the mouth of the Mississippi, he named the region "Louisiana," and formally took possession of it in the name of God and

---

[2] N. Y. Col. Docs., IX, 701.

[3] A footnote in Margry, II., 164, says that the discoverer returned to the West by the Lake Simcoe route. Parkman says the same thing, without citing any authority. ("La Salle," ed. 1889, p. 273.) Our quotation from Le Clercq is the narrative of Membré.

King Louis XIV, there were with him four of the men who had first come in his service to the Niagara in 1678 and remained faithful ever since: Tonty, Father Membré, Dautray, and François de Boisrondet. The others were Jacques Cauchois, Gilles Meneret, Jean Dulignon, Nicolas La Salle, and La Métairie, the notary from Fort Frontenac.

It is to be noted that La Salle, on reaching the Arkansas, in March, 1682, took formal possession of the country, with civil and religious ceremonies and the raising of a cross. Similar observances, in April, at the mouth of the Mississippi, proclaimed the discovery and claimed the region for France. But never did he or those under him, hold such service on the Niagara or the Great Lakes. It was the customary proclamation of discovery; and had been made on the north shore of Lake Erie in 1669 by Galinée and Dollier de Casson; but no such proclamation, nor any claim to priority in the Niagara region was ever put forward by La Salle.

La Salle retraced his way up the Mississippi, and after a long illness reached Mackinac, whither he had sent Tonty. The first news which came east of his exploration of the Mississippi to its mouth came from Tonty, who at Mackinac announced the great achievement. The lateness of the season caused La Salle to abandon his plan of proceeding to Quebec; with his lieutenant he returned to the Illinois, where the winter of 1682–83 was spent in fortifying Starved Rock, in trade, and in attempts to strengthen the little colony. In the meantime Count Frontenac was recalled and was succeeded as Governor of Canada by La Barre, who was no friend to La Salle, nor inclined to give any aid in his undertakings. On the contrary, he wrote disparagingly of him to the Ministry, prevented supplies from being sent to him, and in the spring of 1683 confiscated Fort Frontenac and all that La Salle had there. In the fall of that year the explorer passed eastward; by which route seems nowhere to be specified. He reached Quebec in November, and finding his case hopeless in Canada, soon after sailed for France. He was never again in the region the history of which we here trace.

Assuredly, of all leaders of really great undertakings, who

did achieve a measure of success, and whose names are the enduring endowment of history, Robert Cavelier de La Salle was in some respects the most unfortunate. The ordinary hardships of exploration were the least of his troubles. He could meet fatigue and starvation with a light heart. The coldness and austerity which repelled many, seemed to win him the respect and in some cases the devoted allegiance, of the Indian. But from first to last, throughout his great American adventure, he was beset by a succession of misfortunes most of which, it would seem, ordinary care and good management could have averted. His vessels were wrecked, his goods were lost, his possessions at Fort Frontenac were confiscated, his enemies were busy at Court. His men robbed him, burned his buildings, and deserted. Some to whom he gave his trust, turned traitor, and finally one of his miserable followers shot him in the back and he died in a Texas swamp. He had a perfect genius for making enemies and a knack of defeating his own aims by surrounding himself with untrustworthy and incompetent men.

Of the few who remained faithful, one alone stands conspicuous. That one was the Italian, Tonty. He supplied the sort of ability La Salle did not possess, and he served the adventurer with patient and sturdy fidelity. There are few characters prominent in Niagara history which stand scrutiny better, or more enlist the admiration than the Knight Henri de Tonty, the Man with the Iron Hand. His part in the history of the region here under study rivals La Salle's in importance and extends over a longer period of years.

Although there is no satisfactory or adequate biography of Tonty, there is, seemingly without exception, among students and writers, high appreciation of his worth.[4] He was a son of the Neapolitan banker Lorenzo Tonti whose name

[4] See especially "*Les Tonty*," by Benjamin Sulte, Trans. Roy. Soc. Canada, vol. XI; also the pamphlet, "The Man with the Iron Hand," by Henry E. Legler. (Milwaukee, 1896.) Parkman says much of him, always with warm appreciation: "There are very few names in French-American history mentioned with such unanimity of praise as that of Henri de Tonty. Hennepin finds some fault with him, but his censure is commendation." ("La Salle," ed. 1889, p. 441 note.)

is preserved in the word tontine, descriptive of the insurance system he devised. Born in 1649 or 1650, Henri became a cadet in the French army in 1668. It was perhaps French influence which led him to change the spelling of his family name, numerous autographs exist showing it written " Tonty." He also sometimes spelled his first name " Henry." He saw much active military service and in Sicily, in 1677, at the siege of Messina, according to accepted accounts, his right hand was torn away by a grenade. He afterwards wore a hand of metal, covered by a glove. One esteemed writer [5] says it was of silver, others say it was of iron; so that the wearer of the metal member has come to be commonly styled " the Man with the Iron Hand," by which picturesque and suggestive phrase La Salle's capable administrator is designated in many works. But if we may trust the earliest chronicler who mentions it, the false hand was neither of silver nor iron, but copper. Bacqueville de la Potherie, contemporary with Tonty, says in his history published in 1722: " The Chevalier de Tonty had a wrist of copper covered usually with a glove. This gentleman, in an engagement at Messina, received a sabre-stroke on the fist and was made prisoner. He himself cut off the [wounded] hand with a knife, without waiting for a surgeon to perform the operation. . . . The Indians greatly feared it; they called him Iron-Arm [*Bras-de-Fer*]; he often broke their heads and teeth with a blow of the fist when he had difficulty [*démêlés*] with them. They did not know, at first, that he had this wrist of copper." Parkman speaks of the efficacy of this gloved member as a corrective influence among the savages and adds that they regarded Tonty as a " medicine " of the first class. It is clear, however, that Tonty's ability to deal with men, be they red or white, did not depend on his prowess in cracking skulls or knocking out teeth.

It was the Prince of Conti who recommended Tonty to La Salle. That the explorer found him satisfactory may be gathered from a letter which La Salle wrote to his great pa-

[5] " Duluth was a cousin of Tonty with the silver hand." Winsor, " Cartier to Frontenac," p. 273.

tron, soon after reaching America. It is dated " Quebec, October 31, 1678," and says:

" You well know Tonty's honorable character and agreeable disposition, but perhaps you would not have thought him equal to tasks which call for a hardy constitution, knowledge of the country and the use of both hands. Nevertheless, his energy and cleverness make him equal to everything. At this moment, when everybody dreads the cold, he is beginning the construction of a new fort, 200 miles from here, to which I have taken the liberty of giving the name of Conti. It is situated near the great cataract, more than 120 toises [6] in height." This letter shows what La Salle proposed for Tonty, rather than what he had yet done. Tonty was still at Fort Frontenac; and when the Niagara was reached, as preceding pages show, his chief charge was the construction of the *Griffon*.

The prince to whom this letter was addressed was Louis-Armand de Bourbon, eldest son of Armand, the first Prince of Conti, and nephew of the great Condé. Born in 1661 he was in his eighteenth year when in 1678 he appears as La Salle's patron. To what extent he aided the explorer, either with funds or influence, is not known; but that there had been substantial proof of his interest and friendship is evident from La Salle's letters, and from the great honor which he sought to bring to his patron by bestowing on his fort, on the great cataract, and on the lake which we know as Erie, the name of Conti. If these were bestowed in the hope of favors to come, there is nothing in the subsequent fortunes of La Salle to indicate that he profited from thus adding to the map of America the name of one of the greatest families of Europe's most brilliant court. The name Conti — or " Conty," for it appears both ways with equal authority — did not long stay on the map. Apparently no one but La Salle himself used it for the designation of Niagara Falls. In the very year of La Salle's death it was replaced, as the name of the fort at the river's mouth, by Denonville, who was not too modest to give his own

---

[6] That is, more than 750 feet! Father Hennepin's exaggeration in this matter is familiar; but the reader will note that La Salle's letter was written two months before Hennepin saw the Falls.

name to the fort he built where the feeble Fort Conti had been. For some years the name was retained for the lake; but geographers soon settled upon one spelling or another of the Indian name which for a century and a half has been written " Erie."

The youthful prince whose name was so evanescent a part of our regional history was the least distinguished of a very distinguished line. There is a striking incongruity between the broad plans and far-reaching ambitions of La Salle and the relative insignificance of his patron. The few lines that history accord him deal chiefly with his faults. Like many a noble youth of his time, he seems to have played a man's part while little more than a boy. But if frivolous and dissipated at court, he was brave and capable as a soldier. He served in the imperial army in the campaign of Hungary against the Turks and took a brilliant part in the battle of Gran, 1685. He died in that year, some two years before La Salle was murdered; and is probably remembered far less for the aid he gave to exploration in America than for the fact, mentioned in all notices of him, that he married M'lle de Blois, a natural daughter of Louis XIV and M'lle de La Valliére. The great beauty of his wife has been celebrated in verse and prose by La Fontaine and Mme. de Sevigné.

It is unnecessary to trace in detail the service of Tonty during the years that followed. Much of it has already been indicated. It was he who built Fort Crèvecœur, as it was he who built the *Griffon*. He was left in command when, in March, 1680, La Salle, Dautray and others set out for Canada. Cares and privations on the Illinois brought on a long sickness. In the summer of 1681 he was in Montreal, with La Salle and Membré. Returning westward in August, their loaded barque sailed from Frontenac to Trajagou.[7] Of this passing Tonty wrote: " The father and I went on board, and landed the first day at Niagara, below the fall of the river; there we were forced to put our baggage and merchandise upon sledges, and so conduct them to the Lake Herié, where we reembarked in a canoe to the number of 20 persons, as well soul-

[7] On Bellin's map of 1745, Tejaiagon, near present Toronto.

diers as mariners." By the same account, they gained the Miami, where La Salle joined them in November.

In 1682 he accompanied his chief to the mouth of the Mississippi, and on April 9th signed his name to the *procès-verbal* by which the country was claimed for France. He came again to the Niagara in 1687, to share in the expedition of Denonville against the Senecas; but the chief scene of his activities, for some years, was Fort St. Louis of the Illinois. He appears to have visited Montreal in 1696, but we have no note of his presence on the Niagara later than 1687. In 1702 he joined Iberville in Louisiana, and in 1704, apparently in the vicinity of Mobile, he died. He never received any recompense from his Government for his long and faithful service in America.

Henri de Tonty has sometimes been confused with his younger brother Alphonse, who was commandant at Detroit in 1704, and later, bearing for many years an important part in that colony. A yet younger brother bore the name of Henri, but has no part in the history of our region.

That the example of the restless and dauntless La Salle exerted an influence over the young men of his time, is certain. Many a less worthy adventurer sought to follow his course; less indeed by way of exploration, than in prosecution of the Indian trade. The Government of the colony found nothing more difficult to cope with, than the unlicensed, law-defying *coureur de bois*. In 1682, there was a marked outbreak of this fever for the forest. Many young men secretly went into the Indian trade, without Government permits, and greatly to the disturbance of licensed traffic. The Sieur de La Chesnaye who at heavy cost had fitted out several canoes for western barter complained to La Barre, who was so influenced by La Chesnaye's representations that he issued an order addressed to the Iroquois, giving them leave to appropriate all the goods and peltries which they might be able to seize from French voyageurs, if the latter were not able to show passports like one which he sent to them. It was an extraordinary commission to put in the hands of savages, and it resulted about as might have been foreseen. As two of La Chesnaye's canoes, coming from the country of the Ottawas, laden with furs, and in the charge of Beauvais de Tilly, essayed to pass the Niagara, they were promptly stopped by the alert Senecas posted there, and ordered to show their passes. As ill luck would have it, they had either lost or left them; whereupon the grim sentries of the Niagara, listening to no explanation, promptly appropriated all there was, and sent the Frenchmen on to Montreal, emptyhanded, to tell La Barre that his agents on the Niagara were carrying out his orders. When La Barre sent De Longueuil to the Niagara, to explain the situation and recover the goods, the Indians retorted, " fiercely," that their young men had but carried out the Governor's orders; and even the adroit De Longueuil had to return empty-handed. " Behold," says a memoir of the time, " the first preliminary step to the cruel war which we have sustained in consequence and which has even threatened the abandonment of the colony." [8]

In 1680 La Salle had taken his second departure from Lake Ontario. His establishment at the mouth of the Niagara had burned, yet the spot was one of frequent resort by Indians of the West, and offered too much in the way of trade to be neglected. After his chief had gone, La Fleur, at Frontenac, stocked the barque and sent it up the lake for furs. Its reception at the mouth of the Niagara was notable. " Some of the Sinnekes," says a quaint English record, " and some of the Onnondages went aboard of a French barque att Onnyagaro, that was come to trade there, and took out of the said Barke a Caske of Brandy and cutt the Cable." The date of this pleasantry is fixed by a statement that " this was done in the Gover'nt of Sir Edmond Andrews [Andros]." [9]

It was not the only lawless seizure at the mouth of the Niagara. Some three or four years later a similar incident is reported. During an examination at Albany in 1687 the Senecas acknowledged that " about a year agoe," a Frenchman named Grandmason — an Anglicised spelling — came with a

[8] "*Mémoire sur le Canada,*" 1689.
[9] Statement of the Five Nations to Gov. Dongan, Albany, Aug. 6, 1687. N. Y. Col. Docs., III., 441. Andros ceased to be Governor of New York Colony in October, 1680.

partner "to a place called Aquarage neer to Onnyagaro," where the Senecas and Onondagas took a hundred beaver skins away from him; but they justified this act as having been done under orders, "hee having noe passe neither from His Excell'cy the Govr nor the Govr of Canada"; but, said the Indians, we gave the hundred beavers back again. The poor Indian was never more perplexed than in these days of budding rivalry for the fur trade.

"Aquarage" can not be more definitely located than that it was near Niagara.

No authority is found to show that Count Frontenac ever voyaged beyond the Bay of Quinté on the north, or Oswego on the south, in the lake that for many years was designated by his name.[10] He knew of the portage at Niagara, but was misinformed as to its length. "A person can go," he wrote, November 14, 1674, in reporting Joliet's discoveries, "from Lake Ontario and Fort Frontenac in a bark to the Gulf of Mexico, there being only one carrying-place, half a league in length, where Lake Ontario communicates with Lake Erie. A settlement could be made at this point and another bark built at Lake Erie."[11]

The few records that have come down to us, of this period on the Lakes, are wholly of acts of violence. Lake Erie was

[10] The allusion in a note in the Jesuit Relations (Thwaites ed., LX., 319) to a voyage of Frontenac to Niagara in 1676, is beyond question an inadvertence. The authority on which the editor makes the statement, is a letter of Louis XIV. to Count Frontenac, Apr. 28, 1677; but that letter, as printed in the N. Y. Col. Docs., IX., 126, speaks only of the Governor's "voyage to Fort Frontenac."

The historian Brodhead makes the missionary Garnier a visitor at Niagara in 1683. "Garnier," says Brodhead, "who for three years had been left alone among the Senecas, now [1683] felt no longer safe, and escaped from Niagara to Fort Frontenac." ("History of the State of New York," 1st ed., II, 378). But the document Brodhead cites, states that Garnier "escaped in the bark which was anchored in a little river seven leagues from their village, and where all the Iroquois used to come to trade." (De Meulles to De Seignelay, Quebec, July 8, 1684.) This anchorage probably was Irondequoit, which is approximately the distance mentioned from Garnier's mission at Gandougarae, a few miles from present Canandaigua; but it was more than 100 miles from the mission to the mouth of the Niagara.

[11] N. Y. Col. Docs., IX, 121.

still too little under the sway of the white man fairly to come as yet into history at all; but on Lake Ontario various encounters took place, some of them vaguely recorded, while of many more, beyond question picturesquely melodramatic, no tale can be told. By 1682 the Iroquois, irritated by various acts of the French, were spurring up their bravery in frenzied dances and proclaiming their purpose " to put Onontio in the kettle." Theft and murder became common incidents, and no white man could count his life safe in the region through which the Senecas ranged. Even Father Carheil was mobbed. Not the least stirring episode of 1682 happened in the Niagara River, where the Sieur La Marque had anchored the little barque. He had sailed hither from Cataraqui, probably for trade; but the playful Senecas boarded the vessel in force, trussed up the pilot, beat the Frenchmen and made off with 1300 livres' worth of goods.[12] Soon after the warrior Black Kettle, with his band appeared at Cataraqui itself, broke into the storeroom and carried away a quantity of clothing. Offenses of this sort and worse gradually accumulated, until, as De Courcelles handed the colony over to La Barre, there was deemed ample warrant for an expedition of chastisement.

At this time there was three primitive sailing craft on Lake Ontario, making their base at Fort Frontenac, which was little more than a store for the Indian goods. Not merely the sailing-craft, but fleets of laden canoes, were sent to the wild and hazardous shores to the westward, to trade with the Indians. The mouth of the Niagara was a favorite place for this trade; in 1683, according to the report above cited, " there were seven or eight canoes trading at the Falls of Niagara for the interest of the said fort," by which statement the fault-finding De Meulles sought to show that Frontenac was using the fort and the trading facilities of the lake, not for the King, but for his own profit.

There were ever to be met the hazards of a hostile frontier, even at Fort Frontenac. In May, 1684, a band of Senecas beached their canoes on the strand, and carried their peltries

[12] The Abbé de Belmont records this affair, without further detail. No mention is found of it elsewhere.

to the fort, where the storekeeper, one Champagne, made barter with them; but when, through fear or niggardliness, he refused them drink, the stalwart and reckless savages made rough-house of the whole fort. They stole everything they could lay hands on; then, according to the old chronicle, " supposing we were at profound peace, they restored all the merchandise," but this incredible renunciation was not until their sportive humor had been somewhat appeased, " after having given Champagne and the handful of people there a sound drubbing, and drank as much brandy as they pleased; which clearly proves," triumphantly concludes our disgruntled official, " that the General uses this Fort only as a store for the trade throughout Lake Ontario." [13]

From the days of La Salle and Denonville down to the reestablishment of the French on the Niagara, the story of Lake Ontario appeals by its very meagerness to the imagination. Never wholly deserted by traders, it was, as we have seen, more than once the theater of scenes of violence and outlawry. The French, realizing more and more its splendid possibilities, sent into it goodly store of trading goods; and, at least until the temporary abandonment of Fort Frontenac, kept in commission one or two primitive brigantines, which skirted the forested shores, made port of call wherever barter could be had, and cruised without hindrance and with no mean seamanship these lonely wilderness waters. Wind and wave and seasons' changes, seemingly so fickle, were then as now; but the intrepid navigator of those distant years had little to rely on save his own resources and the Providence which attends the daring. There were no charts to show channel or reef, rock or shoal, save such as he might sketch from his own discoveries; no lights to warn or guide; no harbors even, save such as nature made; yet every glimpse we have of the life of old, shows the lake sailors of those days as a happy-go-lucky crew who knew the ins and outs of Ontario's shores, rocky isles and tortuous channels, as no manner of men have known them since, and who bore into every bay and anchorage the white flag of the Bourbon kings.

[13] Ib.

To-day, the leisured yachtsman making holiday, moors his shining craft in some pellucid cove. As evening falls, the lap of the wavelets at his vessel's side, the incense of his ruminative pipe, lull his soul into a receptive sense of sights and sounds unheeded in the bright and busy day. Dimly through the dusk, around the neighboring point he sees a strange-shaped vessel glide. He hears the creak of a gaff, the muffled clatter of lowering sail, calls and commands in a tongue half known, half strange; the splash of an anchor and the rhythm of a running chain. The August moon makes silhouette of a distant pine, the drowsy breeze brings refrain of some foolish, haunting melody of the old régime, of the days when the hardy sons of France, sailing these wilderness waters as their own, still like the children they were, sang the songs of Anjou, of Brittany or Lorraine. Lulled to the border-land of sleep, our summer sailor vows to seek at daybreak the unknown craft — but with the first sun-glint, his thought is for the morning plunge, the glorious swim; and like the vanishing wisps of mist, fades the memory of his brief and shadowy comradeship with the old-time voyageurs and sailors of the Ontario sea.

CHAPTER VII

LA BARRE'S FIASCO

PERROT BRINGS "THE ARMY OF THE SOUTH" TO NIAGARA — AWAKENING OF ENGLISH INTEREST IN THE REGION — TRADE RIVALRY DEVELOPS A TRAGEDY — MISADVENTURES OF JOHANNES ROOSEBOOM.

THE student of Great Lakes history under the French is familiar with the attempt made by Governor La Barre, in the summer of 1684, to discipline the Iroquois for certain outrages they had committed against the French. Many chroniclers of these events have set forth the story of La Barre's advance, as far as the mouth of Salmon River — the *La Famine*[1] of old chroniclers — at the southeast of Lake Ontario; where they ran short of food, and sickened and died of fever, while he concluded a truce with the Iroquois, having gained nothing from them save their contempt. The expedition, which was to have struck terror to the hearts of the Five Nations, ended (as the early historian Colden delightfully sums it up), in " a Scold between the French General and an old Indian." Nothing ever attempted by the French in America was more futile; yet at the outset, however lacking he may have been in ability, La Barre displayed abundant zeal. He talked of crushing the Iroquois; and to this end sought to enlist all the French allies to the westward. In June two messengers, the Sieurs Guillet and Hébert, were sent by the Ottawa route to the posts and missions of Mackinac and Green Bay, with orders to Durantaye and Du Lhut, to gather as many as possible of the Ottawas, Hurons and other western enemies of the Iroquois, and come to his aid. They were to

[1] The exact site has been subject of much discussion. The shore formation, north of Salmon River, is largely the steep sand dunes, with swamps behind them — a formation characteristic of many places on the Lakes, especially the east end of Ontario, and the eastern part of the north shore of Erie.

rendezvous at Niagara whence they were to advance under French escort, to operate with La Barre's force.

It was at best a costly and difficult project to carry out. The western allies — often allies only in the fancies of the French — were by no means eager to meet the Iroquois in the latter's own stronghold. At Niagara they were on the border of a region which they had learned to shun. What followed the spreading of La Barre's order among the tribes of northern Michigan and Wisconsin, has been much less dwelt upon by historians than the episode of La Famine; yet the events in the west and at Niagara proved, in sequel, of very grave consequence to the French colony, and demand a place in the story of the region here under special consideration.

From this point of view, it is not La Barre who is the principal actor, nor even his great captains, Durantaye or Du Lhut, but a picturesque expert of the wilds, Nicholas Perrot.

Born in 1644, we only know, of his early years, that he came to Canada, a mere lad, received some smattering of education and was soon in the service of the Jesuits as *donné* or *engagé*. Accompanying a priest to a distant mission, he became the practical man of the establishment, looking after the necessaries of life while the missionary was more concerned with things spiritual. Some years of this service, the latter part of it among the Pottawatamies, naturally qualified Perrot for independent action. By 1665 he had left the mission service and was a recognized trader, and for half a century or so his story, for the most part, belongs to Wisconsin. At times, service for the colony, or the undertakings of trade, carried him far to the west and north and east; but not the least adventurous of his experiences was his coming to the Niagara in the summer of 1684.

La Barre had sent, none too lavishly, presents to the Ottawas and other tribes whose help he wished. They took the guns and blankets and tobacco, but found excuses. Du Lhut and Durantaye had in large measure failed to rouse them for the expedition. The former meeting Perrot at Mackinac, urged this difficult recruiting upon him. No one, said Du Lhut, was so well qualified for this work as Perrot, "because," says that worthy, "of the ascendency I had over their minds."

Perrot thereupon set out, "on a Sunday, after holy Mass, to go among these nations, who listened to me and received my presents." They only delayed to get their canoes ready, so that eight days later 400 Ottawas, including their chiefs and veteran warriors, were in rendezvous in Saginaw Bay. Other bands were induced to join in; one chief visited the villages in the vicinity and after haranguing them, came back followed by 100 young men. Perrot was acclaimed leader of the Ottawas; besides whom there was a horde of the Foxes ("People of the Bay") and Hurons, with a considerable retinue of Frenchmen, gathered from these distant posts.

The great flotilla set out for Niagara, but the passage down the Lakes was a succession of difficulties. The third day out from Saginaw a French soldier accidentally shot himself and the Ottawas saw in his death presage of evil to come. A little later, among the islands of the Detroit River, a herd of deer was seen, swimming, and a young man, firing upon them from a canoe, broke his brother's arm. "This second accident," writes Perrot, "made such an impression on the Ottawas that they would have turned face-about if I had not persuaded the father of the wounded man to oblige his son to declare publicly that he had only left his own country in the resolve to perish, arms in hand, facing the Iroquois." He did, in fact, die later of his wound, and it required all of Perrot's tact and persuasion to hold the Ottawas.

In Lake Erie, tempestuous weather drove them ashore, two leagues from Long Point, and during the eight days that they waited the Ottawas grew more and more restive, complaining that, if they were away from home so long, their families would starve. As they appeared quite on the point of deserting, Perrot taunted them with cowardice.

"It is not without reason," he jeered, "that you weep for your women. . . . It is surprising that you have come even this far. You are dastards who know nothing of war, you have never killed men, you have never eaten one unless he were given to you bound hand and foot."

It was a bold course to take, surrounded thus by hundreds of angry savages, but Perrot knew his ground. They did not lay hands on him, but they did retort with every vile word which shame and anger could suggest. " You shall see," they cried, " whether we are men, when it comes to fighting, and if you don't do your duty, like us, we will break your head."

" You need not take that trouble," answered Perrot, " for at the first war-cry you will take to your heels."

A result of these taunts was that the Ottawa chiefs stirred up their braves, and strove among themselves as to which should lead the others, in the great battle with the Iroquois, to which La Barre had summoned them. Unaware of it, Perrot had somewhat overshot the mark, and was soon to find himself in grave danger from an excess of zeal, more embarrassing than the cowardice of which he had accused them.

Another *contretemps* befell. During the detention at Long Point, some Ottawas in the woods, amusing themselves by whistling like deer, were mistaken by some Frenchmen for the animals they imitated; a glimpse of white, seen through a thicket whence the whistling came, was taken by the Frenchman for the breast of a stag, at which he fired; wounding not only the wearer of the shirt, but another Ottawa who followed him. Once more the camp of the Ottawas was thrown into a fever of excitement, anger and fear contending; they were plainly foredoomed; but some of the bolder accused the French of treachery: it was high time to abandon the expedition when the French had begun to kill them.

Once more Perrot assembled the chiefs and reasoned with them. The wounded man was brought forward to prove that though wounded he was not dead. Under Perrot's stimulating influence this one declared that he was going to die further on —beyond the Niagara, in the land of the Iroquois — and that he had left his own country for that purpose. One of the braves, uncle to the wounded man, addressed the crowd. " You may all quit and go home," he cried, " but as for me and my nephew, we shall follow the French everywhere." An example of this sort sufficed. Once more the Ottawa hordes were placated, and all continued the route.

Could one have stood, on a September day of that long-vanished year, on the sightly bluff where now citizens of Buffalo love to resort of a summer evening, overlooking the outlet of Lake Erie, he would have gazed upon a wonderful sight. Paddling around the point of the western (now the Canada) shore, and gliding into the swift current of the Niagara, came canoe after canoe, the large decorated war canoes of the Upper Lakes, manned by a horde of lithe, stalwart, naked warriors, with much, no doubt, of grease and vermilion, something of feathers and bear-claw necklaces, and beyond question, occasionally a din of yelling. More and more they came, an endless flotilla, until the river as far as eye could scan, was alive with them; borne swiftly down, until, where the river divides and slackens, above Grand Island, they swept into the western channel, crossing at Buckhorn Island, and before long landed above the Falls and began the great portage. There were more than 700 warriors, all told: Some 600 Ottawas, Foxes, Sacs and Hurons; with 150 French, summoned from many a remote post of western lake and prairie, scarcely less wild than their red-skinned comrades; and with them, among other officers, Du Lhut, the greatest of the *coureurs du bois,* Durantaye, and Perrot. Red men and white, it was the greatest oncoming the Niagara had known within recorded days. No such retinue attended La Salle, or the arduous progress of the missionary priests. The West had come, under special spur, and in league with France, in angry mood, to smite once and for all, the mighty League of the Iroquois.

While this "Army of the South," as La Barre called it, was making the portage around the falls, spies were sent down to the mouth of the river, not so much to look out for enemies, as to see if any vessels had come. While still in their wigwams at Mackinac or Green Bay they had been made expectant of finding here, arms, ammunition and food. They found nothing, nor sign of any boat or messenger. The French, then, had deceived them, perhaps entrapped them! Bringing their boats and burdens by the old path down Lewiston Heights, and paddling down the quiet stretch of river to

Lake Ontario, came the horde of western tribesmen, and with them the perplexed French. Flaming with passion, the Ottawa chiefs demanded a council.

"You have told us," cried their spokesman, "that we are not men. We will show you, Frenchmen, that we are brave; and we tell you, that since you have lied to us, promising us fine things which we don't see, we are going to the Iroquois village."

Perrot and his companions tried to dissuade them from the rash attack which their threat implied, and urged them to wait. "The vessels have been delayed by head winds," they said, but the Indians doubted. Then it was proposed that the chiefs go on with the French in their canoes by the north shore, to Fort Frontenac, "where the French would give us news of the army; and there we would await the army or follow it if it had taken the field." The Ottawas now taunted the French, for lack of valor; and while some were for going to Frontenac, others clamored for an advance on the Iroquois, the braves making a great hubbub. The French argued that it was imprudent to lead 300 Frenchmen against 1500 Senecas, under the escort of the Ottawas, already exhausted with the march and under the influence of bad omens. Messengers went to the Ottawa camp, to reason with them. As soon as they were told that the French, who until then had been masters of the march, now gave them liberty to lead, "they did not hesitate," says the old historian La Potherie, " to put their canoes in the water and set out on the north shore route, which they had ardently wished to do, leaving behind those of a contrary opinion."

Camp was made that night on the lake shore. At midnight they were startled by the report of a gun across the water opposite the camp. "To arms!" they cried. "The Ottawas showed their zeal by running to the guards. Then they heard a voice which said in the Ottawa tongue, that a French vessel had come to Niagara. Everything that had passed was forgotten and joy became universal. Eight Ottawas arrived immediately in a canoe, and reported that a barque had anchored the evening before in view of Niagara. The officers dispatched a canoe to inform [the vessel] of the arrival of the Ottawas, who would at once repair there."

"When the Ottawas learned, on returning to Niagara, that peace had been made with the Iroquois, they belched a thousand abuses upon the French, who however persuaded the more important chiefs to go to Montreal to see the Governor General."

There appear to be but two contemporary or original accounts of the coming of the western tribes to the Niagara in 1684: Perrot's own journal, and the history of La Potherie, first published in 1722. Both are at times obscure. La Hontan, who was with La Barre in the expedition to La Famine, merely alludes to the western recruits. La Barre himself, in his memoir dated Quebec, October 1, 1684, says: " I had ordered one of the barks to go to Niagara to notify the army of the South to return by Lake Erie to Missilimakinack; she had a favorable passage; found it had arrived, only six hours previously, to the number of 700 men, 150 French and the remainder Indians." A number of the chiefs accompanied the French officers to Montreal where La Barre did what he could to placate them. As for the horde of disappointed savages, they made their sullen way up the Niagara and back over the hundreds of weary miles to their western lodges. There was no heart left in them, in spite of all their boasting, for an attack on the Iroquois; but there was kindled a great resentment towards the French.

In 1683 there was issued from the Paris printing shop of Sebastian Huré's widow, " Rue St. Jacques, at the Picture of St. Jerome, near St. Severin," the first and most trustworthy of Father Hennepin's works, the " *Description de la Louisiane.*" This little duodecimo, long since become one of the scarce and costly Americana sought for and treasured by discriminating bibliophiles, not only gave to the world the first circumstantial account of scenes and events in the incomparable Niagara region during La Salle's visits, sojourn and departure, 1678–9, but made plain alike to France and to her jealous neighbors, the audacious enterprise with which the courtiers of Louis were pressing on in the far wilderness of America to gain new dominions for his crown. It is a striking fact that, although the adventures of La Salle, as graphically narrated by the Recollect, must have attracted considerable attention, and could hardly have escaped the cognizance of Charles II. and his ministers, yet no English publisher seemed to think it worth while to make what no English public called for — an English translation of the book. True, the English of that day, who could read at all, were quite as likely to know French as English; yet translations were then published of other French works. The "*Louisiane*" was not translated. New editions did not follow each other in the Sixteenth century with the rapidity of the present, but their issuance was perhaps more significant. In 1684 another Paris printer, Amable Auroy, issued more copies of the priest's wonderful adventures, and four years later still another Paris edition appeared. The work was printed in Italian at Bologna, in 1686, in Dutch at Amsterdam in 1688, and in German at Nuremberg in 1689 and again in 1692. Of this and Hennepin's other works edition followed edition, in several languages and with many variations, to test or tantalize the modern bibliographer; yet the "*Louisiane*" was not reprinted in England, nor has it been from that day to this; though to no people in the world, the French excepted, did these inland exploratory enterprises carry so much significance. To the English it was the significance of a menace. The only edition of Hennepin's "*Louisiane*" in the English tongue was published in New York in 1880, by the translator, the indefatigable John Gilmary Shea.

It was in the same year that the now quaint and rare "*Louisiane*" was sent out from the Widow Huré's shop, that Colonel Thomas Dongan was sent out by the British Crown to be Governor of the colony of New York. The colony had been English less than 10 years; it was still only English by treaty, rather than by any preponderance of English population. Up to his coming, the Niagara frontier, as a vantage ground for trade or a strategic point for war, seems not to have attracted the attention of either the English or the Dutch. But Dongan immediately turned his thoughts to the far western regions inhabited by the Five Nations whose allegiance was so essential not only to the security of the English towns, but to the prosecution of the fur trade. In 1684, at Albany, a treaty was held with these nations. The Senecas were represented and formally submitted to King Charles and by that acquiescence nominally put the region under the British rule. It may be noted, in passing, that the next year when the Duke of York came to the throne, he decreed that the Archbishop of Canterbury should hold ecclesiastical jurisdiction over the whole colony of New York. Those students who delight in determining the first visitor, the first settler, the first in authority and the like, for a given region, will not fail to note the significance of the above decree. As a matter of fact, however, nothing is more unlikely than that the Senecas who sojourned on the Niagara at this period, or even the Dutch and English traders who gave them rum for beaver-skins, ever heard of the Archbishop of Canterbury, or cared a copper for his ecclesiastical jurisdiction, either on the Niagara or even in the settlements on the Hudson.[2]

Many a student of this period of American history has found delight in the correspondence between Governor Dongan of New York, and La Barre's successor, the Marquis de Denonville. Their letters are not only delightful, but exceedingly illuminating. The official exchange of epistles began with formality and courtesy; but presently each was accusing the other of bad faith and underhand dealing. Strong feeling was developed, and as it blazed into wrath, the truth came out. Chief among matters in dispute was the right of the English, which Dongan claimed and Denonville indignantly denied, to trade with the Western tribes. Dongan, on the other hand, taxed the French with violation of treaty agreements in

[2] Dongan's instructions laid emphasis on the necessity of winning over the Iroquois from the French. See, Sir John Werden to Dongan, Nov. 1, 1684; same to same, Dec. 4, 1684; etc. In August, 1685, we find Dongan recommending that the English build a fort "on this side of the great lake," i. e., Ontario; and in Feb., 1687, that one be built at "Oneigra."

attempting to establish themselves on the Niagara. The contention, involving as it did, the British claim to right of access to the Lakes, has received some attention from historians, but not, as is called for in the present study, with particular regard to the Niagara region.

What with the work of the missionaries, of La Salle and his companions, the French had come to look upon the Great Lakes as their own. Dongan, caring only for the region because of the beaver trade, ignored and denied these sweeping claims. He knew something of La Salle's operations on the Niagara. Now early in 1686 word came to him by a deserter from Canada that the French proposed to establish themselves there once more; whereupon he wrote from Albany, May 22d, to Denonville:

"I am informed that you are intended to build a fort at a place called Ohniagero [Niagara] on this side of the lake within my Master's territorys without question (I cannot beleev it) that a person that has your reputation in the world would follow the steps of Mons. Labarr, and be ill advised . . . to make disturbance . . . for a little pelttree."

Denonville replied that the deserter's story was "devoid of all foundation," yet wanted it understood that the region in question was indisputably under French control. "Certainly you are not well informed," he wrote, "of all the entries into possession [*prises de possessions*] which have been made in the name of the King my Master, and of the establishments of long standing which we have on the land and on the lakes; and as I have no doubt but our Masters will easily agree among themselves . . . I willingly consent with you that their Majesties regulate the limits among themselves, wishing nothing more than to live with you in good understanding; but to that end, sir, it would be very *à propos* that a gentleman, so worthy as you, should not grant protection to all the rogues, vagabonds and thieves who desert and seek refuge with you, and who, to acquire some merit with you, believe they cannot do better than to tell you many impertinances of us, which will have no end so long as you will listen to them."

Dongan was not the man to let such an observation pass

without retort. He did more: he fitted out an English expedition and sent it up the Lakes after furs. It is the first known appearance on these Lakes of any white men save in French interest.

No detailed account of that expedition is known. We do know that in the fall of 1685 Dongan licensed certain men of his colony, to trade English goods among the tribes to the westward. He granted such a permit to Abel Marion la Fontaine, one of the deserters of whom the French Governor had complained. His name appears in various forms in the early records, but the "Marion" of one report, the "Abell Marrion" of another and "La Fontaine Marion" of a third, are one and the same. As he had experience on the Lakes, his present service was to act as guide and interpreter. Leadership of the expedition was entrusted to Johannes Rooseboom, a young Dutchman of Albany, member of a family long prominent in New York colony. Eleven canoes, laden with goods for barter and the indispensable rum, set out from Schenectady, made their way up the Mohawk and by the Oneida lake route to Ontario. Skirting the south shore to Niagara, they made the great portage and paddled into Lake Erie — the first white men, not French or in French service, known to have reached these waters. It was a bold and hazardous undertaking, but Rooseboom proved equal to it. A swift course was taken to the Upper Lakes, where they were welcomed by the Hurons and Ottawas, who had never received so much for their furs, or tasted a more agreeable liquor than the rum which answered its purpose even better than the Frenchman's brandy. With canoes deeply laden with furs, Rooseboom made his way back, unharmed, notwithstanding that Denonville sent an officer to Niagara to stop him. Rooseboom merits some distinction in the annals of the Great Lakes, for this achievement. The expedition had been accomplished in three months, and Dongan was so pleased that he proposed another for the next year.

His correspondence with Denonville, after this adventure, naturally did not abate in plain speaking. Both gentlemen were Catholics, and the French Governor had counted on this unity of faith for some coöperation, at least in matters pertaining to the spiritual welfare of the savages: but Dongan, good Catholic as he was, was ever alert for the interests of his own king and colony.³ Moreover, he had the Irish gift of wit. When Denonville indignantly wrote: "Think you, Sir, that Religion will make any progress whilst your merchants will supply, as they do, *eau de vie* in abundance, which as you ought to know, converts the savages into demons and their cabins into counterparts and theatres of Hell," Dongan blandly replied: "Certainly our Rum doth as little hurt as your Brandy and in the opinion of Christians is much more wholesome."

In due time — nor was it long, for news spread fast even in those days — Denonville learned of this English invasion. Reporting it to the Minister, Seignelay, he urged the construction of a strong French post at Niagara, to put a stop to further English expeditions.

The year 1686 was a year of preparation. Denonville had no intention of repeating La Barre's fiasco of 1684. Immediately on declaring war, he wrote, early in the year, to the Minister, his intention was "to fortify in the best possible manner the post at Niagara; this is of the greatest consequence in order both to furnish the people facilities of getting their peltries from the Outawas and other distant places, and to secure a retreat for the Illinois, in case they be pressed by the Iroquois. But it would be proper to send masons from France, as the wages of those of this country are 3 livres and 3 livres 10 sous a day, and they are moreover indifferent workmen. It is so much the more necessary to fortify that post," he added, " as it is to be feared that the English will seize on it, if not anticipated." The general apprehension of all Canada spoke in that sentence. Since the advent of the vigorous Dongan the apparition of the English on the Niagara haunted every hour of the French. The Minister replied in due season that His Majesty approved of fortifying the mouth of the Niagara, but the Governor must be very careful to keep expenses down; and the faithful Colbert lays down two things to be observed:

³ A tablet in Gov. Dongan's memory, erected in 1911, on St. Peter's church in Barclay Street, New York City, by the Knights of Columbus, is a merited if tardy tribute to his worth and services.

First, Denonville was not to build but one fort a year, beginning with the most urgent; second, he was to " construct only slight fortifications, suitable for warding off a surprise, as he has not to do with any power capable of carrying on a siege, so that a simple wall with loop-holes (*créneaux*), and a ditch and palisades outside, are the only works admissible in that country." The King further told the Governor that he must make the soldiers do the work, but that " 4 or five masons and 20 laborers " should be sent. It is touching to find, in this same letter, an anxious inquiry from the King as to the whereabouts of La Salle. " Let him [Denonville] communicate every particular he will learn of that gentleman, and afford him every protection he will stand in need of, should he return."

When Denonville upbraided Dongan, that vigorous administrator warned him not to build any fort " at a place called Ohniagero [Niagara] on this side of the Lake — within my Master's territories, without question," and immediately set about fitting out another expedition.

Operations were planned on a more ambitious scale than in the preceding year. The adventurers were to go up the Lakes and among the western tribes, in two divisions. The first division left Albany September 11, 1686. Captain Rooseboom again led the party, with the refugee La Fontaine as guide. Some Englishmen may have been included, but most of the men were youths of Albany, members of prominent Dutch families. Among them were sons of Arent Schuyler, and Johannes, eldest son of Jan Jansen Bleecker. Numbering 34 in all (" 29 Xtians, 3 Mohoukes and 2 Mahikander Indians "— *i. e.* Mohawks and Mohicans), with 20 canoes, the expedition came as before, up the Mohawk and through Oneida Lake, its passage being promptly reported to Denonville by the Jesuit James de Lamberville; but though the French might learn of their passing they could not stay them. Rooseboom and his band, which included two Indians from each of the Five Nations, were to winter among the Iroquois, proceeding to their western trade in the spring. This they appear to have done, though no record is known of their experiences until spring. Having passed through Oneida Lake in the fall, as we know from

LA BARRE'S FIASCO 99

Lamberville's report, and relying on their canoes for further progress, they probably wintered in the vicinity of the Oswego, coming on to the Niagara in the spring; unless they had passed the Niagara before winter checked them, in which case they msut have hibernated at some spot on the north shore of Lake Erie. In either event they were the first white men, not French, to sojourn in the region. In May they continued their way towards Mackinac.

As soon as the waterways were free from ice, in the spring of 1687, Dongan dispatched a second division of this party of traders, entrusting its command to an interesting character, " a Scotch gent named McGregor." Dongan's " Scotch gent " was Colonel Patrick MacGregorie, who had come to America from Scotland, with a number of followers, in 1684. According to Dongan, he had formerly served in France, and, plausibly, brought with him certain prejudices which in the New York colony did not impair his value for the bold service he was now to undertake. After an apparent residence on Staten Island he removed to the Highlands, turned his attention to the Indian trade and mastered the Indian tongue — probably the Mohawk. It is plain that he enjoyed the friendship of Dongan, who in 1686 appointed him Muster Master General of the Militia of the Province of New York, and soon after, in the same year, commissioned him for this expedition. Dongan gave him orders " not to disturb or meddle with the French. I hope," he adds, " they will not meddle with him." The hope was natural but futile, for the Scotch colonel was considerably meddled with before he got back.

MacGregorie's band set out with 20 laden canoes. Like Rooseboom's party, they made the dread Niagara portage — dreaded both for its toil, and for the risk of attack — and passed swiftly through Lake Erie, unharmed. Promptly learning of their passage, Denonville sent Desbèrgeres and an armed force to the Niagara, to intercept their return. Desbèrgeres and his men haunted the lower reaches of the river, but events to the westward made their precautions unnecessary.

The two English parties had been ordered to join forces at

or near Mackinac, and on completing their trading to return by the Niagara route to Albany, under the command of MacGregorie. All would have gone well had the French been less alert; but Denonville, having resolved to attack the Iroquois in this summer of 1687, had sent orders to his lieutenants at western posts to come on to Niagara, with such French and Indian forces as they could muster, and join his army in its proposed raid. Obeying these orders, early in May, La Durantaye with a horde of savage followers, paddling south along the Lake Huron coast some 60 miles from Mackinac, suddenly encountered Rooseboom's party, bound north. No special correspondent or moving pictures have recorded for us what happened, nor is there any very graphic account of it. Something of struggle, fierce and picturesque, there inevitably was. Rooseboom and his men were all made prisoners and their goods " which would have bought 8,000 beavers," were confiscated and pillaged. There appears to have been a return to Mackinac, no doubt a debauch and a distribution of English goods on far easier terms to the savage recipient than even the unlucky Dutchmen had contemplated.

Soon Durantaye and his greatly augmented company, including the prisoners, took their exultant way once more down Lake Huron. Below Fort St. Joseph, " at the Détroit of Lake Erie," they fell in with DuLhut, from the Detroit post, and Tonty who had come on from the Illinois country, with his wild recruits. All then coming on towards the Niagara, they encountered MacGregorie and his party. The disparity of force was too great for long resistance. The three French officers now had a horde of savages — by one account 1500. That MacGregorie was a stout-hearted adventurer, may be granted; but surrender was preferable to death. The French appropriated all his trading goods, " which by computation would have purchased to that Troop eight or nine thousand Beavers "; and with the two parties of English captives, continued on the way to Niagara. Both divisions of Dongan's force had been well supplied with rum, which some of the western Indians had never tasted. " The French divided all the Merchandize among the Indians, but kept the Rum to themselves, and got all drunk," says Colden's early chronicle. It was a critical time, for while the carouse was on, a part of the Indians were trying to persuade another part to kill the French and cast in their lot with the English. These arguments failed, and as soon as the rum allowed, the consolidated expedition continued its way toward Niagara.

It is a picture which the imagination may be allowed to dwell upon: the triumphant French, with their English and Dutch prisoners under guard, if not in thongs, and none too tenderly cared for; the horde of exultant and painted savages from the north and west. The advance was by canoe, a picturesque train of crowded barques, the red warriors making the wooded walls of Lake Erie echo with their cries. French, Dutch, English and Indians together, it surpassed in diversity and in numbers La Barre's "Army of the South" of 1684.

It was no slight achievement for Durantaye, Tonty and Du Lhut to have gathered this host of western Indians, and to bring them in fair accord to the banks of the Niagara, scene of their disappointment of three years before. That these officers had thus been able to overcome the natural resentment of the western tribes towards the French speaks well for their tact and ability in so difficult a service. The savages were no doubt strengthened for the time being in their allegiance to the French by the two-fold victory on the Lakes. For the moment, among the motley horde at the mouth of the Niagara, British influence had disappeared.

Whoever attempts to trace the story of the Niagara frontier at this period in all its bearings will find himself led far afield. While Dongan was so stoutly maintaining his sovereign's rights, that sovereign himself, swayed by the exigencies of European politics, was taking steps which largely nullified Dongan's efforts. Louis had sent to London a special ambassador, the Count d'Avaux, "on purpose" to bring about an amicable settlement of disputed boundaries in America — which meant Hudson's Bay to the north, the Niagara and Lakes region to the south. It was found "a thing which it was not possible to decide." Later, King James through his Ministers proposed a Treaty of Neutrality. This treaty, signed at Whitehall November 26,[4] 1686, pledged the rival Powers to maintain peace between their subjects in America, and that neither should interfere with the other in his war upon " wild Indians." The treaty did not mention the Iroquois as subjects of Great Britain, and therefore virtually authorized Denonville to continue his operations against them, while it restrained Dongan from interfering. This treaty was received at New York, and published as law required, June 8, 1687. Anthony L'Espinard of Albany was dispatched to Canada with a copy of it for Denonville's edification. That official however had already received a copy of it direct from King Louis, with orders to execute it. More important yet was the coming of 800 French regulars, under the command of Philippe de Rigaud, Chevalier de Vaudreuil, a soldier who is to play an important part in our story. Thus strengthened both by royal approval and by troops, Denonville hastened his preparations for a campaign against the Iroquois.

The Treaty of Neutrality weakened the British cause in that it did not specify that the Iroquois were British subjects. While the French had good ground for disputing it, the mere claim, if it had the sanction of a treaty, would have given Dongan ample warrant for arming the Iroquois and for insisting on a British establishment for trade on the Lakes or the Niagara. Without that warrant, he assumed rights which the treaty did not give him, and continued to deal with the Iroquois so far as they would consent, as though they were acknowledged subjects of his king.

[4] Nov. 10, O. S.

CHAPTER VIII

DENONVILLE'S CAMPAIGN

THE EXPEDITION OF 1687 — THE CASE OF MARION LA FONTAINE — THE BUILDING AND ABANDONMENT OF FORT DENONVILLE — FATHER LAMBERVILLE'S NARRATION — CONFLICTING RECORDS.

DENONVILLE's great captains of the West — Durantaye, Du Lhut, Tonty and La Forest — with their traders, *coureurs de bois* and savages, and with the militant Jesuit from Mackinac Mission, Rev. Jean Enjalran, made camp at the mouth of our river, June 27th. De la Forest, who on many occasions was the messenger, hastened by canoe along the north shore of Lake Ontario, to inform Denonville that the western allies were at Niagara. The day before he set out from Niagara a barque had sailed for that point from Frontenac, loaded with provisions and ammunition. Denonville heard with satisfaction of the capture of the English and Dutch traders, and hastened the preparations for his great assault upon the Iroquois. His army which with great toil and some loss had been 18 days in coming from Montreal to Frontenac, mustered about 2,000 men, regulars, militia and Indians. Leaving a reserve force at this post, he set out July 4th for the south shore and on the 10th landed at the appointed rendezvous, now known as Irondequoit Bay. As his 400 canoes and bateaux drew near shore, they were joined by the force from Niagara. From Quebec on the east, from villages on the Upper Lakes a thousand miles removed to the westward, the two forces had chanced to reach the appointed rendezvous at the same hour. It was not merely the red man who saw in this fortunate arrival omen of a successful undertaking. The party which had come down the Lakes included " about 180 of the most active men of the colony and about 400 savages." These figures, reported to Denonville by La Forest, must be accepted as more trustworthy than the 1,500, which was reported by some of the captives.

As soon as camp was made Denonville considered the cases

of the prisoners, in whose abject persons he saw the humiliation of his redoubtable rival, Dongan. Men like MacGregorie and Rooseboom were dangerous encumbrances especially at the opening of a doubtful campaign against the Iroquois. All of the prisoners therefore were sent on to Frontenac, under guard; all except the Frenchman, La Fontaine, who in a way was held accountable for the intrusion of the first English force into the region of the Great Lakes. By Denonville's order, he was shot.

There is no mention in Denonville's journal of the execution of La Fontaine. Even a great general, in relating his own deeds, may be reticent on such a point; especially, as was the case in this instance, when it was freely denounced as without warrant. There was in Denonville's expedition, a most interesting character, the Baron La Hontan, in whose adventures the curious student of the history of our region will find much entertainment. Years after, in 1703, in a book published at Amsterdam, La Hontan told the story of the military murder of La Fontaine. He was " unjustly shot to death," says La Hontan. " His case stood thus: Having traveled frequently all over this continent, he was perfectly well acquainted with the country, and with the savages of Canada; and after the doing of several good services for the King, desired leave from the Governor-General to continue his travels, in order to carry on some little trade; but his request was never granted. Upon that he resolved to remove to New England, the two Crowns being then in peace. The planters of New England gave him a very welcome reception; for he was an active fellow, and one that understood almost all the languages of the savages. Upon this consideration he was employed to conduct the two English convoys . . . and had the misfortune to be taken along with them. Now to my mind, the usage he met with from us was extremely hard; for we are in peace with England; and besides, that Crown lays claim to the property of the Lakes of Canada."

De Baugy, who was aide de camp to Denonville, explicitly says in his journal:[1] " This same day [July 11] a French-

[1] "*Journal d'une expédition contre les Iroquois en 1687*," etc. This in-

man was made to 'pass by the arms.' He had been captured with some of the English and had been a deserter from the colony for several years. He was executed in conformity with an order which M. the Marquis had received from His Majesty." [2]

In the Rooseboom party were two Dutchmen, Nanning Harmetsen and Fredrych Harmetsen. In MacGregorie's command was Dyrick van der Heyder. These three worthies, after many adventures, reached New York, where on September 7, 1687, they were summoned before Mayor Nicholas Bayard and made a sworn statement of what had befallen them. To this statement we are indebted for some of the foregoing particulars. The Dutchmen averred that all the members of Rooseboom's and MacGregorie's parties were carried prisoners to Niagara, where the French had now (at the time of their deposition) built a fort. From Niagara all of the prisoners save one were sent to "Cadarackque" (Kingston). There they "were very barbarously treated . . . by the French Commander inforcing them to labour grievous hard in drawing the Bark to bring materialls for to strengthen and building the Fort and otherwise." They were afterward sent to Montreal, then to Quebec, where they "were put out to farmers and others for to work for their victuals." If Rooseboom and MacGregorie were better treated than the rest the narrative does not reveal it. The three Dutchmen and one other made their escape in the night from Quebec and five days later reached Albany, making the journey by water. They had other experiences interesting in themselves, but less intimately associated with our immediate subject than the fate of the one prisoner above excepted. The Dutchmen said they all "were sent from Onyagra [Niagara] to Catarackque a Fort beyond the Lake, except Abell Marrion one of Captain Rooseboom's

teresting and useful journal had its first and only publication in Paris in 1883 — 296 years after it was written. No translation has appeared.

[2] According to an undated Memoir on Canada (No. 474, MS. in Quebec Provincial Archives) La Fontaine underwent still another form of death: "Le conseil de guerre fut tenu qui condamna La Fontaine Marion à avoir la teste cassée; ce qui fut exécutée sur la champ."— *Coll. de Manuscrits . . . relatifs à la Nouvelle France*, I, 561.

Troop was by sentence or order of Gov'r De Nonville shott to death because hee was Frenchman born, altho' a subject of his Majesty of England and having a passe from his Excellcy [Dongan] with the rest of the Troop." From this the inference would be warrantable that "Marrion" was shot at Niagara — the first of war's victims under the English flag on the Niagara border. It is not safe, however, to rest conclusions even on such a contemporary affidavit. The Dutchmen were ignorant men; they were prisoners themselves when at Niagara and no doubt swore, in their statement before Mayor Bayard, not only of things they themselves had seen, but to what they had merely been told at Cataraqui, Montreal and Quebec. The narratives of La Hontan and De Baugy leave no room for doubt in the matter.

Rooseboom and MacGregorie were taken to Montreal. Later in the same year they were released, under orders from France, and lost no time in returning, the former to his family [3]

[3] See "A Brief History of the Ancestors and Descendants of John Rooseboom (1739–1805) and of Jesse Johnson (1745–1832)," Cherry Valley, N. Y. [1897]. The first American Rooseboom (the name being variously spelled, in early records, Roosenboom, Rooseboom, Roseboom) was Hendrick Yannsen Rooseboom, who appears to have come from Holland about 1655. In 1662 he bought a house and lot "in the village of Beverwyck on the hill," now a part of Albany. All of the Albany Roseboooms are descended from him. His son, Captain Johannes the trader, was probably born in Albany in 1661. After the episode above recorded he appears to have settled down at Albany to less adventurous ways. He married Gerritje Coster in 1688. In 1692 he was an assistant alderman and in 1700 alderman of the 2d Ward, holding office several times. In 1700 he was serving at Fort Albany as Lieutenant in Captain Johannes Bleecker's Company. . . . He was "buried in the church," Jan. 25, 1745, aged about 84. It is worthy of note that a grand-nephew of Captain Johannes Rooseboom (grandson of his younger brother Myndert), was the Major (afterwards Colonel) Myndert Rooseboom who was adjutant, or assistant adjutant of the division of General Amherst's army which in 1759, under Prideaux, went against Fort Niagara. An original Order-book which he kept on that expedition begins April 13th, with the troops at Albany, the orders being given by Colonel Corsa, under Colonels "Pridieu," Johnson (afterwards Sir William), and Bradstreet. Some of the regiments are as given by Roseboom, "the 44th, L. Royals, late Forbeses, Inniskillings, Royal Highlanders, Abercrombie's, Mury's, Pardoe's and four battalions of Royal Americans." Only a part of these went to Niagara. Leaving Albany May 8th, he is with the troops as they march through the Mohawk Valley, the supplies being carried in whale-boats and bateaux on the river, and reaching Oswego on June 27th, where the book closes.

in Albany, the latter to New York. Sir Edmund Andros sent him, the next year, against the Indians east of Pemaquid. He was eventually killed in the city of New York, in March, 1691, in an attempt to reduce the Leisler party, which held the fort against the Government. The last trace of Patrick MacGregorie is a statement that he was buried with public honors.

The men who came to Canada in 1685 with Denonville (350 soldiers, 20 officers) formed neither a regiment nor a battalion, but were added to the militia under the misleading title, " Detachment of the Marine." They were not a detachment, but a corps complete of themselves, and formed no part of any regiment from France. They were not of the Naval service ("*La Marine*"), but were equipped and paid by the " Bureau of the Marine and the Colonies " which governed Canada. The permanent militia which from 1670 to 1760 furnished the small garrisons of Canada came also to be called " the Marine." Originally the service of the Detachment was that of scouts and skirmishers (*éclaireurs, tirailleurs*), being exempt from ordinary maneuvers of battalion and regiment. It was an ideal troop for the American service, though Denonville's experience of 1687 may have somewhat shaken his faith in it. The officers, originally all French, were gradually replaced until, from about 1710, they were all Canadians. When occasion required more men for service, these officers assumed command of the militia recruits who in time of peace were farmers and small tradesmen. At the close of the French régime the Marine, soldiers and officers alike, were all Canadian, and with few exceptions remained in Canada under English rule. This perhaps explains why in the military archives of France, little or nothing is to be found of them.

It is foreign to the purpose of the present narrative to enter upon the detail of Denonville's warfare against the Iroquois. The story of this inglorious episode has been more than once recorded, with all possible fullness, by competent hands; it suffices here to summarize its principal features.

Leaving a force of 400 men to garrison the redoubt which had been thrown up on a point of land at the entrance of the bay, and sinking their boats under its protection, Denonville on July 12th began his march with some 1,600 troops and Indians southward through the woods. On July 13th they engaged the enemy, who made an unsuccessful attempt to ambush the invaders. According to Denonville's own account there were of the Indians 800 men under arms in this engagement, of whom he was told 40 were killed, more than 50 wounded. Other minor encounters followed, but the Senecas were illusive and many soon fled beyond the reach of the invader. The principal engagement took place near the present town of Victor. Denonville's soldiers burned three other villages, one in East Bloomfield, another near West Mendon, Monroe County, the third not clearly located; they destroyed the old corn and the growing crop, to an amount estimated at the incredible total of 1,200,000 bushels. They feasted on green corn and roast pig, many hogs being found in these Seneca towns; and suffering more from their own indiscretion than from the assaults of the enemy, they marched back to Irondequoit Bay, reaching the redoubt on July 24th.

The chastisement which Denonville was to have visited upon the Senecas had ridiculously failed. He had broken a wasps' nest, but had thereby only stirred up and angered the wasps. The villages he had burned would be quickly rebuilt. The heaviest loss he had inflicted lay in the destruction of the crops, but not even that meant serious discomfiture to the Senecas, allied as they were with all the undisturbed fraternity of the Long House — and was there not Dongan at Albany, where the King's warehouse overflowed with gifts for the Senecas?

One statement in Denonville's journal calls for our attention. At the entrance of the small village of Gannounata (apparently some two miles southeast of the present village of East Avon), "we found the arms of England, which the Sieur Dongan, Governor of New York, had placed there contrary to all right and reason, in the year 1684, having ante-dated the arms as of the year 1683, although it is beyond question that we first discovered and took possession of that country, and for 20 consecutive years have had Fathers Fremin, Garnier, etc., as stationary missionaries in all their villages."

It was at the Albany treaty of July, 1684, that the Mohawks, Oneidas, Onondagas and Cayugas had asked Dongan to give them the arms of the Duke of York, to put up on their " castles." Dongan was alert to pledge them this " defense " against the French. Later, in August, the Seneca sachems reached Albany, shared in the treaty-making, and received like assurances of protection and good will. " I sent the arms of his Royal Highness now his Majesty," Dongan wrote later, " to be put up in each Castle as far as Oneigra [Niagara], which was accordingly done." From his point of view, shared neither by the French nor his Indian protégés, all of Central and Western New York, as far as the Niagara, came under British domination by formal treaty of August 5, 1684. On that day, in a speech at Albany, the Senecas thanked the Governor for the Duke's arms, which he had given them " to be put in our castles as a defense to them."

Just what sort of fabrication these " arms " were, one hesitates to say. No historical museum is known to contain one of these early relics, no history trustworthily pictures them. However made, painted or graven, they evidently pleased the Indians, who could fasten them to a post by the principal path entering the village, or over the door of the chief sachem's lodge. Probably the Indians themselves brought them into Western New York; nor is it likely that any was put up farther west than the Seneca villages of the Genesee Valley, notwithstanding Dongan's assertion that this emblem of authority was to be seen " as far as Oneigra," for at that period the Senecas had no " castles " in the vicinity of the Niagara.

At Irondequoit, July 25th, Denonville's first care was to send off a barque with the sick and wounded, among them Father Enjalran, to Frontenac and thence down the river, with news of the expedition to date. The redoubt that had been thrown up was leveled, the palisades broken down and burned, that nothing might be of service to the enemy. The boats were made ready and on the 26th the army was on its way to Niagara. Denonville had trouble with his Indian allies who feared to go to Niagara, not daring to hunt on the borders of the enemy's country. They were finally persuaded, but their reluctant and shifty attitude decided the Marquis to do quickly what he had resolved upon at Niagara, and get away as soon as possible. When his force was embarked, the regulars and the Ottawas led the way; the militia were so slow that he left them in the rear. Only 10 leagues did the flotilla of canoes make the first day. On the 27th, they were halted by a gale. On the 28th, the boats with the militia having come up, all went forward again, but wind and wave made progress slow; and finally, on the night of the 29th, they went into camp three leagues from Niagara. Taking advantage of the lull of the night hours (the lake breeze being found to come up with the sun), they broke camp at moonrise; and through the calm, hushed hours of the summer night, lighted by the harvest moon, the army paddled and rowed its myriad small craft along the high bank which formed the shore, and at five in the morning of July 31st reached the entrance of our river and quickly made camp on the commanding spot which La Salle had occupied nine years before.

Two Mohawk Indians who had served with the French in Denonville's campaign, were that summer taken prisoners by the English and carried to Albany, thence down the river to New York, where, in Fort James, August 31, 1687, they were examined before Stephen van Courtland [Cortland] regarding Denonville's expedition and the plans of the French. They both gave long accounts of the battle with the Senecas and the destruction of villages and crops. As interpreted by Akus Cornellius, a Schenectady Dutchman, their stories are none too lucid. One of these Indians, Kakariall, had served with the French on the expedition, but on reëmbarking at Irondequoit, was in a canoe with others who refused to go to Niagara. "Two dayes," his statement runs, " they stayed at Irondekatt, then the Govr. gave orders to go by water to Oniagoragh [Niagara], which the Christian Indians refused and went back to Cadaraghie, but 10 or 12 canoes with French went after them, who at last persuaded them to go along to Oniagoragh, except two Cannoes (whereof this Deponent was one) and some River Indians, who escaped." He adds particulars about the fort building at Niagara, but as they are hearsay, may be omitted.

DENONVILLE'S CAMPAIGN 111

His companion, Adandidaghko, was taken to Niagara, and gave some details:

The Govr. gave orders that the whole army should goe directly to Oneageragh, butt the Xtian Indians refused itt butt would returne to Kadaraghie, and soe went that way, the Govr. forthwith followed them with seven Canoes [in] each seven Menn, and stopt them saying,
"What is the matter that you leave us? it is better that wee goe and returne together."
Butt they would not, till one Smiths John stood up and spoke very loud, saying to the rest of the Xtian Indians:
"You hear what the Governor's will is, that wee should go up with him; if wee doe not, he will force us to it; come, you are lusty Men, let us goe with him."
Soe they were perswaded, and returned back with the Govr. Severall Canoes endeavoured yett to escape, butt were so watched by the French, that they could not except two or three Canoes that stole away; so were forced to go with the French along the shore side of the Lake till they came to Oneagoragh, being two days by the way, where the French made a Fort, and put two great gunns and several Pattareras in itt, with fouer hundred Men to bee there in Garrison.[4]

Never before has so distinguished a company gathered on the banks of the Niagara. For the moment, the military branch of the administration of New France is centered here. With Governor de Denonville and the Marquis de Vaudreuil is Denonville's second in command, the Knight Louis Hector de Callières-Bonnevue, Governor of Montreal, a veteran of 20 years' military service before he came to Canada in 1684; he is destined later to succeed Count Frontenac as Governor of Canada. Here too is the Chevalier de la Troye, another veteran who has successfully led an expedition against the English on Hudson's Bay; Denonville, the year before, writing to the Minister, Seignelay, had spoken of de la Troye as "the most intelligent and most efficient of our captains; he has that excellent tact required for the exercise of all qualities needed to command

---
[4] Board of Trade, N. Y. papers, (London docs.), III, N. Y. Col. Docs., III, 433-435.

others." Still another interesting figure in the group is La Forest, Major of Fort Frontenac, where La Salle had left him in command in 1679. When La Barre seized that fort, La Forest returned to France, but at the present period of our story, Fort Frontenac has been restored to him. He has served in the Illinois country, and later is to command at Fort St. Louis (present Peoria) and Detroit. His early service is peculiarly identified with Lake Ontario. No one knew it better than he, and his services were much in demand when a capable messenger was to be sent across its uncertain waters.

In command of one battalion is Dorvilliers, an experienced officer who had gone at the head of his troop in 1682 to Fort Frontenac. He had reconnoitered Lake Ontario and the Seneca country and made a plan, showing the location of the Indian villages before La Barre set out on his attempt of 1684. In that expedition Captain Dorvilliers had commanded the rear guard. The experiences of the sick camp of La Famine were his; and he was La Barre's special messenger to France, to report on it all to Louis and his counsellors. His praises are sounded in many letters of the time. Denonville styled him "a man of much prudence and intelligence," and sent him to command at Fort Frontenac, successor of La Forest. Note has been made of the service he was called to perform in guarding the Niagara pass against the MacGregorie expedition. However he may have failed in that, he had gained an acquaintance with the region perhaps as intimate as was possessed by any one in Denonville's command.

Denonville's entire force, that landed this August morning where now Fort Niagara stands, consisted of four battalions of regular troops, each battalion made up of four companies; three battalions of militia, recruited from the *habitants* — for the most part the untrained Canadian farmer and villager; and four distinct bands of savages, known respectively as of the Mountain [Montreal], the Sault, Sillery and Arhetil. According to De Baugy, there were 353 Indians, not counting the Ottawas and others from the West who although they no doubt tarried at Niagara were not held there for any service.

The companies of soldiers and militia were small. The larg-

DENONVILLE'S CAMPAIGN

est, a militia company headed by Captain de la Ferte, in the battalion of Longueuil, numbered 58 men; the smallest, that of De Repentigny in the battalion of La Valterie, also militia, had but 36 men. The regular troops ranged from 41 to 46 men per company. De Baugy, who gives a detailed enumeration of the entire force, says there were 843 regulars, 804 militia, and 353 Indians, not counting those from the west; and that this force arrived at Niagara in 142 canoes and 198 bateaux; but his totals do not agree with his details. The total force was about 2,000 men. There were two extra heavy bateaux, each of which carried a small cannon and 15 men (*habitants*).

To Denonville, this attainment of Niagara was the fruition of long-cherished hopes. From the hour of his arrival in Canada, he had planned, and worked, for the armed occupation of this frontier. His reports to De Seignelay contain, over and over, allusions to it. He had not counted on destroying the Seneca nation by his raid; but he had hoped to achieve something substantial by occupying the Niagara. "It is an indispensable necessity," he had written in November, 1686, "to establish and maintain a post of 200 men at Niagara, where married farmers ought, in my opinion, be placed to make clearances and to people that place, in view of becoming, with barks, masters of Lake Erie. I should greatly wish to have a mill at Niagara." He believed Dongan was about to plant a company of his English, Scotch and Dutch adventurers there, and he so told the Minister. "Were the English once established there, they must be driven off, or we must bid adieu to the entire trade of the country." And he begged for "two good battalions and the funds necessary to sustain the movement and to occupy the post at Niagara." King Louis gave personal study to the region, as we know from the Royal endorsals on the documents; approved the fortifying of Niagara, and the necessary expense therefor; but Denonville was cautioned by his Majesty "to construct only slight fortifications, suitable for warding off a surprise, as he had not to do with any power capable of carrying on a siege, so that a simple wall with loop holes [*créneaux*] and a ditch and palisades outside, are the only works admissible in that country." He was further admonished to employ the soldiers and "to oblige those of the country to work."

The preceding year he had ordered Dorvilliers to Niagara, with the Sieur de Villeneuve, a draughtsman sent out from Paris. Denonville's estimate of this man is striking. "Though a very good, very correct and very faithful draughtsman, he has not, in other respects, a well-ordered mind and is too narrow to be qualified to furnish any views for the establishment of a post, and to be entrusted with the exclusive superintendence of it." In a subsequent letter he calls him "a fool, a rake and a debauchee who must be tolerated because we have need of him." Denonville begged that Vauban might send him a better man, a request evidently not granted, for it was Villeneuve who surveyed the site and drew the plans for the works which Denonville now set about creating.

"I have selected the angle on the Seneca side formed by the Lake and the river," he wrote, a little later; "it is the most beautiful, the most pleasing and the most advantageous site on the whole of that Lake; the map and plan of which you will have if Sieur de Ville Marie [*sic:* Villeneuve] will take the trouble, for I tormented him considerably for it."

Beautiful and advantageous it seemed to Denonville, this August morning as he landed with his army. Although the men had toiled all night at the oars, there was no time for rest, for the Governor was determined to show to the Indians, especially those from the West, that here was to be "a secure asylum, in order to encourage them to come this winter to war in small bodies." He was also spurred by the fear of Seneca attack.

M. de Villeneuve's plan was simplicity itself. A square, with bastions at the angles, to be surrounded by a high and stout palisade, was traced out on the level ground in the natural angle of lake and river. It was a treeless spot then as now, denuded in days immemorial by countless Indian camps which at certain seasons had been pitched there. The regular soldiers were set at clearing the bushes and small growth; the militia were set at work making the pickets. Denonville notes as the chief inconvenience of the site, the distance that timber and

DENONVILLE'S CAMPAIGN

firewood had to be brought. This work, he says, was the more difficult, "as there was no wood on the ground suitable for making palisades, and from its being necessary to haul them up the hill." Two thousand [5] pickets, 16 feet long, sharpened at one end, were cut and conveyed to the ground. This work was accomplished on the 30th, meanwhile the soldiers had dug the trench where they were to be planted. The next day the soldiers set 700 of them, using four crude pile-drivers which they made. "We wished to make two or three chevrons," says De Baugy, "but the necessary tools were lacking, the barques not being able to come in because of contrary winds." Finally, a canoe was sent out to the little wind-bound vessels, two leagues away, for the tools.

The next day the wind allowed the vessels to draw in, and work went faster. The French soldiers trimmed and sharpened the palisades, the militia set them in the earth. This day three bastions were begun; and Denonville, deeming that some measure of security was gained, ordered the militia to embark.

Denonville was thoughtful of many things. He sent off Du Lhut [6] and one companion to the Detroit River to engage the Indians of that region to bring game to the garrison during the winter. Tonty was sent out to warn friendly tribes near by to be watchful of the Iroquois. The Italian came back at night to report that he had seen, lurking in the vicinity, Iroquois in white shirts, an unheard of thing for savages "who go naked, and smear themselves with clay, in order to be less easily seen." Denonville sent Tonty forth once more, this time with a company of 60 men and three or four drummers, to scare off the enemy — if there were any. Protected thus by martial rub-a-dub in the neighboring forest, the militia departed "right after dinner" (*sur l'après disnée*), while the regular soldiers continued the work, which was to be known as Fort Denonville. A permanent garrison of 100 men was detailed for the post under command of De Troyes as senior cap-

[5] I cannot reconcile De Baugy's figures. His words are: "*On a tiré la place, d'un quarré que l'on veut entourer de 100 pieux; pour cet effet, les habitants ont eu ordre d'un faire 2000*," etc.

[6] De Baugy has "du Hault," but Du Lhut is evidently intended.

tain, with another captain and two subalterns. Leaving also Vaudreuil on the spot for a few days to complete the fort and get in a supply of firewood, Denonville and his officers and some troops departed.

Setting out from the mouth of the Niagara very early in the morning, the flotilla skirted the shore to the westward, as the militia had done, and as, a little later, Vaudreuil and the rest of the army were to do, the entire force returning to Frontenac by way of the north shore. They had no mind to attempt the Iroquois side of the lake. Band after band, the western savages took their way up the Niagara and through Lake Erie, or overland by the forest trails to the Detroit; and the little garrison of Fort Denonville, a timorous, depressed, ineffective company, buried in the hostile wilderness, took up the petty details of routine on which life itself depended.

The first day out, Denonville and his retinue made rapid progress —" 13 good leagues," says De Baugy, with greater accuracy than is sometimes the case in his journal. This brought them to the traverse across Burlington Bay, which they made by moonlight " for fear the wind would surprise us." Camp that night was at Point Onoron,[7] where the Marquis overtook the militia. A thunder storm delayed them on the 5th. They were also delayed by the feebleness of the men. " In each canoe that had six men, not more than three were able to row." On the 6th, they saw the barque which had taken the sick and wounded from Irondequoit to Fort Frontenac; it was now on its way to the Niagara with provisions for the garrison, in charge of one Gaillard. On the 8th, they were overtaken by the two barques which they had left at Niagara, now bearing Vaudreuil and the last of the army; and on the 9th they all made Frontenac. Without accompanying the army farther east, we must return to the cheerless huts that were huddled within the palisades of Fort Denonville.

Scarcely had the commissary, Gaillard, unloaded his stores and sailed away, leaving De Troyes and his men to themselves, then it was discovered that the provisions were bad. Some of the casks were soaked with sea water, the flour had got wet, the

[7] Not identified.

DENONVILLE'S CAMPAIGN 117

biscuits were full of weevils. A feeble attempt was made to raise vegetables, but the season was now late, and what few seed they had, scarce sprouted. The soldiers proved indifferent fishermen and worse hunters; fear of the Iroquois took the heart out of them. They dared not send out small parties; one such party lost two men by the ever-watchful Senecas; another party that ventured into the forest was never heard from. Summer waned, autumn faded into the chill and dreary winter; and as the days dragged on, with no visits from their western allies, bringing game, the scurvy looked in upon them, starvation came and took command. If any attempt was made to get relief from Frontenac or Montreal, the inadequate old records do not tell of it. Father Jean de Lamberville, to whom this flock looked for counsel and encouragement, early fell desperately sick. The veteran De Troyes sickened and died. Death was a familiar caller at all the cabins within the palisades. In six weeks the garrison lost 60 men. In March, 20 more died; and the handful of wasted men remaining would soon have joined their fellows, but for the arrival of a Miami war party, led by Michitonka. Twelve out of the 100 were all that were left. Two or three of the strongest, the priest among them, set out with some of the Miamis and made their way by the margin of the lake to Frontenac; and the lake being open, early in April, a relief boat was sent to the unhappy post. With the relief came Captain Desbergères and the Jesuit priest Milet.

It was near the end of Lent, and one of Father Milet's first acts was to mark out the site for the erection of a great cross. Hewn of oak, it was 18 feet tall, and on the crosspiece Father Milet himself traced the symbols for the legend:

Regnat, Vincit, Imperat Christus.

These words, abbreviated, were cut in the oak, and midway of the line, the symbol of the Sacred Heart. On Good Friday the cross was set up and blessed, in the middle of the square, among the graves where lay De Troyes and 80 of his men.

The renewed garrison included some capable men — the sieurs De la Mothe, LaRabelle, Demuratre de Clerin, de Gemerais,

Chevalier de Tregay, all lieutenants or other officers, and others of repute; and the summer passed without incident, save that Iroquois war parties constantly hung about, keeping the garrison under tension. Meanwhile its fate was considered in Paris.

As it was a question of giving up either Frontenac or Niagara, Denonville decided to maintain the former, and to abandon Niagara. With the slight means at his command, the revictualing of Niagara was expensive. His hope, too, that western tribes would make it a base of incursions into the Iroquois country of central New York, had not been realized. Louis approved; and so, in September the bark *La Générale* sailed to the mouth of the Niagara, but not with reinforcements or provisions — she had come to take away Desbergères and his homesick garrison. The guns were put on board, as were the other meager effects of value. The palisades on the south and east sides of the fort were broken down. Elsewhere the wind had already done this work, so that, had an Iroquois war party appeared, they might readily have entered. But the cabins and other buildings were left standing, with doors ajar, to welcome who might come, Iroquois or wolf. Father Milet took from above his door a little sun-dial. "The shadow of the great cross falls divers ways," he said; and leaving all stripped and forlorn, with the great cross standing in the little square, on the morning of September 15th, the melancholy garrison sailed away. Before embarking the men were gathered about the cross by the priest, who said a final Mass. The last recorded act at Fort Denonville was one of devotion.

The foregoing account is based on Denonville's own narrative [8] of the establishment of Fort Denonville; on the statement of the "Condition in which the Fort of Niagara was left in 1688" [9] witnessed by the Rev. Jean Milet, Desbergères and others; and related papers. There exists however another document [10] which gives many additional details and merits attention.

[8] "Mémoir of the voyage and expedition . . . against the Senecas," 1687.
[9] Paris Docs., IV, N. Y. Col. Docs., IX; 386–388.
[10] "*Mémoire pour 1690*" in *Collection de Manuscrits . . . relatifs à la Nouvelle France,*" vol. 1, published by the Legislature of Quebec, 1883.

According to this narrative, a messenger reached Montreal in February with word that the garrison at Fort Frontenac were all sick with the scurvy. De Callières fitted out a company of militia with supplies, which set out from Montreal early in March. They were detained at La Chine for some weeks, then proceeding by canoe, a force of 80 in all — 30 soldiers, six officers, six navigators, the rest *voyageurs* commanded by M. de St. Cirq. The commander of the whole relief expedition was the Chevalier D'Eau. The memoir continues:

We arrived at Fort Frontenac about the 20th of April, where we found the garrison reduced to 12 or 15 persons, which made us conclude that Niagara would be no better off. A vessel was promptly made ready; meanwhile St. Cirq set out with his Canadians and some of the sick. When at the isle of Tonniata [11] several canoes set off to hunt, two of them fell into an Iroquois ambuscade which killed one party and carried off the other. It was impossible to go to their aid; the rest of the company hastened on to Montreal.

Finally the barque was equipped with 15 soldiers and four officers, a Jesuit, the captain and 10 sailors. As the captain missed his route in leaving the fort, because he had drunk too much wine, we did not reach the Niagara until the 12th of May, at midnight. One of their officers came alongside and told us that all the garrison was well, but when we were in the fort we saw quite the contrary, since there were more than 80 coats hung along the palisades. Indeed there were but three officers and four soldiers who were well, and five or six dying men whom they put on board the barque. One of them died while being carried, the others were soon cured.

There were 80 Miamis whom we found camped there who had come about the end of April. The garrison believed they would all have died, had not the savages often gone hunting, so that there was no lack of deer and wild turkey.

They told us that Monsieur de Troyes, commandant, had died May 8th, and that it was to him they ascribed the principal cause of the sickness; because the previous autumn he had cut down the rations, and refused to kill a cow he had; except for this they would

Although the memoir is headed "1690" there can be no question that the incidents related are of 1688.
[11] Probably the Grenadier island of to-day. "Five or six leagues from La Galette is an island called Tonihata."— Charlevoix, III, 194.

have had the hay which was to have been put in the soldiers' mattresses, but this obliged them to sleep on the ground.

This severity made the garrison resolve to mutiny, to cut the throats of the commandant and several other officers with whom they were not pleased, and to choose a commander who should lead them to the English at New York. Of all the garrison, only three refused to join in the plot. The evening before this plan was to be carried out, a large Iroquois war party [12] appeared before the fort, who kept up a skirmish and held the garrison in suspense for several days. This made them delay their plan, and several falling sick, the scheme was abandoned.

The 80 Miamis who were camped about the fort did not wish to return to their own country without making an attempt against the Iroquois. About 65 of them set out to surprise some Seneca villages. When they were near they fell into an ambuscade, there was an exchange of shots and the Miamis fled. There was but one Iroquois killed, whose scalp they took. The first who returned to the fort told us that all the Miamis were defeated. Their women, who had remained at the fort, began to wail and kept it up for three days, when the fugitives began to come in one after another, so that only one man was missing.

The next day they made ready to depart. We set them across the river in bateaux, and from there they went on through the woods to the Detroit, crossing from there to their own country.

Four days later the missing man appeared. He had been eight days without food, and had an arrow through his thigh. Our surgeon pulled it out, drawing it through the thigh, the savage not flinching, and in a few days he was healed.

About the middle of September two barques arrived with orders to the commandant to burn the fort, to bring back all the effects to Frontenac and to send the garrison to Montreal; all of which was accomplished in four days. So we returned to Frontenac, and took a bateau for Montreal, carrying the Miami with us.

There is nothing in this account which cannot be reconciled with Denonville's official report, except the burning of the fort. It is substantially the account of Gédéon de Catalogne, who in 1686 had served at Hudson's Bay under the Chevalier de Troyes. He was at Frontenac or Montreal in the spring of

[12] Belmont says 40 canoes.

DENONVILLE'S CAMPAIGN

1688 when it was resolved to send a relief force to Niagara. He took service in it.

According to long accepted records, the Jesuit Jean de Lamberville was with the afflicted garrison at Fort Denonville, was attacked by the scurvy and removed to Fort Frontenac, being succeeded at Niagara in the spring of 1688 by Father Milet. Let us examine the testimony bearing on the priest Lamberville's part in the campaign.

The memoirs of neither Denonville nor De Baugy refer to Jean de Lamberville as having been at Niagara. The latter makes no mention of him at all. The former alludes to his Onondaga mission, and to his return to Fort Frontenac, June 30th, from Onondaga, with Indian hostages. Denonville set out on his expedition against the Senecas, July 4th. He does not say he was accompanied by any chaplain, although Father Enjalran joined him at Irondequoit, having come from the West with Tonty. Receiving a serious wound, he was sent down to Fort Frontenac, and did not return to Niagara.

Although it was the custom to assign a chaplain to a garrison whenever possible, and although Father de Lamberville is generally stated to have ministered at Niagara until he was incapacitated by disease, satisfactory proofs in the matter have not been found. On the other hand, a letter by De Lamberville, lately come to light, appears to show that he first went to Niagara on the vessel that carried supplies, in the autumn of 1687, and that he returned with it to Fort Frontenac.

It nowhere appears that he was with Denonville in the Seneca country. The Rev. Jacques Bruyas either accompanied Denonville, or joined him at Irondequoit; but returned from Irondequoit to Frontenac, not coming to Niagara.

At Totiakton, the largest of the Seneca villages, July 19th, the Rev. François de Gueslis Vaillant, with Denonville and his officers, signed the formal Minute of taking possession of the Seneca country.

Both Vaillant and Bruyas were at times intimately associated with the elder Joncaire. Father Vaillant's mission work, prior to Denonville's raid, and for some years afterward, was carried on among the Senecas; no other Jesuit of the New York missions is known to have labored nearer the Niagara; but no mention is found of the presence on this river of either of these priests.

So far as appears, Denonville and his army came to the Niagara unaccompanied by any chaplain; but De Lamberville soon came, with the vessel bringing supplies, from Frontenac. His own account of the voyage [13] is one of the most graphic narratives we have of early adventure on Lake Ontario, and is best given, in main part, in the priest's own words:

The day before our departure from Cataroqui, the Iroquois, who were hemming us in, had fired on the crew when yet at the wharf, and wounded a sergeant, who died after receiving the last Sacraments. Hardly had we doubled the point than an Iroquois fired at us. It was the signal for the Indians to leave their camp, where they had been for several days enjoying the good cheer they had taken from the French near the Rapids.

A great number had been invited to witness the attack on our barque. If they took it they would starve out our friends at Niagara. Several canoes pursued us and made for a little island, intending to intercept us, for on account of the shallows we had to pass very close to it. Other Indians ran along the shore to capture us in case we landed. Suddenly the wind dropped, and we were becalmed. The savages were all around, but out of gunshot. We prayed, and I exhorted the men to fight to the death rather than be taken and tortured. We had four cannon called *pierriers* for discharging stones, twelve muskets, with two arquebuses and six grenades. We determined not to fire all at once, but one after the other; while two of us were to keep loading. Our deck had no guards, so we had to lie down while fighting. A shower of bullets swept over us. We replied by a volley from both sides of the barque. Some of the Indians fell in their canoes and were carried off, but their place was taken by others.

Four canoes bolder than the rest came close up to us, but we stopped them with our arquebuses and the *pierrier,* which had thirty stones in it. That discharge riddled the canoes and made them

[13] The original MS. is in the British Museum. It does not appear in the "Relations" as edited by Thwaites, but is quoted in a more recent work, "Pioneer Priests of North America," by Rev. T. J. Campbell, S.J., who speaks of the manuscript as "recently discovered."

DENONVILLE'S CAMPAIGN 123

draw off to the island to attend to the wounded and repair the damage to their boats. They came again to the charge, not doubting that half of our number had fallen under their furious fusillade. But no one had yet been hit. Just then they remarked that there was no fire from the stern and they made for it, but a cry, "they are boarding us!" from one of the soldiers caused a rush in that direction with swords and grenades, but at that moment a slight wind sprung up and we began to move.

I was engaged in loading the muskets and sticking out two arquebuses from the stern to scare the invaders. The puff of wind gave us courage, and we drifted slowly past the island.

Just then a chief started out with five or six canoes to head us off. He stood up brandishing his weapons and then aimed at the pilot and a sailor who were defending the bow, but they dodged in time and escaped the shot, and immediately aimed at him and tumbled him over with a shot in the neck and another in the body, as I afterwards learned. But his companions would not withdraw, when one of our soldiers, a Breton, who had been in the German wars, rushed to the *pierrier* and at the risk of his life, for he had to stand up, applied the match, and in a flash a shower of stone balls sunk the canoe to the bottom. The Breton was not hurt, but two Indian bullets passed through his hat.

It was the last effort of the savages. The wind freshened, and the distance widened between us, and they, fearing to go out in the open, withdrew. The fight had lasted three-quarters of an hour. Three hundred bullet holes were in our sails; many of the ropes were cut, but thanks be to God, none of our halliards was injured. We were a league away and were again becalmed, but the Indians did not follow us.

Next morning we started with a west wind and a cloudy sky. Off in the distance we saw the fires of the Iroquois. We kept out in the lake, for a storm was approaching. The lake was soon like the ocean in its fury. Great waves washed over us, but we did not dare to put in, for fear of the enemy. Often we thought we were going to the bottom. Finally, after fourteen days of hard weather, we saw in the distance the flag of Fort Niagara. Our joy may be imagined. We could see the Iroquois skulking around as we landed.

We had scarcely unloaded when the Commandant thought it would be advisable to return, because the wind was favorable and our friends at Cataroqui would be anxious. On the 18th of October we reached Cataroqui. The Indians had been hanging about the fort all the time, behind 200 cords of fire wood which we had heaped up. They were waiting for our return, but lost patience and decamped the day before we arrived, after setting fire to all our wood and killing a soldier, whose death revealed their ambuscade.

It is clear, by the priest's own account, that he returned to Frontenac in October. Who then was chaplain at Fort Niagara during that terrible winter of scurvy and starvation? Was there a later passage of a bark from Frontenac to Niagara, bringing the priest, De Lamberville, a second time, to stay through the winter? Where the records are not obscure, they are silent; and conjecture is not history.

Years afterward, when De Lamberville was in Paris, he wrote a long letter [14] to a friend in China, in which he recalled some of his experiences in the Lake Ontario region. The battle with the Indians on the lake, above related, is again told in different language, and the statement made that the little bark was attacked by 800 Iroquois, in their canoes; "they were about to overwhelm us with their numbers, when Heaven was favorable to our prayers and sent us a wind which swept us away from their fury when they thought to grasp their prey, and to avenge upon us the death of their comrades."

In this letter he continues: "I was afterward obliged, through obedience, to remain in this ill-fated rendezvous with 140 soldiers, whose chaplain I was." This appears to refer not to Niagara, where the garrison had never been more than 100 men, but to Frontenac. De Lamberville in this letter mentions neither place by name, but proceeds with a long account of how they (in the unnamed fort) were beset by the Iroquois, so they "could get neither wood, water, nor fresh food." He tells how the scurvy broke out in the garrison and "carried off about a hundred men." He says that he caught the disease and was near dying, when "an officer of our troops unexpectedly came over the snow, with 30 men, 15 of whom were Iroquois, friends and Christians." He does not state where they came from, but says "they had marched 80 leagues

[14] Dated "Paris, this 23d of January, 1695." The name of the missionary to whom he wrote is not known.

DENONVILLE'S CAMPAIGN

over the snow, with their food, clothing and arms." Allowing 2½ miles to the league, this about as closely approximates the distance from Montreal to Frontenac, as it does that from Frontenac to Niagara, if the latter journey were shortened by crossing the western end of the lake on the ice. In other words, it does not help to clear up the mystery. De Lamberville continues with a graphic account of his removal from the afflicted fort, which runs in part as follows:

They found us in a very bad condition; and for fear of remaining themselves in this fort,— where the unwholesome air made them feel, from the first, the beginning of this singular malady,— they resolved to depart immediately, and to make all possible haste, that they might not be surrounded or encountered by the enemy. This officer, who was my friend, having learned from the surgeon that I had only one or 2 Days to live if they did not get me away from this post, undertook to remove me who was half dead. He refused to accord the same favor to some others, even officers,— who afterward died, but who were less ready for death than I was,— alleging the length of the journey, and the inclemency of the season; the necessity of carrying their arms, provisions, and blankets; and the necessity for making great haste on account of the enemy, who were following in their track. He undertook to do for me what he would not do for another. Having entreated him to let me die, and to consent to substitute in my place a sick officer, he absolutely refused.

Accordingly, as I had become useless from that time, on account of the condition in which I was, the rest of the garrison received general absolution, while they supported me by the arms; then having bound me upon a sledge, to which 2 great dogs were harnessed, they set out, passing over a frozen lake. The ice broke, and, carefully bundled upon this sledge, I was in this condition plunged into the water. The dogs which were attached to it kept me above the ice, to which they held fast with their claws. To rescue me from this peril needed carefulness, because the ice which surrounded me was broken on all sides. Finally, when they were drawing me out of the water, the rope broke, and I ran the risk of being drowned. Being withdrawn from the water and again placed upon the ice, the dogs were too much fatigued; and some French Canadians and soldiers who were with us took the trouble to drag me, now over the ice, now over the snow, by turns,— without discontinuing their march, because the Iroquois were following in their track; and because they wished to keep the advantage that they had over them, for fear that they might attack us.

The narrator says that the journey lasted seven and a half days, when they reached Montreal. "It was in February, 1688, that this occurred." He was taken to the Seminary of St. Sulpice, but did not recover from the effects of the ordeal for two and a half years.

A winter journey on foot from present Kingston to Montreal in seven days and a half means 35 miles a day; a thing within reason; but a journey from Niagara to Montreal in that time and under the desperate conditions that existed, is inconceivable. Accepting Father De Lamberville's letters as wholly trustworthy, the conclusion is inevitable that his affliction did not occur at Fort Denonville, the Niagara of to-day.

This conclusion overthrows a story which appears to have been accepted from the days of La Potherie and Charlevoix. Our examination of the matter, an effort to discover the truth, has at least shown in some measure the existing conditions at this most critical time in the fortunes of New France. Denonville's ineffective raid into Central New York gave to French enterprise on the Lower Lakes a serious set-back. It so roused the ire of the Iroquois that Fort Denonville was abandoned, and Fort Frontenac greatly reduced. Nearly a third of a century is to elapse before the French again venture to establish themselves on the Niagara.

Still another version there is of the fate of Fort Denonville, which may have place here, if only to illustrate what a wide variety of statements may be given currency and accepted as trustworthy facts. In a memorial prepared by the Commissioners of Trade and Plantations in 1697, regarding the rights of the British Crown over the New York Indians, occurs the following statement:

A new war broke out and those Indians made divers inroads into Canada, blocked up the Fort of Onyagra and starved the French garrison in it; so that a priest was the only man that survived, and

DENONVILLE'S CAMPAIGN

cutting all communication between the French and their fort at Cadaraqui, forced the garrison (about the beginning of this present war with France) to quit that place; in doing which the French blew up one of the bastions, and left the rest entire, which with a quantity of ammunition came into the Indians' possession.[15]

One aspect of Denonville's ill-fated venture on the Niagara demands a word. It is unique in the early annals of the region in not having trade as its chief occasion and impetus. It was a part of Denonville's ineffective attempt to discipline the Iroquois by fighting them. Could the garrison on the Niagara have been spared long enough to feel secure, trade operations would naturally have sprung up; but nothing of the sort appears in the short and tragic history of the post. Its real purpose shows forth in a Government communication, written a few months before its abandonment: " His Majesty highly approves their [Denonville and Champigny] having caused one [fort] to be built at Niagara, and is persuaded that it will afford friendly Indians, and particularly the Illinois, an opportunity to harass the Iroquois this winter by small parties who will find a sure retreat in that post." [16] But when the resentful Iroquois sent an angry delegation to Montreal, to demand the demolition of the fort, Denonville, knowing he could not maintain it, acceded to their demands.

The officer who had been placed in command of the rescued garrison merits further notice. Raymond Blaise Desbergères de Rigauville, born between 1655 and 1660, was of the parish of St. Pierre, city of Orleans. He had married, about 1680, Anne Richard de Goigni, by whom he had a son, Nicolas, born about 1682. The father ranked as lieutenant. In 1685 he was made captain and came to Canada in the troops of Denonville. On the death of De Troyes, he came with the relief party to Fort Denonville and commanded on the Niagara until the abandonment of the post. In July, 1689, he fought a duel with Captain François Lefebvre, Sieur Duplessis, in which he received a sword cut; it is recorded that Duplessis

[15] N. Y. Col. Docs., V, 76.
[16] The Minister (Seignelay) to Denonville and Champigny, Mch. 8, 1688.

afterwards paid him 600 francs. In 1691, with his family, he is at Chambly, where he was in command, 1692-95. His wife had evidently died, for in 1694 he married Jeanne-Cécile Closse, widow of the fort major Jacques Bizard. She died in 1700. Desbergères rebuilt the fortifications of Chambly and later complained that the Government had not reimbursed him for large personal outlay. In the summer of 1696 we find him with a military expedition on Lake Ontario and in Central New York, making war on the Onondagas. In 1709 he again commands at Fort Chambly, and on November 13th of that year, at the isle Dupas in Lake St. Peter, takes a third wife, Marguerite Vauvril de Blazon, widow of Major Lambert Boucher de Grandprè. The next year he was made Major of Three Rivers, which rank he held at death. He was buried at Montreal July 21, 1711. His son Nicolas, spoken of as Rigauville, is to have a part in our regional history scarcely less important than that of the father, being in command at Fort Niagara for many years.

An incident connected with the service of Desbergères has been preserved, which though trivial, somewhat illustrates soldier life at these frontier posts.

When he came to the relief of the Niagara garrison in 1688 Desbergères brought with him a favorite dog named "*Vingt-Sols*" (Twenty Sous), which rendered good service as sentinel. A son of this dog was called by the soldiers "*Monsieur de Niagara.*" Taken by his master to Chambly, he developed a fondness for running through the woods to a neighboring post, La Prairie de la Madelaine, where there was another dog. Seeing that he went and came faithfully, the soldiers fastened letters to his collar, which never failed of delivery. In this way was established the dog-post (*poste à pataud*) which was so useful and became so famous that Desbergères applied to the Intendant at Quebec for the allowance of a daily ration for *Monsieur de Niagara*, and it was granted. Further, he was formally added to the garrison list, and at roll-call would reply — or some one would reply for him if he was not there —" *En course* " or " *à la chasse.*" It is edify-

DENONVILLE'S CAMPAIGN

ing to read that " this continued, even several years, after his death." [17]

[17] The story of "*Monsieur de Niagara*" has been a favorite one with French Canadian writers, and has been retold with variations and details here omitted, for two hundred years. Sometimes it is ascribed to Chaussegros de Léry, who lived long after "*M. de Niagara*" had trotted his last course. It really originated with Gédéon de Catalogne, who was both author and soldier, and who came to Niagara with Desbergères and may be said to have "personally known" this useful servitor of the King.

CHAPTER IX

WILDERNESS STRIFE

ENGLISH CLAIMS REASSERTED — ADVENTURES OF THE BARON LA HONTAN, EXPLORER OF THE SOUTH SHORE OF LAKE ERIE — THE REVENGE OF DUBEAU — FRONTENAC'S RAID OF 1696.

IT will readily be believed that after the stirring events of this summer of 1687, the correspondence between the rival governors did not abate in vigorous expression. On hearing of MacGregorie's expedition, Denonville had written in broad terms, accusing Dongan of perfidy. The English Governor replied: " I have been informed that you are told I have given to Indians orders to rob the French wherever they could meet them. That is as false as 'tis true that God is in heaven." Denonville refused to release MacGregorie and the other prisoners, on the ground that Dongan was supplying the Senecas with guns and ammunition. If he was not doing so directly, it became easy for the Five Nations to get these and other goods at Albany. August 21st the French Governor wrote again, upbraiding Dongan for sending the expeditions to Mackinac, " where no Englishman ever had put a foot and where our Frenchmen have been established over 60 years." Dongan replied that he had given no passes for his people to trade at Mackinac, but among the Ottawas, " where I thought it might be as free for us to trade as for you." " 'Tis a very hard thing," he observed in a subsequent letter, " that all the Countryes a Frenchman walks over in America must belong to Canada." This conception of the French theory and practice of occupancy evidently pleased him, for he uses the idea often in his letters. In reply to Denonville's agents, in February, 1688, speaking of MacGregorie's seizure, he observes: " I am sure it was out of the Government of Canada, except a Frenchman by tredding upon the earth makes itt belong to that Collony."

Finally Denonville sent back Major MacGregorie, and

with him, at Dongan's suggestion, two agents, Father Franciscus Valiant, a Jesuit, and Elambert Dumont, a layman, to treat with Dongan and try to reach terms of agreement. It does not appear that they met to discuss the situation; but they exchanged a series of papers in which the claims of the respective colonies were urged sometimes with vigor and adroitness, sometimes with evasion and sophistries. Dongan demanded the "breaking down" of the fort at Niagara; the restoration to his men of all they had been robbed of, or its equivalent; and the return of the prisoners. The arguments were long, and their exchange continued through the month of February, 1688. At length Father Valiant "demanded" that the points at issue be referred to the two kings, and that a truce for 15 months be agreed upon: "within this time we shall hear what the two kings shall have agreed upon concerning the limits, the Fort of Niagara, and the restitution of the goods . . . if they command the forts to be demolished, the goods to be restored, then those shall be demolished and these be restored." "Governor Dongan," urged Father Valiant, "says that he had power to send Major Maggregorys and others to the Ottowawas, because he does not acknowledge them for the subjects of the King of France. Had not we the selfsame reason to say we had power to build a fort on Niagara to make war with the Indians, seeing for better reasons we do not acknowledge them for subjects of the King of England?" Addressing Dongan the priest continued:

"You demand, first, the fort in Niagra to be demolished. This cannot be granted; first, because it is built there by the command of the Most Christian Kinge, and therefore it must be demolished by his command; secondly, because it would not be reasonable to demolish it before there be a general peace, since in the meantime we have need of the fort to protect ourselfs from the Indians untill there bee something concluded concerning the limitts. This only I can declare and grant, that foresaid fort does not give us any other right to those Indians, than what we pretend to have longe since." And the other points in Dongan's demand were as stoutly and ingeniously argued, only to be as ably rebutted by the redoubtable Dongan. In his last paper to the French agents occurs this striking sentence: "[As] for the 5 nations of Indians being the Kinge of Englands subjects, I know no better judges than themselves, and very ancient records of there [their] submission which is a very just title and farr better than that of yours (of a poore Frenchmans goeinge with a pack upon his back) to Onyagro."

In less than a month after Denonville built his fort at Niagara, Governor Dongan had known all about it and was taking council with the Iroquois for its overthrow. He gathered the chief men of all the Five Nations in the city hall at Albany, August 5th, discussed with them Denonville's raid and fort-building at Niagara, and told them he was laying these things before the King. "I think it very necessary," he added, "for the brethren's security and assistance, and to the endamageing the French, to build a fort upon the lake, where I may keep stores and provisions in case of necessity," and he urged them to tell him "where he might build," and to "looke out sharpe for fear of being surprized" as "the strength of the French will be at Cadarahqui and Onyagaro, where they build a fort now."

Dongan submitted the whole weary dispute to the Earl of Sutherland, Lord President of the King's Privy Council, sending his report over to London by John Palmer. The succeeding half century was to see many special messengers dispatched to Whitehall in behalf of British claims on the Niagara and the Great Lakes, but none of them was a more picturesque figure in our colonial history than Palmer. An English lawyer, he had come to New York about 1675 from Barbadoes. He is soon spoken of as "Captain" Palmer; was made King's Ranger for Staten Island and held other offices. He was a close friend of Governor Dongan, who in 1684 made him the first judge of the New York Court of Oyer and Terminer. The story of his imprisonment in later years is part of a very stirring chapter of New York and Massachusetts colonial politics, but it was as "Judge" Palmer, one of the most influential men in Dongan's administration, that he now visited London, and laid before Sutherland Dongan's representation of what should be done to secure the Niagara region to Great Britain. The following extracts from the Governor's long report will suffice to illustrate the arguments relating to the Niagara and the Lakes, as well as the singular spelling of that period:

My Lord: When his Maj'ts Commands came to my hand a Father and another gent were here who came along with Magregory from ye Gov'r of Canida. They would not come to any agreement to demolish the ffort at Onijagaro [Niagara] nor to restore the Goods alleadgeing it was set up by ye French Kings Direction, and that they had no orders for pulling it downe, all there drift was to gain a cessation for 15 Monthes and that the matters in Difference might be referred for a Decision at home: upon which I called the chieffe of the five nations of Indians together who are now with me, and I proposed it to them, to see what there opinions would be, who unanimously agreed not to consent to any thing 'till these Demands were complyed wth also they desyred that what goods were taken from them they might be returned, and another fort that lyes in ye way of there Bever hunting broaken downe, for say they wee are in prison so long as they are standing, and further that ye Fort at Cadaracqui might also be destroyed saying ye French had no right to it, and that they only gave leave to one La Sall to have a man there to Dress there armes as they came from hunting, and since the French have built a stone fort there; as to Onyagaro they have not the least pretense of right to it, only that a poor Frenchman went there to trade with ye Indians; they may have the like pretence to all those parts of America, for they doe the same almost everywhere.

Considering how feeble and helpless if not hopeless the establishment was, the student peruses with some skepticism the glowing reports that were sent to France. One questions whether Denonville believed all he wrote. There even was prepared a "Memoir on the advantage of the establishment of a Fort at Niagara," inspired if not written by the Governor, in which, after setting forth that the British were seeking to seduce the Iroquois and to possess themselves of the control of the Lakes and the fur trade, it was stated:

Now, that things are changed by the favor of God, and the King takes care of that country, it appears very easy to return the compliment to those English if, as there is reason to hope, his Majesty's arms are victorious over the Iroquois, and these are reduced; particularly by erecting a fort at Niagara with a strong garrison for the protection of the settlers who will establish themselves there in order to clear the land, which is most excellent, and to carry on the trade in furs with the Iroquois Indians, who do all their hunting on the lands belonging to the King's domain. The English will thus be deprived of a trade in peltries amounting to 400,000 livres yearly, which will be very beneficial to the French colony.

All the inhabitants of said Niagara will pay to the revenue (*ferme*) of his Majesty's domain the duty of one fourth of the beavers, and one-tenth of the moose (*orignaux*) the same as at Quebec. This will increase, by a large sum, the King's revenue in said country, and should his Majesty think fit to leave it to a private person when the Iroquois are pacified, inasmuch as the establishment of the said Niagara must be considered a newly discovered country. Persons will be found who will give a considerable sum for the privilege of receiving the duties on the beaver and moose which will be reported from said Niagara.

Among the followers of Denonville who shared with him the campaign against the Senecas and the building of Fort Denonville on the Niagara, was the young Gascon already mentioned, Louis-Armand de Lom d'Arce, better known as the Baron de La Hontan, the seigneurial designation being derived from his ancestral village of La Hontan in the Basse-Pyrénées. Coming to America in 1683, a lad of 17, he served in Canada for ten years. His career as a whole, his picturesque personality, and his vivacious writings in many editions have been made so familiar to students of that period that it may suffice here briefly to narrate the incidents of his career on and near the Niagara.

Fort Denonville, he tells us, was built in three days. On August 1, 1687, Denonville's savage allies took leave of him with elaborate speech-making, of which La Hontan made report. The western tribes assured Denonville that they were pleased to see a fort so conveniently placed, since it would " favor their retreat from any expedition against the Iroquois."

WILDERNESS STRIFE 135

They urged him to continue to make war, winter and summer, upon the Iroquois, and pledged their help. " Mr. Denonville," says our chronicler, " gave them fresh assurances of his intention to carry on the war, in spite of all the efforts of the Iroquois, and, in a word, protested that he would prosecute this design so vigorously that in the end these barbarians should be either quite cut off, or obliged to shift their seats," i.e., remove elsewhere.

On the very day of this impressive leave-taking, Denonville dispatched La Hontan on service to the westward. A company of picked men was assigned him. His brother officers, he says, " made me presents of Cloaths, Tobacco, Books, and an infinity of other things, that they could spare without any inconveniency, because they were then upon their return to the Colony." The story of his American adventures, as afterwards published, purports to be a series of letters to his relatives; that from which we quote, though probably penned in Portugal in 1694, is dated " Niagara, August 2, 1687," at which time he was undoubtedly on our river. " The Men of my Detachment," he continues, " are brisk proper fellows, and my Canows both new and large." In company with Duluth and Henri de Tonty, and followed by a horde of savages, the young officer embarged at Niagara, August 3d. At the entrance to Niagara gorge, where navigation stops, they met Claude Grisolon de la Tourette, brother of Duluth, who had come with a single canoe alone all the way from Mackinac, to join Denonville's army.

La Hontan tells at length of the passing of the portage. " Before we got at any beaten or level Path, we were forced to climb up three Mountains, upon which an hundred Iroquese might have knocked us all on the head with stones." Before the portage was accomplished they discovered, he says, " a thousand Iroquese that marched towards us. . . . We were in danger of losing our Lives as well as our baggage; for we had not embarked above the Fall half a quarter of an hour, when the Enemy appeared upon the Streight side. I assure you, I 'scap'd very narrowly; for about a quarter of an hour before, I and three or four Savages had gone 500 paces out of our Road to look upon that fearful Cataract; and 'twas as much as I could do, to get at the Canows before they put off. To be taken by such cruel Fellows was to me no trifling thing," and he quotes with the aptness of the scholarly wit he was:

"'*Il morir e niente, ma il vivere brugiando troppo.*'"[6]

La Hontan's much quoted description of the Falls, which he found "seven or eight hundred foot high," may here be omitted. After rowing all night, their party "arrived next morning at the mouth of the Lake, which appeared to be indifferent rapid. Then we were secure from all danger, for the Iroquese Canows are so dull and large that they cannot sail near so quick as those made of Birch-bark. The former are made of Elm-bark, which is very heavy, and their form is very aukard; for they are so long and broad that 30 Men row in them, two abreast, whether sitting or standing, and the sides are so low that they dare not venture 'em upon the Lakes, tho' the wind be very slack." We may smile at La Hontan's "800-foot" Niagara Falls, and hesitate to accept the 1000 Iroquois on the portage; but we cannot deny the accuracy of his pages in countless other matters. He was a close observer, a clear and entertaining writer. There is no record of his time more valuable in many ways.

The boats skirted the north shore of Lake Erie, portaged across Long Point instead of going around it, and on September 6th entered the Detroit River. For some months La Hontan was stationed at the little Fort St. Joseph on the St. Clair at the entrance to Lake Huron — the fort which Duluth had built in 1686, to keep the English out of the upper Lakes. The Jesuit missionary, Avenau, joined him; and he says he "waited with impatience for the arrival of one Turcot and four more of the *coureurs de bois*" whom Denonville had promised to send, to hunt for the post. They did not come, but four Canadians, expert hunters, brought in game enough to keep them alive. It may be observed in this connec-

[6] "To die is nothing, but to live in the midst of fire is too much," alluding to the Iroquois custom of burning prisoners.

WILDERNESS STRIFE

tion that had the garrison at Niagara in 1687-8 consisted of fewer French soldiers and more Canadians, they probably would have come through in better condition. The former, knowing nothing of American forest life, were infantile in their inefficiency and timorous inability; the latter knew how to hunt, and to live; and, as the coming years were to prove, were a better reliance for frontier fighting than the troops of France.

Turcot we have already met, with La Salle's deserters. Outlaw that he was, he was probably no worse than many others of his time, harbored in Indian lodges and at distant posts. La Hontan would have preferred him to the priest. In December there came in upon him a band of Hurons led by one Saentsouan. The season being too late to proceed further in their canoes, these and their " baggage " were left with La Hontan, while they marched overland to Niagara, doing the 300 miles in 10 days. Somewhere in the Iroquois country they fell upon a village, killed many, carried off 14 prisoners and four women, and returned with a loss of but three men. " Among the Captive Slaves, there were three who had made part of the number of the 1000 Iroquese who mean'd to appear before my Post without any delay." This news, he says, " gall'd me to the last degree," and made him very careful of his corn. But the Iroquois did not trouble him. In the spring of 1688 he went to Mackinac, for corn; then appears to have wandered, with hunting and war parties, to Sault Ste. Marie, and far east of Lake Huron, not returning to his post on the St. Clair until July 1st. On the 3d he set out again, apparently with only an Indian escort, " and stood to the south side of the Lake Erie."

This is the first account we have of any exploration of the south shore; the pity is, it tells us so little, and some of that so wrong. La Hontan claims to have crossed through the islands of the western end of the lake, thence to have skirted the shore as far as the " River of Condé," where he says they arrived July 17th. On the map published in his book, a dotted line shows his route. The Condé is drawn as a large stream, entering the lake from the southeast at the extreme southeastern point of the shore. Its actual prototype is probably the Cattaraugus, although La Hontan says it was 20 leagues (about 50 miles) from the outlet of Lake Erie. It "runs 60 leagues in length without cataracts," says our explorer, "if we may credit the savages, who assur'd me that we may go from its source to another river that falls into the sea, without any other land-carriage than one of a league in length, between the [one] river and the other." There is here evidently some vague notion of the Allegheny but no clear idea of distance. La Hontan's "river of Condé" found little acceptance with geographers; on most of the maps, later than his, it is not shown; but it does reappear, many years after, to the great misleading of certain theorists; as will be duly related.

La Hontan says he saw only the mouth of the Condé, where they landed July 17th, and "the savages fell to work cutting down trees, and making a redoubt of stakes, or pales, for the security of our canows and baggage, and for a safe retreat to our selves in case of necessity." He stayed in the redoubt while a war-party marched off, up the river, intending to surprise a village of Cayugas, who came there to fish. Two days later his Indians came running back, pursued by "not less than 400" Iroquois. There follows an involved account of their further progress by canoe to a little island, where they found shelter in a creek; though one is at a loss to locate this at the eastern end of the lake, unless indeed they had turned westward and were on the peninsula opposite Erie.[7] There were several encounters between La Hontan's Ottawas and the Iroquois, who had with them 18 Miami prisoners. There was an ambuscade and an attack. Owing to the haste of the Ottawas in firing most of the enemy escaped, " abating for 10 or 12 whose heads were brought into the little fort where I stayed. The Slaves indeed were all retaken, and so rescued from the Cruelty of these Tygers." With this La Hontan says he rested satisfied; the captives were stowed in the canoes and the party steered for the Detroit which was

[7] La Hontan's map shows an island in Lake Erie at the entrance to the Niagara, but the dotted line, indicating the voyage of 1688, does not reach it. The map does not show Presqu' Isle peninsula.

WILDERNESS STRIFE

gained August 13th; some days were spent in hunting, and on the 24th they were at Fort St. Joseph.

Despite its confusion and the exaggeration of the river Condé, the account of this expedition along the south shore of Lake Erie is too explicit and circumstantial in many respects to be regarded as fiction. When La Hontan invented his narrative he did not give precise dates for incidents such as are indicated above. Of those who had sailed Lake Erie before him, Joliet, Galinée, Tonty, La Salle and Dautray make up the honor-roll, but none of them had touched the south shore; nor do we find record of any white man who had, prior to this coming of La Hontan in 1688.

Arrived at his lonely and neglected post of St. Joseph, La Hontan found awaiting him Michitonka and his band of 80 Miamis, just come from Niagara, where they had saved the remnant of the garrison from utter starvation, as already narrated. Michitonka's people were wild with joy at receiving from La Hontan their captive tribesmen, of whose plight they had not known. On his part La Hontan first heard from the chief what had befallen at Niagara. "Michitonka acquainted me," he writes, "that after he went to the Fort of Niagara, with a design to make some Expedition into the Country of the Tsonontouans [Senecas], he found that the Scurvey had made such a terrible havock in that Fort, that it had swept off the Commander and all the Soldiers, bating 12, who had the good luck to get over it, as well as M. De Bergères [Desbergères], who by the advantage of a hale Constitution had stemm'd the raging Violence of that Distemper." We have noted the fact that Desbergères came to Niagara in the spring, with the relief party. The Miami chief further reported, not quite accurately, that Fort Frontenac was as badly off as Fort Denonville.

La Hontan reflected on this and other news that Michitonka gave him; nor did it take him long to decide that his proper course was to abandon Fort St. Joseph, service at which he had always found irksome. He called a council which "came to this Resolution: That since the Marquis de Denonville had a mind to clap up a Peace, and the fort of Niagara was abdicated, the fort I then commanded would be of no use." He had ammunition and provisions for not more than two months. He decided to abandon his charge, a decision which he assures us, " afforded matter of Joy to the Soldiers, who were afraid of being obliged to a more rigorous course of Abstinence in that Post than they had formerly undergone; for the measures of a critical Abstinence do not sit well upon a Soldier's Stomach." Loading what they could into their canoes, they set fire to the fort, August 27th, and as the smoke of the burning huts and palisades rolled above the clearing, they paddled off for Mackinac. The following winter, according to his own account, he spent in travels far west and south. He claims to have explored a great river which he calls " Long," coming into the Mississippi from the west; but this part of his narrative lacks the explicitness of the voyage along the south shore of Lake Erie, and is commonly regarded as fiction. He reappeared at Mackinac in May, 1689, and at Montreal in July, going down by the Ottawa River route. Instead of being censured or broken in rank because of the irregularities of his western service, he was chosen by the Governor (Frontenac) as a special messenger to Paris to announce the failure of the English expedition under Phips. He is back again in Canada in 1691, but does not again come into our region, nor need we here follow further his personal adventures.

In a letter which purports to have been written at Nantes, October 25, 1692, first printed in his work in 1703, La Hontan outlines a plan for fortifying the Niagara and adjacent lakes, which he says he submitted " above a year agoe," say in 1691, to Frontenac, " and is what he would have me still to undertake ":

I project, therefore, to build and maintain three Forts upon the course of the Lakes, with some Vessels that shall go with Oars, which I will build according to my Fancy; but they being light, and of great carriage, may be managed either with Oars or a Sail, and will also be able to bear the shocks of the Waves. I demand 50 Seamen of the French Biscay, for they are known to be the most dexterous and able Mariners that are in the World. I must also have 200 soldiers, chosen out of the Troops of Canada.

WILDERNESS STRIFE 141

I will build three little Castles in several places; one at the mouth of the Lake Errie, which you see in my Map of Canada, under the name of Fort Supposé, besides two others. The second I will build in the same place where it was when I maintained it, in the years 1687 and 1688 . . .; and the third at the Mouth of the Bay of Toronto, upon the same Lake.

"Fort Supposé" is shown on La Hontan's map on the east bank of the Niagara at the outlet of Lake Erie — obviously on the high bank where the United States Government in 1844 built Fort Porter. Our young officer evidently recognized the strategic and commanding value of that point. He was the second writer (Hennepin being conceded the first) to allude to the site of the present city of Buffalo.

His second fort or "little castle" was to have stood on the site of the burned Fort St. Joseph where Fort Gratiot was afterwards built, at the entrance to Lake Huron; the third apparently on Georgian Bay, which he calls Toronto. In La Hontan's time Lake Simcoe bore that name, which was also applied to the portage to Lake Huron. The end of the portage on Georgian Bay is evidently the site designated. He asked for 90 men for the defense of these forts, and argued that by means of the vessels on the Lakes he could easily bring a horde of Western savages to the Niagara — unloading them, doubtless, under the guns of Fort Supposé — and fall with such irresistible fury on the Iroquois that these enemies of the French would be forever quieted, or annihilated. This fantastic project, submitted to Frontenac, won such approval that — according to La Hontan — it was seriously laid before Ponchartrain; but that great Minister found many reasons why it should not be undertaken: First, France could not spare the seamen La Hontan asked for. Second, the King had ordered Frontenac to make peace with the Iroquois, not to kill them. Third, not least of the reasons, because when the forts and vessels were ready the friendly savages would prefer war to beaver trapping and the French Ministry thought it better to promote the fur trade than feuds among American savages.

Thus La Hontan's project, the first ever devised for the defense of the upper Niagara, the site of Buffalo and the neigh-

boring lake, came to naught; whereupon he, not one whit
cast down, turned to other employments and adventures, where
we may not follow him. Still it is with some regret that we
dismiss him from our story. He was no doubt a rather improper young man, if his living were as free as his writing;
but he was certainly a clear-headed man who did his own thinking, with a wit all the more enjoyable because used at the expense of ponderous, conceited folk who took their sham selves
seriously. His mocking spirit made him no friend of the clerics. A youth, fond of adventure and abounding in vitality,
he wrote with the cynicism of an aged courtier who had discovered that the world is hollow. About to make a most
promising marriage, La Hontan deserted the waiting maid, to
the great scandal of Quebec. "A solitary life is most grateful to me," he boasts, "and the manners of the savages are
perfectly agreeable to my palate." Into the wilderness of the
Lakes and the Niagara he brought books, some of the world's
greatest, and quoted from Homer or from his beloved Lucian
to illustrate the traits of the savages. He came to know several Indian tongues as he knew Greek, Latin, Italian and his
native French, and discovered a beauty and nobility in the
aborigines' philosophy of life which made him ever more satirical and contemptuous of the follies and shams of European
society. A victory over the English — at Placentia — being
ascribed to his genius and valor, he declared there was no
just ground for such praise; and when Louis XIV recognized
his services by making him Lieutenant of Newfoundland and
Acadia, he insisted that it was an honor mistakenly bestowed.
His career to the end is full of ups and downs, and the sum
of his achievements is not great. He stands alone in the early
history of our region, conspicuous for his jaunty humor, his
freedom from cant and pretense, and as our study of his work
inclines us to conclude, for his priority as an explorer of the
south shore of Lake Erie.[8]

[8] It will suffice here to refer the reader who seeks further of La Hontan,
to two excellent studies: J. Edmond Roy's "*Le Baron de La Hontan,*" in
Can. Roy. Soc. Proceedings, 1894; and Thwaite's Introduction to the
edition of La Hontan's "New Voyages," published by McClurg, Chicago,

In these early years the Indians who appeared on the lower Lakes and the Niagara were quite as apt to be of western tribes as of the Iroquois, with which people, especially the Senecas, we have come to associate the region. The Missisaugas, who had villages to the west of the Niagara, were of Algonquin stock. The Miamis, whose war parties often roamed hither, and who saved the remnants of the garrison of Fort Denonville, were a people of southern Michigan and neighboring lands. The Ottawas, Sauteurs, and other tribes from the Northwest, came down the Lakes for war or trade. The Foxes and Sauks went west from the Niagara region.[9]

Not long after the abandonment of Fort Denonville, one Dubeau, a Canadian half-breed, son of a Frenchman and a Huron woman, who is described as "one of the strongest men in the country," was taken captive by the Iroquois, who bound him and guarded him closely. As he could speak their language he gained their good-will, so that they trusted him a little and guarded him less closely. "One night, as they were near Niagara, all being asleep and the fire dying down, Dubeau arose, took a hatchet, killed all eight of them, and made his way to the Ottawas."[10] A brief record of a tragedy typical of the region and the time.

There are few annals of Lake Erie at this period. Cadillac, after three years at Mackinac, went down to Quebec in 1697, where he reported that he had "put several parties in the field against the Iroquois, and our allies came back from them victorious, having killed or taken prisoners 102 warriors of the tribe of the Sonnontouan [Senecas]. The last fight took place on the water, in Lake Erie, with equal numbers; and it

1905. Of the very many editions of La Hontan the English edition of 1703 (the year in which the first French issue appeared), is rather better reading than the French; few books give us better the English idiom of the period; and it admirably preserves the manner and spirit of the original. La Hontan at his best wrote with a classic pen; the grossness and indecencies found in a part of his work are by some attributed to an alleged colaborator or editor, the publisher Nicolas Gueudeville, an unfrocked French friar.

[9] Coll. Wis. Hist. Soc., III, 265.

[10] The incident of Dubeau is recorded in the *Mémoire* ascribed to Catalogne.

was so fierce that, both sides having come to land with their canoes, they dispatched each other with their knives. There remained on the field 40 Iroquois and there were 15 prisoners; our allies sustained a small loss."[11] Here is a rare chapter of Lake Erie history, the details of which may only be found in the imagination.

We do not undertake here a minute study of events at Fort Frontenac, elsewhere recorded by competent hands. It will suffice to note that its destruction was ordered in 1688, when Niagara was abandoned. Denonville, writing in 1690, says he " sent orders to the captain commanding Fort Cataracouy " — apparently Valrenne —" to abandon that post after having sapped the walls by piling timber well smeared with tar against them." Instead of burning the fort, Valrenne undertook to blow it up. The garrison withdrew to Montreal, but enough of the structure remained to serve as shelter for the Indians of the neighborhood.

The year before, three barks had sailed the lake; two of them built at La Salle's orders, now scarcely seaworthy; a third built by La Barre. During the temporary abandonment of Fort Frontenac, they probably made their base at what was later known as La Galette, near present Ogdensburg. It was not until 1696 that the ruinous fort was repaired and newly garrisoned.

The student cannot fail to observe a singular inconsistency in the policy and conduct of the French, for many years after their entry into the Lower Lakes as a theater of action. Dependent in large measure for the success of their undertakings on the good will of the aborigines, over and over again they thwarted their own ends by antagonizing the natives on whom they must rely. Often the pretext was, that the Indians were the allies of the English; but the result was none the less disastrous. Even if no tradition lingered of Champlain's murderous invasion of 1615, Denonville's raid on the Seneca vil-

[11] Frontenac to the Minister for Colonies, Oct. 15, 1697. Some further reference to this fight is contained in an unpublished narrative by M. de Champigny of events in Canada, 1696–97; it is stated that there was an ambuscade and fight on Lake Erie, in which 60 Iroquois were slain or drowned. (*Coll. Moreau St. Méry*, Vol. VI.)

WILDERNESS STRIFE

lages in 1687 not only made all French operations within striking reach of the Senecas more hazardous, but naturally inclined the Senecas to view with favor the friendly offers of the English, who like themselves were treated as enemies by the French. There were numerous episodes of the sort, which do not fall within the scope of our narrative, the effects of which were like that of the raid of 1687. In the summer of 1696 the veteran Frontenac, in retaliation, made an expedition against the Onondagas which was in effect a repetition of the unhappy achievement of Denonville nine years before. It must have mention here, as it marks another step in the gradual entry of the French into Lake Ontario. With a motley force of French regulars, Canadian militia and Indian allies, Frontenac set out from Montreal, July 4th. Twelve days brought his army to Fort Frontenac, 12 more to the mouth of the Oswego. Passing up this river, they gained the villages in the vicinity of Onondaga Lake, but the nation had fled. A lame girl and an old man were taken, and the latter tortured to death. Villages of the Onondagas and Oneidas were burned, and crops destroyed. Then the "army" retraced its way, crossed the eastern end of Ontario and regained Quebec, to await proofs that the blow had produced a chastened and friendly feeling throughout the Six Nations.[12]

[12] It was this expedition of 1696 which inspired Alfred B. Street's once popular metrical romance, "Frontenac." With all its erudition, real or assumed, it mingles many statements which will perplex the reader who has regard for the facts; as for instance, in Canto III.:

> In the soft twilight's darkening glow,
> Near the wild shores of Ontario. . . .
> . . . . a brigantine creeps
> Round one of the points to the push of
>   her sweeps.

Only by poetic license can a brigantine be found on the lake at that date.

CHAPTER X

JONCAIRE THE ELDER

THE DOMINANT FIGURE OF HIS TIME ON THE NIAGARA — THE EMBASSY OF CLERAMBAUT D'AIGREMONT — TWO NATIONS STRIVE FOR TRADE CONTROL — RAUDOT PICTURES JONCAIRE.

IN tracing the history of the Niagara region, one comes to a time when records seem to vanish and exploits to cease. The story of the early cross-bearers and explorers is much more than twice told. The splendid adventuring of La Salle has been made the most familiar chapter in the annals of the Great Lakes. After him, in the closing years of the seventeenth century, a few expeditions, a few futile campaigns and fated undertakings, have been meagerly chronicled. We read of La Barre's foolish and fruitless plans, of Denonville's pathetic and calamitous establishment at the mouth of the Niagara. But with the passing of La Salle from the pages of our regional history, the light wanes, the shadows deepen. We are come to the Dark Decades on the Niagara.

So one may fairly designate the first forty years of the eighteenth century. Speaking broadly, they are a part of the century-long strife between France and England for American supremacy. There were periods, it is true, in these decades, when the rivals were nominally at peace. The Treaty of Ryswick, after King William's War, proclaimed a peace that was kept from 1697 till 1702; and following Queen Anne's War, the Treaty of Utrecht warded off armed hostilities from 1713 to 1744. Thus for thirty-five years — seven-eighths of the period under notice — there was political peace between France and England; but on the Niagara, and the Great Lakes which it joins, there was never a day in all those forty years when the spirit of commercial warfare was not active.

During these years, the American colonies of the rival Powers were developing along widely divergent lines. France established her distant posts, throughout the lake and trans-

Alleghany region, her very energy weakening her for future defense. The English colonies, and New York in particular, devoted themselves more to developing the home territory. Both cajoled and bargained with the Indians, both exhausted themselves in fighting each other. It was the time when the slave trade was encouraged; when piracy flourished. But recently were the days when Captain Kidd and Morgan and Blackbeard and their kind " sailed and they sailed "; and the attention of New York's Governors was divided between lawless and red-handed exploits on the seas, the quarrels of their legislative councilors, and the interference of the French in their reach for the fur trade.

Throughout these Dark Decades there is a figure in our regional history which, strive as we may, is at best but dimly seen. Now it stands on the banks of the Niagara, a shadowy symbol of the power of France. Now it appears in fraternal alliance with the Iroquois; and anon it vanishes, leaving no more trace than the wiliest warrior of the Senecas, silently disappearing down the dim aisles of his native forest. Yet it is around this illusive figure that the story of the Niagara centers for forty years.

This man is the French interpreter, soldier, and Seneca by adoption, commonly spoken of by our historical writers as Chabert de Joncaire — more accurately, as Chabert de Joncaire the elder. He never attained high rank in the service; he was a very humble character in comparison with several of his titled superiors who were conspicuous in making the history of our region during the time of his activity hereabouts. But it was primarily through his skilful diplomacy, made efficient by his peculiar relations to the Indians, that France was able to gain a foothold on the Niagara, for trade and for defense, and to maintain it for more than a quarter of a century.

His baptismal name was Louis Thomas de Joncaire; his seigneurial title, Sieur de Chabert. The son of Antoine Marie and Gabriel Hardi, he was born about 1670,[1] in the little town of St. Remi, of the diocese of Arles, in Provence. As a child,

[1] Tanguay gives this date. A report of 1732 says he was born in 1668.

he may have played amid the mighty ruins of Roman amphitheaters and palaces, and have grown up familiar with monuments of a civilization which antedated by many centuries the Christian era.

The date of his coming to America is uncertain; possibly with the troops of the Marine, largely from Provence, which accompanied the Chevalier de Vaudreuil in 1687. Some years his senior, Vaudreuil often appears as his patron and staunchest friend, defending his character when vilified, and commending him for favor and promotion. Other evidence tends to indicate that he accompanied Frontenac to America in the capacity of quartermaster (*maréchal-des-logis*) in the autumn of 1689. We find him holding this rank in the Governor's Guard in 1700. June 14, 1704, the King at Versailles named Joncaire an ensign in the colonial troops and approved his going, the following winter, to live with the Senecas. From 1706 he is a lieutenant of the Marine. In an official letter of 1738 he is mentioned as having served as interpreter since 1701.

At an early period Joncaire and several companions were taken captive by the Iroquois. The exact date does not appear. In view of his relations to Vaudreuil, he may have accompanied that officer in the expedition against the Senecas in 1687; but his capture by the Senecas was probably in 1692 or 1693. The earliest account of Joncaire's early years appears to be that contained in a letter written by M. Raudot the younger — son of the Intendant Raudot, and for a time joint administrator with him — to the Minister, Ponchartrain.[2] Under date of Quebec, November 1, 1709, M. Raudot informed the Minister that " The Sieur Jonquaire, officer of the troops of this country and interpreter of the Iroquois, who has the confidence and friendship of M. de Vaudreuil, does not conduct himself, as it appears to me, for the good of His Majesty's service. I have the honor of giving you his history and of

Another, of 1735, speaks of him as 60 years old, which would make his birth year 1675.

[2] Preserved in the *Correspondance Générale*. So far as I have noted, it has never been published.

JONCAIRE THE ELDER

showing you his character; you can judge him for yourself." Raudot continues:

> He is a man who talks much, who brags, and even lies. He boasts a great deal of his influence with the Senecas, and makes it appear as great as possible.
>
> If an upright man, he cannot possess these traits; but he adds to them something of ingratitude, not refraining on every occasion to show contempt for his benefactor. He thinks thereby to increase his own importance, insinuating by his talk that it was necessary to come to him in Iroquois matters; but the most reputable men think differently, believing that if he had not been consulted, affairs would have gone better.
>
> He has been a soldier in this country, and was taken captive by the Senecas. As they were fastening him to a stake, to burn him, without knowing what he did, he gave a blow of his fist on the nose of one who held him. It made the savage's nose bleed, averted the tragedy and saved his life, since he was soon adopted, the savages admiring a man who dared, alone, defend his life among many enemies.
>
> It is from him, Monsieur, that I have drawn this history, which seems to me fabulous, it being the custom of the Indians to burn people whom they think brave, treating them more cruelly than others. But, at any rate, he was adopted, remained with them, gained their regard and confidence, and did not return to the colony until we made peace with these nations.

M. Raudot continues with an account of Joncaire's subsequent service, which will presently be related. The passage quoted above is the earliest known account of Joncaire's captivity, and was derived from him. Some years later the historian Bacqueville de La Potherie published a somewhat different version:

> He was taken in a battle; the fierceness with which he fought a war chief who sought to bind him in order to burn his fingers, until the death sentence could be carried out, induced the others to grant him his life, his comrades having all been burned at a slow fire. They [the Iroquois] adopted him, and the confidence which they had in him thenceforth, led them to make him their mediator in all negotiations.[3]

[3] La Potherie was a contemporary of Joncaire, and his "*Histoire de*

This passage, which is apparently the basis of versions of the affair by modern writers, has been variously "enlarged and improved"; but it is worth noting that the man who wrote down Joncaire's own much simpler account in 1709 declared that he did not believe it. Raudot, however, was just then trying to make a case against Joncaire. There is no reason to doubt that worthy's captivity, however writers may have decked it with imaginary incidents. On that captivity, and Joncaire's subsequent adoption, depended the course of history in Western New York for half a century. Joncaire passed much of his subsequent life among the Senecas, and though he won distinction for his service to his king and the cause of Canada, he seems never to have forfeited the confidence of his red brethren. He did not, like many prisoners of the period, wholly sever his connection with his own people. On the contrary, his intimacy with the Senecas proved of the greatest value to Canada in the promotion of her plans for trade.

Whenever Joncaire may have been taken prisoner, he was released in the autumn of 1694, with twelve other prisoners, one of whom was M. de Hertel,[4] a French officer whose services were of some note at a subsequent period. Father Milet, who

L'Amerique septentrionale," published in Paris in 1722, contains the fullest early account of Joncaire's captivity after Raudot's I have been able to discover. La Potherie is apparently Parkman's authority; yet I find no other basis than the passage above quoted for the following, in "Frontenac and New France under Louis XIV": "The history of Joncaire was a noteworthy one. The Senecas had captured him some time before, tortured his companions to death, and doomed him to the same fate. As a preliminary torment, an old chief tried to burn a finger of the captive in the bowl of his pipe, on which Joncaire knocked him down. If he had begged for mercy, their hearts would have been flint; but the warrior crowd were so pleased with this proof of courage that they adopted him as one of their tribe, and gave him an Iroquois wife." Evidently the historian has read into the meager account of La Potherie certain picturesque — and highly probable — details drawn from his own knowledge of Indian customs and character. As for Joncaire's Indian wife, her existence is also highly probable; but I find only circumstantial proof of it in contemporary records.

[4] "*Orchouche, avec les Ouiengiens, ramène 13 esclaves; entre autres, M. de Hertel et M. de Joncaire.*"— Belmont, "Histoire du Canada," p. 36. The Abbé de Belmont was Superior of the Seminary at Montreal, 1713 to 1724. His MS. history is in the Royal Library at Paris.

JONCAIRE THE ELDER

had been held a prisoner among the Oneidas since 1689, was returned to the French at the same time. Joncaire had then lived among the Senecas for several years, and had been adopted by a Seneca family to fill the place of "a relative of importance," whom they had lost. "He ingratiated himself so much with the nation," says Colden, "that he was advanced to the rank of a sachem, and preserved their esteem to the day of his death; whereby he became, after the general peace, very useful to the French in all negotiations with the Five Nations, and to this day they show regard to his family and children."[5] There is no implication here, nor in any other writer who may be called contemporary with Joncaire, that he married a Seneca woman. On March 1, 1706, at Montreal, he married Madelaine le Guay, by whom, from 1707 to 1723, he had ten children,[6] several of whom died in infancy, and but two of whom came to bear a part in their country's history. The eldest child, Philippe Thomas de Joncaire, born January 9, 1707, is known by his father's title, Chabert, and by many writers the two are more or less confused.[7] The seventh child, Daniel, "Sieur de Chabert et Clausonne," sometimes called Clausonne, was born in 1716. Both of these sons followed in their father's footsteps, and for many years are conspicuous figures in the history of the Niagara region.

The first public service in which we find the senior Joncaire employed was not until six years after his release by the Iroquois. He was at the conference in Montreal, July 18, 1700, between the Chevalier de Callières and six deputies from the Iroquois, two from the Onondagas and four from the Senecas.

[5] Colden's "History of the Five Indian Nations of Canada" (London, 1747), p. 179.

[6] Tanguay, "Dictionnaire Généologique." The following data are given regarding Joncaire's children: Philippe Thomas, b. Jan. 9, 1707; Madelaine, b. May 8, 1708, d. 1709; Jean Baptiste, b. Aug. 25, 1709, d. 1709; Louis Romain, b. Nov. 18, 1710; Marie Madelaine, b. April, 1712, d. 1712; Louis Marie, b. Oct. 28, 1715; Daniel, b. 1716; Madelaine Thérèse, b. March 23, 1717; Louis Marie, b. Aug. 5, 1719; François, b. June 20, 1723. The family home seems always to have been at or near Montreal. Madame de Joncaire, mother of these children, is buried in the church at Repentigny.

[7] In Parkman's "Half Century of Conflict," Joncaire and his oldest son are spoken of as the same person, and no distinction is made between them in the index.

Pledges of peace were made in the figurative language employed on such occasions. Callières was solicitous about certain Frenchmen and Indian allies of the French who were still held in the Iroquois country. The deputies declared their willingness to restore them, and asked as a special favor that Joncaire return with them, to fetch out the captives. This request was granted, Father Bruyas and the Sieur de Maricourt being also sent along, the two former to the Onondagas, Joncaire to the Senecas. "Our son Joncaire," the chiefs called him; and before the council broke up, they solemnly gave to Callières three strings of wampum. "We give these," they said, "in consequence of the death of Joncaire's father, who managed affairs well, and was in favor of peace. We inform Onontio, by these strings of wampum, that we have selected Tonatakout, the nearest blood relation, to act as his father instead, as he resembles [him] in his disposition of a kind parent." We are to understand that this father who had died was the adoptive father, according to the Seneca custom. The Governor expressed sympathy; approved the appointment of the new father; and gave the Senecas a belt "in token of my sharing your sentiments; and I consent that Sieur Joncaire act as envoy to convey my word to you and to bring me back yours."[8] This so pleased the chiefs that they consented that four of their people should remain at Montreal until their return.

Callières at this period was more concerned in making a firm peace with the savages south of Lake Ontario than with getting any foothold on the Niagara. In fact, for the time, he avoided any movement in that direction. The next spring, when he sent La Mothe-Cadillac and Alphonse de Tonty to make their establishment at Detroit, he had them follow the old Ottawa route, "by that means," he announced beforehand to Pontchartrain, "avoiding the Niagara passage so as not to give umbrage to the Iroquois, through fear of disturbing the peace, until I can speak to them to prevent any alarm they might feel at such proceedings, and until I adopt some measures to facilitate the communication and conveyance of neces-

[8] N. Y. Col. Docs., IX, 711.

saries from this to that country through Lake Ontario." Callières knew that the Minister had very much at heart the success of the project on the Detroit; it was not politic to urge at the moment the advantages to be gained from a hazardous experiment on the Niagara. The band that built Fort Ponchartrain, thereby laying the foundations for the city of Detroit, went thither by the Ottawa route; and although there was an occasional passage by way of the Niagara — a few of which we can trace, more of which, no doubt, we are ignorant of — yet for some years from the time we are now considering, the principal coming and going between the Upper Lakes and the lower St. Lawrence was by the northern route.

Joncaire spent the summer of 1700 among the Senecas in the furtherance of his mission. There were no permanent Seneca villages at this time west of the Genesee. By September 3d he was back again at Montreal, with Father Bruyas and Maricourt from the Onondagas, nineteen "deputies" of the Iroquois and thirteen prisoners for restoration to the French.

Joncaire had found no little trouble in inducing them to return. Many a French soldier was brought by the fierce Senecas a trembling, fainting captive into their lodges, only to be adopted as one of the nation. An alliance with a young squaw, by no means always uncomely, quickly followed. The rigors and discomforts of the frontier post and wilderness campaign prepared him to accept with philosophy if not with entire satisfaction, the filth and rudeness of savage life. In the matters of cruelty and barbarity, the French soldier of the period was too often the equal to his Indian brother. The freedom of the forest life always appealed to the Gallic blood. There was adventure, there was license, there were often ease and abundance among his savage captors. If at times there were distress and danger, these, too, he had known in the King's service. Small wonder, then, that among such captives as saved their scalps by reason of some exhibition of a dauntless spirit, there were many who preferred to abide with the red men, in their villages pleasantly seated in the beautiful valleys of Central New York, to a return to the duties and privations of service in Canada. Once more among the French, they knew they need never look for mercy again from the Iroquois into whose hands they were ever likely to fall. Their point of view must have been entirely familiar to Joncaire; though on this and subsequent occasions he seems faithfully to have sought to induce them to return.

The matter of Indian wives, which hardly calls for our further consideration save in relation to the family of Joncaire, did receive at one time and another, a good deal of attention from the Canadian Governors. Officially Canada always opposed these alliances, as did the Church. Actually, they occurred with great frequency wherever the two races were thrown into such social intimacy as pertained to the frontier and the wilderness. Frontenac himself was said to have had half-breed descendants, of whom were the prominent family of Montour; but this statement, much repeated by writers, is apocryphal. Vaudreuil, in 1706, issued an order forbidding Cadillac to let his men in the Detroit settlement take Indian wives because " experience showed they became good-for-nothings and their children the same." A report of 1709 says of Vaudreuil: " He has had to order Joncaire to get rid of one Montour, who springs from such a marriage. It appears that all children born of it make all the trouble possible for the French."

Whatever may have been Joncaire's course, he kept a singularly strong hold on the affections of the Senecas. With the party that went up to Montreal in September, the Senecas sent along a young man. " When Joncaire was in our country," said one of their spokesmen to the Governor, " the father of this youth whom we restore, was his master; but now it is Joncaire who is master of this young man. We give him in order that if Joncaire should happen to die, he may be regarded as his nephew and may take his place. Therefore it is that we give him up to Onontio, whom we beg, with the Intendant, to take care of him and to confine him should he become wild." And Callières, as in duty bound, promised to care for the youth, and to " furnish him everything he shall require to qualify him for filling some day said Sieur Joncaire's place."

For some years following Joncaire was much employed on

missions of this sort; now sojourning among the Onondagas or the Senecas, to secure the release of prisoners or to spy on the emissaries of the English; now back at Montreal, interpreting at councils. In the negotiations of the time he was indispensable.

At the general council at Montreal in the summer of 1701, at which assembled not only representatives of the Iroquois, but the tribes from Mackinac and the West, Joncaire found himself for the time being in an embarrassing position. The western tribes, after great difficulty, had been induced to send hither the French and Iroquois prisoners, for exchange. Here appeared the Rat, that greatest and most eloquent red man of his day, of whose eloquence, intelligence and nobility of character many writers from La Potherie to Parkman have testified. The Rat handed over to Callières his Iroquois prisoners, and demanded to know why the Five Nations were not delivering up theirs; they were not acting in good faith, he said. The Iroquois replied, through their orator Teganeout, that their young men had charge of the prisoners, and that the latter were unwilling to leave the lodges where they had lived since childhood; were they French or Western Indian, it mattered not; they had forgotten their own people and were attached to those who had adopted them, significantly adding that Joncaire had not very strongly urged their return.

Joncaire arose in the council, acknowledged his fault, and begged the Senecas, his brethren, to help him accomplish the matter hereafter. High words followed, but later reconciliation was effected.

A few days afterward, the council being still in session, the Rat died. In the obsequies that followed, Joncaire was singularly conspicuous. The body of the great Huron chief lay in state at the Hôtel Dieu, in an officer's uniform, with side arms, for he held the rank and pay of an officer in the French army.[9] After the Governor General and Intendant had sprinkled the corpse with holy water, Joncaire led sixty warriors from Sault St. Louis to the bier, where they wept for the dead, bewailing him in Indian fashion and " covered him," which figurative

[9] Charlevoix, Shea's ed., V, 147.

expression signifies that they gave presents to his tribesmen. After the imposing funeral, at which the ritual of the Roman Catholic church was blended with military usage and Indian rites, Joncaire led another band of Iroquois to condole with and compliment the Hurons, with significant gifts of wampum.

In these acts Joncaire was undoubtedly at work, not only for his Government, but for the Senecas and his own interests, which from now on center more and more on the western boundary of the Five Nations cantons. French interests on the Niagara were not to be jeopardized by a needless rupture with the Hurons.

At a council at Onondaga, in September, 1701, Joncaire encountered Captain Johannes Bleecker and David Schuyler, sent out from Fort Orange, as their report has it, " to hinder the French debauching of our Indians." The English reports of these transactions are less formal and correct than are those of the French; but their vigorous phraseology, heightened by the ignorant or whimsical spelling of the time, adds a reality and picturesqueness to the chronicle which the Paris documents lack. Joncaire had brought an abundance of the goods which the Indian craved, a part at least of the store intended for the families who consented to release their prisoners in exchange. Captain Bleecker and his companion were irritated at the success which Joncaire and his fellows had among " our Indians." " We understand," said Bleecker, " the French are come here to trade. Do you send for us to come with such people, if you send for us for every Frenchman that comes to trade with you, wee shall have work enough and if you will hearken to them they will keep you in alarm Continually we know this is the contrivance of the Priests to plague you Continually upon pretense of Peace and talk [to] you until you are Mad, and as soon as these are gott home, the Jesuits have another project if you will break your Cranes [craniums?] with such things; we advise you brethren when the French comes again, lett them smoak their pipe and give them their bellyfull of Victualls and lett them goe."

The Dutch emissaries of the English on this occasion heard

JONCAIRE THE ELDER

Joncaire take the Indians roundly to task because they promised more than they performed in the matter of returning prisoners. He spoke as one who had nothing to fear, and consequently his words had weight. After some days of it, " Monsieur Jonkeur went his wayes," says the English record, and the Dutchmen wènt back to Albany, their chief concern being, as from the first, to secure the trade of the Five Nations to themselves. Their plans for that trade, even at this period, involved the control of the Niagara River.

From further worry over the friendship of the Iroquois, Callières was spared by death, May 26, 1703; and a new and stronger Onontio took his place at the head of the administration in Canada. This was the Chevalier de Vaudreuil, whose part in the history of our region is to continue important for many years.

Like his predecessor, he had had experience with the Seneca in his native wilds. As we have seen, Vaudreuil had come out from France just in time to join Denonville's expedition of 1687. He shared in that inglorious campaign, coming to the Niagara at its close, and helped to build the fort which was destined to be the scene of one of the most tragic episodes in the history of French occupancy in America. Vaudreuil's personal knowledge of the Niagara pass had no doubt its influence in shaping his policy towards the Iroquois. In a letter to the Minister, Pontchartrain, November 14, 1703, his first communication after the death of Callières, he speaks of Joncaire's recent return from a three months' sojourn among the Senecas, and declares the intention of sending him back to winter among them. This he did, but at the first breaking up of the ice in the spring, Joncaire appeared at Fort Frontenac with the news that the English were preparing to hold a general meeting of the Iroquois at Onondaga.

The neutrality of the Five Nations had now become the chief object of solicitude for the French. Joncaire was speedily sent back to the Senecas, and with him the priest Vaillant, that their combined efforts might defeat the seductive overtures of the English. Once more at Onondaga, the great capital of the Iroquois, he met his old adversary, Peter Schuyler.

The Indians were as ready to listen to overtures from one party as the other. This attitude alarmed the French. Joncaire posted off to Quebec to inform Vaudreuil, and was sent back with messages to Ramezay, at Montreal.

Under the sanction of the French at this time Indian parties fell upon certain New England settlements with dire results. We must accord to Joncaire a share in the instigation of these attacks. He was also an intermediary in negotiations with the Senecas, regarding an attack upon them by the Ottawas; we find him writing to the Governor, from the Seneca capital, under date of July 7, 1705, that " the partisans of the English in these villages do all in their power to induce the young men to avenge the attack made by Outtaouais on them, and that they are restrained only by the hope of recovering their prisoners, and by the proceedings they have seen me adopt."

The King and his Ministers at Versailles came to have great interest in the peculiar services rendered by Joncaire. " His Majesty," wrote Pontchartrain to Vaudreuil, June 9, 1706, " approves your sending Sieur Jonqueres to the Iroquois, because he is esteemed by them and has not the reputation of a Trader. . . . I have no doubt of the truth of the information Sieur Jonquieres has given you respecting the intrigues of the English among the Iroquois. Continue to order him to occupy himself with breaking them up, and on your part, give the subject all the attention it deserves."

There is among the Paris Documents [10] of the year 1706, a paper entitled: " Proposals to be submitted to the Court that it may understand the importance of taking possession of Niagara at the earliest date, and of anticipating the English who design to do so," etc. It is unsigned. It does not appear to have been written either by Vaudreuil or the Intendant, though it was probably by the order of the former that it was sent to Versailles. It shows that now, seventeen years after the abandonment of Denonville's enterprise, the expediency of again attempting a permanent establishment on the Niagara was being considered. It is worth while to

[10] N. Y. Col. Docs., IX, 773–775.

note the principal points in favor of the proposition, as they were drafted for the edification of the King.

Niagara was claimed to be the best of all points for trade with the Iroquois. It would serve as an entrepôt to the establishment at Detroit. With a bark on Lake Ontario, goods could be brought from Fort Frontenac to the Niagara in a couple of days, thus effecting a great saving in time, with less risk of loss, than by the existing canoe transportation. " It is to be considered," argues this document, " that by this establishment we should have a fortress among the Iroquois which would keep them in check; a refuge for our Indian allies in case of need, and a barrier that would prevent them going to trade with the English, as they begin to do this year, it being the place at which they cross."

The foregoing statement fixes, if not exactly the date at which traders in the English interest made themselves a factor on the Niagara, at any rate the date when the French began to think they had, and seriously to fear them. In this crisis, they turned to Joncaire, whom the writer of these " Proposals " cites as " an officer of the Marine forces in Canada, who has acquired such credit among the Iroquois, that they have repeatedly proposed and actually do suggest to him, to establish himself among them, granting him liberty to select on their territory the place most acceptable to himself, for the purpose of living there in peace, and even to remove their villages to the neighborhood of his residence, in order to protect him against their common enemies." This was no doubt true, and goes far to show how closely affiliated with the Senecas Joncaire had now become. But the proposition that follows is a singularly guileless and child-like specimen of statecraft.

It was urged that the English would take no alarm if this good friend of the Senecas, this soldier who lived with the Indians in their lodges, should go to the banks of the Niagara " without noise, going there as a private individual intending simply to form an establishment for his family, at first bringing only the men he will require to erect and fortify his dwelling, and afterwards on pretence of conveying supplies and merchandise there, increasing their number insensibly, and when the Iroquois would see that goods would be furnished them at a reasonable rate, far from insulting us, they would protect and respect us, having no better friends than those who supply them at a low rate." The document goes on to show how a monopoly of the beaver trade at Niagara may be secured, and to discuss the necessity of underselling the English, a thing which the French at this period could not do, especially in the price of powder and lead, which the English furnished very cheaply to the Indians.

It is suggested in the "Proposals" that the King "grant ten or twelve thousand weight of gunpowder and twenty or thirty thousand weight of lead, which would be yearly reimbursed to him at the rate his Majesty purchases it from the contractor. This would counterbalance the price of the English article; and then as our powder is better, we would thereby obtain the preference; become masters of the trade and maintain ourselves at peace; for it cannot be doubted that those who will be masters of the trade will be also masters of the Indians, and that these can be gained only in this way."

All of this was to be accomplished by Joncaire's clandestine establishment at Niagara. The King was reminded, somewhat presumptuously, that the Niagara enterprise, on a liberal scale, "would be of much greater advantage and less expense than carrying on a war against Indians excited by the English." Though obviously true, this was hardly the way in which to win favor with the war-racked Louis. The "Proposals" conclude as follows:

After having exposed the necessity of the establishment of this post; the means of effecting it without affording any umbrage to the Iroquois, and the most certain means to maintain peace and union with the Indians, it remains for me to add, as respects the management of this enterprise, that it would be necessary to prevent all the improper Commerce hitherto carried on, by the transportation of Brandy into the forest, which has been the cause of all existing disorders and evils. In order to avoid these it would be proper, that the Court, had it no other views, should give the charge of this business to our Governor and Intendant who in order to maintain the King's authority in Canada and to labor in concert for the public peace, would always so coöperate that the whole would be accomplished in a manner profitable to religion, trade and the union with the Indians, which are the three objects of this establishment.

There is in this a suggestion of priestly authorship. The whole document smacks more of the clerical theorist than of the soldier, the trader or the practical administrator of affairs. Its recommendations were not followed, though it had its effect, along with other causes, in bringing about an investigation into the state of affairs, not only on the Niagara, but at other points of trade on the Lakes.

In 1707 Joncaire was sent farther afield, on a mission among the Illinois. When complaint was made of his conduct by one Riverin, the Minister wrote back that the accusation against Joncaire was false, and that Riverin himself was not above joining in cabals. No further hint is found of the nature of the affair. A promise, in this year, that Joncaire should have promotion,[11] bespeaks a continuance of official confidence in him. To Joncaire himself the Minister wrote: " I have received your letter of September 3d of last year. M. de Vaudreuil informs me of what you have done among the Iroquois in the journeys you have made by his order, and I am satisfied with your conduct. Continue punctually to execute the orders of M. de Vaudreuil and I will remind the King of your services; but at present there is no vacancy in the Canadian troops."

A document of the time of singular interest, is a letter from the Minister, Pontchartrain, to La Mothe-Cadillac, in which, replying to a proposal of the latter to connect Lakes Erie and Ontario by a canal, it is remarked: " It does not seem to me that we can at present undertake the junction of the Lake Ontario with Lake Erie by a canal, as you propose, because of the expense. However, send me an analyzed statement (" *un mémoire raissonné* "), with a plan and estimate of cost." [12]

[11] The Minister to de Vaudreuil, June 13, 1707; same to Joncaire, June 30, 1707.
[12] The Minister to Cadillac, June 30, 1707.

As early as August, 1705, we find the English complaining of "Jonkeur the French interpreter who lives in the Senekas country." As he first went to the Senecas in the winter of 1704, his advent on the Niagara was probably about that time. From that time also, date the references, in both French and English records, to trade on the Niagara. It was in a sense a renewal of the earlier occupancy which had ended so lamentably with the abandonment of Fort Denonville. French occupancy of the region then ceased, nor was it resumed for 30 years; but in that period there was probably never a season when some attempt at trade on the river or at its mouth, was not made by the French. A few of these attempts, sometimes disastrous, are noted in our narrative. It was the presence of Joncaire, or of traders who relied on his influence with the Indians, that drew to the vicinity in 1707 bands of those uncertain nomads whom we vaguely know as Mississagas. Their later occupancy of the Niagara region is less definite than that of the Senecas. They were probably the people who had greeted La Salle in 1678; and seem to have shifted about in the region east of Lake Huron and north of Lake Erie, as conditions of sustenance or warfare suggested; but in 1707 word was carried to Albany that two sachems of a western nation "called Wississachoos"— which is held to mean the same as Mississagas —" were come to the Senecas country & acquainted the 5 Nations, that there were Three Castles of their Countrymen come to settle at a place about 8 Miles above Jagare,"[13] that is, Niagara. The reference is not to the falls, but to the mouth of the river, and the proposed settlement appears to have been what was later known as the Mississaga village near Chippewa Creek.

The English had frequent reports not only of the deeds but of the designs of the French in the Niagara region. The New York Indian records [14] often contain entries that read as

[13] N. Y. Indian Records, Wraxall's Abridgment.
[14] By "New York Indian Records" I mean specifically the manuscripts so styled, being records of transactions of New York's Indian Commissioners and the Indians from 1678 to 1751. In 1754, Peter Wraxall wrote an abridgment of a part of these records, which was preserved in four folio manuscript volumes. The fire in the Capitol at Albany, in 1911, destroyed

though the French had not merely a trading-post but a fort even, on the river, some years before Joncaire actually built there. These reports no doubt arose from the temporary sojourns which traders made, in a neighborhood so favorable for their purpose. In May, 1708, word reached Albany that the French were about to build "at Oghjagere or the Great Falls."[15] In July of 1708 the English were warned against "a fort at Ochjajare."[16] A truer revelation of what the French were actually doing is found in an Indian complaint, July 5, 1715, "that there are some evil designs intended by the French, who keep a party of men at the Carrying Place of Jagare."[17] Such records, many of which might be cited, sufficiently establish the presence of French traders on the Niagara, some years prior to the time when Joncaire built his trading-post.

Louis XIV was by no means satisfied with the information he received through regular channels regarding the condition and prospects of the lake posts. He accordingly devised a plan for a fuller and more trustworthy report. Under date of June 30, 1707, instructions were sent from Versailles to M. de Clerambaut d'Aigremont at Quebec, imposing upon him a task which called for no little perspicacity and tact. This gentleman, who was serving as sub-delegate to the Intendant, the Sieur Raudot, was directed to visit Fort Cataracouy (*i. e.*, Frontenac, now Kingston, Ont.), Niagara, Detroit and Missilimackinac, "to verify their present condition, the trade carried on there and the utility they may be to the Colony of Canada." The letter of instructions was long and explicit on many delicate matters regarding which the King wanted light. The administration of La Mothe-Cadillac at Detroit was especially to be inquired into, as many complaints

them. Fortunately, they had been copied, for Professor Charles H. McIlwain of Harvard University, who in 1915 published them, with a scholarly introduction and many useful notes, under the title "An Abridgment of the Indian Affairs," etc. In view of the destruction of Wraxall's MSS., citations from them in my narrative are referred to Professor McIlwain's printed volume.

[15] McIlwain's "Wraxall," 54.
[16] *Ib.*, 57.
[17] *Ib.*, 105.

and contradictory reports had reached the Court. Of Niagara the letter of instructions said:

His Majesty is informed that the English are endeavoring to seize the post at Niagara, and that it is of very great importance for the preservation of Canada to prevent them so doing, because were they masters of it, they would bar the passage and obstruct the communication with the Indian allies of the French, whom as well as the Iroquois they would attract to them by their trade, and dispose, whenever they please, to wage war on the French. This would desolate Canada and oblige us to abandon it.

It is alleged that this post of Niagara could serve as an entrepôt to the establishment at Detroit, and facilitate intercourse with it by means of a bark on Lake Ontario; that in fine, such a post is of infinite importance for the maintenance of the Colony of Canada, and that it can be accomplished by means of Sieur de Joncaire whom M. de Vaudreuil keeps among the Iroquois. His Majesty desires Sieur d'Aigremont to examine on the spot whether the project be of as great importance for that colony as is pretended, and, in such case, to inquire with said Sieur de Joncaire, whether it would be possible to obtain the consent of the Iroquois to have a fort and garrison there, and conjointly, make a very detailed report of the means which would be necessary to be used to effect it, and of the expense it would require; finally to ascertain whether it would be desirable that he should have an interview with said Sieur Joncaire, and that they should have a meeting at Niagara.

Word had reached Louis, which he was loth to accept, that Vaudreuil kept Joncaire among the Iroquois for the purpose of carrying on profitable trade with them, and of destroying the establishment at Detroit. Not the least difficult commission with which d'Aigremont was charged was to inform himself as to Joncaire's conduct, and report thereon.

There were further instructions, in a letter from the Minister, Pontchartrain, July 13th; but for some reason, probably because the season was far advanced, d'Aigremont did not undertake his mission until the following summer. On June 5, 1708, he set out from Montreal in a large canoe, amply provisioned but carrying no merchandise for trade. It was in fact the King's express; and so well did his sturdy men ply their paddles, up the swift St. Lawrence, through the tortuous channels of the Thousand Isles, coasting the uncertain lakes — fickle seas even in midsummer — making the great carry around the cataract of Niagara, and hastening by lake and river, that they accomplished the journey as far as Missilimackinac, stopping at the designated points long enough to observe and take testimony, and were back again at Montreal, September 12th. D'Aigremont's report, addressed to Pontchartrain, is dated November 14th; so that, allowing an average passage to France, more than a year and a half elapsed from the day when the King made known his will regarding a special investigation into the lake posts, till he received the report of his emissary.

That report is a document of exceptional value for the exact data it affords. At Fort Frontenac, where Captain de Tonty was in command, d'Aigremont took the depositions of Indian chiefs and other principal men, much of it tending to show that Tonty pursued an arbitrary and selfish policy in his dealings both with Indian hunters and French soldiers; " yet it is to be remarked," writes the King's reporter, " that notwithstanding all these petty larcenies, Mr. de Tonty is deeply in debt; an evident proof that they have not done him much good. What may have driven him to it is, the numerous family he is burdened with, which is in such poor condition as to excite pity." After pointing out the difficulty of keeping the Indians from carrying their peltries to the English, and the advisability of maintaining and strengthening Frontenac, d'Aigremont goes on to tell of his visit at Niagara.

He had left Fort Frontenac on June 20, 1708, and on the 27th rounded the point that marks the mouth of the Niagara; it had taken him a week to follow the north and west shores of the lake from Tonty's disturbed establishment. Joncaire had been appraised of his coming. " I found him," writes d'Aigremont, " at the site of the former fort." " After conversing some time respecting this post, he admitted, My Lord, that the advantages capable of being derived from it, by fortifying it and placing a garrison there, would be, namely — that a number of Iroquois would separate from all their villages, and establish themselves there, by whose means we could always know what would be going on in those Villages and among the English, and that it would be thereby easy to obviate all the expeditions that could be organized against us.

"That the Iroquois would trade off there all the moose, deer and bearskins, they might bring, as these peltries could not be transported to the English except by land, and consequently with considerable trouble.

"That the Mississaguets settled at Lake Ste. Claire, who also convey a great many peltry to the English, will not fail in like manner to trade off their moose, deer and bearskins there.

"That the Miamis having, like the Mississaguets, demanded by a Belt of the Iroquois a passage through their country to Orange to make their trade, would not fail to sell likewise at Niagara the skins that are difficult of transportation by land, and this more particularly as the English esteem them but little. But, My Lord, these considerations appear to me of little importance in comparison with the evil which would arise from another side. This would be, that all the Beaver brought thither by any nations whatsoever would pass to the English by means of their low-priced druggets, which they would have sold there by the Iroquois without our being ever able to prevent them, unless by selling the French goods at the same rate as the English dispose of theirs, which cannot be.

"It is true that this post could be of some consideration in respect to Detroit to which it could serve as an entrepôt for all the goods required for purposes of trade there, which could be conveyed from Fort Frontenac to Niagara by bark; a vessel of forty tons being capable of carrying as many goods as twenty canoes. Though these goods could, by this means, be afforded at Detroit at a much lower rate than if carried by canoes to Niagara, the prices would be still much higher than those of the English. This, therefore, would not prevent them drawing away from Detroit all the Beaver that would be brought there.

"The post of Niagara cannot be maintained except by establishing that of La Galette [on the St. Lawrence, a little below present Ogdensburg], because the soil of Fort Fron-

JONCAIRE THE ELDER 167

tenac being of such a bad quality, is incapable of producing the supplies necessary for the garrison, its last one having perished only from want of assistance, as they almost all died of the scurvy."

D'Aigremont discussed at length the advisability of creating an establishment at La Galette as a base of supplies for Niagara; but he did not think a post could be established at Niagara at this time with entire success: " At least great precautions would [need be] taken at the present time, and whoever would propose an extensive establishment there at once would not fail to be opposed by the Iroquois. Such cannot be arranged with them except by means of Mr. de Longueuil or of Sieur Joncaire, one or other of whom could propose to settle among them at that point, as the Iroquois look on these two officers as belonging to their nation. But my Lord," d'Aigremont significantly adds, " the former would be preferable to the latter because there is not a man more adroit than he or more disinterested. I do not say the same of the other, for I believe his greatest study is to think of his private business, and private business is often injurious to public affairs, especially in this colony, as I have had occasion frequently to remark."

D'Aigremont thought there was so little prospect that the post of Niagara could be established, that he did not take the trouble to report an estimate of the expense such a project would incur; but bearing in mind the King's remarks regarding the motives which led Vaudreuil to keep Joncaire among the Iroquois, he replied to this point as follows:

" I do not think the Iroquois will suffer the English even to take possession of that post [Niagara], because if they were masters of it, they could carry on all the trade independent of the former, which does not suit them.

" The Marquis de Vaudreuil sends Sieur de Joncaire every year to the Iroquois. He draws from the King's stores for these Indians powder, lead and other articles to the value of 2,000 livres, or thereabouts, which he divides among the Five Nations as he considers best. Some there are who believe that he does not give them all, and that he sells a portion to them;

or at least that he distributes it to them as if it were coming from himself, thereby to oblige these Indians to make him presents. What's certain is, that he brings back from those parts a great many peltries. I am assured that they reach fully 1000 annually; in the last voyage he made, he brought down two canoes full of them. He left one of them at the head of the Island of Montreal [" *bout de l'isle* "], and had the peltries carted in through the night. As for the rest, My Lord, I do not know whether the Marquis de Vaudreuil has any share in this trade."

The Minister acknowledged this report in due time. Writing from Versailles, July 6, 1709, he said: " In regard to the post of Niagara, it is not expedient under any circumstances; and as there is no apprehension that the Iroquois will take possession thereof, it is idle to think of it. Therefore we shall not require either Sieur Longueil, or Sieur Jonquair [*sic*] for that "; and he added that he would have the latter " watched in what relates to the avidity he feels to enrich himself out of the presents the King makes these Indians, so as to obviate this abuse in future." Even though Joncaire were chargeable with undue thrift, Pontchartrain evidently felt that he was by all odds the best man to manage the Iroquois in the French interest.

We here encounter insinuations against the character of Joncaire. In the King's service, he was charged with using his opportunities to enrich himself. There are many allusions to this not very surprising matter, from now on. He continued for several years to come, in much the same employment as that which we have noted. He never lost the confidence of Vaudreuil — possibly, as the foregoing correspondence may have suggested to the reader, because they were allied for personal profit in a surreptitious fur-trade. In November, 1708, we find the Governor commending him in a letter to the Minister. " Sieur de Joncaire," he writes, " possesses every quality requisite to ensure success. He is daring, liberal, speaks the [Seneca] language in great perfection, hesitates not whenever it is necessary to decide. He deserves that your Grace should think of his promotion, and I owe him this justice, that he attaches himself with great zeal and affection to the good of the service."

Joncaire at this period, 1708-9, was much of the time at Onondaga, doing what he could to counterbalance English influence. This was a task which yearly grew more and more difficult. Although Joncaire to the end of his days retained the good will of the Iroquois, and especially of the Senecas, he saw the hold of the French upon them gradually weakened, the temptations of English trade gradually and effectively strengthened.

Conflicting reports reaching the Minister regarding Joncaire, he wrote for enlightenment: " There is in Canada an officer named Joncaire, interpreter with the Iroquois. His conduct is equivocal. Some say he is a man not merely necessary but faithful, worthy of all confidence. Others declare that he abuses the trust placed in him, in the distribution of goods, and that he turns Government supplies to his own profit." [18] He ordered the Governor to investigate: " If guilty, have him make restitution, and put an honest man in his place."

In compliance with this order, a long report on Joncaire was written by the younger Raudot, son of the Intendant. From it we have already drawn the story of Joncaire's escape from the stake, and Seneca adoption. Raudot, evidently willing enough to paint the interpreter as black as possible, told the same story that d'Aigremont had included in his report — that Joncaire unloaded his furs at the head of Montreal Island and had them carted into the town secretly by night.[19] He even undertook to sketch Joncaire's public service.

He had been, wrote Raudot, one of Frontenac's guardsmen, until he became exempt from service. Callières had made him an officer, and both of these Governors had employed him as interpreter with the Iroquois. He had been sent to the Senecas with presents, and to reside, whereas Maricourt lived among

[18] Orders of Pontchartrain, Versailles, July 6, 1709.
[19] The date of Raudot's long letter to Ponchartrain, giving virtually the history of Joncaire's earlier years, is Nov. 14, 1709. D'Aigremont's report bears date Nov. 14, 1709. The accusations against Joncaire were no doubt matters of common knowledge.

the Onondagas. When this officer died, Joncaire, becoming the chief representative of France among the Iroquois, undertook to move the chief council-place of the Iroquois from the Onondagas to the Senecas. This stirred up the Onondagas; and as for a time they saw no more French coming to them with presents, they more readily inclined to the overtures of the English. Raudot made it appear that the Onondagas were ready to "raise the hatchet" against the French. He even pretended to fear that the other Iroquois nations would join with the Onondagas, "with the exception of the Senecas, who have always been firm in our alliance." This Joncaire, who was thus pictured as responsible for great risks to his country, and the raising of many enemies, was being paid 400 livres a year as interpreter, besides which he received 300 livres for outfit, etc., for each journey he made. Raudot thought he should be required to pay this back "when peace comes." "No one doubts, Monseigneur," added this informer, "that the Sieur de Joncaire receives gifts from his savages, in return for those he gives, or that he trades with them, since besides the gifts he carries them from the King's storehouse, he takes along quantities of other merchandise. They claim there is never a journey that does not bring him in two or three thousand francs (*deux à trois cents pistoles*). I cannot however believe that he gives the King's presents as coming from himself, the Indians knowing very well who sends them; but he could mix a part of them with his own trade — or, rather, as he is beloved by these savages, receive large presents from them for what he gives. It is a difficult thing," is the informer's smug and somewhat superfluous observation, "to know the truth."

CHAPTER XI

ACTIVITIES OF JONCAIRE

THE MURDER OF MONTOUR — JONCAIRE WINS ENGLISH ENMITY — A TRADE EPISODE OF 1717 — THE HOUSE BY THE NIAGARA RAPIDS — A STORMY VISIT FROM LAWRENCE CLAESSEN.

MEANWHILE, there came a critical time. Schuyler and others in the English interest, were very active at Onondaga; reports reached Vaudreuil that the Iroquois were declaring against the French, that troops were about setting out from Fort Orange to strike a blow. The French missionaries, Lamberville and Mareuil, were frightened or cajoled into leaving. A party of drunken Indians burned the chapel and priest's house at Onondaga, being set on thereto, the French believed, by Schuyler. Joncaire and his soldiers were at Sodus Bay, some 45 miles away, when this happened. He sent word of it, June 14, 1709, by canoe to M. de la Fresnière, commanding at Frontenac. His letter [1] shows that he was thoroughly

[1] The letter referred to, sent from Sodus Bay ("Bay of the Cayugas") to M. de la Fresnière, commanding at Fort Frontenac, is one of the few documents written by Joncaire known to be in existence. Its phraseology helps us form a just idea of the writer, who expresses himself, not as a rough woods-ranger might, but as one accustomed to letters and good society. This letter, as printed in N. Y. Col. Docs., IX, 838, is as follows:

BAY OF THE CAYUGAS, 14 June, 1709.

SIR — Affairs are in such confusion here that I do not consider my soldiers safe. I send them to you to await me at your fort, because should things take a bad turn for us, I can escape if alone more readily than if I have them with me. It is not necessary, however, to alarm Canada yet, as there is no need to despair. I shall be with you in twenty or twenty-five days at farthest, and if I exceed that time, please send my canoe to Montreal. Letters for the General will be found in my portfolio, which my wife will take care to deliver to him. If, however, you think proper to forward them sooner, St. Louis will hand them to you. But I beg of you that my soldiers may not be the bearers of them, calculating with certainty to find them with you when I arrive, unless I exceed twenty-five days.

The Revd. Father de Lamberville has placed us in a terrible state of embarrassment by his flight. Yesterday, I was leaving for Montreal in the best possible spirits. Now, I am not certain if I shall ever see you again.

I am, sir and dear friend, your most humble and most obedient servant,

DE JONCAIRE.

alarmed for the safety of himself and men. Regaining his assurance, he went back to the Senecas.

Towards the end of April, 1709, as Joncaire and his men were at a place "called by the Indians Ossaroda being upon the Creek that lyes opposite Cayouges," that is, Sodus Bay, they encountered the half-breed interpreter Montour, with 10 sachems of western tribes on their way to Albany. Here was a clash of rival interests, the story of which is best told in the language of the old record [2] which preserves it:

> The sd French Interpreter Jean Coeur advised Montour to turn back again otherwise he would oblige the 5 Nations to kill him, upon wch he replied he would perform his Journey to this Place [Albany]. Jean Ceur then desired him to smoak, he replied he had no Tobacco. Jean Ceur then gave him a little, Montour took out his knife to cut it, Jean Ceur then asked what he did with such a little Knife & desired Montour to give it him & he would give him one that was better. As soon as Jean Ceur had the Knife he flung it away at the same time there stood a French Man behind Montour with a Hatchet under his Coat who cut the sd Montour into his Head & killed him, whereupon the 10 Sachems come to Cayouge with Montour would have killed the French Interpreter Jean Ceur & all his Company if it had not been for the sd Montours Brother in Law who prevented it.

Joncaire's return to the Senecas at this time won for him more warm praise from Vaudreuil, who wrote to Pontchartrain that Joncaire, "by his return to the Senecas, has given evidence of all the firmness that is to be expected from a worthy officer who has solely in view the good of his Majesty's service." One reason for Joncaire's enmity towards Montour was that the latter had turned traitor to the French, and not only thwarted their aims among the Iroquois, whenever he could, but induced bands of western Indians, bringing furs for trade, to carry them to Albany, rather than make barter with Joncaire.

Later this year Joncaire went to Montreal with Father d'Heu and a French blacksmith who had been for some years

[2] Wraxall's "Abridgment of Indian Affairs." The details here given have been nowhere else noted.

ACTIVITIES OF JONCAIRE

in the Seneca villages, and a band of some forty Senecas as escort.

In July, 1710, the French took alarm lest the Iroquois should join the English in a threatened expedition against Canada. Longueuil and Joncaire, with ten other Frenchmen and some Indians, hastened to Onondaga, where the French, through Joncaire, as interpreter, made an exceedingly vigorous harangue, threatening the Indians with dire vengeance if they shared in the hostile movement. "If you do," said Joncaire (as reported in the English documents), "we will not only come ourselves, but sett the farr Nations upon you to destroy you your wifes and Children Root & Branch. . . . Be quiett and sett still." There was a divided sentiment in this council, but finally the French influence appeared to prevail, though a delegation of Indians soon appeared in Albany to inform Governor Robert Hunter of all that Joncaire had said, and to receive English assurances of friendship. On the other hand, a little later, Vaudreuil reported the matter to the Minister.[3] He begged of Monseigneur Pontchartrain that he specially remember the services of Joncaire and Longueuil, "who expose themselves to being burnt alive, for the preservation of the country in keeping peace with the Iroquois, who without them would inevitably make war." Joncaire, he added, has the same influence among the Senecas that Longueuil has with the Onondagas. Notwithstanding that Joncaire, the preceding summer, "was obliged to stay among them, and to send back his soldiers, in fear lest they would be put in the kettle, exposing himself alone to the caprice of these people in order to endeavor to keep the peace," yet he still continued to receive their favor, "as if himself a Seneca." At this time, the French flattered themselves that they could count on the friendship of all of the Five Nations except the Mohawks, who were most under English influence.

We find Joncaire, in September, carrying messages from M. de Ramezay, commandant at Frontenac, to Vaudreuil at Montreal. It was from Joncaire that the Governor received

[3] Vaudreuil to Pontchartrain, Nov. 30, 1710. There are numerous allusions to the matter in the documents.

the first intelligence of the preparations which the English were making at Boston and elsewhere, to attack Canada.

When Ramezay, in 1710, marched against the English, Joncaire commanded the Iroquois from Sault St. Louis and the Mountain, who made up the rear of the army; and he was probably with Vaudreuil, in September of that year in the advance to Chambly in quest of the English. More urgent matters in the East for a time withdrew the attention of Government from the Niagara and its problems. Still, no emergency could arise which could make Vaudreuil forgetful of the Iroquois.

For the next few years Joncaire continued to go back and forth between Montreal, where he acted as interpreter, and the Seneca villages, where he was supposed to be at work to offset the influences of the English, chiefly as made manifest through Peter Schuyler. We find record that he was among the Senecas in 1710 and again in 1711.

At a great war-banquet in Montreal, in August, 1711, at which 700 or 800 warriors assembled, "Joncaire and la Chauvignerie first raised the hatchet and sang the war-song in Ononthio's name." This was on receipt of the news that the English were preparing to attack Quebec. Many of the Indians answered the cry of the warlike Joncaire with applause, only the Indians from the upper country hesitating, because they had, almost all, been trading with the English; but in the end, twenty Detroit Hurons taking up the hatchet, all who were present declared for the French. The incident shows of what great value Joncaire was to the cause of the French at this critical time, in holding for them the good will of the Iroquois and tribes to the westward.

The next year, 1712, he was for a time in command at Fort Frontenac, in place of the Sieur de la Fresnière, who was incapacitated by fever. At this time the Senecas were much disturbed over matters to the westward. They feared, in the event of an outbreak against Detroit or by the tribes at the Sault, that they would be beset on the Niagara side. They sent a large delegation to Montreal, but declared to Vaudreuil "that they should not speak unless Sieur de Jon-

ACTIVITIES OF JONCAIRE 175

caire were present." That officer arrived from Fort Frontenac in September. We have not the details of the conference that followed; but the Senecas made their usual pledges of confidence in the French. At the same time, other tribes assembled at Onondaga were showing decided preference for the English, and sending word to the Indians at the Sault, requesting them " to remain passive on their mats, and not to take any sides," whatever might happen.

For the next few years I find little trace of Joncaire; but there is no reason to suppose that he did not continue in the same service as for the preceding years.

By his influence among the Iroquois, Joncaire was enabled to render a peculiar service in the summer of 1715. The post of Michilimackinac was distressed through lack of provisions. An appeal was made to Dubisson, commanding at Detroit; but he sent word that the corn supply had run so short that he had been obliged to send the Sieur Dupuy to the Miamis to try to buy of them, but it was doubtful if they could supply enough. In this extremity Ramezay appealed to Joncaire, who went among his Iroquois friends in the villages of Central New York and bought 300 minots of corn — about 900 bushels. This he made the Indians carry to the shore of Lake Ontario, some twenty leagues from the place of purchase. There it was loaded into the canoes for Capt. Deschaillons and dispatched to the distressed post; but all of this occasioned such delays that a hundred Frenchmen and Canadians were allowed to leave Mackinac and go down to Montreal to winter.

In the autumn of 1716, on his return to Montreal from the Iroquois cantons, Lieut. de Longueuil had called the attention of MM. de Ramezay and Bégon to the need of a "little establishment" "on the north [east] side of Niagara, on Lake Ontario, 100 leagues from the fort of Frontenac, a canoe journey of seven or eight days." Such a post, he claimed, would attract the Mississagas and Amicoues to trade with the Iroquois, when the latter went to hunt in the vicinity of Lake Erie. He also proposed that a barque should be built to serve as a transport between Frontenac and Niagara, claiming that it would be a sure means of conciliating the Iroquois and of gaining a great part of the fur trade which now went to the English. With such a post at Niagara, it would be possible to keep the *coureurs de bois* from trading in Lake Ontario, either by seizing their goods or arresting the traders, who were working mischief for the traffic at Fort Frontenac. De Ramezay, in communicating these views to Vaudreuil, commented that if such a post were approved, the trade there should be kept to the King's account.[4] The Marquis de Vaudreuil would not agree to establish this post at Niagara until the Iroquois should ask for it. The council approved, granting permission to proceed as suggested, if the Senecas wished it. This proposed establishment was never built, but we have in Longueuil's suggestions another form of the project which some four years later was to take shape in the *Magazin Royal* at Lewiston, and nearly ten years later in the permanent foundation of Fort Niagara. Due recognition must be taken of Longueuil's foresight at this time. Apparently to him, and not to Joncaire, is due the suggestion which later ripened into the Niagara establishment. Though employed for many years in similar service, the one among the Onondagas, the other with the Senecas, and though equally commended, in dispatches to the Minister, for their zeal and sagacity, a certain distinction attaches to Longueuil and his part in our history, which is not shared by Joncaire; a distinction due no doubt to family and social standing, rather than to native ability or devotion to the service.

Perusal of the New York Indian records for the first three decades of the Eighteenth century — down indeed to the day of his death — discovers endless complaints of Joncaire and his activities. His usefulness to the French can in a way be demonstrated from the trouble he made for the English, and for the Dutch traders at Albany, and the Indians in English allegiance. One tale that was told of him was that he had tried to stir up the Senecas " to kill and plunder all the farr Indians " that came to the Niagara or Lake Ontario to

[4] MM. de Ramezay and Bégon, at Quebec, to the Council of Marine, Paris, Nov. 7, 1716.

ACTIVITIES OF JONCAIRE 177

trade.[5] Albany lent a ready ear to anything that was alleged against this arch-enemy; who went his way, in the service of King and country, with singular zeal and amazing influence.

Coming from Montreal to what is now Western New York, in December, 1716, he found the Seneca villages ravaged by small-pox. A band of 300 warriors, which set out to attack the Illinois, returned because their chief had died of this disease, which more than once, in the years we here study, took heavy toll from the Iroquois and the tribes to the south and west. The evil reports which the English had spread, regarding Joncaire, so influenced even his Seneca friends, that they questioned if he had not come among them as a spy; and when he went back to Montreal a high chief accompanied him, to learn if the French were preparing to attack them.[6]

October 24, 1717, at a conference, apparently held at Onondaga, the Senecas made the surprising inquiry, if Joncaire were not among them "only as a Spy." He had spent the winter of 1716-17 in the Senecas' country. In spite of his affiliation and long-standing friendship with the Senecas, "a rumor prevailed that he had been sent thither to amuse them whilst preparations were being made to march against them in the Spring."[7] This suspicion of Joncaire was undoubtedly due to the influence of the English, which by this time had become predominant among the eastern Indians of the Federation. Even the Senecas were wavering and doubtful. Joncaire, when charged with being a spy, "did all in his power to disabuse them; but though highly esteemed among and even adopted by them, he could not succeed in removing their suspicion, for at the moment of his departure for Montreal, they sent a chief of high character with him to know from him whether it were true that he designed to attack them."

So reads the somewhat obscure document. The object of

[5] McIlwain's "Wraxall," 68.

[6] Record of the incident is preserved in the *Correspondance Générale*. (MS. vol. 38.)

[7] Proceedings in the Council of the Marine, June 25, 1718, signed L. A. de Bourbon and Le Maréchal D'Estrées. The document is marked: "To be taken to my Lord the Duke of Orleans." *See* N. Y. Col. Docs., IX, 876-878,

the embassy to Montreal was obviously to learn, not from Joncaire but from Vaudreuil, if any steps were to be taken hostile to the Senecas. Later, a delegation of chiefs and forty others arrived and were given audience by Vaudreuil. With elaborate ceremony they bewailed the death of the old King,[8] gave to Vaudreuil a belt which they begged he would send to the young King, whom they asked to take them under his protection; and did not omit the usual request at these conferences, that Joncaire, the de Longueuils, father and son, and de la Chauvignerie, " Should be allowed to go into their villages whenever they would wish to do so, or should be invited by their nations. They added, that they were fully aware that there were some people (meaning the English) whom this would not please, but no notice must be taken of such; that they were the masters of their own country, and wished their children to be likewise its masters, and to go thither freely whenever M. de Vaudreuil should permit them." This declaration of mastery in their own country illustrates anew the unstable and bewildered state of mind in which the Five Nations then were. Some years since, they had formally deeded their country to William III; and on more than one occasion they had acknowledged the authority of the French.

In June, Alphonse de Tonty left Montreal for Detroit, at which post he had been granted the privilege of trade, on condition that he would confine his operations to the jurisdiction of Detroit, nor send goods for sale to distant tribes. In crossing Lake Ontario, on his way to Niagara, he met nine canoes, all going to Albany to trade. Three were from Mackinac, three from Detroit and three from Saginaw. Tonty endeavored to head off this prospective trade for the English, and succeeded so well, heightening his arguments by substantial presents, that they all agreed not to go to Albany, but to go with him to Detroit.

Two days later, when this imposing flotilla was within six miles of Niagara, they fell in with seventeen canoes, full of Indians and peltries. In reply to his inquiries, these also admitted that they were going to Albany to trade, though they

[8] Louis XIV had died Sept. 1, 1715.

ACTIVITIES OF JONCAIRE

added that they were coming to Detroit afterwards. Tonty was equal to the emergency. Inspired by self-interest as well as loyalty to his Government, "he induced them also to abandon their design, by the promise that the price of merchandise at Detroit should be diminished, and he would also give them some brandy."[9] There followed a judicious distribution of this potent commodity.

One is tempted to conjure up the scene. Here were twenty-six laden canoes, not counting Tonty's own boats. They had come long journeys from remote and widely separated points, and their one objective point was the Englishmen's trading-place on the Hudson. But no sooner do they come under the blandishments of the Frenchman, and scent the aroma of his brandy-kegs, than these long-cherished plans so arduously followed, are thrown to the winds. They beach their canoes at or near the point of Niagara. A cask of liquor is broached, and Tonty permits the thirsty savages " to buy two or three quarts of brandy each, to take to their villages. But they first agreed that it should be carefully distributed by a trusty person."

In spite of these reassuring precautions, the transaction seems somewhat to have burdened his mind, for he thought it well to explain that " he hoped the council would not disapprove of what he had done, nor of the continuance of the same course, as he had no other intention than merely to hinder the savages from going to the English."

He succeeded fairly well in that purpose. After the distribution of brandy, they all reëmbarked, seven of the canoes promising to go to Montreal. Tonty sent back with them his trusty interpreter, L'Oranger, to keep them from changing their minds as they paddled down the lake. " He was only able to conduct six of them to Montreal; the seventh escaped and went to Orange."

Meanwhile ten canoes joined the commandant's own retinue; all paddled swiftly up the Niagara to the old landing, made the toilsome portage around the falls and pushed on to-

[9] Report of L. A. de Bourbon, secretary, Council of Marine, Oct. 12, 1717.

gether for Detroit, where they arrived July 3d. It was a typical move in the game that was being played, and France had gained the point.

This expedition was notable for its use of the Niagara route. Only a few years before we find Vaudreuil explaining to the Minister that he dispatched the Sieur de Lignery to Mackinac, and Louvigny to Detroit, by the Ottawa River route, because the Senecas had warned him that a band of Foxes lay in wait for plunder at the Niagara portage, or on Lake Erie.[10] If this were not duplicity on the part of the Senecas, it shows that war parties from the West foraged as far east as the Niagara; notwithstanding the supposed jealousy with which the Senecas guarded it.

Again we lose sight of Joncaire for a time; but the events of 1720, a date of great importance in the history of the Niagara, indicate that he was long busy with plans for giving the French a foothold on the river, and that even his Seneca friends had increasing cause to regard him with suspicion.

The attention of the Government was turning more seriously than ever before, to the Niagara passage as a means of reaching the upper posts. A " Memoir on the Indians of Canada, as far as the River Mississippi, with remarks on their manners and trade," dated 1718, affords an interesting glimpse of our river at that period:

The Niagara portage is two leagues and a half to three leagues long, but the road, over which carts roll two or three times a year, is very fine, with very beautiful and open woods through which a person is visible for a distance of 600 paces. The trees are all oaks, and very large. The soil along the entire [length] of that road is not very good. From the landing, which is three leagues up the river, four hills are to be ascended. Above the first hill there

[10] Vaudreuil to the Minister, Oct. 15, 1712. In a subsequent letter, Nov. 6, 1712, Vaudreuil speaks of the band of Otagamis (*i. e.* Outagamis, otherwise Foxes or Sacs), led by one Vonnere, who lay in wait at the Niagara portage, so that an expedition for Detroit led by M. de Vincennes was sent by the Ottawa River route, "not only to avoid these savages, but to prevent the convoy from being pillaged by the Iroquois," etc. The name " Vonnere " is found elsewhere in the more probable form " *Le Tonnerre,*" *i. e.*, " Thunderbolt."

ACTIVITIES OF JONCAIRE

is a Seneca village of about ten cabins, where Indian corn, beans, peas, watermelons and pumpkins are raised, all which are very fine. These Senecas are employed by the French, from whom they earn money by carrying the goods of those who are going to the upper country; some for mitasses,[11] others for shirts, some for powder and ball, whilst some others pilfer; and on the return of the French, they carry their packs of furs for some peltry. This portage is made for the purpose of avoiding the Cataract of Niagara, the grandest sheet of water in the world, having a perpendicular fall of two or three hundred feet. This fall is the outlet of Lakes Erié, Huron, Michigan, Superior, and consequently of the numberless rivers discharging into these lakes, with the names of which I am not acquainted. The Niagara portage having been passed, we ascend a river six leagues in length and more than a quarter of a league in width, in order to enter Lake Erié, which is not very wide at its mouth. The route by the Southern, is much finer than that along the Northern shore. The reason that few persons take it is, that it is thirty leagues longer than that along the north. There is no need of fasting on either side of this lake, deer are to be found there in such great abundance; buffaloes are found on the South, but not on the North shore.

This valuable Memoir, long and full of explicit information regarding the lake region, and the country and peoples to the west as far as the Mississippi, is of unknown authorship. It was probably written by some French officer assigned to a western post. As regards the Niagara, it antedates by three years the visit of the Jesuit Charlevoix, and it gives us our first information of Seneca settlement on the banks of the river. Although throughout these earlier years and for some time yet to come the Ottawa route was used more than the Niagara, yet there can be no doubt that, prior to 1720, many an expedition to the West had passed this way. Many a canoe, coming now singly, now in pairs, now in numbers, had no doubt carried the *coureur de bois*, and the trader with his merchandise, from Lake Ontario up the beautiful stretch of green water till stopped by the rapids in the gorge; had made

---

[11] According to O'Callaghan, this is another instance of the adoption of Indian words by Europeans. *Mitas* is not a French but an Algonquin word for stockings or leggings, in the "Vocabulary" of La Hontan, II, 223.

the steep climb up those "mountains" and followed the well-worn path of the long portage until, in navigable water above the great cataract, a new embarkation could be made with safety. Many a voyageur, too, returning from the West, as messenger from one of the upper posts or with canoes laden with packets of skins, had no doubt braved the dangers and difficulties of the Iroquois route, that he might sooner reach Frontenac and the settlements down the St. Lawrence. Some of these expeditions we have traced; but when one studies the history of Detroit and Mackinac and the various establishments on Lake Michigan, and notes the frequent communication they kept up with Montreal, he can but conclude that, notwithstanding the known use of the Ottawa route, there must have been many a hardy traveler on the Niagara of whose presence there is no more record in history than there is trace of his keel in the waters he traversed. Joncaire himself, known and welcomed throughout the country of the Senecas, was probably on the river many a time since his meeting with d'Aigremont, on the site of Fort Denonville; but not until 1720 do we find official record to that effect.

Early in May, 1720, Joncaire appeared at Fort Frontenac. The previous year, at the beginning of harvest, he had laden his canoe with trinkets, "small merchandizes," powder, lead, not forgetting the useful belts of wampum and the equally useful brandy, and had crossed over to the Long House of the Iroquois. Here, in the heart of our New York State, he had wintered, part of the time at the great Seneca village and part of the time at the little village.[12]

It was by the instructions of Vaudreuil and Begon that he made this sojourn, the design being that he should win for the French such favor that they might carry out undisturbed the

[12] In 1720 "the great Seneca village" was apparently at the White Springs, one and one half miles southwest of Geneva. It later removed to a location some two miles northwest of Geneva, where it was long famous as the Ga-nun-da-sá-ga of the Senecas, otherwise Kanadesaga. "The Seneca castle called Onahe," mentioned further on in our narrative, was at this period about three miles southeast from the present village of Canandaigua. These locations are in accordance with conclusions reached by the late George S. Conover of Geneva, than whom probably no one has made a more thorough study of the subject.

orders which the Court had promulgated in 1718, namely, the building of magazines and stockaded houses at Niagara and other Lake Ontario points.

The winter had been well spent. He brought back with him to Frontenac not merely several bundles of peltries, but good tidings which a council was quickly summoned to hear. The Senecas were most favorably disposed towards their father Onontio, and to the uncle Sononchiez, by which name they had come affectionately to designate Joncaire. Their father and their uncle, their message ran, were masters of their land. " The Indians consented not only to the building of the House of Niagara but also engaged themselves to maintain it. And if the English should undertake to demolish it they must first take up the hatchet against the Cabanes of the two villages of the Sennekas." [13] Such, at any rate, was the message as delivered to the delighted council.

No time was lost. In " 10 or 12 days " a canoe was packed with goods: " Some pieces of Blew Cloth three dozen or thereabouts of white Blankets for the use of the Indians half a Barrel of Brandy &c "; and with eight soldiers and young La-Corne — son of Captain de La Corne, Mayor of Montreal — the expedition set out gaily for our river. The season was propitious, the voyage short and successful. They entered the mouth of the Niagara and pressed on up the river to the head of navigation. Here, at the beginning of the portage on the east side of the gorge, where Lewiston now stands, " the Sieur de Joncaire & le Corne caused to be built in haste a kind of Cabbin of Bark where they displayed the Kings Colors & honored it with the name of the *Magazin Royal*."

Joncaire did not linger long, but went very soon to confirm his peace with the Senecas, leaving La Corne in command. From the Senecas' village he hastened back to Frontenac. There he took into his canoe as *compagnon du voyage* John Durant, the chaplain of the fort, from whose memorial are drawn in part the data for this portion of our narrative. They voyaged together to Quebec, arriving September 3d, and Joncaire was granted early audience with Vaudreuil and the In-

[13] Durant's Memorial, N. Y. Col. Docs., V, 588.

tendant, to whom he told what he had done. Vaudreuil was pleased, and the next day bestowed upon him the title of Commandant at Niagara, and bade him hasten back to that precarious post. There was joined to this new dignity an order for the inspection of the magazine " established in the Lake of Ontario. This Magazine is situate on the west of the Lake for the Trade with the Missasagué otherwise called the Round Heads distant about thirty leagues from that of Niagara. The House at the bottom of the Lake [14] was built by the Sieur de Anville a little after that of Niagara." [15] The Sieur Douville had built another house, for trade with the Ottawas, at

[14] *I. e.*, foot, west end. The allusion is probably to a trading station at Burlington Bay, designated in some French maps as "*Le fond du Lac.*"

[15] The builder of the trading-post at the head of Lake Ontario, the builder of the trading-post on the Bay of Quinté, and the officer who spent the winter of 1720–21 on the Niagara, are apparently the same man, variously designated in the printed documents as "the Sieur de Anville," "the Sieur D'Agneaux," and "the Sieur D'Ouville." The name is also to be found written 'd'Auville" and "d'Agneaux." Some of these variants are doubtless due to illegible manuscript, or inaccurate copying. He appears to have been the same officer who, at a conference with the Iroquois at Quebec, Nov. 2, 1748, signed his name "Dagneaux Douville." He was a lieutenant in the detachment of Marine troops serving in Canada. In 1750 he is spoken of as "Sieur Douville," commandant of Sault St. Louis; and in 1756, when he shared in another conference with Indians at Montreal, as "Lieut. Douville."

I find it impossible, from the allusions in the records, to be definite regarding French officers in the Canadian service, who are designated as "Douville." Philippe Dagneau Douville, Sieur de la Saussave, born 1700, was commandant at Toronto in 1759. His brother, spoken of also as Sieur de la Saussaye, was at Niagara, *en route* for Detroit, in 1739. The latter appears to have been the Alexandre Dagneau Douville who served among the Miamis, 1747–48; who was sent out from Fort Duquesne in 1756, on a foraging expedition, and was killed the next year in an attack on a fort in Virginia. A "Douville" was second ensign under Capt. Duplissis in 1729; was with De Villiers at Green Bay in 1730, in which year he married Marie Coulon de Villiers. "Douville" was also interpreter at Fort Frontenac in 1743. If, as seems probable, it was Philippe who was at the conference in Quebec in 1748 — Alexandre being among the Miamis in that year — then it was probably Philippe whose connection with the trade on Lake Ontario is noted in the text. The confusion is increased by the record that in 1728 "Rouville la Saussaye" was the lessee of the trading-post at Toronto; but whether there is any relation between Rouville la Saussaye, the trader, and Douville de la Saussaye, the soldier, I leave for future determination, or those who may have more exact information in the matter.

ACTIVITIES OF JONCAIRE

the foot of the Bay of Quinté. "They leave to winter in all their new forts," says Chaplain Durant, "but one Store Keeper and two Soldiers." Here indeed, was service for the King, a living immurement in the wilderness; yet the careers of men like Joncaire show how alluring this forest life, in spite of all its hardships and hazard, proved to many a soldier of New France.

Joncaire set out from Montreal, about the middle of October, 1720, to winter at Niagara. His two canoes were laden deep with goods from the King's storehouse. His escort numbered twelve soldiers, but at Frontenac six were left behind. There were evidently delays, at Frontenac or beyond, for as he skirted the south shore of Ontario his journey was stopped by ice thirty-five leagues from the Niagara. He put in at the Genesee and wintered there.

Into what extremity this failure of expected relief plunged the occupants of the bark cabin at the mouth of the Niagara gorge, we are not told. La Corne does not appear to have wintered there, for Durant records that "the Sieur D'Ouville had stayed there alone with a soldier, waiting the Sieur de Joncaire." Probably the friendship of the Senecas preserved them, but Joncaire's failure to arrive in the fall with goods to trade kept the storehouse empty till spring, to the no small embarrassment of the French and disappointment of the Indians.

There exist of this episode, as of many others that form our history, two official accounts, one French, the other English. In the abstract of Messrs. de Vaudreuil and Bégon's report on Niagara for 1720, it is set forth that "the English had proposed to an Iroquois chief, settled at Niagara, to send horses thither from Orange, which is 130 leagues distant from it, for the purpose of transmitting goods, and to make a permanent settlement there, and offered to share with him whatever profits might accrue from the speculation. The English would, by such means, have been able to secure the greatest part of the peltries coming down the lakes from the upper countries; give employment not only to the Indians who go up there and return thence, but also to the French." The reader will note the delightful impudence of this last proposition. The report continues: "They [the French] have a store there well supplied with goods for the trade; and have, by means of the Indians, carried on there, up to the present time and since several years ago, a considerable trade in furs in barter for merchandise and whisky.[16] This establishment would have enabled them to purchase the greater part of the peltries both of the French and Indians belonging to the upper country." It is clear that the English were about to attempt an establishment on the Niagara, had not the French forestalled them.

It is not easy to reconcile the various dates, or lack of dates, in the English and French records of this establishment. It was on October 26, 1719, that Vaudreuil sent Joncaire to carry to the Five Nations a favorable word from the King, and the presents above mentioned. He was charged to tell the Senecas that if the English came to Niagara they — the Senecas — should fall on them and seize their goods. It was agreed with Bégon that La Corne the younger and an *engagé* should spend the winter of 1719–20 on the Niagara, and that they were to open trade the following spring, on the Royal account. Their presence, it was argued, would keep the English away, and help the trade at Frontenac.

An Indian reported at Albany, in July, 1719, that the French were building at Niagara. He had been at the Seneca Castle called Onahe, within a day's journey of Niagara, and there met some Ottawas who had asked the French at Niagara, how they came to make a fort there without asking leave of the Five Nations; and the French had replied, " they had Built it of their Own Accord, without asking any Bodys Leave and Design'd to keep Horses and Carts there for Transportation of Goods," etc.[17]

Either the date of the above is too early by a year, or it refers to a structure built some time in 1719, which was succeeded by the larger *Magazin Royal*, which, according to explicit accounts, both French and English, was built in the lat-

---

[16] "*Eau de vie de grain.*"
[17] N. Y. Col. MSS. in State Library, Albany, Vol. LXI, fol. 157.

The Niagara at Lewiston, Looking North. Joncaire's "*Magazin Royal*" was Beyond the East End of the Bridge, on the First Level Above the River

ter part of May, 1720. In the report sent by Vaudreuil and Bégon to the Minister, under date of October 26, 1720, it is stated that " on the representation made by the Sieur de Joncaire, lieutenant of the troops, as to the importance of this post and of the quantity of furs which could be traded for there, they are making there a permanent establishment (" *un établissement sédentaire*"). We have charged him to have built there by the savages a picketed house ("*une maison de pieux* ") to which [construction] he pledged them last spring." The same report recites the visit to the Senecas of Messrs. Schuyler and Livingston, their names appearing — grotesquely distorted, as is usually the case with English or Dutch names in the old French documents — as "*le Sr. Jean Schult, commandant, et le Sr. L. Euiston, maire à Orange*"*!* The bark house was obviously surrounded by palisades — a strong, high fence of sharpened stakes. If the text of the French report may be accepted, the Indians themselves bore a willing hand in its construction.

Durant's memorial makes no mention of a visit at *Magazin Royal* in behalf of the English, but there was one. The work on the bark house under the Niagara escarpment was no sooner begun than word of it was carried eastward through the lodges and villages of the Six Nations. In April of 1720, Myndert Schuyler and Robert Livingston, Jr., had set out from Albany for the Seneca Castle, to hold one of the conferences which the Commissioners of Indian Affairs so frequently ordered at this period. Here, May 16th, they took the Indians to task because the French " are now buissey at Onjagerae, which ought not to be Consented to or admitted." The English emissaries went on to remind their Seneca brethren of the promises that had been made " about twenty-two years agoe to secure their Lands and hunting Places westward of them . . . to the Crown of great Brittain to be held for you and Your Posterity." The French, they continued, " are now buissy at onjagera which in a Manner is the only gate you have to go through towards your hunteing places and the only way the farr Indians conveniently came through where Jean Coeurs [Joncaire] with some men are now at work on building a block house and no Doubt of a Garrison by the next Year whereby you will be so Infenced that no Room will be Left for you to hunt in with out Liberty wee know that in warr time they could never overcome you, but these proceedings in building so near may be their Invented Intrigues to hush you to sleep whilst they take possession of the Heart of Your Country this is Plainly seen by us therefore desire you to Consider it rightly and sent [send] out to spy what they are doing at onjagera and prohibite Jean Coeur building there, for where they make Settlements they Endeavour to hold it so that if he takes no notice thereof, after given in a Civil way, further Complaints may be made to your brother Corlaer, who will Endeavour to make you Easy therein."

This ingenuous appeal having been emphasized, according to custom, by giving a belt of wampum, the sachems retired to think it over. Six days later — May 22d — the sachems of the Senecas, Cayugas and Oneidas assembled, and in behalf of their own peoples and of the Mohawks and Onondagas, spoke to the English delegates at length and with the customary Indian grandiloquence. Regarding the French intrusion at Niagara they said, in part:

"You have told us that you were Informed the French were building a house at Onjagera which As you perceive will prove prejudiciall to us & You. Its true they are Either yett building or it is finished by this time wee do owne that some Years agoe the Five Nations gave Trongsagroende Ierondoquet & onjagera and all other hunting Places westward to ye Crowne to be held for us and our posterity Least other might Incroach on us then we also partition the hunting Places between us and the french Indians but since then they are gone farr within the Limits and the french got more by setling Trongsagroende and we must Joyne our Opinion with yours that if wee suffer the french to settle at onjagera, being the only way to ward hunting, wee will be altogether shut up and Debarred, of means for our lively hood then in deed our Posterity would have Reason to Reflect on us there fore to beginn in time wee will appoint some of our men to go thither to onjagera and Desire you to send one along so that in the

ACTIVITIES OF JONCAIRE 189

name of the five Nations Jean Coeur may be acquainted with the Resolve of this Meeting and for biden to proceed any further building, but ordered to take down what's Erected."

Having thus confirmed the English in their assertions, and pledged their own friendship, the sachems through their spokesman gave the belt of wampum and passed on to other matters. At the end of the conference three chiefs were appointed to go to Niagara to expostulate with the French; and Messrs. Schuyler and Livingston deputed to go with them their Dutch interpreter, Lawrence Claessen.

This man, whose name in the old records is variously spelled Claessen, Clawsen, Clausen, Claese, Clase or Clace, acquires some importance in our record from the fact that he is the first representative of English interests known to have visited the Niagara in other than a clandestine way. With the exception of Rooseboom and MacGregorie and perhaps one or two others of their class, he is the first white man, not of France or in the French interest, known to have reached the region. Moreover he is a typical example of a class of men who at this period were indispensable alike to the English and French. He was an Indian interpreter, a go-between, the medium of communication between the English and the Indians. Though not a soldier, he was for his people in other ways the counterpart of Joncaire among the French; and although his experiences appear to have been less hazardous and romantic than were that adventurer's, yet his life, for a score of years before we find him at Niagara, had been successfully devoted to a calling which demanded exceptional knowledge and tact, and which brought no lack of arduous experiences.

As early as 1700 he was serving the English as interpreter in their councils and treaties with the Five Nations. He was apparently even then no novice at the trade, for the next year the Mohawks gave him about three acres on small islands in the Mohawk, in proof of their gratitude because of his fairness as an interpreter. He was a witness, July 19, 1701, to the deed by which the Five Nations conveyed their beaver-hunting grounds to King William. It is a strange document, containing among the attached signatures the pictographic

190   AN OLD FRONTIER OF FRANCE

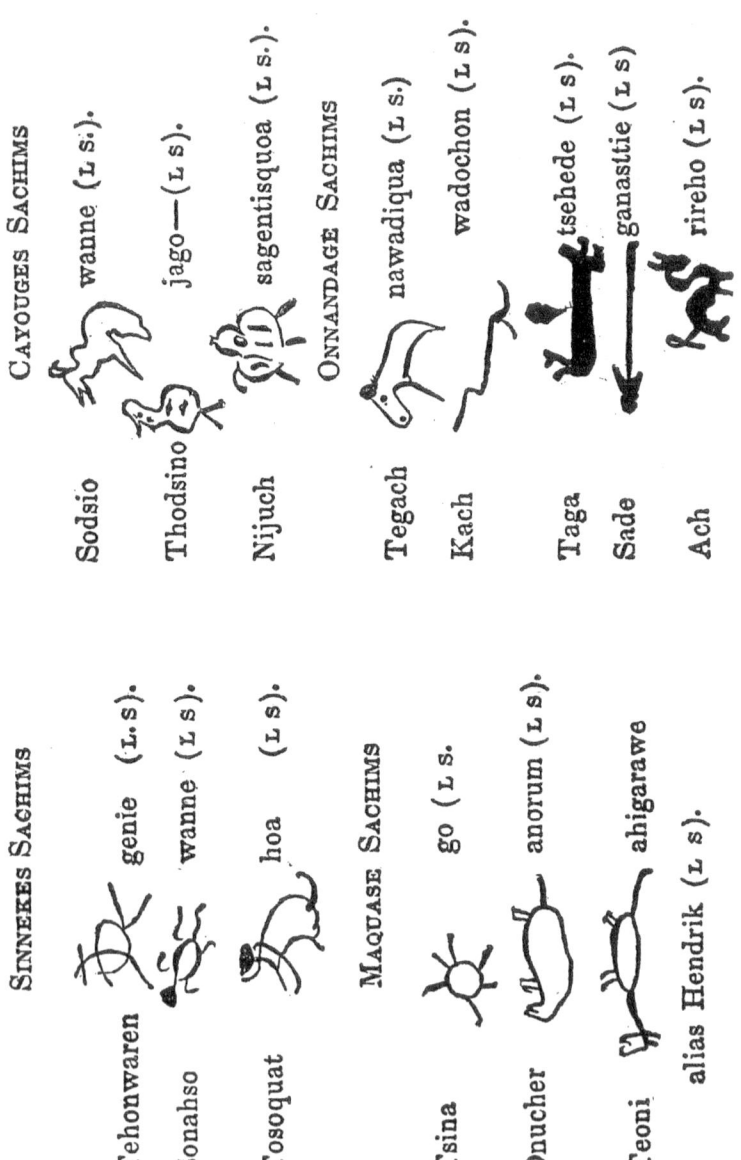

Some of the signatures attached to the Five Nations' deed of July 19, 1701   (N. Y. Col. Docs., IV.)

ACTIVITIES OF JONCAIRE 191

devices of sachems of each of the Five Nations; and quit-claiming to the English Crown all the country of the Iroquois south of Lakes Ontario and Huron, on both sides of Lake Erie and as far west as Lake Michigan, " including likewise," specifies the deed, " the great falls oakinagaro " [Niagara]. This vast area, 400 miles wide by 800 miles long, an empire in itself and now the seat of millions of people, the home of commerce and of culture, but then the wilderness which the Iroquois claimed as his hunting-ground, and because of its resources of fur the bone of contention between Europe's greatest Powers, was absolutely given, with every rivet and clamp of legal verbiage which the language of the law, redundantly profuse then as now, could command —" freely and voluntarily surrendered delivered up and forever quit-claimed . . . unto our great Lord and Master the King of England called by us Corachkoo and by the Christians William the third and to his heires and successors Kings and Queens of England for ever." And the sole compensation for this transfer was to be liberty on the part of the Five Nations to hunt as they pleased in this domain, and to be protected by the English in the exericise of that right.

From this date on for many years Claessen continued to act in a confidential capacity and as interpreter. The colonial records afford many glimpses of him. In 1710 he was sent to the Senecas' country, " to ye five Nations to watch ye motions of ye French & to perswade those Indians to give a free passage to ye farr Indians through their Countrey to come here to Albany to trade."

On this mission, at Onondaga, July 17th, he encountered Longueuil and Joncaire. He was among the Indians at Onondaga again in the spring of 1711. Two years later we find him, with Heinrich Hanson and Captain Johannes Bleecker, holding an important conference at the same great rendezvous.

Whenever the Indians went to Albany to confer — and that was often, at this period — Claessen was summoned to interpret. On such occasions, the communications from red men to Governor, or vice versa, were made through successive interpretations. Thus it was customary, on these occasions, for the sachem to make his speech, paragraphed, so to say, by the gift of wampum belts. This speech Claessen, who, perhaps alone of all the white men present, understood the Five Nations dialects, repeated, more or less accurately, in Dutch. Usually it was Robert Livingston, secretary for the Indian Commissioners, who knew both Dutch and English, but not Indian, who translated what Claessen had said, for the benefit of Governor Burnet, who understood only English.

Sometimes there was still further interposition of lingual media. Such was the case at a conference at Albany in 1722 between Governor Spotswood of Virginia and the Indians. On this occasion there was speech-making by the Delawares. Here Claessen's knowledge failed him, so another interpreter, James Latort, was called in, to convert Delaware into Mohawk or Dutch.

More tedious yet was the work of the interpreters at a conference held at Albany in 1723 between the commissioners of Indian affairs and representatives of western tribes — the "farr Indians" of the quaint old records. Claessen could not understand them, but a Seneca who had been a prisoner among them could, and interpreted to Claessen, who in turn interpreted to the commissioners; thus after three transformations the message reached a record in English. The wonder is, not that there were so many misunderstandings, but — if one may judge from the dispatch of business — that there were so few.

There were other interpreters employed by the English at this period; among them Captain Johannes Bleecker and Jan Baptist van Eps, a man who was sent on important missions among the Senecas, and may not unlikely have found his way to the Niagara; his name, in some of the reports of Indian speches, appears rather startlingly as John the Baptist. There was even a Dutch woman, Hilletje van Olinda, employed as "interpretress" at Albany in 1702. But none other in his time seems to have borne so important a part as Lawrence Claessen. In 1726 he was one of the witnesses to a trust deed by which the Onondagas, Cayugas and Senecas confirmed to Governor Burnet, as representative of King George, the quitclaim deed which the Five Nations had executed in 1701. The terms of the latter instrument are not so sweeping as in the former case. The country deeded is from the Salmon River, in Oswego County, New York, to Cleveland, Ohio, a strip sixty miles wide back into the country from the water front, and carefully specifying that it includes "all along the said lake [Erie] and all along the narrow passage from the said lake to the Falls of Oniagara Called Cahaquaraghe and all along the River of Oniagara and all along the Lake Cadarackquis," etc.[18] Small wonder, in view of these sessions in good faith, that the English vigorously contested all French establishment on the Niagara.

Two years after the signing of this deed, Claessen was invited to Oswego, to mark out a land grant for the King. "We know none so proper," said the sachems to Governor Montgomery, "as Lawrense Clausen the Interpreter, who is one of us And understands our Language." "I consent," replied his Excellency, "that Lawrence Clausen the Interpreter go up with you as you desire to mark out the Land you are to give his Majesty at Oswego, And as he [the King] is your kind father I expect you will give him a Large tract." This was on October 1, 1728. As late as November 23, 1730, we find him just returning to Albany from Onondaga and reporting to the Indian Commissioners the latest news regarding Joncaire, which will be noted presently as we trace the career of that worthy.

In all the thirty years during which we have sight of Lawrence Claessen, no service on which he was employed is recorded with greater detail than that which brought him to the Frenchmen's "*Magazin Royal*" on the banks of the Niagara in the spring of 1720. In his journal of that visit he has left a pretty vivid account of the way in which his mission sped.

After a week of travel from the Seneca town Claessen and the three Seneca chiefs, on the last day of May, arrived at the "*Magazin Royal.*" They found it a good-sized house, "Forty Foot long and thirty wide," but it was not ample enough to afford them a hospitable reception. It was occupied, according to the English account, by a French merchant

[18] From the original roll in the office of the Secretary of State, Albany.

and two other Frenchmen — one of them Douville. Joncaire does not appear to have been there when Claessen arrived. The French account says that the Englishman (Claessen) told La Corne, " whom M. Bégon appointed to trade at that place, to withdraw, and that they were going to pull down that house. La Corne answered them that he should not permit them to do so without an order from Sieur de Joncaire, who on being advised thereof by an Indian, went to the Senecas to prevent them consenting to that demolition."

The argument between Claessen and La Corne was a heated one. Claessen told the latter he had been sent, in company with the sachems, " to tell you that the Five Nations have heard that you are building a house at Octjagara [Niagara], and the said sachims having considered how prejudicial that a French Settlement on their Land must consequently prove to them and their Posterity (if not timely prevented) wherefore they have sent me and them to acquaint you with their resolution that it is much against their inclination that any buildings should be made here and that they desire you to desist further building and to leave and demolish what you have made."

The French merchant was at no loss for defense. " We had leave," he replied, " from the young fighting men of the Senecas to build a house at Niagara. My master is the Governor of Canada. He has posted me here to trade. This house will not be torn down until he orders it."

The three sachems with Claessen scouted the idea that the young fighting men of their nation had given or could give permission for the French to establish themselves on the bank of the Niagara. " We have never heard," they said, " that any of our young men had given such leave for making any building at Octjagara."

Claessen did not tarry long. Returning by way of Irondequoit, he there encountered new evidence of French enterprise in a blacksmith whom the Governor of Canada had sent among the Senecas to work for them " gratis, he having compassion on them as a father," and in three French canoes loaded with goods, bound up for Niagara. By June 7th he was back at

ACTIVITIES OF JONCAIRE

Seneca Castle, where he called together the chiefs and young warriors for a council. When they met, Joncaire appeared with them. Claessen told the assembly what had been said at Niagara; whereupon the Indians, old sachems and young warriors alike, joined in a disclaimer. The French, they said, had built the house at Niagara without so much as asking their leave, and they desired " that their brother Corlaer may do his endeavour to have ye said House demolisht that they may preserve their Lands and Hunting." They suggested that the English at Albany write to the Governor of Canada and insist that the house be destroyed.

Here Joncaire broke in. He had listened to the Senecas' disclaimer, but now he assumed a taunting tone. Interrupting Claessen he exclaimed: " You seek to have the house at Niagara torn down only because you are afraid that you — you traders at Albany — will not get any trade from this Seneca nation and from the Indians of the far West. When we keep our house and people at Niagara we can stop the Senecas and the Western Indians too from trading with you. That is the trouble with you. You are not afraid that we keep the land from the Senecas."

" The French," disputed Claessen, " have made this settlement at Niagara to encroach on the Five Nations, to hinder them in their hunting, and to debar them from the advantage they should reap by permitting a free passage of the Western Indians through the Seneca castles. What is more, you impose on these people in your trade. You sell them goods at exorbitant rates. For a blanket of strouds you demand eight beavers, for a white blanket six, and other goods in proportion; whereas they may have them at Albany for half those prices." And the assembled Indians gravely affirmed that it was so.

Lawrence Claessen went back to Albany, leaving Joncaire for the time victorious. He prevailed on the vacillating Senecas not only to spare but to protect the house by the Niagara rapids, arguing that they themselves would profit from it, and emphasizing the argument, we may be sure, by a discreet bestowal of gifts.

For the Senecas, this occurrence was but another step towards an inevitable end. For the French, it was a great achievement. The adroit Joncaire had crowned the efforts of more than forty years; for ever since La Salle had built his first house on the river the French had longed for its permanent possession. The achievement won for Joncaire new expressions of regard. In the report of the Governor and Intendant for 1720 one may read: "No one is better qualified than he [Joncaire] to begin this establishment [Niagara], which will render the trade of Fort Frontenac much more considerable and valuable than it has ever been. He is a very excellent officer; the interpreter of the Five Iroquois Nations, and has served thirty-five years in the country. As all the Governors-General have successfully employed him, they have led him to hope that the Council would be pleased to regard the services he will have it in his power to render at this conjuncture." [19]

[19] Local tradition fixes the site of *Magazin Royal* on the present Bridge Street at Lewiston, a few rods east of the tracks of the International Railway Company, and within a stone's throw of the bank of the Niagara. Here, at the south side of the road, just at the edge of the steep slope that stretches to the upper heights, one may yet trace the outlines of what appears to have been a well, and of the foundation of a building; scarcely however of Joncaire's cabin, but very plausibly of a house which later occupied the site, regarding which the late Rev. Joshua Cooke, for many years a resident of Lewiston, wrote to the present chronicler: "I have a particular interest in the spot, for in 1802, eighty-one years after Joncaire built, my grandfather built his pioneer home on the spot — the first white man's home on the Niagara, after Joncaire." The old ferry road followed the general direction of the present Bridge Street, but ran a little to the north of it, in a ravine of which a portion still remains, at its junction with the river. Within recent years the building of the electric road along the river bank, the reconstruction of the suspension bridge at this point, and the cutting and grading incident to this work, have greatly changed things thereabouts.

CHAPTER XII

NIAGARA AND THE WEST

EARLY TRAVEL BY THE NIAGARA ROUTE — FIRST WHITE WOMEN OF THE WEST — THE BRITISH COVET THE NIAGARA TRADE — THE HUGUENOT SPY OF THE NIAGARA.

THE reader who has followed our narrative thus far may long since have concluded that it deals only with strife and contention. Such in truth is its chief character to the very end; but a few glimpses of the region in its more peaceful aspect may be had. On the Niagara the French made no attempt at settlement, save in very limited fashion under the protection of Fort Niagara and at the upper and lower ends of the portage. Here were never laid the hearthstones of a peaceful community, nor is there found in the documents of the time any serious proposition for the establishment of a settlement on the Niagara which might in a few years raise its own grain, vegetables and live stock, and become measurably self-supporting, as was Detroit. The development of that settlement brought to the Niagara as travelers many who were to be prominent in the early annals of the City of the Straits. No doubt the real aristocracy of Detroit — if so typically democratic a community has an aristocracy — may be made up of descendants of the 50 soldiers and 50 Canadians who went with Cadillac in 1701; and to that list would belong the wives of Cadillac and Alphonse de Tonty who with their retinue passed up the Niagara the following year.

From about the close of the Seventeenth century the Niagara route to the West was more and more used, superseding the more difficult way of the Ottawa River. That northern route was followed, although, it is recorded, against his will, by Antoine de La Mothe-Cadillac in 1701, when with his fine company he went to found the present city of Detroit. Leaving La Chine May 5th, the banks of the Detroit were reached July 24th. The Founder of Detroit has no place in the story of the Niagara, save that, in later years, he passed this way. When in the summer of 1701 his wife resolved to join him in the West, she chose to go by the Niagara route. She was Marie-Thérèse Guyon-Dubuisson, a Quebec maiden, daughter of a well-to-do merchant. She married La Mothe-Cadillac in 1687, and is often mentioned, in the documents of the time, as Madame de La Mothe. Setting out from Quebec, September 10, 1701, with her little son, she was joined at Montreal by the wife of Alphonse de Tonty, who before marriage was Anne Picoté. With a few other women, wives of soldiers and servants, and an escort of Canadians, they came on to Fort Frontenac, where they passed the winter. As soon as the ice allowed, in the spring, they followed the south shore of Ontario and entered the Niagara. There were no horses on the great portage, and unless Madame Cadillac was carried, sedan-chair fashion, or drawn on a hand-sled, a device much used on the portages, she and her women companions must have climbed the Lewiston heights and plodded on foot the eight miles of forest path that brought them to the river's marge above the cataract. The white men of the party and the Indian boatmen carried the canoes and supplies; and re-embarking, all passed up the river into Lake Erie and vanished to the westward. There very likely was at least one night's sojourn on the river, and a visit to the Falls; but we have no record of it.

Madame Cadillac, Madame Alphonse de Tonty and their attendants were the first white women on the Niagara, the first to pass through any of the Great Lakes.

Very few women come into our story, from first to last. Rarely is it possible to trace the influence of feminine association in all the annals of this region under the French. All the more conspicuous, therefore, becomes this visit of the First Woman of the West, one who by all accounts, was lovely in person, energetic and capable to an exceptional degree. A pleasant glimpse of her is afforded by a letter from the Jesuit Father Joseph Germain,[1] who wrote to Cadillac at the time of the departure of his wife on her great journey: "Every-

[1] Germain to Cadillac, Quebec, Aug. 25, 1701.

one here admires the magnanimity of these two ladies who certainly have courage to undertake so laborious a journey to go and join their husbands, without fearing the great difficulties or the fatigue or other inconveniences which must be endured by roads so long and so rough for persons of their sex. Well! Sir: is it possible to show more sincere conjugal affection or a firmer attachment? Some one said pleasantly to them the other day that they would pass for heroines. But on some other ladies, more fastidious, saying to Madame de La Mothe, in order to dissuade her from this journey, that that would be well if they were going to a pleasant and fertile country, where they could always get good company, as in France, but they could not understand how people could make up their minds to go to an uncultivated and uninhabited place where they could not but have a very dull time of it in such great solitude, she very discreetly replied that a woman who loves her husband as she ought to do has no attraction more powerful than his society in whatever place it may be; all the rest should be indifferent to her; those are her opinions."

If the ladies of Quebec were astonished at the temerity of Mesdames Cadillac and Tonty, the Iroquois of the Niagara were much more so. "It is certain," wrote Cadillac,[2] "that nothing [ever] astonished the Iroquois so greatly as when they saw them. You could not believe how many caresses they offered them, and particularly the Iroquois who kissed their hands and wept for joy, saying that French women had never been seen coming willingly to their country." They reasoned that the proclaimed peace was indeed sincere, since women of this rank came amongst them with confidence.

Robert Reaume, Joseph Trotier *dit* Desruissaux, and Toussaint Pothier *dit* Laverdure, were engaged by written contract, September 5, 1701, to escort Mme. de La Mothe-Cadillac, Mme. Alphonse de Tonty and their children, from Montreal to Detroit, and at the same time to accompany Francis Mary Picoté de Belestre " and his equipages " on the same trip. Robert Reaume did not settle in Detroit but his sons Hyacinth and Peter did.

[2] Cadillac to Pontchartrain, Quebec, Sept. 25, 1702.

Happy dames, to make that momentous journey under the escort of servitors whose very cognomens spoke to them of rushing streams and forest greenery! Favored of Fortune was Madame Cadillac, thus to pioneer her sex into that Great West, which has now become — may we not say — more than any other part of the globe, the Woman's world!

Cadillac himself was no stranger to the Niagara region, first passing through the river, apparently, in 1702. Although he first went to Detroit by the Ottawa route, he subsequently passed back and forth through the Lower Lakes, more than once. Of one experience, in the summer of 1706, his letters hold some record. Returning from Quebec, while on Lake Ontario, four or five boats did not get on so well as the others, and finally disappeared. Cadillac sent one of his men, Mons. de Figuer, to find them and say that Cadillac would wait for them at " the fort of the Sables," that is, Irondequoit, a convenient stopping-place, but not a fortification. There he did wait, eight days. Finally he went on, with a Seneca escort of 26 men, led by a chief, Touatacoute. Reaching Detroit, Cadillac wrote to the Marquis de Vaudreuil, asking that the deserters be arrested: " I hope you will send back the wives of Chanteloup and La Roche de St. Ours; also the men St. Jean and Parisien of my company, with their wives, these two rascals having deserted or taken a holiday out of mere wantonness." He further says that these men, in coming through Lake Ontario, had put in at the bay of Goyagouin — that is, Sodus, " and visited the large village of Sonontoua to take letters to the Jesuit who resides there, who apparently charged them to take the answers to Montreal." The Iroquois had promised Cadillac that they would escort the missing Frenchmen " up to the portage at Niagara "; St. Jean did indeed present himself at Fort Sables, while the others apparently went down the river. Cadillac thought they deserved to pass the winter in prison, but wanted them sent back to Detroit in the spring.[3]

[3] These and other details are given in a letter of Cadillac to de Vaudreuil, Aug. 27, 1706; *see also,* account of a "talk" between de Vaudreuil and the Senecas, Sept. 4, 1706.

Among the things which Cadillac thought essential to the welfare of Detroit was the destruction of Fort Frontenac, a new fort to be built "25 leagues lower down at a place called La Palette" [*sic:* Galette], near present Ogdensburg; and, to be rid of the difficulties of the Niagara portage. On this point a document of 1708, summarizing certain letters of Cadillac, says: "It would be necessary to make a junction between Lake Erie and Lake Ontario. He says that he knows, for that [purpose], a way and a canal which has remained unknown to everyone else until now." He may have had the Grand River and western end of Lake Ontario in mind; if not, one is at a loss to know what he did mean. Two years later the Sieur d'Aigremont, reporting on conditions at Lake posts, wrote:

When I passed the portage at Niagara it did not appear to me that any communication between Lake Ontario or Lake Erie could be made that could avoid this portage, and if M. de la Mothe knows a means of doing so, I think he is the only man in the country who does. But, My Lord, even if it were true that a communication with Lake Ontario or Lake Erie could be made it could only be done with very great expense and it would not follow from that, that Detroit would be able to obtain from Montreal any help it might need in case of war with the Iroquois, for such help could not even be given to Fort Frontenac, which has to be passed through on the way to Detroit.[4]

We know from his own letters that the Jesuit missionary François Vaillant[5] was on the Niagara in 1701. Writing to Cadillac from Fort Frontenac, September 23, 1701, the priest speaks of meeting "Mme. de la Mothe," the wife of Cadillac, and adds: "On Lake Erie I met Quarante Sols, the Huron. . . . As regards the Iroquois whom we met on the way, we did not find them much opposed to your settlement; some even testified to me their joy that when going hunting on Lake Erie, they will find at Detroit [in exchange] for the skins of the

[4] D'Aigremont to Pontchartrain, Oct. 18, 1710.
[5] The name often occurs as Vallant or even Valliant; but the priest's own signature is as above; more fully, François Vaillant de Gueslis. He went to Canada in 1670; died at Moulins, Sept. 24, 1718.

roebuck, stag and hind, all they want." As fear of the Iroquois had been one reason for the tardy use of the Niagara route, Father Vaillant's report was reassuring. The Huron chief Quarante Sols — in plain English, Forty Sous — seems to have been constantly passing up and down the Lakes, and beyond question was a familiar and influential figure in the Niagara region. Father Marest, at Mackinac, October 8, 1701, wrote that Father Vaillant " was much mortified that he was not able to pass this way, either going to Detroit or returning," evidence that the priest returned to the western mission by the way of Niagara and Lake Erie. Many another Jesuit of those early years undoubtedly knew our region of whose passing or temporary sojourn on the Niagara no record is preserved. Among them was Father Claude Aveneau, who appears to have passed through Lake Erie to his Miami mission on the St. Joseph, where he served from about 1702 to about 1708. One might conjecture that Point Abino on the north shore of Lake Erie near the Niagara, formerly spelled " Abeneau " (and several other ways), derives its name from some association with this missionary; but proof is lacking.

In the 58 years that followed the establishment of Detroit, prior to the English conquest, there was a constant migration thither. After the first few years, practically all of it was by the Niagara route. Under the protection of the midsummer Convoy, at first one or two families ventured the hazards of wilderness and of wave, to join husband, father or sweetheart in the West. As the Niagara portage was made safer, and travel facilities improved, this class of travel greatly increased. From the precious records of Ste. Anne's church, Detroit, running back unbroken to that beginning year of 1701, and from numerous public or family documents, the patient antiquarian might compile a long list of the families who thus passed the Niagara portage in the first half of the Eighteenth century. It was the first well-defined migration into the Middle West, and it was for the most part of fine quality. Much has been said of the lawless and evil character of forest rangers, unscrupulous traders and loose-living boatmen and soldiers, in this region; one may not conclude that such was the character of all. Many who figure here were of the other social extreme. Most of the officers of the military, and many a civilian, called by duty to these lakes, bore names long honored among the *noblesse* of France. Many a younger son of a noble family turned to service in America, tempted by the certainty of adventure or the chance of preferment and distinction, if not by the substantial offers of land-grants and bounties with which Louis XIV lured them on. Thus it came about that even as the feudal system was dying out in France it was revived and continued, in some of its features, in Canada, by the granting to prominent colonists or soldiers of achievement, of tracts of land, called seigneuries. Most of these, on the St. Lawrence and its tributaries, were of a half league water front, with a depth of two or three leagues. To these " seigneuries " were given the ancestral or place names with which the family had been identified in France. As the seigneuries were divided for sons and sons' sons, so seigneurial designations multiplied, so that brothers figure in our history by different appellations, and sons lose their patronymic in common usage. The royal grant to Cadillac was not called a seigneury, nor do we find any on the Lakes, save La Salle's at Kingston and one to the Chevalier Le Gardeur de Repentigny, at Sault Ste. Marie. No grant, however called, was made on the Niagara; but Cadillac in 1703 asked that one be made to him on the north shore of Lake Erie:

> The Grand river, thus called in Lake Erie, near to the end of this Lake . . . is supplied on its banks and in the interior with large numbers of mulberry trees, the ground also is perfectly suited to them. If you will have the goodness to grant me six leagues frontage on both sides and as much in depth, with the title of Marquis, and with higher, middle and lower jurisdiction, with hunting, fishing and trading rights, I will establish a silk industry by sending for suitable people from France for that purpose who would bring the necessary number of silk worms. If you grant me this favor, I will take steps to bring them over by the first ships so that they may arrive here before winter.[6]

[6] Cadillac to Pontchartrain, Aug. 31, 1703.

Note has been made of the journey of Mesdames La Mothe-Cadillac and Tonty by the Niagara route in 1702. In the years following, wives, children, and other relatives of officers, soldiers and tradesmen at Detroit, similarly passed, usually with the Convoys. Sometimes the relatives went with the officers, a great family party; and if there were hardship and danger, we may be sure there were gayety and good cheer as well. So went, in 1705 or '06, the family of Peter Maillet and his stepson John Francis Peltier; in 1706, Peter Robert, moving his family west two years later; in 1707, Stephen Campeau; Michel and Jacques Campeau, about 1710; and in other early years, Cuillerier de Beaubien, Trotier des Ruisseaux, Chesne St. Onge, Godefroy de Roquetiade, Godefroy de Marboeuf, Charles and Pierre Barthe, Godé de Marentette — the list might be greatly extended.

In 1706, after Cadillac had been given exclusive control of the settlement on the Detroit, there was a notably large migration thither from the old St. Lawrence towns. One list [7] enumerates 48 persons who with their possessions went in this summer to share the fortunes of the new colony. Beyond question, most of them journeyed by the Niagara route. In May, 1706, two brothers, Jean and Paul Lescuyer, brought 10 head of cattle and three horses, the first domestic animals known to have been taken west of Lake Ontario.

The greatest travel to the westward, in any one year during the period of French control in our region, was in 1749. A record of 1750 mentions the passing of 12 families, composed of 57 persons, up the Niagara, bound for Detroit.

Most, perhaps all of the commanders at Fort Pontchartrain (or Detroit) after Cadillac, and at many other western posts, passed up and down the Niagara and through our lakes, some of them many times. Some of these belong to the story of the Niagara as well as the Detroit, and will be duly noted. When Picoté de Belestre went out to his post in 1712, his wife Catherine went with him. She was of the family Trotier de Beaubien, and a former husband was Jean Cuillerier. These

[7] Compiled by C. M. Burton; in Mich. Hist. Colls. XXXIII, 271.

are ancestors of a numerous line, prominent to this day in Detroit and vicinity.

Notes of this sort might be greatly multiplied; but these may serve to remind the reader that all was not strife on the Niagara in those distant days; may help somewhat to fill out the picture with reminders of the ever-swelling stream of passers-by, many of whom were of noble lineage, many more of whom were to found large and worthy families in the heart of America. It was usually the son, sometimes the grandson of the original settler from France, who made this second migration. Most of those who went to the Detroit and elsewhere in the West, in the early years of the Eighteenth century, were born on the lower St. Lawrence — Quebec, Three Rivers, Montreal; but their parents as a rule were born in Normandy or neighboring provinces.

That it was the day of small things, in trade as in war, may be illustrated by a statement of provisions, munitions and merchandise sent to the Lake Ontario posts — Frontenac, Niagara, head of the lake, and Bay of Quinté — for the year 1722–23. The total Government outlay for the three sorts of supplies was 29,800 livres, 17 sous, 6 deniers. Furs from these points, not including Quinté, in 1722, netted 18,178 livres; in 1723, 22,732 livres. This of course was by exchange. In the same season, wages of employees at Frontenac came to 900 livres; the storekeeper at Niagara received 400 livres per annum and the gunsmith the same. The pay of six soldiers was 180 livres each. In the two years named, there was charged to transportation on Lake Ontario, 1050 livres. The total expense of administering these posts, 1722–23, was 35,-210li, 17s, 6d; total receipts from sale of peltries 40,911li, 8s, 6d — a profit of 570li, 11s — or a little over $1000 a year! This was the trade for which Joncaire labored and lived with the Iroquois, for which the Niagara was occupied, for which two great Powers contended!

The day of small things, it indeed was; but of great things potentially. Far greater figures the fur trade was presently to yield, although the Eighteenth century did not think in millions, as the Twentieth is compelled to. A handful of soldiers could seize half a continent; another handful could dispossess them. Nothing is clearer, in our study, than that France did much, with a small force. The significance of events and achievements was independent of numbers.

Projects for lake navigation, of which, for some years after the disastrous ending of La Salle's venture, nothing is heard, naturally enough were revived in connection with the establishment of Detroit An unsigned and undated document, probably by Cadillac, sets forth that if a settlement were made on the Detroit, " it has been determined to build boats at Katarakoui to convey the necessary articles as far as Niagara where a fort will be constructed in order to keep carters there who will carry out the portage of them; they will be received by other boats which will convey them here," that is, to Detroit. Another document, on the necessity of a post on the Detroit, is endorsed: " These plans are to have barges at Fort Frontenac for navigating Lake Ontario, and at the fort that would be established for navigating the lakes above the Fall of Niagara." But control of the Niagara portage was essential, and that was slow in coming. Detroit had existed 20 years before Joncaire gained a permanent lodging on the Niagara, and was a quarter century old before the building of Fort Niagara offered some encouragement to Detroit and other western posts that shipping facilities by way of Lake Erie might be improved. Although sundry proposals are found, for the construction of sail vessels above the Falls, nothing of the sort was ever accomplished by the French, who down to the Conquest used nothing larger on Lake Erie than canoes and bateaux, some of them, it is true, large for such craft, and fitted with sails. Detroit seems to have made no effort to build even the smallest of schooners. The *Griffon* was not only the first deep-water bottom sailed by the French on Lake Erie, but it was the last.

The British plans for getting a foothold on Lake Erie and the Niagara at this time are revealed in various documents. A " Representation of the Lords Commissioners for Trade and Plantations to the King upon the State of His Majesties

Colonies and Plantations on the Continent of North America," dated September 8, 1721, sets forth at length that it would be of great advantage to build a fort in the country of the Seneca Indians, near the Lake Ontario, " which, perhaps, might be done with their consent by the means of presents, and it should the rather be attempted without loss of time, to prevent the french from succeeding in the same design, which they are now actually endeavouring at." We have already alluded to other forms in which this design was shown. It reappears in various ways, in numerous documents and publications of the time.

There ensued between the Marquis de Vaudreuil in behalf of Canada, and Governor Burnet, an exceedingly spirited correspondence; one of those epistolary dialogues — duels, rather — which by their exhibitions of human nature do so enliven the record of the long strife for supremacy in America. Joncaire had left Montreal in September, 1720, for the house by the Niagara rapids. He carried with him a generous stock of articles of trade, powder, lead and brandy, for he had heard, among the Senecas the preceding autumn, that the English were coming to carry on trade at Niagara. He was to stay on the Niagara and among the Senecas until the following June and had orders to pillage the English, if they appeared. Governor Burnet, down in New York, was quickly apprised of it, and made known his mind to Vaudreuil. He began with compliments worthy of a French courtier. He had come to his post in September last, he wrote, with an inclination to salute his neighbor to the North by a cordial notification of his arrival. " I heard such a high eulogium of your family and of your own excellent qualities that I flattered myself with a most agreeable neighborhood, and was impatient to open a correspondence in which all the profit would be on my side. But I had not passed two weeks in the province when our own Indians of the Five Nations came to advise me, that the French were building a post in their country at Niagara; that Sieur de Joncaire was strongly urging them to abandon the English interest altogether and join him, promising them that the Governor of Canada would furnish better land near Chambly, to those who would remove thither; and would uphold the rest against the new Governor of New York, who was coming to exterminate them; . . . that an effort was making to persuade them to close the passage through their country, to the English, in case the latter should disturb the post at Niagara, and that M. de Longueuil had gone thither for that purpose, and to complete the seduction of the Indians from their ancient dependence on Great Britain." He explains why he has not waited for instructions from the Court before writing in the matter, and continues: " You will perceive, by the Treaty of Utrecht, that all the Indians are to be at liberty to go to trade with one party and the other; and if advantage be taken of the post at Niagara to shut up the road to Albany to the Far Indians, it is a violation of the Treaty which ought justly to alarm us, especially as that post is on territory belonging to our Indians, where we were better entitled to build than the French, should we deem it worth the trouble." He charges Vaudreuil with unseemly haste in seizing " disputed posts "; renews his expressions of regret, and adroitly adds that he believes that " most of these disorders are due to this Joncaire, who has long since deserved hanging for the infamous murder of Hontour [Montour] which he committed. I leave you to judge whether a man of such a character deserves to be employed in affairs so delicate."

Canada's Governor replied, *seriatim,* to all the counts which Burnet undertook to score against him. Burnet, he said, was " the first English Governor-General who has questioned the right of the French, from time immemorial, to the post of Niagara, to which the English have, up to the present time, laid no claim." He declared that the French right there had continued since La Salle's first occupancy; that Fort Denonville was given up in 1688 because of sickness, " without this post, however, having been abandoned by the French "; a claim which, to say the least, shows that Vaudreuil possessed qualifications that would have made him an adept in certain occupations of the law. He denied that there had been any dispute between the French and Indians as to the erection of Joncaire's trading-house, denied that there was any infraction of the treaty of peace, or that French occupancy of the Niagara interfered in the least with the Western Indians who could still carry their trade to the English if they saw fit. As to Joncaire, Governor Burnet was assured that he had been misinformed as to that useful man's character and qualities, " as he possesses none but what are very good and very meritorious, and has always since he has been in this country most faithfully served the King. It was by my orders that he killed the Frenchman named Montour, who would have been hanged had it been possible to take him alive and to bring him to this colony." The letter concludes with formal expressions of esteem, and the rather superfluous hope that the explanations would be satisfactory.

He himself had the satisfaction, the next year, of having his conduct approved by the King. "His Majesty has approved of the measures M. de Vaudreuil adopted to prevent the execution of the plan formed by the English of Orange to destroy the establishment at Niagara; and of the steps he took to dissuade the Iroquois from favoring them in that enterprise, and thereby to hinder the English undertaking anything against that post or against those of the Upper Country. His Majesty recommends him to endeavor to live on good terms with the English, observing, nevertheless, to maintain always His Majesty's interests."

A document of 1720,[8] on the need of a trading-post at Niagara, makes the interesting statement that the English had proposed to an Iroquois chief, residing at Niagara, to send him horses, if he would turn the trade to them, and to divide profits with him. It accuses the English of sending 20 hogsheads of rum annually to the Senecas, besides what they forwarded through the Senecas to tribes west of the Niagara. A few weeks later,[9] the French had word that the English were coming with 200 men to demolish Joncaire's trading-post, and that four of the Iroquois nations had joined with them to do this. Vaudreuil wrote to Peter Schuyler, who commanded at

[8] "*Mémoire sur la necessité de faire un Etablissement au bas du Portage de Niagara à deux lieues du Lac Ontario pour y faire la traitte avec les Sauvages,*" etc. It bears date Oct. 26, 1720.

[9] "*Conseil de Marine,*" Jan. 1, 1721.

Albany in the absence of the Governor, asking as to the truth of this report, and making the usual defense of French claims to the Niagara. Belief in this alliance against them was evidently general and genuine among the French, for in April we find Joncaire himself informing the Baron de Longueuil that the Oneidas, Onondagas, Cayugas and Mohawks had agreed to join the English in an assault on the house by the Niagara rapids, but that the Senecas had refused to join them. Vaudreuil promptly issued orders (April 18, 1721) for an expedition to proceed to Niagara, to hold a conference with the Indians there, to show them that it was to their interest to maintain the house " for which they have asked, and which they helped to build," and not permit the English to make any establishment on the river. This conference ended, he was to proceed to the Onondagas, taking Joncaire with him.[10]

A spectator, on May 19, 1721, looking lakeward from the high bank where now old Fort Niagara keeps impotent guard, would have seen, swiftly skirting the shore from the eastward, a flotilla of King's boats and bark canoes, some crowded with soldiers, others laden deep with merchandise. Not in many a year had so imposing a company come to the Niagara. The lower reaches of the river are quickly accomplished, and as the voyagers make landing below *Magazin Royal*, they receive hearty welcome from Chabert Joncaire, surrounded by delighted and greedy men, women and children from the Seneca and Mississaga lodges on the river bank. The first greeting, a deferential one, is for Charles Le Moyne, Baron de Longueuil, lieutenant governor of Montreal. With him are the Marquis de Cavagnal, son of the Governor-General of Canada, Captain de Senneville, M. de Laubinois, commissary of ordnance, Ensign de La Chauvignerie the interpreter, de Noyan, commandant at Frontenac, and John Durant, state chaplain at that post. Each of the three King's boats brought six soldiers, and there were valets and cooks, so that Longueuil's party numbered twenty-eight or more. Besides these, two bark canoes had each borne eight men and a load of merchandise, one destined for the storehouse at Niagara, the other for trade

[10] *Corr. Gén.*

among the Miamis at the upper end of Lake Erie. Still another canoe brought, with De Noyan and the chaplain, four soldiers and an Indian.

For Longueuil, it was, as above indicated, a diplomatic visit of grave import. He and La Chauvignerie were also under orders from the Court to join Joncaire at Niagara and go with him among the Senecas to distribute presents and thank them for the good will they had shown the French in permitting the construction of *Magazin Royal*. For the Marquis de la Cavagnal and Captain de Senneville, it was largely a pleasure trip: they "had undertaken that voyage only out of curiosity of seeing the fall of the water at Niagara," says Chaplain Durant, thus indicating probably the first sight-seeing tourists, as distinguished from all other travelers on the Niagara.

It was not in the nature of things, however, that young men of the spirit and enterprise of Cavagnal and Longueuil should rest content with sentimental gazing. They had, in fact, the serious purpose, in compliance with an order laid upon them by the Governor himself, "to survey Niagara and take the exact height of the cataract." This apparently had never been done before. It is plain, from their wild guesses and exaggerations, that neither Hennepin nor La Hontan attempted it, nor do they report an attempt by any one connected with the expeditions of La Salle or Denonville.

It is matter of regret that no official report of this first measurement of the falls is known. We learn of it from a verbal interview which took place in Albany five months later. On October 10th of this year the Hon. Paul Dudley of that town gleaned some facts from one Borassaw — so the English report spells his name. This man (a French Canadian, probably a boatman or possibly a trader), said he had been at Niagara seven times, and was there the last May, when the height of the falls was taken by Longue Isle, St. Ville and Laubineau — in which perverse spelling of the Hon. Paul Dudley we may recognize Longueuil, Captain de Senneville and Laubinois. They used, the Frenchman said, a large cod-line and a stone of half a hundred weight, and they found the perpendicular height " no more than twenty-six Fathom; his

Words were *vingt et six Bras.*" This height, 156 feet, indicates that the measurement was made at the eastern edge of the American Fall, which spot, known in our day as Prospect Point, was undoubtedly the natural and most frequented place of observation, from days immemorial. The height which de Cavagnal and his companions reported in 1721, was within a few feet of the height as known today.

Mons. " Borassaw " told still further of Niagara wonders. He thought that if the total descent of the river, including the lower rapids, were taken into account, the earlier reports of the height of the fall might not be far out of the way. He mentioned the terrible whirlpools, and the noise, which Mr. Dudley decided was not so terrible as Father Hennepin had reported, since one could converse easily close by; and dwelt especially upon " *la brume,*" the mist or shower which the falls make: " So extraordinary, as to be seen at five Leagues distance, and rises as high as the common Clouds. In this Brume or Cloud, when the Sun shines, you have always a glorious Rainbow." The Canadian's graphic account of Niagara phenomena served a good purpose in toning down the earlier exaggerations; but, reported Mr. Dudley, " He confirms Father Hennepin's and Mr. Kellug's Account of the large Trouts of those Lakes, and solemnly affirmed there was one taken lately, that weighed eighty-six pounds." [11]

Two or three days [12] after the arrival of Longueuil and his retinue, there came two other canoes; one laden with merchandise bound for Detroit; in the other were four traders and the famous Jesuit, Father Charlevoix.

It was "two o'clock in the afternoon" of May 22d that Charlevoix reached the mouth of the Niagara. He had passed the neglected waste, the site of Denonville's and La Salle's

[11] *See* " An Account of the Falls of the River Niagara, taken at Albany, Oct. 10, 1721, from Monsieur Borassaw, a French native of Canada. By the Hon. Paul Dudley, Esq., F. R. S.," in *Philosophical Transactions,* Royal Soc., London, 1722. Dudley's record of Borassaw is also given in Vol. III, " The Gallery of Nature and Art " (6 vols.), 2d ed., London, 1818. *See also* Vol. XIII of La Roche's " *Mémoires litér. de la Grande Bretagne,*" La Haye, 1721–26.

[12] Durant says May 21st; Charlevoix says he arrived at Niagara on the afternoon of May 22d.—" *Journal Historique,*" Letter XIV.

earlier establishments, not stopping until he reached Joncaire's cabin —" to which," he wrote a few days later, " they have beforehand given the name of fort: for it is pretended that in time this will be changed into a great fortress." There were here now, all told, some fifty Frenchmen, a most distinguished company to be found, this May evening of the year 1721, harbored together in a rough house under the Niagara escarpment at the edge of the rapids. Here these comrades in arms and adventure feasted together on fresh fish which Seneca and Mississaga boys brought them from the river, with roast venison or other provision from the forest, well prepared by Longueuil's own cooks; not forgetting the comfort of French liquors or other luxuries which the traveler of quality was sure to carry with him into the wilderness. They gave the priest a welcome at the board, and he, being no ascetic, was glad to join them. It is a pleasure to conjure up the jovial gathering — a rare occasion in a history which usually presents to the student a dismal and distressed aspect, often deepening into tragedy.

The French officers were extremely well satisfied with what they found on the Niagara. A council was held at which the Senecas made their usual facile promises and Joncaire spoke " with all the good sense of a Frenchman, whereof he enjoys a large share, and with the sublimest eloquence of an Iroquoise."

The officers were to set off on their mission the next day. That evening a Mississaga Indian invited them to a " festival," as Charlevoix calls it; and although by this time he was not without some acquaintance with Indian ways, the priest found it " singular enough." As this is the first " festival " on the banks of the Niagara which has been reported for us, the reader may find pleasure in joining the party, with the Jesuit historian for mentor:

" It was quite dark when it began, and on entering the cabin of this Indian, we found a fire lighted, near which sat a man beating on a kind of drum; another was constantly shaking his *chichicoué*, and singing at the same time. This lasted two hours and tired us very much as they were always repeating the same thing over again, or rather uttering half articulated sounds, and that without the least variation. We entreated our host not carry this prelude any further, who with a good deal of difficulty showed us this mark of complaisance.

"Next, five or six women made their appearance, drawing up in a line, in very close order, their arms hanging down, and dancing and singing at the same time, that is to say, they moved some paces forwards, and then as many backwards, without breaking the rank. When they had continued this exercise about a quarter of an hour, the fire, which was all that gave light in the cabin, was put out, and then nothing was to be perceived but an Indian dancing with a lighted coal in his mouth. The concert of the drum and *chichicoué* still continued, the women repeating their dances and singing from time to time; the Indian danced all the while, but as he could only be distinguished by the light of the coal in his mouth he appeared like a goblin, and was horrible to see. This medley of dancing, and singing, and instruments, and that fire which never went out, had a very wild and whimsical appearance, and diverted us for half an hour; after which we went out of the cabin, though the entertainment lasted till morning." The discreet father naïvely adds to his fair correspondent: "This, madam, is all I saw of the fire-dance, and I have not been able to learn what passed the remainder of the night." He speculates at length on how the chief performer could have held a live coal in his mouth; the Indians, he is told, know a plant which renders the part that has been rubbed with it insensible to fire, "but whereof they would never communicate the discovery to the Europeans." With the known properties of cocaine and some other drugs in mind, this explanation would seem in a degree plausible; against the theory is the fact that the pharmacopæa has pretty thoroughly tested all the plants which the Indian of these latitudes could have known. There was probably a good deal of charlatanry about the exhibition which so puzzled the good priest.

To Charlevoix, the environs of *Magazin Royal* were far from pleasing. Most of the modern visitors who resort to the vicinity in thousands every summer, find the prospect un-

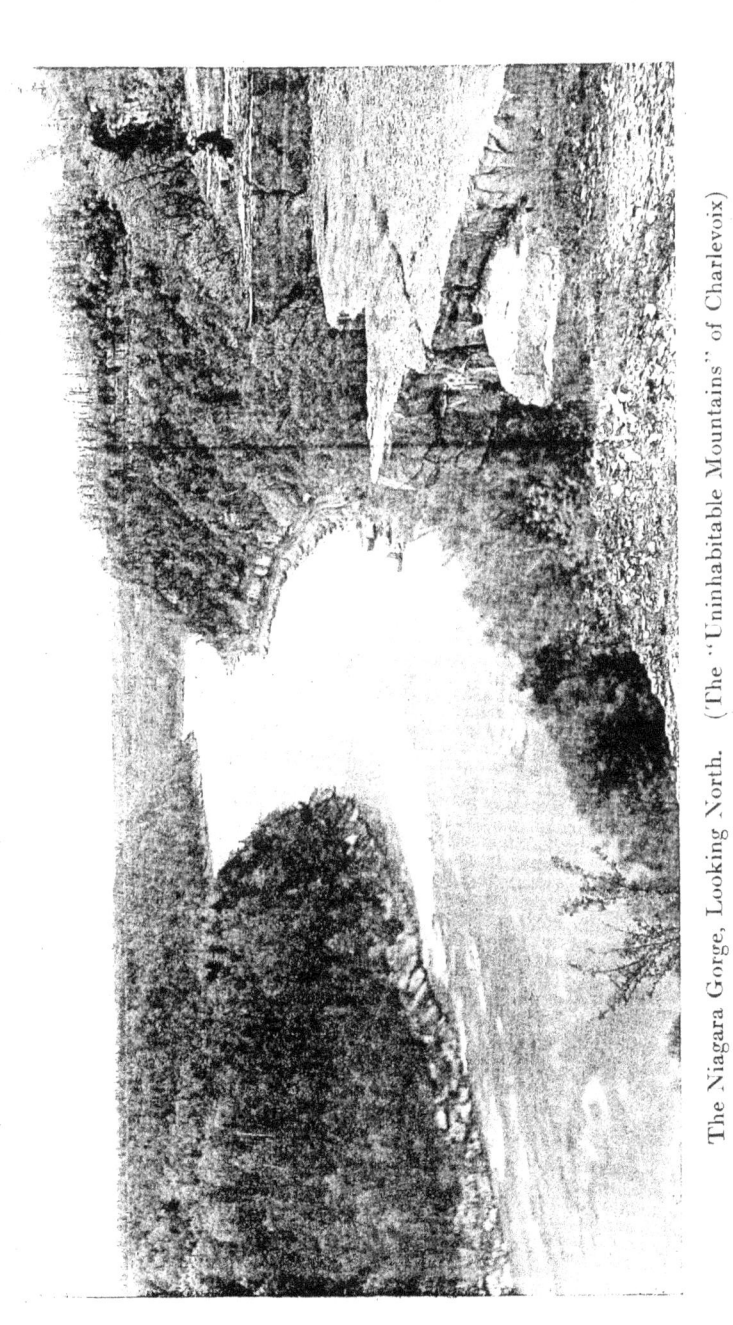

The Niagara Gorge, Looking North. (The "Uninhabitable Mountains" of Charlevoix)

commonly attractive. Here the wild gorge of the Niagara ends, and between alluvial banks the beautiful river, as if wearied with its struggles above, continues at a slower pace toward the blue Ontario. At landings, on the Lewiston or Queenston sides, are steamers with flags a-flutter waiting for the throngs of tourists. Trolley-cars shuttle back and forth, their road-beds scarring and changing the old slopes. On the Canadian side, cedars and other wild growth still soften the outlines of the heights, crowned with a noble Corinthian shaft in memory of the heroic Brock. A bridge, the second that has swung across the river at the mouth of the gorge, and, on the American side, a steam railroad, have still further contributed to the obliteration of natural outlines. But nothing short of a cataclysm can destroy the beauty of the place. The heights are green and pleasant, easily reached by winding roads, crowned with grain-fields and orchards. Below are the quiet, picturesque villages of Lewiston and Queenston, and all the low country is a garden.

Not so did it appear to Charlevoix, who protested that "nothing but zeal for the public good could possibly induce an officer to remain in such a country as this, than which a wilder and more frightful is not to be seen. On the one side you see just under your feet, and as it were at the bottom of an abyss, a great river, but which in this place is like a torrent by its rapidity, by the whirlpools formed by a thousand rocks, through which it with difficulty finds a passage, and by the foam with which it is always covered. On the other, the view is confined by three mountains placed one over the other, and whereof the last hides itself in the clouds. This would have been a very proper scene for the poets to make the Titans attempt to scale the heavens. In a word, on whatever side you turn your eyes, you discover nothing which does not inspire a secret horror." This shows a favorite form of the exaggeration to which the priest was addicted; he has elsewhere described mere oak trees as reaching " to the clouds."

After the departure of the officers, he made the long portage and continued his journey. Once up the heights, he acknowledged a change of sentiment. " Beyond those uncultivated and uninhabitable mountains, you enjoy the sight of a rich country, magnificent forests, beautiful and fruitful hills; you breathe the purest air, under the mildest and most temperate climate imaginable." His passage up the Niagara, it will be remembered, was at the end of May. He visited the falls, of which he wrote on the spot a long description, sending it back to Montreal by some *voyageurs* whom he met at the entrance to Lake Erie; whence, on May 27th, he continued his long canoe voyage to the westward. The goods for trade and for the post at Detroit were laboriously packed over the portage. Boatmen and Indians, sweating and straining, bore inverted on their shoulders the long bark canoes, up the steep heights and along the forest path to quiet water above the cataract.

Setting out in the other direction, our tourist officers, with De Noyan, Laubinois and Durant, departed on the 22d, and on reaching the lake turned their prows westward, to make their way to Fort Frontenac along the north shore of the lake.

Nearly a month later Chaplain Durant, making his way to Albany with a delegation of Indians, met Joncaire at the mouth of the Oswego River. "I asked him," the chaplain writes, "what he had done with these savages upon the subject of the voyage he had undertaken to them. He answered me, 'I have beat the Bush and Mr. de Longueuil will take the birds. Our voyage will do him honor at the Court of France,' and explained himself no further." A little advanced on his way, above the Oswego falls Durant met Longueuil and La Chauvignerie. "Have you succeeded," he asked, "in engaging the Five Nations to defend the Post of Niagara?" They answered that the chiefs of the Senecas, Cayugas, Oneidas and Onondagas had given them "good words," promising to tell him further at Montreal, and hurried on towards Lake Ontario.

The French officers were little inclined to make a confidant of the priest, and with good reason, for he was then, as he had been at Niagara, virtually a spy in the English interest. John Durant was a Recollect, a Frenchman who claimed to be of Huguenot family, which, perhaps, accounts for his resolve to change both his country and his religion. Apparently his Niagara visit suggested the way to him. He had been stationed at Fort Frontenac, and returned thither from Niagara; but on June 13th he deserted that post and his charge, and with an Indian escort set out for Albany, where he stated his case to Governor Burnet, and gave him a journal of what he had seen and heard at Niagara. It is from that journal that a portion of the foregoing narrative is drawn.[13] Burnet made Durant the bearer of his own report to the Lords of Trade in London, together with a letter commending the author for favor and suggesting reward for his services. In due time the thanks of the Lords of Trade were sent back to Governor Burnet, with the assurance that " we have done what we could for his [Durant's] service, tho' not with so much success as we cou'd wish ";[14] and we hear no more of Chaplain Durant, the Huguenot Spy of the Niagara.

William Burnet was appointed Governor of the Colonies of New York and New Jersey, April 19, 1720. He was no sooner established in his new office than he began a zealous campaign against the advances of the French. In his first communication to the Lords of Trade, September 24, 1720, just one week after his arrival in New York, he stated that " there may be effectual measures taken for fortifying & securing the Frontier against the French, who are more industrious than ever in seducing our Indians to their Interests & have built trading Houses in their country." In November, reporting the result of the Legislative Assembly of 1720, he declared it his intention to build a new fort at Niagara and a small one at Onondaga. He complained that the French " tryed to seduce the Sinnekees " by sending priests among them, grotesquely declaring this to be a breach of the treaty which required the French " not to molest the Five Nations "! " This," he added, " besides their continuing to fortify at Niagara shews how much they take advantage of the unsettled state of the limits between the Crowns."[15]

[13] *See* Durant's Memorial, etc., N. Y. Col. Docs., V, 588–591.
[14] Lords of Trade to Burnet, Whitehall, June 6, 1722.
[15] Burnet to the Lords of Trade, June 18, 1721.

"When I get the King's presents to the Indians, which I hope will be dispatched," he suggestively wrote, "I propose to go into the Indian country through the five nations and give them these presents at their own homes when I come among the Sinnekees I will propose to them my design to build a Fort at Niagara & leave a whole company of souldiers to guard it and be a defence to the Indians against the French and to make this succeed the better I intend to give land to the officers and souldiers & to the Palatines and all others that will go there by this means in a year or two the country which is very fruitful will maintain itself and be the finest Settlement in the Province because it is seated in the Pass where all the Indians in our dependance go over to hunt and trade with the Farr Indians it will likewise make it practicable to have another settlement above the Fall of Niagara where vessels may be built to trade into all the Great Lakes of North America with all the Indians bordering on them, with whom we may have an immense Trade never yet attempted by us and now carried on by the French with goods brought from this Province."

The project does credit to the Governor's zeal and enthusiasm, but it came to naught, so far as Niagara was concerned. In a representation to the King the following year, the advantage is urged of building a fort "in the country of the Seneca Indians, near the Lake Ontario, which, perhaps, might be done with their consent by the means of presents, and it should the rather be attempted without the loss of time, to prevent the French from succeeding in the same design, which they are now actually endeavoring at"; [16] and the King's attention was especially directed to Burnet's Niagara scheme, but no royal encouragement was given. The Governor himself, in his report to the Lords of Trade for 1721, reviews at length the protest he had made to the Canadian Governor because of the French establishment at Niagara, but says nothing more of his own proposition for that river. He had sent instead a small company to carry on trade at Irondequoit Bay. The Palatines, whom he had considered as available Niagara colonists, had objected to such an exile in a distant and prob-

[16] "State of the British Plantations in America," 1721.

ably hostile wilderness, and had been given their now historic lands on the Mohawk.

One phase of the establishment at Irondequoit must be noted in tracing the history of the Niagara. The company of seven young Dutchmen who spent the winter of 1721–22 at Irondequoit, were under the command of Captain Peter Schuyler, Jr. To him Governor Burnet gave explicit instructions for the regulation of trade and the control of his party. In a postscript to his letter of instructions he wrote:

"Whereas it is thought of great use to the British Interest to have a Settlem^t upon the nearest part of the lake Erée near the falls of Iagara you are to Endeavour to purchase in his Majesty's name of the Sinnekes or other native propriators all such Lands above the falls of Iagara fifty miles to the southward of the said falls which they can dispose of."

If young Schuyler made any efforts to make this purchase, the record of it is not known. When he returned with his band to Albany in September, 1722, Joncaire still continued commandant at *Magazin Royal*, and trade-master of the Niagara region.

In June, 1722, the Lords of Trade, replying to Burnet's proposition of a year and a half before, hoped that the fort which he would build on the Niagara would effectually check the efforts of the French at that point, but advised him to "take the consent of the Indian Proprietors" before he built. A year later — June 25, 1723 — Burnet wrote that if he could get the Two-per-cent. Act confirmed, he should be "very ernest to build a Fort in the Indian Country among the Sinnekees," but subsequent events showed that he no longer thought Niagara the place for his establishment. The statement of a contemporary English historian, that a number of young men were at this time sent into Western New York "as far as the Pass between the Great Lakes at the Falls of Iagara to learn the language of these Indians & to renew the Trade,"[17] — that is to build up a direct traffic with the Western Indians which had been neglected for the easier barter of English goods to the French — apparently refers to the short-lived establish-

[17] Colden's "Account of the Trade of New York," 1723.

ment at Irondequoit, already referred to. Evidence is lacking to show that the English or Dutch gained any foothold on the Niagara at this period.

In 1724, with due consent of the "Indian Proprietors," Burnet made his famous establishment at the mouth of the Oswego River, which was the foundation of the present city of Oswego. At the time no one was dreaming of future cities. It was but a new move in the century-long game for the fur trade. One might say, with some accuracy, that it was Joncaire's trading-house on the Niagara that provoked the English to make a like establishment, though much better built, at Oswego; and it was the English at Oswego that spurred the French to hasten the construction of the stone Fort Niagara. A broader statement of the situation, however, would show that these establishments by no means represented all the efforts which the rivals were putting forth at this period to secure the Indian trade.

The English in particular were successful in other ways. One of the first legislative acts passed under Burnet had aimed to put a stop to the direct trade between the English and the French. It had long been the custom for Albany traders to carry English-made goods to Montreal, selling them to the French who in turn traded them to the Indians. The English could supply certain articles which were more to the savage taste than those sent over from France; and they could afford to sell them at a lower price. Having stopped the peddling to the French, Governor Burnet made strong efforts to draw the far Western Indians to Albany for trade direct with them. In these efforts he was fairly successful. Bands of strange savages from Mackinac and beyond, accompanied by their squaws and papooses, presented themselves at Albany, where their kind had never been seen before. They had come down Lake Huron, past the French at Detroit, and through Lake Erie; and paddling down the swift reaches of the navigable Niagara had made the portage, reëmbarking below the heights and at the very doorway of the French trading-house; with some interchange, no doubt, of jeers and imprecations, but none of furs for French goods; and following the historic high-

NIAGARA AND THE WEST

way for canoes, they skirted the Ontario shore to the Oswego, then passed up that river, through Oneida Lake and down the Mohawk, until they could lay their bundles of beaver skins before the English, on the strand at Albany.

This was, indeed, a triumph of trade. They spoke a language which the traders there had never heard, but they brought many packs of furs; and with, perhaps, a double interpretation, the business sped to the entire satisfaction of the English. These people came in various bands; about twenty hunters, in the spring of 1722; and in the spring of 1723 over eighty, besides their numerous train of women and children; with sundry other parties following. They traveled over 1,200 miles to get to Albany.

Burnet was delighted with this proof that even with their *Magazin Royal* at the foot of the Niagara portage, the French did not by any means have a monopoly of the business. The English emissaries in the country of the Five Nations were as active as ever was Joncaire, and at this period appear to have been even more successful. Burnet attributed the increased trade to the stoppage of the English-French barter above mentioned and to " the Company whom I have kept in the Sinnekees Country whose business it has been to persuade all the Indians that pass by to come rather to trade at Albany than at Montreal, and as the Indians that come from the remote Lakes to go to Canada are commonly in want of Provisions when they come below the falls of Niagara, they are obliged to supply themselves in the Sinnekees Country where our people are and then they may take their choice where they will go, which considering the experience they have now had of the cheapness of Goods in this Province, we need not fear will be universally in our favor." [18]

So well disposed were these Western Indian traders towards the English, that they entered into a " League of Friendship " at Albany, which both Governor Burnet and Surveyor-General Colden construed as a desire to join the Six Nations, " that they may be esteemed the seventh Nation under the English Protection "— a matter for which the English were presumably

[18] Burnet to Lords of Trade, June 25, 1723.

far more eager than was the ancient League of the Iroquois, now, alas, past the splendid meridian of its strength. Its remaining energies were to be dissipated in the strife of the usurping strangers.

Burnet's dealings with the Five Nations were conspicuous for fairness and sagacity. In order to thwart the French, and bring the Western fur trade to the New York Colony, he could afford to be generous, especially to the Senecas, whose aid was indispensable. In his first meeting with them, at Albany, in September, 1721, he so won their good will that they declared they would not let the French fortify Niagara. The French, they protested, had deceived them there some thirty years ago, pretending to get permission to build a storehouse, and then fortifying it without permission; but, said the Indians, we pulled it down. They did not exactly promise to do so again, but said: " We are resolved as soon as any French come to the Five Nations to tell them to pull down that trading House at Onjarara, and not to come either to settle or Trade among us any more."

The protestations of friendship at this council, on the part of the Five Nations — still referred to as the Five Nations, though since the inclusion of the Tuscaroras in 1715, really become six — were somewhat warmer than usual. The conference was shared in by the Governor " and diverse gentlemen from New York that attended his Excellency," by Captain Robert Walters, Cadwallader Colden and James Alexander of the Royal Council, by the twelve Commissioners of Indian Affairs, headed by Colonel Peter Schuyler, by the Mayor and Aldermen of Albany, and, no doubt, by such unofficial spectators as could gain admission. The Mohawks, Oneidas, Onondagas, Cayugas and Senecas were all represented by painted, be-feathered and greedy sachems. Their chief spokesman was not content, before so august an assemblage, with the more ordinary pledges of friendship.

" We call you Brother," he said, holding out the belt of wampum, " and so we ought to do, and to love one another as well as those that have sucked on [one] breast, for we are Brethren indeed, and hope to live and dye so," and he promised on behalf of the Five Nations "to keep the Covenant Chain inviolable as long as Sun & Moon endure." It is not impossible that the Indians had wind of the great present they were to receive—"as noble a Present," Burnet wrote afterwards, "as ever was given them from His Majesty King George." At the close of the formal proceedings the Indians told the Governor that they heard he had lately been married.[19] "We are glad of it," they said, "and wish you much Joy And as a token of our Rejoycing We present a few Beavers to your Lady for Pin Money," adding with amusing frankness, "It is Customary for a Brother upon his Marryage to invite his Brethren to be Merry and Dance."

The Governor did not disappoint them. The gifts which he now spread before them would have filled a warehouse. The list, which has been preserved,[20] is not uninstructive. There were given to the Indians on this occasion five pieces of strouds [worth at that time £10 per piece in New York and upwards of $13 at Montreal], five of duffels, five of blankets, four of "half thicks," fifty fine shirts, 213 Ozibrigg[21] shirts, fifty red coats, fifty pairs of stockings, six dozen scissors, fourteen dozen knives, four dozen jack-knives, five dozen square looking-glasses and thirty dozen of round hand-mirrors, twenty-eight parcels of gartering and twelve of binding, twenty pounds of beads, twenty brass kettles, fifty guns, 1,000 pounds of powder in bags, 200 pounds of bar lead, ten cases of ball, 1,500 gun-flints, twelve dozen jewsharps, six and one-half barrels of tobacco, and last, but very far from least, a hogshead of rum. There were besides private presents to the sachems, including guns, powder, shirts, laced coats and laced hats, and special portions of liquor. Even this was not enough.

[19] He had married a daughter of Abraham Van Horne, a prominent New York merchant.

[20] Minutes of Conference at Albany, Sept. 7, 1721, kept by Robt. Livingston, Sec'y for Indian Affairs.

[21] A coarse linen much used in the Indian trade. The name is often written "Oznabrigg," but the correct form is Oznaburg, after the city so named in Germany, whence these linens were originally imported. The name came to be applied to coarse linens made elsewhere. "Duffels" were coarse woolen cloths, the name probably derived from Duffel in the Netherlands.

Governor Burnet " in the name of his Majesty, Ordered them some Barrls of Beer to be merry withall and dance, which they did according to their Custom and were extreamly well Satisfyed."

And back to their several villages the loaded retinue went; up the Mohawk, to Onondaga; the diminishing party continuing, now by lake and stream, now filing along the old trails, to the Seneca towns in the valley of the Genesee and to the westward. Red coats, hand-mirrors and new guns were hard arguments to be overcome by the pinched French at *Magazin Royal.*

It was on the strength of the good will of the Senecas, won at this conference, that Burnet ventured to send his young men, under Captain Schuyler — son of Peter Schuyler, President of the Council — to attempt a settlement at Irondequoit on Lake Ontario. Burnet hoped that others would join him there; but caused it to be clearly understood that the place was indisputably in the Indians' possession. It was merely to serve as a depôt of English goods, where Western traders, who would pass by the French establishment on the Niagara, were to be supplied on terms far more liberal than the French could afford. With the one possible exception of powder, the English could furnish everything used in the Indian trade more cheaply than the French, supplying, of course, rum instead of brandy, a substitution to which the red man made no demur, so long as the quantity was ample.

CHAPTER XIII

"A HOUSE OF PEACE"

THE BUILDING OF FORT NIAGARA — SERVICES OF JONCAIRE, LONGUEUIL AND DE LÉRY — JONCAIRE'S LETTERS FROM THE FORT — AN IMPORTANT OUTPOST FOR FRANCE IN AMERICA.

WE are now come to the point in our story where the testimony of the ancient manuscripts is quickened, vivified by an existing landmark. The stone house popularly known as the "castle," the most venerable of the group of structures in the Government reserve of Fort Niagara, dates, in its oldest parts, from 1726. It is the oldest edifice in the Northern United States, west of the Mohawk. Vaudreuil conceived the project of it; Longueuil the younger and Joncaire gained the uncertain consent of the Five Nations for its erection; and Gaspard Chaussegros de Léry, the King's chief engineer in Canada, determined its exact location and superintended its construction.

Joncaire's efforts to secure for the French a more efficient stronghold on the banks of the Niagara than his palisaded storehouse under Lewiston Heights, began at least as early as 1723. They probably were unceasing from the time of his first occupancy of the neighborhood, but in the year named the correspondence shows that his efforts were directed toward definite achievement. On August 23d, Joncaire wrote from Niagara to the Governor that the Iroquois had agreed that a regular fort should be built on the Niagara, " but that it should be a little fort of palisades, in which 300 men could defend themselves."

This was but an entering wedge for the more substantial structure which the French had resolved to build. When Vaudreuil learned, December 8, 1724, of the operations of the English at Oswego, he realized that another move in the game must be made by the French if they would retain even a share of that portion of the fur trade which made the Great Lakes its highway to market. Joncaire's feeble establishment was in danger of eclipse, of being cut out, by the rum and other superior inducements which the English were so lavishly offering. It is evident that the Governor studied the situation thoroughly that winter. By spring he had made up his mind. He wrote to the Minister, May 25th, that, should the English undertake to make a permanent establishment at Oswego, nothing remained but to fortify Niagara. He could say "fortify" to the Minister, though to the Iroquois declarations must continue to be made, that their devoted father — Onontio — sought only to build a trading-house — a storehouse — anything, so long as it was not called fort. He proposed first to build two barques on Lake Ontario, which should not only carry materials for the proposed construction at Niagara, but could cruise the lake and intercept Indian parties on their way to trade with the English. The building at Niagara, the Minister was informed, " will not have the appearance of a fort, so that no offense will be given to the Iroquois, who have been unwilling to allow any there, but it will answer the purpose of a fort just as well."

The Intendant, M. Bégon, approved the project. Under date of June 10, 1725, he wrote to the Minister, that in view of the great importance of doing everything possible to prevent the English from driving the French from Niagara, " we have determined to build at Fort Frontenac two barques to serve in case of need against the English, to drive them from that establishment [Niagara] and also to serve for carrying materials with which to build a stone fort at Niagara, which we hold to be necessary to put that post in a state of defense against the English" as well as against the Iroquois. He added that these boats would be very useful in time of peace, sailing between La Galette, Frontenac and Niagara, and carrying provisions, munitions of war, merchandise for trade, and peltries, reducing the expense below that of canoe service. " They will serve also as far as Niagara for the transport of provisions, merchandise and peltries for all those belonging to the posts in the upper country, or who go up with trade per-

A "House of Peace:" The Castle or Mess House at Fort Niagara, Built 1726

"A HOUSE OF PEACE"

mits. The freight which they will be able to carry will compensate the King for the cost of construction.

"I sent, for this purpose, in February last, two carpenters and four sawyers, who arrived at Fort Frontenac, traveling on the ice, the 26th of the same month. I am informed that during the winter they cut the wood needed and have barked and sawed a part of it. I have also sent nine other carpenters and two blacksmiths, who set out from Montreal on the 15th of last month, to hurry on the work, that these boats may be ready to sail the coming autumn." [1]

A postscript to this letter adds: "Since writing, M. de Joncaire has come down and tells me that the Iroquois will not interfere with building the boats, and will not oppose the Niagara establishment, asking only that there should not be built there a stone fort."

As the years passed, it was Joncaire who more and more represented the power of France on the Niagara. He it was to whom the Governor of Canada entrusted the delicate business of maintaining amicable relations with the Senecas; and on his reports and advice depended in considerable measure the attitude of the French towards their ever-active rivals. In November, 1724, Vaudreuil had written to the Minister that in order to retain the Five Nations in their "favorable dispositions," he thought he "could not do better than to send Sieur de Joncaire to winter at Niagara and among the Senecas. According to the news to be received from Sieur de Joncaire," added the Governor, "I shall determine whether to send Sieur de Longueuil to the Onontagués, among whom he has considerable influence."

That Joncaire's news was favorable, is evident from the sequel; for Longueuil was sent to the Onondagas, from whom he gained a dubious consent that the French might build a fort at the mouth of the Niagara. In June, 1725, Joncaire went down from the Seneca Castle — near present Geneva — to

[1] These barques were commanded by sailing-masters Gagnon and Goueville. Each had four sailors, with six soldiers to help. A memorandum states that the operations of the vessels in 1727 cost 5775 livres, 3 sols (sous), 11 deniers. A sailor received for a season's work 530 livres, the masters 803 livres each.

Quebec, where he assured the Intendant, Bégon, that the Iroquois were pledged not to interfere with the construction of the two barques then building at Fort Frontenac, " nor oppose the establishment at Niagara, only requiring that no stone fort should be erected there." According to the French reports, this last stipulation was soon set aside, for in the dispatches of Vaudreuil and Bégon to the Minister, dated May 7, 1726, telling of Longueuil's mission to the Five Nations, one reads as follows:

" He repaired next to Onontagué, an Iroquois village, and found the Deputies from the other four villages there waiting for him; he got them to consent to the construction of two barques, and to the erection of a stone house at Niagara, the plan of which he designed."

This mission of Longueuil proved an eventful one. He was charged to cross Lake Ontario to order the English to withdraw from Oswego. A curious meeting ensued. At the mouth of the river he found 100 Englishmen with sixty canoes. They stopped him, called for his pass, and showed him their instructions from the Governor of New York, not to let any Frenchman go by without a passport. Then the doughty Canadian, not relishing the idea of being under English surveillance, turned to the Iroquois chiefs who were present, and taunted them with being no longer masters of their own territory. His harangue had the desired effect. The Indians, galled by his words, broke out against the English with violent reproaches and threats. " You have been permitted to come here to trade," they said, " but we will not suffer anything more." They promised Longueuil that in the event of a French war with the English, they would remain neutral; and the delighted emissary turned his back on the discomfited Englishmen, who dared not interfere, and accompanied by a large volunteer retinue of Indians, continued his journey to Onondaga.

Here the deputies of the Five Nations gathered to meet them. He showed them the plan he had designed for a house at Niagara. The report as subsequently laid before the Minister and Louis XV, says " a stone house." It is by no means certain that Longueuil gave the Indians this idea. According

to the version they gave, when taken to task the next year by
Governor Burnet, the French officer told the Onondagas " that
he had built a Bark House at Niagara, which was old and began to decay, that he could no longer keep his goods dry in it,
and was now come to desire leave to build a bigger house,
wherein his goods might be safe from rain, and said that if they
consented that he might build a house there and have vessels in
Cadaracqui Lake [Ontario], he promised it should be for their
good, peace and quietness, and for their children's children,
that the French would protect them for three hundred years."
The Senecas were reported to have protested; they sent a wampum belt to the Onondagas, with the warning that "in case
the French should desire to make any Building or Settlement
at Niagara or at Ochsweeke [Lake Erie] or elsewhere on their
land, they should not give their consent to it." But the Onondagas, "being prevailed upon by Fair speeches and promises,
rejected the Sinnekes belt, and gave the French leave for building at Niagara." It was Joncaire, as we have seen, who overcame the objecton of the Senecas. Returning from their country, he brought word that they would not hinder the construction, though he had previously cautioned Vaudreuil not to attempt a stone building. But the elder Longueuil, writing to
the Minister under date of October 31, 1725, explicitly says
of his son's achievement: "The Sieur de Longueuil, having
repaired to the Onondaga village, found there the deputies of
the other four Iroquois villages. He met them there, he got
them to consent to the construction of the two barques and to
the building of a stone house at Niagara." It was to be no
fort, but "a house of solid masonry, where all things needed
for trade with the Indians could be safely kept, and for this
purpose he would go to Niagara to mark out the spot on
which this house might be erected, to which they consented."

The sequence of events in this affair affords a striking illustration of the way in which things were taken for granted, or
work undertaken before official sanction was obtained or funds
made available. The two barques, without which the construction of Fort Niagara would have been impossible, were being
built before the Indians had given their consent to it. The

consent of the Indians to the erection of the fort was not gained until after its erection had been fully determined upon by the French; and all of this important work was well in hand long before the Department in France had provided funds for it. The plan of the Niagara house, which is spoken of as designed by Longueuil, was sent to the Minister in France, with an estimate of the cost, amounting to 29,295 livres. Various estimates are mentioned in the dispatches of the time. De Maurepas, perplexed by a multiplicity of demands, endorsed upon these dispatches: "It seems necessary to forego, this year, the grant of 29,295 li., and 13,090 li. for the house at Niagara and the construction of the two barques." At Versailles, April 29, 1727, Louis expressed his satisfaction at the construction of Fort Niagara, and promised to "cause to be appropriated in next year's Estimate for the Western Domain, the sum of 20,430 li., the amount of the expense, according to the divers estimates they have sent, and as the principal house at the mouth of the river must have been finished this spring, his Majesty's intention is, that Sieurs de Beauharnois and Duypuy [Dupuy] adopt measures to rebuild the old house next Autumn. This they will find the more easy, as the two barques built at Fort Frontenac will aid considerably in tranporting materials. His Majesty agrees with them in opinion that the Iroquois will not take any umbrage at this, for besides being considered only as the reconstruction of the house already there, it will be used, at least during the Peace, only for Trade. They will, meanwhile, adopt with those Indians such precautions as they shall consider necessary, to neutralize any new impressions of distrust the English would not fail to insinuate among them on this occasion. This must prompt them to have the work pushed on with the greatest possible diligence." The King afterwards disapproved of any further outlay for "the old house," and Joncaire's establishment at the head of the lower navigation on the Niagara was never rebuilt.

It was true then, as now, that building expenses do not always work out according to specifications. In October, 1727, we find Dupuy trying to explain his heavy expenses: "The house at Niagara cost infinitely more than the 29,295 li.

"A HOUSE OF PEACE"

granted for last year. The expeditions which we have had to send there in 1726 and this year have greatly increased the cost of freight and transportation of provisions needed there." Vaudreuil had hoped to have the vessels on Lake Ontario ready by the autumn of 1725; but no record is found stating that they sailed to the Niagara that year. The testimony of the correspondence, so far as known, shows that the vessels did not carry building material or workmen to the Niagara until navigation opened in the spring of 1726.[2] The Baron de Longueuil wrote, October 31, 1725: "The two barques have been finished this autumn, they will be ready to sail next Spring, and to carry the stone and other material needed for building the stone house at Niagara," etc. They were to take out on their first voyage, ten masons and four carpenters and joiners, besides the 100 soldiers with six officers detailed for the enterprise. A report of the Intendent Bégon, May 20, 1726, says: "The two barques built at Fort Frontenac are ready to sail, they will carry to Niagara the materials necessary for building the house."

Vaudreuil, as we have seen, had written that Longueuil had designed a plan for the proposed establishment on the Niagara, and it may have been in accordance with the suggestions of this soldier that the work was begun; but for such a construction as was desired, expert engineering ability was required. There was but one man in Canada qualified to undertake the task, and to him the Baron de Longueuil — then Governor *ad interim*, wrote under date of March 28, 1726:

"I beg Monsieur Chaussegros de Léry, engineer, to work without let-up in building the Niagara house, which he will place wherever he shall judge it most advisable. It is a work of absolute necessity, the old house being of wood and offering no means of preservation, unless it is fortified. It is moreover of the greatest consequence to profit by the favorable

[2] The local histories and narratives relating to Fort Niagara usually give the date of its commencement as 1725. There is some discrepancy of dates in the documents, or copies of original documents, which I have examined; but it is plain that work on the "castle" was not begun until June, 1726. That the reader may know on what I base my conclusions, I have given in my narrative ample extracts from the documents themselves.

disposition of the Iroquois in regard to us. I undertake to have this expense approved by the Court."

Gaspard Chaussegros de Léry, who now becomes an important figure in the story of the Niagara, was the son of an engineer of Toulon, where he was born, October 13, 1682. Trained to his father's profession, we find him, in 1706, serving in the army of Italy, and gaining glory and a wound at the siege of Turin. A later service in the squadron of the Marquis de Forbin, took him to the coast of Scotland and won him a captain's rank in the infantry regiment of Sault. When the navy board (for so we may render "*le conseil du marine*") decided in 1716 to undertake a more extensive system of fortifications in Canada, it chose de Léry to carry out the royal plans. These included an elaborate refortification of Quebec, the building of a wall around Montreal and subsequently of other works at Chambly, Three Rivers and other points, as well as the construction of prisons and public buildings. De Léry came at once to the scene of his labors, perfected the plan of what he proposed to do at Quebec, and returning to Paris, submitted it to the King. His plans and estimates were approved and he returned to Canada to press forward the work. The correspondence of the time shows that he was much embarrassed by lack of sufficient appropriations; a fact which gives special point to the closing statement in M. de Longueuil's letter, assigning him to Niagara. Not having received any order from the Court to undertake this work, de Léry was apprehensive that the King would not approve. However, relying on the assurance of Longueuil, he devoted himself to it in the summer of 1726. Under date of July 26th of that year the Baron de Longueuil wrote to the Minister:

"It is for me to inform you of the measures which I took this last spring for the establishment of the post of Niagara . . . and of my plan for sending to Niagara as soon as navigation was open, in order to forestall the English, and to begin early to work on the house of which we have had the honor to send you the plan, in order that it may be completed this year. M. Bégon assured me that he would send the workmen

"A HOUSE OF PEACE"

I had asked for, as soon as the ice went out, and that M. de Léry would come to Montreal at the same time. He arrived here in March; and in April I sent the workmen with a detachment of a hundred soldiers, commanded by my son and four other officers. As soon as they arrived at Niagara, I learn by these officers, M. de Léry had laid out the house in another place than that which I had proposed to him, and which had seemed to me most suitable in order to make us masters of the portage, and of the communication between the two lakes. He will no doubt give you his reasons.

"The work has been very well carried on and the fortifications are well advanced. The barques which were built last year at Frontenac have been of wonderful aid. They sent me word the tenth of this month that the walls were already breast high everywhere. There has been no opposition on the part of the Iroquois, who on the contrary appear well satisfied to have us near them; but the English, restless and jealous of this establishment, have seduced and engaged several Seneca chiefs to come and thwart us with speeches of which I send herewith a copy, and which have had no other effect than to reassure us of the good will of the Iroquois." He expresses the hope that the house at Niagara will be finished this year, refers to the Dutch and English at Oswego, and adds: "The uneasiness I have felt, because of the English and Dutch, who had threatened to establish themselves at Niagara, and my fears lest the Iroquois would retract the word they gave last year, have not permitted me to await your orders for the construction of this house. I beg you to approve what I have done through zeal for the good of this colony."

One of the "four other officers" referred to in the foregoing letter, as having shared in the building of Fort Niagara, was the Sieur de Ramezay, "Chevalier of the Royal and Military Order of St. Louis," etc., as later memoirs recount his titles. He was only an ensign in the colonial troops in 1720, when he entered upon his Canadian service; and he remained in the garrison at Montreal until the spring of 1726, when he was appointed lieutenant and sent to Niagara. Another who shared in this undertaking was a son of Lieutenant Le Verrier.

The youth " showed good qualities in his service at Niagara," but becoming sick was sent back to Quebec. Still another unfortunate was the Sieur de la Loge, who received so severe an injury in one of his eyes, at Niagara in this summer, that it was feared he would lose the sight of both; he was sent to Quebec and thence to Paris, that he might have the attention of the famous oculist, St. Yves.

On April 28, 1726, the Baron de Longueuil appointed his son Charles Le Moyne (then a captain, afterwards second Baron de Longueuil) to be the first commandant of Fort Niagara — not then built, but destined to be the focal point of all our regional history under the French. The letter making the appointment directed the young man to repair to Niagara with a detachment of troops, to superintend the construction of the fort; and called upon the officers and soldiers of the detachment, and especially upon Joncaire, and upon all travelers passing by way of the Niagara, to acknowledge his authority.[3]

On September 5th the new commandant wrote from Niagara that the new house was very much advanced, and would have been finished had it not been for the sickness that broke out among the workmen, 30 of whom had been ill; but that the place was then enclosed and secured.

De Longueuil, who knew the region well, had proposed that the stone house should stand farther up the river, and on going to the Niagara, after his successful conference at Onondaga, had decided to place it " on a most advantageous elevation, about 170 feet from the old house, and some 130 feet from the edge of the river; the barques could there be moored to shore, under the protection of the house, of which they could make later on, a fort with crenelated enclosure or wooden stockade "; but de Léry decided otherwise, holding that the angle of the lake and river not only commanded the portage and all communication between the lakes, but enabled the French to keep watch over Lake Ontario, so as to prevent the English from

---

[3] The letter, which is of peculiar interest, since it records the appointment of the first in the long succession of commandants at Fort Niagara, will be found in the Appendix.

going to trade on the north shore of that lake. The English could not cross the lake in their bark canoes; to reach the north side, the natural route was by skirting the shore, from Oswego to Niagara and westward. Hence, even though de Léry had placed the fort at the portage, the English might easily have seized the mouth of the river, and by controlling Lake Ontario, have blockaded the French in their fort and starved them into a surrender. They could have made it impossible for assistance to reach it from the base of supplies, Frontenac, or the river towns; and they could have made it equally impossible for the garrison of Fort Niagara to withdraw. The two barques which the French counted so greatly upon, for communication with the new establishment, would often find it a tedious if not impossible matter to beat up to the portage against seven miles of steady current; whereas the post, if placed at the mouth of the river, would always be accessible, these vessels making the passage from Fort Frontenac and return, in fair weather, in about fourteen days. All of these reasons are so cogent that one can but wonder that an officer of Longueuil's experience should have considered any other spot than that fixed upon by de Léry. The latter's capabilities as a military engineer were sométimes called in question. Montcalm, more than a quarter century later, spoke of him not only as " a great ignoramus in his profession," adding, " it needs only to look at his works," but declared that he " robbed the King like the rest " of the men who served as engineers-in-chief in Canada.[4] Be that as it may, de Léry's judgment in locating Fort Niagara was justified by the circumstances.

When the foundations of the stone house were laid and the walls were rising, de Léry traced a fort around them. He made a map of the lake, showing the mouth of the river, and prepared plans and elevations of the house. The drawings were forwarded to the King, and are described in the abstract of dispatches. The portion of the works which it was found impossible to complete, before the winter of 1726-27 set in,

[4] Montcalm to M. de Normand, Montreal, April 12, 1759. Paris Docs., X, 963.

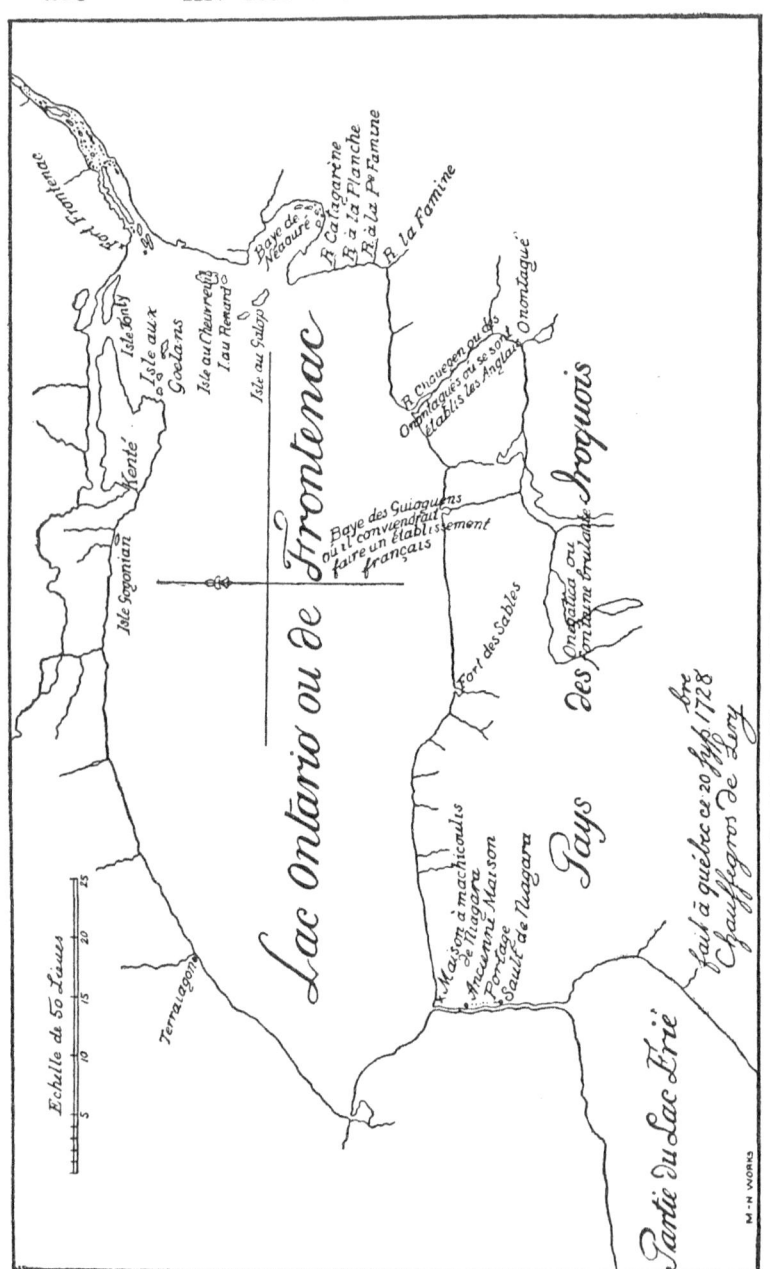

De Léry's Map of Lake Ontario, 1728.

he colored yellow. He may have procured part of his stone from the Heights ("*Le Platon*"), his timber from the marsh west of the river; but most of the stone was brought from the vicinity of Fort Frontenac, in the two barques. With the map there was also sent a memoir "to make plain my reasons for placing the house ["*maison à machicoulis*"] at the [entrance of the] strait, where it now stands, and where the late Marquis de Denonville, Governor-General of this country, had formerly built a fort, with a garrison." He sent also a plan and estimate for a small house at the Niagara portage, adding: "This house will be useful in time of peace, but in case of war with the Indians, it could scarcely be maintained, on account of the difficulty of relieving the garrison." The memoir continues:

"I arrived, June 6th, with a detachment of troops, at the entrance to the river Niagara. The same day I examined it, with the masters of the barques. We found it not navigable for the barques." The examination must have been most superficial, for once past the bar at the mouth, they would have found a deep natural channel for seven miles.

"I remarked, in beginning this house, that if I built it, like those in Canada, liable to fire, should war come and the savages invest it, as was the case formerly with Mons. Denonville's fort, if it caught fire the garrison and all the munitions would be wholly lost, and the [control of the] country as well. It was this which determined me to make a house proof against these accidents. Instead of wooden partitions ["*cloisons*"] I have had built bearing-walls ["*des murs de refend*"], and paved all the floors with flat stones. . . . I have traced around a fort of four bastions; and in order that they may defend themselves in this house, I have made all the garret windows machicolated; the loft ["*grenier*"] being paved with flat stones on a floor full of good oak joists, upon which cannon may be placed above this structure. Though large it would have been entirely finished in September, had not some French *voyageurs* coming from the Miamis and Illinois, in passing this post, spread the fever here, so that nearly all the soldiers and workmen have had it. This has interfered with the construction so that it has not been completed in the time that I had expected. There remains about a fourth of it to do next year. This will not prevent the garrison or traders from lodging there this winter." That his own services should not be overlooked he added: " I have the honor to inform you, Monseigneur, that my journeys to Niagara have occupied nearly five months."

Two sets of plans of this building, drawn by de Léry, are still preserved in Paris. One set is dated Quebec, January 19, 1727 — while the great house was under construction. Later plans, dated 1738, endorsed by de Léry and son, show substantially the same interior arrangement; thus indicating that for a number of years the structure was used as originally designed.

The rear of the structure was towards Lake Ontario. The main or south front had three doors, two of them long since converted into windows. On the ground floor, at the right of the middle vestibule, were the store where barter with the Indians was carried on, and the clerk's room. Opposite was the guard-room. The bakery, with its outside oven, store-room for provisions, two other store-rooms and a powder magazine, were ranged along the north side of the corridor, in the middle of which was a well. The elevation shows that the windows of the ground floor were protected with iron bars.

An interesting feature of the floor above was the chapel with its altar, at the southwest corner of the building. This was discontinued after a separate chapel was built. A guard-room and chambers filled most of this floor, except at the northeast corner, where was a kitchen, the old fireplace of which may still be seen.

The stairs are to-day as originally drawn by de Léry. The roof and great chimneys show changes, including a part of a structure at one time used by the United States Government as a lighthouse.

The old "castle," or "mess house," as it is indifferently called, still stands, probably the oldest building in the northern United States west of the Mohawk, the scene and center of stirring and significant events not only in the days of the French but through the stormy vicissitudes of the American Revolution and the War of 1812.

"A HOUSE OF PEACE"

De Léry's apprehensions regarding official approval of his choice of site for Fort Niagara were set at rest the next spring by the following letter from the new Minister of Marine:

> The Marquis de Beauharnois and M. Dupuy have forwarded to me the maps and plans which you sent to them, with data explaining your reasons for building the Niagara house where the late Marquis de Denonville had reared a wooden fort, which time has destroyed, instead of placing it at the portage where the old house stood. His Majesty is pleased to approve it. He is gratified with your zeal and the diligence with which you have conducted the work. . . . The Marquis has asked for you the Cross of St. Louis.[5]

While the King's engineer was busy with the plan and actual construction of the fort, Joncaire and his long-time friend and associate, the younger Longueuil, were fully occupied in keeping the savages in good humor. There is no known basis for the story that the French, resorting to stratagem, planned a hunt which should draw the Indians away from the spot until the building had progressed far enough to serve as a defense in case of attack.[6] Such a story does not accord with Joncaire's known relations with the Senecas.

It was a singular council that was held on the Niagara — probably at the old house at Lewiston — on July 14, 1726, between the younger de Longueuil and representatives of the Five Nations. Addressing himself to the officer, one of the chiefs referred to the conference of the preceding spring, and holding out a wampum belt, said: "I perceive my death ap-

[5] Maurepas to Chaussegros de Léry, Brest, May 13, 1727. In later letters it is stated that M. de Léry was to receive the coveted decoration on Sept. 25, 1727.

[6] "It is a traditionary story that the mess house, which is a very strong building and the largest in the fort, was erected by stratagem. A considerable, though not powerful, body of French troops had arrived at the point. Their force was inferior to the surrounding Indians, of whom they were under some apprehensions. They obtained consent of the Indians to build a wigwam, and induced them, with some of their officers, to engage in an extensive hunt. The materials had been made ready and while the Indians were absent the French built. When the parties returned at night they had advanced so far with the work as to cover their faces and to defend themselves against the savages in case of an attack."—" The Falls of Niagara," by Samuel DeVeaux, Buffalo, 1839.

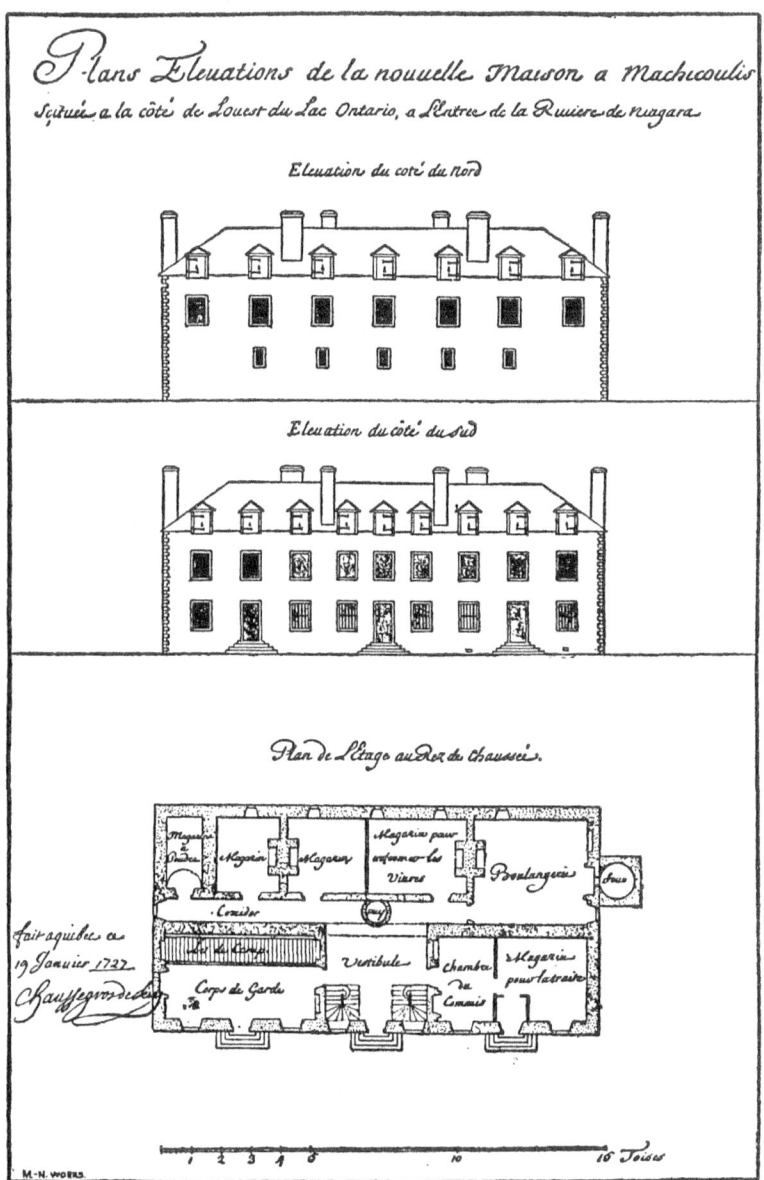

The great stone house at Fort Niagara, 1727.
From the original plans of Chaussegros de Léry, preserved in the Archives of the Colonies, Paris.

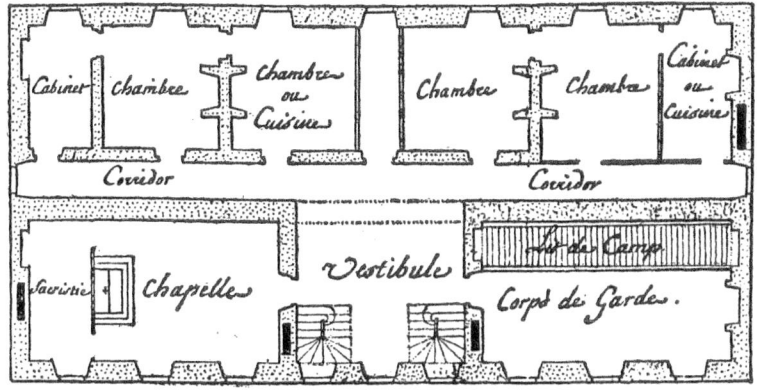

Second story of the great house, as planned by De Léry. The lower story ("Rez-de-chaussée") is shown on the opposite page.

proaching. It is you and the English who come to destroy us. I beg you, cease your work until I may hear your voice another time. Put the time at next September, when I will show you what is in my heart, as I hope you will open yours to me."

The shrewd commandant of Niagara was not to be diverted from his purpose. "Here is your belt, my son," he said, taking up the wampum. "I fold it and put it back in your bag." The return of the wampum always signified a rejection of proposals. "I put it back, not purposing to discontinue the works which they have sent me to do here. I hold fast to your former word, which consented that there should be built here a new and large house, to take the place of the old one, which can be no longer preserved.

"I do not consider these words you now speak as coming from you Iroquois, but as an English speech which shall not stop me. See, here on the table are wine and tobacco, which go better than this affair, which must be forgotten and which I reject."

As this "talk" was not confirmed by a belt, a second council was held at the unusual hour of midnight ("*tenu à minuit*"), at which a much finer belt of wampum was offered and accepted, with longer speeches, in which the Senecas promised to stand by the pledges which the Onondagas had made. "It is not only for the present that I speak," said a chief, " but for always. We join hands for good business, we five Iroquois nations, and may we always keep faith, and you do the same on your side."

At the very outset of this new undertaking, the success of which he had so much at heart, Philippe de Rigaud, Marquis de Vaudreuil, died at Quebec, October 10, 1725, and was buried in the church of the Récollets at Château St. Louis. It would be superfluous here to enter upon a review of his long and on the whole successful administration; but it is pertinent to our especial study to recall his relations to the Niagara region. In France, as early as 1676, he had served in the Royal Musketeers. In the year of his arrival in Canada, 1687, we find him commanding a detachment of the troops of the Marine, engaging in the Iroquois compaign with Denonville, and sharing in the establishment of the ill-fated Fort Denonville at the mouth of the Niagara. The knowledge of the region gained then, undoubtedly affected his direction, throughout many years, of the endeavors of Joncaire and the younger de Longueuil. Soon after his first coming to Niagara, he was promoted to the rank of captain, for gallantry in the defense of Quebec against Phipps. He was decorated with the Cross of St. Louis for a successful Indian campaign; and in 1698, when Callières succeeded Frontenac as Governor of Canada, the Chevalier de Vaudreuil succeeded Callières as Governor of Montreal. It was in 1703 that he again followed Callières, in the highest office of the colony. Though not a Canadian by birth, his connections by marriage were Canadian, and more than any other Governor up to that time, he identified himself with colonial interests. The French in military or civil office in Canada were by no means always devoted to the welfare of the country; but Vaudreuil seems for the most part to have served it like a patriot. Throughout the twenty-two years of his administration, he had ever in view the promotion of the fur trade, the extension of French influence on the Lakes. His master-stroke in these efforts was to be the establishment of Fort Niagara, regarding which Louis XV had written to him with his own hand: "The post of

"A HOUSE OF PEACE" 243

Niagara is of the greatest importance, to preserve the trade with the upper countries." The King no doubt had derived his impressions from Vaudreuil's representations, but none the less, royal sanction was useful. Now, on the eve of achievement, his hand is withdrawn and another is to take up the work.

Louis XV. selected as the successor of Vaudreuil, Charles, Marquis de Beauharnois, a natural son of Louis XIV. He had been an office-holder in Canada a score of years prior to this date, having in 1702 succeeded M. de Champigny as Intendant. In 1705 he was appointed " Director of the Marine Classes " in France, but he was captain of a man-of-war when, January 11, 1726, Louis XV commissioned him to be Governor of Canada, an office which he was to administer until 1747, thus becoming a factor of no little consequence in the particular history that we are tracing. In the interim between Vaudreuil's death and the arrival of Beauharnois, that is, until September 2, 1726, the first Baron de Longueuil was the chief executor for Canada. He solicited the governorship, but was without influence; the Court, it is said, was advised not to appoint a native Canadian. But the post which was denied him was, later on, to be filled by his son.

Chabert de Joncaire of the trading-house at the portage is spoken of at this period as the commander at Niagara; [7] it is not plain, however, that he was in command of troops at the new fort. In July, 1726, the son of the lieutenant governor of Montreal was sent with a small body of men to garrison the fort and complete the works. This man, with whom begins a succession of commandants of Fort Niagara which continues to the present day, was Charles Le Moyne the second — Le Moyne, it will be borne in mind, being the family name of the Baron de Longueuil. The first of that title was now a veteran of seventy years. The new commandant, too, had seen many years of service for the King in America, and had been on the Niagara before this time. As early as 1716 he had made a campaign beyond Detroit, into the Illinois country, and had been reported as killed. We have noted his great influence with the Indians; but the few glimpses afforded of him

[7] N. Y. Col. Docs., IX, 979.

in the official documents give little idea of his personality, save in one respect; he was, at a somewhat later period than we are now considering, very corpulent, so that, in the language of the chronicle, he was "illy adapted for travel." He was forty years old when he came to command the new fort on the Niagara. Three years later he was to succeed, on the death of his father, to the title and estate of baron.

It should not be overlooked that this new establishment, which marked a new advance of France and was a new expression of that Power, short-lived though it was to be, in the Lake region and Mississippi Valley, identifies with the story of the Niagara a scion of the greatest Canadian family of its period, and, in certain aspects, one of the most important and influential families concerned in making the history of America. Charles Le Moyne the immigrant, son of a tavernkeeper of Dieppe, played his part in the New World as pioneer, interpreter, and trader, marvelously prosperous for his day and opportunities. But the family fame begins with his many sons, several of whom appear on the pages of Seventeenth and Eighteenth century history by the surnames drawn from their seigneurial rights and estates. One of these sons, Charles, was that first Baron de Longueuil whom we have seen as a major in La Barre's expedition; campaigning with Denonville against the Senecas; helping in the establishment of the ill-fated fort on the Niagara which was built in 1687, and subsequently serving his King in many capacities, not least important of which was that as negotiator with the Iroquois, thus paving the way for the erection of the new Fort Niagara. These were incidents in his later years while serving as lieutenant governor of Montreal. In his more youthful days, and while his numerous younger brothers were still children, he had served in France; as one appreciative student has admirably summed it up —"had, with his Indian attendant, figured at Court as related by the Duchess of Orleans in one of her letters to her sister, the Countess Palatine Louise; had married the daughter of a nobleman, a lady in waiting to her Royal Highness of Orleans; and had built that great fortress-château of Longueuil, the marvel of stateliness and elegance

"A HOUSE OF PEACE"

of the day for all Canada; and had obtained his patent of nobility and title of Baron."[8] Of his brothers, six — Iberville, Saint Hélène, Maricourt, Sérigny, Bienville, Châteauguay — have written their names on the continent from Hudson's Bay to the Gulf of Mexico, none more largely or lastingly than Jean Baptiste Le Moyne, who as Bienville is known as the Father of Louisiana. And of his sons, Charles Le Moyne the second, born in 1687, was the captain, the chevalier and (on the death of his father) the second Baron de Longueuil; the adopted son of the Onondagas, the comrade and friend of Joncaire, and the first commandant of the new Fort Niagara.

A glimpse of the fort, during this interesting period of construction, is afforded by a letter written by the younger Longueuil to his father the baron. It is dated "Niagara, 5th September, 1726," and runs in part as follows:

> There are no more English at Oswego or at the little fall. The last canoe which has gone to winter had to go on to Albany to find brandy, and they assure me that there is not one in the whole length of the lake or the river. This is the third canoe that has told me the same thing. If I meet any in the lake or going down, I will have them pillaged.
>
> It will be October before I can leave here, and I do not know when we shall have finished. Sickness has constantly increased. We have now more than thirty men attacked by fever, and I find that our soldiers resist better than our workmen. If they could work, we should not have enough of them to put the house in state of security this month. It would certainly have been finished this year, but for the sickness. I mean the stonework, for M. de Léry having sent away the sawyers, we have not enough planks to half cover it. The master-carpenter is sick and has done nothing for fifteen days. We shall cover what we can, and then close the gable with the joist of the scaffolding. (". . . *bouchera le pignon avec les madriers d'echafaudage.*") If they (the gables) are not entirely enclosed, they will at any rate be protected by the walls all around.

He adds that as soon as possible, he shall send back the married men, who are good-for-nothing weepers ("*les pleureux*

[8] Grace King's "New Orleans," p. 15.

qui ne valent rien "), no doubt a true-enough characterization of the home-loving *habitant*, who in the savage-infested wilderness of the Niagara found himself homesick even to tearfulness.

Among the French officers at Niagara in the summer of 1726 was Pierre Jacques Payen, Captain de Noyan; who wrote, probably in the fall of that year,[9] to the Marquis de Beauharnois, as follows:

> As I believe, monsieur, that you have not recently been informed regarding the establishment at Niagara, I crave the honor of telling you as to the condition of the house when I left there, and such news as I learned on my way.
>
> I set out from Niagara the 8th of this month. The works would have been finished by this time, had not frequent rains and the violent fevers which attacked nearly all our workmen, long delayed their completion.
>
> There remained yet twelve or fifteen days' work of masonry to do, and there is reason to fear that the timber framework is not yet ready to put up. Whatever diligence M. de Longueuil may have been able to use, he could not procure planks enough to cover it.

The letter continues with a graphic account of negotiations between the English and the Iroquois, as it was reported to Captain de Noyan at Fort Frontenac. It is but another version of the unsuccessful negotiations of Peter Schuyler — this time disguised in the old French as " Joan Sckuila." " You know," Schuyler is reported to have harangued to the tribes, " you know that the French are building a fort at Niagara in order to reduce you to slavery — and you are resting with your arms crossed. What are you thinking of? We are all dead, brothers, you and I, if we do not prevent our loss by the destruction of this building. Look at these barques, which will carry you off captive. It is for you to say whether they have been built by your consent." And after listening to more

---

[9] The copy of M. de Noyan's letter which I have followed in the Archives office at Ottawa, bears date Feb. 22, 1726. The original obviously was written some months later than that, probably in September. The old form of indicating September —" 7bre "— may very likely have been misread by a copyist. September 22d also accords with the date of a report by de Noyan, given in an abstract of despatches relating to Niagara.—N. Y. Col. Docs., IX, 978.

"A HOUSE OF PEACE"

in like strain, the Indians returned Schuyler's wampum belt, and replied with cool sarcasm that he always said the same thing to them. " Yes," they added, " it is we who have desired these boats, we consented to what our son [M. de Longueuil] asked of us, we repent of nothing. . . . It is a thing done. We have given our word."

It was at this council that Schuyler asked the consent of the Five Nations for the English to build a trading-house opposite the French post [" *bâtir aussi à Niagara une maison vis-à-vis celle de votre Père* "] ; but to this proposition they returned the wampum, saying they would have nothing to do with it, and Schuyler could arrange as best he might with " Onontio." There is a triumphant tone in Captain de Noyan's letter, reporting this defeat of the English at so critical a time. English enmity now centered on Joncaire, who was regarded as the chief instrument of their discomfiture. It was reported that certain Seneca chiefs were bribed to make way with him. One of the few letters written by Joncaire which are preserved, was written at the end of 1726, at Fort Niagara, apparently to his friend the younger Longueuil, then commanding at Fort Frontenac. It runs in part as follows:

NIAGARA, 26 December, 1726.

I am obliged to you for the notice which you gave me by your letter of December 28th, concerning the council which was held between the Iroquois nations and the Governors of Boston and New York.

Tagariuoghen, chief of the Sault Ste. Louis, and one named Alexis, chief of the Lake of the Two Mountains, have just acknowledged to us the design of the English, and the promises which the Iroquois made to them, concerning the house at Niagara, and me. I learned the same thing toward the end of November at the Seneca village where I had gone, after giving the necessary orders for the Niagara garrison, to reply to a belt which the Iroquois had sent to the Governor at Montreal.

I found in this village only coldness towards us and any good words which I could say to them were scarcely listened to. The next night, toward midnight, they wakened me for a council; and being come there, they begged me to treat peaceably with them, that there was no need of heat on the part of any of us.

First, they said, the house at Niagara did not please them; that they strongly suspected that it was only the Onondagas who consented to its construction, and that the four other nations had no part in it.

Second, that M. de Longueuil had promised to make a present of three barrels of powder and a proportion of balls to each nation, but they had seen nothing of all that.

They held out to me a belt for these things, but I would not touch it, and contented myself with telling them that their belt was a rattlesnake which would bite me if I took it in my hand, and that moreover their father Onontio had sent me to Niagara to listen to good words and not to bad.

As to the house in question, it was the strongest pillar of the five Iroquois nations, since M. de Longueuil had intended in making it to deliver them from the slavery in which they had for a long time been. But [I said], as I saw that I was speaking to deaf men, I told them that they might make their speeches to people who knew how to answer. The Iroquois replied:

"We hear you. You say that we should address Onontio. That was indeed our first thought, for our resolution is made for next spring."

The next day I noised it about that I saw clearly that their minds were divided, but that I hoped that they would find for us, as much as for the English, and that it was useless for them to talk to me of abandoning the building ("*de vider le plancher*"), they could be assured that I should not quit Niagara until they had cut my body to pieces to give pleasure to the English — and that even then they would have to deal with people who would come to look after my bones. I have still a trick ("*un plat de mon métier*") to show them in the spring — I put it aside till then, since my emissaries are not at the village, and whether it succeeds or not I shall promptly send my two oldest sons to Montreal to inform my superiors of the state of affairs in this country.

One must restrain the Iroquois [? Senecas] in every way in this present affair, but it is necessary to interpose the Onondagas, and say to the Iroquois nations: Since when do you make no longer one body with the Onondagas? You have told us every year that what one Iroquois nation does or says, all the others agree to. Since when is all that changed? How comes it that when the English ask you which nation it was that gave permission to the French to build at Niagara, that in the presence of you all the Onondaga replied fiercely, " It was I." How happens it that you did not dispute this before the English?

After all, I hope that the Holy Spirit which commonly gives to those who govern the State more light than to others, will furnish enough means to our superiors to confound the Iroquois and so reëstablish peace.

As for me, trust to my looking out for myself against the assassination which the English have at all times wished to accomplish. Whoever undertakes it will have half the risk. I will serve him as they do in Valenciennes.

I beg you to communicate what I send you to Messieurs de Beauharnois, to the Intendant, and to our Governor at Montreal, and above all to so inform M. de Longueuil that he will be assured of the care which I take in the present affair.

A little later Joncaire wrote again to the younger de Longueuil at Fort Frontenac:

". . . Inform our superiors of what has happened to me in this country. It is for them to direct what I should say and do. The Iroquois will go down to Montreal next spring to demand that we pull down the house at Niagara. If they destroy it," adds Joncaire with a fine touch of the Gascon, " it will only be when I, at the head of my garrison, shall have crossed in Charon's barque — I shall show them the road to victory or to the tomb." Nevertheless, he adds the fervent hope: " May God change the hearts of those who are against us."

It was not until the end of another season — October 17, 1727 — that Chaussegros de Léry reported to the Minister that the house at Niagara was entirely finished, surrounded with palisades and furnished with a guard-house to prevent surprise by the savages. Referring to the English at Oswego, he could not refrain from calling attention to the fact that events had justified his choice of site for Fort Niagara: " The English are established at the mouth of Oswego River, they have built a little fortified work [" *petite redoubt à machicoulis* "] and keep a garrison there. The French have always been masters of this post and of the south side of Lake Ontario. If they had built the stone house as proposed at the portage, it is certain that the English would have made another on Lake Ontario. This house at the portage appears to me useless. The old one, with some small repairs, will serve yet some years." He adds that if he "had been the master" the last year it would have been easy for him to establish the French at Oswego as well as at Niagara; evidently forgetting for the moment that he had not established the French anywhere, however satisfactory from an engineering point of view his services on the Niagara had proved. Our study of the documents makes clear that Fort Niagara was made possible, under the encouraging policy of Vaudreuil, only by the devotion and personal influence of the younger de Longueuil and the elder Chabert de Joncaire.

Left to themselves, without provocation from the English, the Senecas and neighboring tribes would have found Fort Niagara a blessing. They did indeed, so find it for a good many years. At a conference between Beauharnois and the Onondagas, August 19, 1734, the Indians spoke of the goodness of the French Governor in sending Joncaire [10] to them. In the same speech the Onondaga orator, holding out a wampum belt, said:

"Father, here is an old message we bring back to you. It was given to the Five Iroquois Nations, nine years ago, by our late son, Longueuil, when the house at Niagara was built. He promised that it would be a House of Peace for us and for our children, down to the third generation and farther; he assured us also, that we should enjoy the peace that he attached to that House. Nothing afforded us more pleasure, and we pray you to give us assurance of the promise, by renewing it to us."

"I assure you," replied the Governor, "that the House at Niagara will be a House of Peace for you and your children, as long as you please."

[10] Philippe Thomas, eldest son of the Joncaire whose story we have traced.

CHAPTER XIV

A TROUBLESOME TREATY

POLITICAL ASPECT OF THE STRIFE ON THE NIAGARA — THE TACTFUL COURSE OF GOVERNOR BURNET — FORT NIAGARA AND THE FUR TRADE — INCIDENTS OF A PICTURESQUE TRAFFIC.

WHAT may be termed the political situation in the country of the Six Nations, and especially among the Senecas who kept the Western Door of the Long House, in the years from the building of Joncaire's house at Lewiston to the construction and garrisoning of Fort Niagara, 1720–26, admirably illustrates the difficulty of treating with the Indian. Even the noble Iroquois was fickle, given to double-dealing; yet it was a duplicity inherent in a lower degree of social development than that from which his Caucasian tempters approached him. The wisest of their sachems were statesmen in some matters, children in others. The Senecas adopted Joncaire according to their ancient custom, and through him gave the French their foothold on the Niagara. At the same time, tempted by the trade inducements of the English, they helped the Western tribes to go to Albany, to the confusion of the French, and allowed the English to get and to keep a footing in their own territory.

So matters continued until Longueuil, by his *coup de maître* of 1725, gained permission in a council at Onondaga to build what soon proved to be a fort, in Seneca territory. We have already traced the steps of that construction, as recorded in the reports of the French. When Burnet heard of it, as he speedily did, down in New York, he may well have wondered what all his fair speeches to the Indians had accomplished, what all the tiresome councils had amounted to, of what avail the many lavish gifts.

At the September council at Albany in 1726 he took the tribes to task. How is it, he demanded, have you given your consent to the French, to build this house at Niagara? The answer was characteristic, but far from satisfactory. One Ajewachtha, an Onondaga sachem, was the mouthpiece for the occasion. When Longueuil was among the Onondagas last year, said the sachem, the Senecas heard what his errand was, and "sent a Belt of Wampum, . . . that in case the French should desire to make any Building or Settlement at Niagara or at Ochsweeke [1] or elsewhere on land, they should not give their consent to it. . . . The Onondagas being prevail'd upon by Fair speeches and promises, rejected the Sinnekes belt, and gave the French leave for building at Niagara." De Longueuil, the sachem added, had promised that the French would protect them for three hundred years.

Did the land at Niagara, asked Governor Burnet, belong to the Onondagas, or to the Senecas, or to all the Six Nations?

The Seneca sachem, Kanaharighton, replied that it belonged to the Senecas particularly.

Do the sachems of the other Five Nations acknowledge that?

They all said it did; not only the land at Niagara belonged to the Senecas, but the land opposite it, on the other side of Lake Ontario.

What business then, asked Burnet, had the Onondagas to grant the French permission to build there, when the land belonged only to the Senecas?

"The Onondagas say it is true they have done wrong, they might better have left it alone and have left it to the Sinnekes whose Land it is, they repent of it and say that People often do what they afterwards repent of."

The Onondaga further explained that the consent which had been given by his people, without leave of the other nations, was in accordance with their old customs; one nation often spoke in the name of all the rest in the League. If the others afterwards approved of it, it was well; if any of them disapproved, the pledge was void. The Six Nations had sent Seneca and Onondaga sachems with a belt of wampum to the French at Fort Niagara, to protest against the proceedings

---

[1] "Called by the French *Lac Erié*."—Marginal note in New York Council Minutes, XV, 87.

A TROUBLESOME TREATY

and ordering the work to stop. But the French had not the red man's regard for the talking belts. We can not stop work, they said, with what show of gravity and regret may be imagined; "being sent and order'd by the Governour of Canada to build it," they "durst not desist from working." But they readily promised that Joncaire, who was soon going to Montreal, should inform the Governor that the Six Nations wished the work stopped; "he would bring back an Answer at Onondaga by the latter end of September (when the Indian corn was ripe), and then they threw their Belt back and rejected it by which they had spoke, and said they thought they were sent by the Govr of New York, on which they [the sachems] replyed that they were not sent by him, but by the Sachims of the Six Nations, and did not know who had given the French that liberty, that they did not know it, and desired that they would name the Sachims who had given their leave, on which they [the French] did not reply, but said that when the House was finished 30 souldiers would be posted there with Officers and a Priest."

This and much more the Indians told Governor Burnet. In the same breath, the Onondagas took all the blame to themselves, and charged the French with perfidy. The Governor adroitly explained to them that France and England were at peace, and gave them to understand that it was not the English, but the Six Nations, whose interests were threatened by the new fort at the mouth of the Niagara. He read to them that portion of the Treaty of Utrecht which bore on the matter. The chief question, he gravely pointed out, was, whether the fort was prejudicial to them in their hunting, or to the Western Indians who might wish to come for trade. If they said it was not, His Excellency had nothing to say, and the French had done well; but if the Six Nations found it prejudicial to their interests, and complained of it to him, he would lay the matter before the English King. The Indians replied:

"Brother Corlaer, . . . you ask if we approve of the building at Niagara; we do not only complain against the proceedings of the French in fortifying Niagara on our Land contrary to our inclination and without our consent, to pen us up from our chief hunting-place, but we also humbly beg and desire that Your Excell: will be pleased to write to His Majesty King George that he may have compassion on us, and write to the King of France to order his Governour of Canada to remove the building at Niagara, for we think it very prejudicial to us all." And this the Governor agreed to do.

Nothing could be finer than the temper and adroitness with which Burnet conducted this matter. At the opening of the conference his attitude was that of accuser, of one deeply wronged; the attitude of the Indians that of culprits and deceivers. This aspect of their relations was quickly annulled by the calm, judicial air which the Governor gave to his inquiries. With rare insight into Indian character, he so presented the case that they became the wronged parties, the French the sole offenders, and himself merely the gracious friend who sought to do all he could in their behalf.

This conference was held on September 7th. Two days later, the Governor made a long, impressive speech to the sachems. He reviewed the relations of the Five Nations to the French from the earliest days, not failing to show that the latter had been constant aggressors and treacherous enemies, and he pictured the building of the fort at Niagara as a new affront, which endangered the very existence of the Confederacy. His words had their intended effect. The sachems renewed their protestations, in terms of singular earnestness. "We speak now," said Kanackarighton, the Seneca, "in the name of all the Six Nations and come to you howling. This is the reason for what we howl, that the Governor of Canada incroaches on our land and builds thereon, therefore do we come to Your Excellency, our Brother Corlaer, and desire you will be pleased to write to the great King, your Master, and if Our King will then be pleased to write to the King of France, that the Six Nations desire that the Fort at Niagara may be demolished. This Belt we give to you, Our Brother [Corlaer], as a token that you be not negligent to write to the King, the sooner the better, and desire that the letter may be writ very pressing."

Not the least gratifying point to the Governor in this

harangue was the expression " *our* King." The treaty commissioners at Utrecht, thirteen years before, had agreed that the New York Indians were subjects of Great Britain; but the Indians themselves were sometimes provokingly oblivious of the relationship.

Governor Burnet took advantage of the complaisant and suppliant mood of the sachems to suggest that, since they were asking the King of Great Britain to protect them in their own lands, it would be most proper " to submit and give up all their hunting Country to the King, and to sign a deed for it," as it had been proposed to do twenty-five years before. He intimated that had it been done then, they would have had a fuller measure of protection from the English. After consultations, the proposition was accepted, and the deed of trust, which had been executed July 19, 1701, was confirmed and signed by Seneca, Cayuga and Onondaga sachems. Thus at Albany, September 14, 1726, in the thirteenth year of George I, was deeded to the English, a sixty-mile strip along the south shore of Lake Ontario, reaching to and including the entire Niagara frontier.

The mighty League of the Iroquois had atoned for their blunder of letting the French build Fort Niagara in their domain, by giving it to King George. From this time on the " stone house " was on British soil; but it was yet to take the new owner a generation to dispossess the obnoxious tenant.

The Albany conferences ended, after the usual gift-giving and feasting, the Iroquois deputies leisurely departed by trail and river, to their several seats to the westward. Burnet journeyed down to New York, where on September 27th he made report to the Council at Fort George, of all he had concerted with the Six Nations. " I flatter myself," he said, " that I have contributed not a little to fix them in their duty to his Majesty, their affection to this Government, and their just apprehensions of the ill designs of the people of Canada in fortifying so near to them at Iagara." [2] The next winter he sent a man to live among the Senecas, but not to trade with them. Whoever this representative was, or what his success,

[2] Journal, Legislative Council; reprint, Albany, 1861, p. 539.

he counted but little against the activities of Joncaire. A year later (September 30, 1727), Burnet assured the Council that this agent had been "very active . . . that pressing instances might be made at the Court of France against the stone house at Niagara."[3]

The fifteenth Article of the Treaty of Utrecht is as follows:

> The subjects of France inhabiting Canada, and others, shall in future give no hindrance or molestation to the Five Nations or Cantons of Indians, subject to the Dominion of Great Britain, nor to the other natives of America who are in friendly alliance with them. In like manner, the subjects of Great Britain shall behave themselves peaceably towards the Americans who are subjects or friends of France, and they shall enjoy, on both sides, full liberty of resort for purposes of Trade. Also the natives of these countries shall, with equal freedom, resort, as they please, to the British and French Colonies, for promoting trade on one side and the other, without any molestation or hindrance on the part either of British or French subjects; but who are, and who ought to be, accounted subjects and friends of Britain or of France is a matter to be accurately and distinctly settled by Commissioners.

This was assented to by the representatives of England and of France, who signed the treaty of which it is a part, at Utrecht, April 11, 1713. In due time it was promulgated in the Colonies. England in the Valley of the Mohawk, and France on the Great Lakes, were at work, with such seductive influences as they could exert, for the friendship of the savages and a greater profit from the fur trade. It was not, however, until Joncaire's cabin stood at the foot of the Niagara rapids, that the English took genuine alarm at what they regarded as the impudent encroachment of the French, and fell back upon the terms of the treaty for a definition of rights.

It has been related, that in 1721 Governor Burnet made a spirited protest against the establishment of Joncaire's trading house, of which Vaudreuil had made an equally spirited, but not equally logical, defense. Protests of this sort being so obviously of no avail, correspondence on the subject between the

[3] *Ib.*, p. 555.

Governors seems to have ceased. But when word reached Burnet of the new fort at the mouth of the river his ire was kindled afresh. On July 5, 1726, he wrote to M. de Longueuil, then acting Governor, pending the arrival of Beauharnois, a vigorous, but by no means offensive letter on the subject. He had learned, he wrote, that about a hundred Frenchmen were at Niagara, commencing the erection of a fort, " with the design of shutting in the Five Nations, and preventing the free passage of the other Indians at that point to trade with us as they have been in the habit of doing." He expressed his surprise that the French should undertake a project so obviously an infraction of the Treaty of Utrecht; denied that La Salle's brief occupancy of the region gave the French any rights, and reminded the Governor that the lands at Niagara belonged to the Five Nations. " Should the fortifying Niagara be continued," he added in conclusion, " I shall be under the necessity of representing the matter to my Superiors, in order that the Court of France, being well informed of the fact, may give its opinion thereupon; as I have heard that it has already expressed its disapprobation of the part Mr. de Vaudreuil took in the War of the Abenaquis against New England." [4]

Burnet sent his friend Philip Livingston, of the Colonial Council, to Montreal with this letter, and begged of M. de Longueuil considerate treatment of the messenger. The messenger was well enough received, but the reply which the Canadian soldier sent back, under date of August 16th, was far from apologetic. " Permit me, Sir, to inform you," it ran, " that it is not my intention to shut in the Five Iroquois Nations, as you pretend, and that I do not think I contravene the Utrecht Treaty of Peace in executing my orders from the Court of France, respecting the reëstablishment of the Niagara

[4] French translations of several of Burnet's letters are preserved in the *Correspondance Générale;* also a translation of a letter relating to Niagara, from the Duke of Newcastle to Walpole, dated " Vitchall " [Whitehall], May 15, 1726; and the various memoirs regarding Niagara which were prepared during the discussion; one of them makes 20 closely-written folio pages, in the Canadian Archives transcript. Their purport is sufficiently shown in our narrative.

post, whereof we have been the masters from all time. The Five Nations, who are neither your subjects nor ours, ought to be much obliged to you to take upon you an uneasiness they never felt, inasmuch as, so far from considering that the establishment at Niagara may prove a source of trouble to them, they were parties to it by a unanimous consent, and have again confirmed it in the last Council holden at Niagara, on the 14th of July last."

De Longueuil, it will be observed, squarely contradicted the clause in the treaty which declared the Five Nations to be " subject to the dominion of Great Britain." His audacity was symbolical of the entire policy of France on the wilderness frontiers at this period. This feature of Baron de Longueuil's reply may well have surprised the English Governor. It would, no doubt, have surprised him still more had Longueuil meekly yielded to his demands, and promised to leave the Niagara. It was to be expected that he would base the French claim on the flimsy pretext of continuous right from La Salle's day; but that, in addition to this claim, he should have the effrontery to deny and defy the plain declaration of the treaty, was matter for amazement.

As we have seen, at the Albany conferences with the Indians, in September, Burnet had promised to lay the case — their case, as he made it appear to them — before the King. With his unfruitful correspondence with Longueuil fresh in mind he was more than willing to do so. Before the close of the year — presumably by the first ship that served, which happened to be the *Old Beaver*, Mathew Smith, master,— he dispatched long letters on the subject, both to the Lords of Trade and to the Duke of Newcastle, King George's Secretary of State. For the edification of the former, he rehearsed at length all that had taken place; told of the action taken at the conferences with the Indians; exulted a little, as was natural, in announcing that they had signed a deed surrendering the land they lived in to the British Crown; and enclosed a copy of the deed with this explanation of the fact that it was signed by only three of the nations: " The Maquese [Mohawks] and Oneydes live nearest to us, and do not reach to

A TROUBLESOME TREATY 259

the French lake, and therefore there was no occasion to mention the matter to them, and if I had proposed it publickly to them, it might soon have been known by the French, and have produced some new enterprize of theirs, so that I thought it best to do it with a few of the chief and most trusty of the three nations who border upon the Lakes."

He sent to the Lords copies of his correspondence with Longueuil, and called especial attention to that officer's denial of the Treaty. "The Treaty says," wrote Burnet, "'*The five Nations or Cantons of Indians, subject to the Dominion of Great Britain.*' Mr. De Longueuil denys it expressly and says, '*Les cinq Nations qui ne sont ny vos Sujets ny les Nôtres.*' The Five Nations who are neither your Subjects nor ours." He pointed out the other aggravating and inconsistent features of Longueuil's letter.

To His Grace the Duke the Governor made a more concise but equally strenuous report, adding his "most earnest application" that Newcastle would "obtain His Majesty's directions, that strong instances may be made at the Court of France for this purpose, which I hope will be successful at a time when there is so firm an alliance between the two Crowns. . . . This is a matter of such consequence to His Majesty's Dominions in North America that I humbly rely on Your Grace's obtaining such a redress, as the Treaty entitles this Province and the Six Nations to, from the French, which can be [no] less than a demolition of this fort at Niagara." [5]

The Duke of Newcastle put the whole matter into the hands of Horatio Walpole, with instructions from King George that he should present it "in its full light" to the Ministers of the Court of France, "and to use all the necessary arguments to prevail on them to dispatch orders to the officer commanding in Canada to demolish that fort, and His Majesty doubts not but they will comply as soon as they shall be informed precisely of the state of this affair." [6] Walpole prepared a memoir on Fort Niagara which he submitted, May 9, 1727, to

[5] Burnet to the Duke of Newcastle, N. Y., Dec. 4, 1726.
[6] Duke of Newcastle to the Hon. Horatio Walpole, Whitehall, April 11, 1727.

the aged Cardinal de Fleury, Prime Minister of France.[7] In it he rehearsed at length the grievances which Burnet had communicated. Beyond the employment of a more polished style, Walpole's memoir on Niagara added nothing to the facts or the arguments as we have already reviewed them. At the end of his recital of facts, Walpole added the following:

It is to be remarked, that the Nations in question are formally acknowledged, by the Treaty of Utrecht, to be subject to and under Great Britain, and in virtue of the same Treaty they and all the Indians are to enjoy full liberty of coming and going for the purpose of trade, without molestation or hindrance. Now, the pass at Niagara is that by which the Far Indians are able to repair to the country of the Five Nations, and also the only one by which the Five Nations themselves can go into their own territory to hunt; and in spite of the benevolent and innocent views Sieur de Longueuil pretends to entertain in building such a fort, the Indians cannot be reputed to enjoy free trade and passage so long as they are bridled by a fort built on their own territory, against their will, and which absolutely subjects them to the pleasure of the French, wherefore they have recourse to their Sovereign and King, the King of Great Britain, who cannot refuse to interest himself strongly, as well on account of these subjects as for the maintenance of Treaties.

In this smooth, featureless form, the innocuous phrases of a somewhat perfunctory diplomacy, Louis XV received the English protest against the building of Fort Niagara — that protest for which the Iroquois' sachems had gone to Albany "howling," and which they had begged should be "writ very pressing." Kanackarighton, the daubed and greasy Seneca, and Horatio Walpole, the courtier, were vastly farther apart than even the Court of France and the Niagara wilderness — of which it is plain Walpole's ideas were of the vaguest. Many a forest ranger would have laughed at his claim that the fort at the mouth of the Niagara kept the Senecas from their hunting grounds. The germ of this specious plea lay in Burnet's benevolent suggestion to the Senecas, but it helped make a case

[7] De Fleury, formerly preceptor to the King, in 1726 succeeded the Duke de Bourbon Condé as Prime Minister of France, being then seventy-three years old. He lived until January, 1743.

A TROUBLESOME TREATY

against the French, and there were few either at Whitehall or the Court of Louis competent to criticise or likely to question it. Indeed, had the red Indians themselves made their "howl" before the French King and his Ministers, the result, beyond the infinite diversion which they would have made, would scarcely have been different. Even while the English protest was taking its official course, Louis and his Ministers were affirming that "the post at Niagara is of the utmost importance for the preservation to the French of the trade to the upper country," and were considering the amounts to be spent on "the reconstruction of the old house at Niagara [Joncaire's *Magazin Royal*], the expense whereof, amounting to 20,430 li, may be placed on the estimate of the expenses payable in 1728 by the Domain of the West."[8]

King George I died June 11, 1727; and, in Canada, in 1726, the Marquis de Beauharnois had succeeded the Baron de Longueuil; but the Niagara contention continued. Burnet in the spring of 1726 having built and fortified a stone house at Oswego, the new Governor of Canada at once assumed the aggressive; sent a formal summons to Burnet to withdraw his garrison thence within a fortnight, and "to cast down the block house and all pieces of work you raised up contrary to righteousness," "or else His Lordship the Marquis of Beauharnois will take measures against you and against your unjust usurpation as he will think fit." With a fine solicitude for a rigid adherence to the Treaty of 1713, the humor of which must even then have shown itself to Burnet, if not to Beauharnois, the French Governor accused the English Governor of "a plain contravention to the Treaty of Utrecht, which mentions that the subjects of the two Crowns shall not intrench upon one another's land, till the decision of the limits by the judges delegated to that end"— a decision which was never made, for the commissioners contemplated by the 15th Article of the Treaty were never appointed. The English contention, as afterwards formulated by Walpole in his memoir

[8] Abstract of Despatches relating to Oswego and Niagara, N. Y. Col. Docs., IX, 979. The remark quoted above, on Niagara's importance, is a note by the King himself.

on Fort Oswego, was that their fortification at that point was no violation of the treaty, "since the Commissioners to be named would have nothing to determine relative to the countries of the Five Nations, who are already declared by the Treaty of Utrecht to be subjects to the Crown of England." This was a perfectly just deduction from the obvious intent of the treaty.

Burnet replied to the arrogant demand of Beauharnois with his usual spirit and good sense; reminding him that when he (Burnet) had protested against the operations of the French at Niagara, he had been content with writing to Court, for the English Ambassador to make dignified and decorous presentation at the Court of France: "I did not send any summons to Niagara, I did not make any warlike preparations to interrupt the work, and I did not stir up the Five Nations to make use of force to demolish it, which I might have done easily enough." In a long letter, he defended his right, under the treaty, to build at Oswego, and denied again the right of the French to occupy Niagara: "It is true, sir, that I have ordered a stone house to be built there [at the mouth of the Oswego], with some contrivances to hinder its being surprised, and that I have posted some souldiers in it, but that which gave me the first thought of it, was the fortified and much larger house which the French have built at Niagara, upon the lands of the Five Nations."

In due time report of this correspondence reached the Lord Commissioners of Trade. Under date of December 21, 1727, they referred it all once more to Newcastle; and His Grace in turn placed it in the hands of Horatio Walpole. Recalling the memoir on the subject of Fort Niagara which Walpole had made the year before, Newcastle wrote to him:

Both that Memoir and his Eminence's answer to you, promising to give orders to examine this matter, and to decide according to justice, led us to expect that there would not be any more cause for complaint, but as, instead of seeing it remedied, His Majesty has been advised that the French think of encroaching still further on the countries under his obedience in said quarter, he has deemed it expedient that you again apply to the Court of France to induce it

A TROUBLESOME TREATY 263

to transmit the most precise orders to the Governor of Canada to abstain from attempting anything contrary to the Treaties, so that all these differences between the subjects of the two Crowns may be terminated in such a manner that the Indians may visit each other without molestation, and the Five Nations receive such encouragement and protection from His Majesty as they must naturally expect from their Sovereign.[9]

The result of these instructions was Walpole's memoir on Oswego, laid before the Prime Minister of France, March 9, 1728.

The 15th Article of the Utrecht Treaty continued a fruitful source of disagreement for many years to come. In 1748 we find Governor Clinton of New York carrying on an epistolary dispute with La Galissonière, who had succeeded de Beauharnois, over this same debatable Article. The French Governor had his own interpretation of it, alleging that it " does not name the Iroquois, and though it did so, it would be null in their regard, since they never acquiesced therein: we have always regarded them as Allies in common of the English and French, and they do not look on themselves in any other light." " You are misinformed," replied Clinton, " for they have done it [i.e. submitted themselves to Great Britain] in a solemn manner, and their subjection has been likewise acknowledged by the Crown of France in the Treaty of Utrecht."[10] This disparity of view between the two countries continued as long as France held Canada.

For a decade and more following the building of the new fort, Joncaire the elder continued active in matters relating to the interests of the Niagara. He was not military commandant, except apparently for a short period; nor was he in charge of barter with the Indians at that post. Coming and going, now at the Seneca villages, now at Niagara, or again at his home in Montreal, he continued in the military service, but always charged with the special duty, which ac-

[9] Newcastle to Walpole. The letter as printed in N. Y. Col. Docs., IX, 959, is dated "Whitehall, 16th May (O. S.), 1726," but the year should be 1728.
[10] Clinton to La Galissonière, Fort George in New York, Oct. 10, 1748.

corded well with his frequent service of interpreter, of cultivating cordial relations with the Senecas, and of reporting on the movements of the English — duties in which later on his eldest son is to succeed him, when the father is assigned to a new field of activity.

From the day when Chaussegros de Léry broke ground for the great stone building at the angle of lake and river, life on the Niagara became more and more complex. The building operations drew thither hordes of curious and jealous Indians. The trading-post at present Lewiston was still maintained, and in its neighborhood, at the foot of the portage, as well as at the head of the long carry, were settlements of the Senecas, many of whom found profitable employment in helping traders and travelers up and down the steep hills. Although the Mississaugas had not yet made their village across the Niagara from the new fort, they made temporary camp there and haunted the region in numbers during this busy summer. However deserted and desolate these lake and river shores may have been when winter shut down, and the wolf's long howl at the edge of the forest answered the west wind in its sweep over the bleak lake, there was varied life and activity when the ice broke up. Then came endless flotillas of bark canoes, loaded with peltries. The fur trade was old, long before the stone house at Niagara was built. Into the general history and conditions of that trade, it is unnecessary to go in these chapters. But certain features of that trade, and of the attendant life, heretofore unrecorded save in the long-neglected documents, may profitably be set down here in illustration of the conditions of the time on the Niagara and the Lower Lakes.

The great purpose of the French in building the new fort on the Niagara was to regain the fur trade which was fast slipping from them into the hands of the English. The strategic advantage of the military occupation of the strait was not overlooked; but it was far less by way of preparation for a future contest at arms with England, than to secure purely commercial advantage, that the work was undertaken. And, from the French point of view, it was high time that something decisive be done. More and more the Western tribes,

A TROUBLESOME TREATY

who ravaged the great beaver-bearing grounds of the upper lake region, were being drawn to Oswego and Albany by the superior allurements of the English. Longueuil, reporting to his father the baron concerning his Onondaga mission of 1725, wrote that he had seen more than a hundred canoes on Lake Ontario, making their way to Oswego. How to stop this trade was a matter of grave consequence to Canada. Returning from Onondaga, he had encountered many canoes, propelled by Nipissings and Sauteurs from the Huron regions, making their way into Lake Ontario by the Toronto River, and all headed for the mouth of the Oswego. The new barques, he reflected, should stop this. The Baron de Longueuil, in reporting his son's discoveries, added the further information that sixteen Englishmen had gone to trade at the Niagara portage, " where they appear to have wintered, having taken there a large quantity of merchandise. They even came within a day and a half of Frontenac, and have drawn to them by their brandy nearly all the savages, which has done so great an injury to the trade of these two posts that they will not produce this year a half of their usual amount." The French at this time heard some things that were not so. There are many reports that the English intended to establish themselves at Niagara; such rumors had been current at Montreal and Quebec ever since 1720, when the English had proposed to put horses on the Niagara portage; the profits of that enterprise were to be shared with a Seneca chief who was to represent the English. But that project came to naught, nor is there convincing proof that the English, either in 1720, 1725, or at any other time, were on the Niagara in trade, during the French occupancy.

More credible, however, was the further news, gathered by the younger Longueuil in this momentous summer of 1725, that English and Dutch traders at Albany had bought 200 bark canoes from the Ottawas and Mississaugas, tribes which at this period carried most of their peltries to the British. Longueuil saw more than sixty of these canoes, making the Oswego portage. It looked to him as though the English were bent on pushing into the upper country and utterly destroying the French trade, "or to come in superior number to Niagara to make an establishment there, and to prevent that which we plan to do." Longueuil took his hundred soldiers to Niagara in the summer of 1726, not more to employ them as laborers on the stone house, than to patrol the lake and to stop the English canoes which were fully expected to swarm down upon them. The English did not come, but the hundred soldiers were maintained there, apparently, a year or more. Their return to Quebec is noted under date of September 25, 1727.

The French did what they could to check the growing English trade. *Voyageurs* passing through Lake Ontario were commanded to follow the north shore, from Frontenac to Niagara. If found near Oswego, they were liable to seizure and confiscation. In 1729, this order was renewed, emanating from the King himself, and the commandant at Fort Frontenac was cautioned to enforce it. It was proposed that two canoes, carrying trustworthy men, should cruise on the lake and intercept any traders headed for Oswego. In the spring of 1736, Beauvais, commandant at Fort Frontenac, learned that two traders, Duplessis and Deniau, were making for Oswego. Alphonse de Tonty was sent after them. He overtook them four leagues from the mouth of the Oswego River, confiscated the 300 pounds of beaver in their canoe, and carried them back to Frontenac, whence they were sent to Montreal and imprisoned. After a trial and fine of 500 livres each, which they were too poor to pay, they were further imprisoned for three months. The hope was expressed in the dispatches that this example would "always restrain those who might be inclined to drive a fraudulent trade."

At Niagara Captain de Rigauville, whose command of that garrison extended over several troubled years, exerted himself constantly to keep traders from passing along the south shore of the lake. His faithful services at Niagara won for him special recognition in the dispatches. In 1733 promotion was asked for him; but we find him, some years later, still in the same rank and at the same post.

France and England being nominally at peace, the Cana-

A TROUBLESOME TREATY 267

dian officials were wary when it came to actual conflict with their adversaries in trade; they showed a wholesome respect for the English ability and willingness to come to blows; but armed strife would have availed them nothing in the circumstances. The main thing was to draw the Indians. To this end, the Government was urged, time after time, in the annual and special reports of the Governor and Intendant, to provide ample store of goods for Fort Niagara. In 1728, the Minister is specially begged to send goods in great abundance to the new house at Niagara, that the Indians may be kept from going to the English. Year after year this request is repeated in the dispatches. Occasionally the Indians found fault with the quality of the *écarlatines* [11] supplied by the French, or with the price in barter; but the one thing that killed the fur trade at Fort Niagara was the restriction put on the sale of brandy. A report of 1735 says, of the trade at Niagara and Frontenac, that it becomes yearly less and less, in proportion to the expenses incurred for it by the Crown. "These two posts, which some years before had produced 52,000 li. of peltries, for the past four years yielded only 25,000 to 35,000 li." All this loss was charged to the cessation of the brandy supply. The priests were reported to have refused to confess any one engaged in trading brandy to the Indians, and the storekeepers at Niagara and Frontenac were so disturbed by the decree of the bishop, forbidding the traffic, that they preferred to relinquish their posts rather than fall under the ban of the church as a *cas reservé*.[12] Beauharnois, mournfully reviewing the situation, admitted that it was difficult to let the savages have brandy and keep them from getting drunk, "but it is equally certain that nothing so keeps them from trading with the French as the refusal to let them have liquor, for which they have an inexpressible passion." Two years later we read that the trade at Niagara and Fron-

[11] *Ecarlatines, i. e.,* scarlatines, as some of the old records have it; probably coarse woolen stuff. *Cf. écarlates,* an old word for hose or legging. Not to be confused with *écarlate* ("scarlet"), for some *écarlatines* were blue.

[12] *Cas reservé,* a grave offense, decision in which is reserved for the bishop or other superior officer of the Church.

tenac is no better. "The suppression of the brandy trade, added to the bad quality of *écarlatines* and low price of beaver, disgust the Indians who come there to trade — they pass on to Oswego." And still later, in 1740, the Sieur Boucherville, then recently in command of the garrison at Niagara, gave several reasons to the Intendant, Hocquart, to show why trade was so bad at that post. First, he said, for several years past the brandy trade had been forbidden at Niagara; and every year there came down from the upper country many canoes loaded with beaver and deer skins, but if on reaching Niagara the Indians could not get brandy they would not part with their peltries, but continued on to Oswego. Besides that, Indian traders in the pay of the English constantly intercepted the hunters as they came from the west and north, securing their peltries and effectively blocking the opportunities for trade with the French at Niagara.

The Intendant consulted with the Minister at Versailles as to what might be done; but that dignitary was able to suggest nothing more effective than to send messages to the chiefs of the Mohawks, the Oneidas, and the Onondagas, who were the intermediary agents of the English, that they must cease favoring the English trade, or their canoes would be stopped and pillaged. M. de Beaucourt was sent to a council at Onondaga, charged with this delicate mission. The assembled chiefs listened, apparently in complacent humor, and sent him away with the equivocal assurance that they would spread his words among the villages.

In 1740 the Sieur Michael (sometimes written "St. Michael") succeeded Boucherville as commandant at Fort Niagara, being sent there because of his supposed ability to build up trade; but in official circles at Quebec, as no doubt generally in the gossip of the day, the opinion prevailed that if the fur trade at Fort Niagara was to flourish the amount of the annual lease should be reapportioned with regard to the traffic;.and be accompanied by a freer dispensation of brandy.

The fur trade at the posts was carried on in two ways; either by lease (*bail*), the Intendant giving lease-hold to the highest and best bidder for the trade of a post, and the rent giving the exclusive rights to the lessee throughout the extent of his post; or by permits (*congé*), the Governor granting permissions to trade in certain forts. These permits were granted in great numbers to persons whom the Governor judged proper. Those who received permits paid a certain sum (*redevance*) yearly. The proceeds, whether by lease or by *congé*, were received by the Governor, who distributed them in pensions or perquisites to certain officers, in gifts and alms to widows and children of officers, or other expenses of this sort. If at the end of the year, there remained any funds accruing from this source, they were turned into the general treasury.[13]

The posts of Frontenac, Niagara and Toronto at first were leased, but after a trial of that system, they were reserved for the King's trade, because of the keen rivalry of the English in these quarters. The lessees of these posts having put on their goods prices which seemed too high to the Indians, the English sent wampum belts among the tribes, with intelligence of the goods and liquor which they had at Oswego, and which they offered at lower prices than the French. As a consequence, the Indians would not stop to trade at Niagara. To checkmate this move, it was necessary to cancel the lease at Niagara, and at the other trading-posts on Lake Ontario; and by successive reductions in the price of goods, to regain the Indian trade. Niagara was more convenient for the Indians than Oswego, being nearer to their hunting grounds. The reduction of prices at Niagara, however, was carried so far that goods were sold there on royal account at less than they had cost the King. For some years, there seemed no middle course. The French saw that they must submit to this loss at Niagara, or renounce the Indian trade and abandon the whole region to the English. After all, this diminution in the price of merchandise was less a real loss than a diminished profit, because the furs which the King received in trade were sold at Quebec, bringing as much as and sometimes more than the price paid by the King for goods traded to the Indians.[14]

[13] "*Mémoire pour M. François Bigot* . . . ," Paris, 1763, p. 21.
[14] Bigot to the Minister, Sept. 30, 1750.

So unsatisfactory was the state of trade, in the years following the erection of the stone house, that it was proposed once more to change the system of trade there. D'Aigremont wrote to the Minister, October 15, 1728: "I believe it will be advantageous to lease the posts of Niagara and Frontenac, for there is now much loss in the trade made on the King's account, and it will always be so."

In 1727 we find Beauharnois complaining of Dupuy's management of the trading-posts. "He has farmed out for 400 francs the post at Toronto to a young man who is not at all fit. M. d'Aigremont, to whom M. Dupuy sent the agreement for signature, refused to sign, saying that he would talk about it with the Intendant, showing him that this would work great wrong to the trade at Frontenac and Niagara." Notwithstanding all that, Dupuy returned the agreement next day, but he refused to sign, alleging that he knew of another man who for some years past had offered a thousand crowns [15] for the lease. The statement, which M. de Longueuil confirmed, illustrates the favoritism and "graft" for which the administration of the colony was soon to become notorious.

Although the building of the stone house at Niagara did somewhat stimulate the traffic at that point, it by no means removed all difficulties. The King's account suffered much at the hands of incompetent, careless or dishonest agents. In the year 1728 Saveur Germain Le Clerc, who was in charge of the trading at Niagara in 1727, died after a long illness, during which his accounts were so neglected that M. d'Aigremont, reporting on the trade of the posts for that year, was unable to find out what goods or stores had been traded or used at Niagara; and he despaired of being able to tell any better the following year, "M. Dupuy having sent to Niagara to replace the Sieur Le Clerc, a man who is scarcely able to read and sign his name, notwithstanding representations which I have made regarding it. This man is Rouville la Saussaye, to whom was leased last year the post at Toronto for one year for 400 livres. He still has that lease, which is not compatible with his employment as clerk ("*commis*") and store-

[15] "*Mille esous.*" The value of the *écu* is usually given at 2s. 6d. English.

A TROUBLESOME TREATY

keeper ("*garde-magazin*") of Niagara. This lease-hold which is at the foot of Lake Ontario and which has been exploited in the King's interest in past years as a dependency of Fort Niagara, ought not to be leased to the storekeeper in charge of trade at Niagara, because of the abuses which may spring from it — this man may send off to the Toronto post the Indians who come to Niagara, under pretext that he has not in the storehouse there the things they ask for. Furthermore he might make exchanges of good peltries for bad ones, and besides could intercept all the Indians in Lake Ontario, and so utterly ruin the trade at Forts Niagara and Frontenac."

The representations of M. d'Aigremont were not without effect, for Rouville la Saussaye was soon succeeded by one La Force, who held the post for some years, though evidently not greatly to the King's profit. He carried on the barter with the Indians at Niagara, apparently in a loose way, with little or no balancing of books or auditing of accounts, from 1729 till 1738, when the Intendant, Hocquart, suspecting that all was not right, sent the Sieur Cheuremont to Niagara to investigate. The result was that La Force was found to be a debtor to the King's account in the amount of 127,842 *chats*. The *chat* or cat of the French fur-traders was probably the raccoon,[16] and the meaning of La Force's singular indebtedness is best given in the words of M. Hocquart: "According to the traders' method of keeping accounts, the cats are regarded at Niagara as [the unit of] money by means of which they estimate the price of goods and of peltries. For instance, a blanket will sell for eight cats, a pound of beaver-skin for two; similarly with other articles of merchandise and furs." The Sieur Cheuremont informed Hocquart that he had reckoned on La Force's account all the provisions, stores and goods

[16] *Chat* and *chat sauvage* are terms which are very often encountered in the old reports, and would naturally be taken to mean wild-cat — either the *Lynx rufus* or the Canadian lynx, *Lynx Canadensis*. A careful study of the subject by J. G. Henderson, in a paper read before the American Association for the Advancement of Science, 1880, reaches the conclusion that the *chat* of the early traders was really the *raton* of France, or in English, the raccoon. The fisher (*Mustela canadensis*), also often called wild-cat, is believed to be the *pecan* or *pekan* of the French-Canadian traders.

for trade which had been shipped to him, with allowance for all that he had used, and accepting his own figures as to goods sold. The Intendant summoned the involved commissary to Quebec, but when he demanded an explanation of the deficit, La Force could only say that Cheuremont had made such calculations as he chose; as for himself, he had traded according to the established tariff. This tariff, he said, did not take into account the goods which were ruined, and he adduced yet other reasons for his great shortage. La Force had long had the reputation of a man of probity; there was nothing on which to base a charge against him of theft. The Intendant therefore reached the conclusion that there had been nothing worse than great negligence in La Force's conduct of affairs, "and that his numerous family of eight or nine children had considerably increased the expenditures." Cheuremont toiled for three months in a vain effort to straighten the Niagara accounts; meanwhile La Force was asking to be paid 1000 livres which he claimed due him each year, but which were withheld from him.

The Intendant finally in 1739 replaced La Force with the Sieur Le Pailleur, whom he describes as "the most honest man I can find for this employ." And again there were obstacles to a business-like administration of the post. Le Pailleur had scarcely taken up the duties at Niagara when he had an adventure with a mad bull, being dragged over two arpents of road, and thus put *hors d'état* for work, so that for the year 1739 he was unable to keep up his trading accounts or even to make an inventory of merchandise in the storehouse.

There are preserved many reports regarding skins received at the Lake Ontario posts in these years. Niagara, Frontenac and Toronto are often summed up in one schedule. These lists, enumerating the number of each sort of fur received, with the price allowed, are not without interest, for they illustrate not only the state of the market, but the relative abundance of different animals taken by the Indians. Some of the old French names of species are difficult to identify. In the following schedule of furs received at Niagara and Frontenac, season of 1727, "*chat*" has been rendered as raccoon, "*vison*" as mink, "*pecan*" as fisher (*Mustela canadensis*), and "*loup-cervier*" as wolverene (*Gulo luscus*).

KIND.		NUMBER.	VALUATION PER SKIN.
Castor ....beaver		2580	7 li. 6s.
Chevreuil ....buck		295	
Chevreuils verts...buck (green)........		1875	
Bœufs Illinois ....bison		4	
Cerfs ....red deer............		844	
Orignaux ....moose		7	
Chats ....raccoon		448	28s.
Loutres ....otter		167	3 li. 5s.
Loups-cerviers ....wolverene		8	7 li.
Loups-de-bois .....wolf		4	3s.
Martres ....marten		247	3 li. 9s.
Grands ours.......bear		378	3 li. 12s.
Oursons ....cub		52	} 60@38s.
Ours moyens .....bear, half-grown.....		8	
Pecans ....fisher		84	4 li. 9s.
Pichoux ....polecat		104	55s.
Reynards rouge....red fox		6	55s.
Visons ....mink		5	10s.
Rat musqués......muskrat		8	1s. 6d.

The above is one of many lists and schedules to be found in the reports of the trading-posts. Niagara and Frontenac are invariably coupled, and no separate mention is made of Toronto, which for trade purposes was regarded as a part of Niagara. Toronto was at first treated as a separate leasehold. Later, it was made virtually a branch of Niagara. In 1729 we find the storekeeper at Niagara directed to send goods to Toronto as needed, the accounts to be included with those of his own post.

While the beaver market continued good, and the animals themselves abundant, many other fur-bearing animals whose skins are now highly prized, appear to have been neglected by the trappers. The beaver was the great staple and object of trade, although at times the market so fell off that there was little if any profit in the business as carried on by the French,

Of all our fur-bearing animals the beaver was the most widely distributed. Wherever the conditions of lake or pond, marsh or forest supplied him with the means for his natural habitat, there he was to be found. But the records, even at the very beginning of the French occupancy on the Niagara, indicate that at that time the beaver-hunting grounds were some distance west and north of the old Iroquois stronghold of Central and Western New York. In Joncaire's day the main supplies for the trade at Niagara appear to have been brought by Indians from the territory north of Lake Erie, the country around Lake Huron, and the remoter regions of the Lake Superior section. In 1739 we find Beauharnois making strenuous efforts to increase the beaver trade by establishing posts among the Sioux. In that year, as at some earlier periods, war between tribes had interfered with the hunting; while other tribes, which gleaned some of the best beaver grounds, the Ottawas and Saulteux of Lake Huron, persistently refused to stay their loaded canoes at Fort Niagara, drawn to the English " by the brandy distributed without measure, and cheap goods."

The attention paid to the beaver trade in the official correspondence of Canada, even in its relation to the Lower Lake posts during the years we are considering, would fill an ample volume. The larger aspects of that trade cannot be considered, here, the present aim being only to remind the reader that the quest of the beaver, more than anything else, brought Fort Niagara into existence.

There were amusing difficulties, in those days, on the part of the storekeepr at Niagara, and his brother traders elsewhere, in trying to make the Indians understand the basis of exchange. They could never be made to recognize the distinction between the skins of the full-grown and half-grown animals. One exasperated report compares the confusion growing out of this classification, to the selling of an old *robe de chambre*, of which the sleeves and bottom of the gown are sold at one price, and the back and facings at another, " according as the parts of this robe were near the body." At a meeting of agents and merchants at Château St. Louis in

A TROUBLESOME TREATY 275

Quebec in 1728, it was agreed that, beginning January 1, 1730, full-grown and half-grown beavers should be taken on a valuation of 3 li. 10s. per pound, and " *castor veulle* " (undressed fur) at 48s. per pound; a reduction from rates than prevailing. At this meeting was again heard the inevitable complaint that any effort to make the Indians recognize distinctions in beaver pelts made them carry their furs to Oswego.

The famine of 1733 contributed to the diminution in the receipt for beaver, and by a fire in April of that year at Montreal, more than 2000 pounds were burned.

The combined trade at Forts Niagara, Frontenac, and the head of the lake during the season of 1724–25 showed a profit of 2382 livres, 3 sols, 9 deniers — about $476 on the present basis of values. A report of 1725 says: " Two hundred and four 'green' deer-skins and twenty-three packets made up of various furs are left at Fort Frontenac or Niagara, which is a mere trifle, and shows how the English have taken nearly all the trade away from Niagara. They even come to trade within ten leagues of Frontenac. Moreover the price of furs has so fallen that bear-skins have been sold this year for 47s. apiece." It is difficult to fix the purchasing power of the sol (*sou*) at that day, but at its nominal value of a half-penny (English), it puts the price of a bear-skin in 1725 at less than half a dollar.

The falling off in trade in 1725, over 1724, is striking. Furs from the three posts above designated realized, in 1724, 29,297 li. 10s.; in 1725, only 9,151 li. 15s. 6d. Against the total receipts of 38,449 li. 5s. 6d. in the two years, there were charged 36,067 li. 1s. 9d. for expenses, leaving the balance of profit as above given. One item of expense was the salary of 600 livres paid to the storekeeper or agent at Niagara. In these figures and many others to like purport which are contained in the records, are to be found the real reason for building the stone Fort Niagara. The effect of that enterprise was immediate. In 1726, long before the new work was finished, we read: " The house at Niagara had a good effect on the beaver trade." Yet for that year, receipts from Niagara, Frontenac and " head of the lake " were only a little over 8,000 li., with expenses of over 13,000 li. "This trade," says a note of October 20, 1726, " is so poor only because the English were all the spring and part of the summer in the neighborhood of Niagara and gathered in all the best skins. There were also *coureurs de bois* from Montreal who spent the winter in trade at Fort Frontenac, who made a good deal of money there. Added to all that, the price of skins has greatly fallen."

CHAPTER XV

ANNALS OF THE WILDERNESS

THE VENTURES OF JOSEPH LA FRANCE — THE NIAGARA MUTINY OF 1729 — FATHER CRESPEL AT NIAGARA — DEATH OF JONCAIRE THE ELDER — THE MYSTERIOUS RIVER CONDE.

A NOT infrequent source of disturbance and annoyance at Fort Niagara was the passing of unlicensed voyageurs and traders, many of whom brought retinues of savages, their canoes fur-laden, and tauntingly defied the commandant at the river's mouth. As early as 1727 we found record of men of this class from Louisiana, coming down Lake Erie on their way to Montreal, and of Canadians passing up the Niagara on their way to the Mississippi, making off with cargoes of goods for which they had not paid. Efforts were made at Niagara to arrest this class of free-booters. One Claude Chetiveau de Roussel, who came up the Mississippi and through the Lakes without a passport, was arrested, put on board ship at Quebec, and sent to the Rochefort prison. In 1732 peremptory orders were given to the commandant at Niagara, that the goods of all traders seeking to pass up or down the river without a permit, should be seized.

As the great stone house neared completion and life at the mouth of the Niagara passed from the bustle of construction to the routine of a small garrison, Longueuil relinquished command once more to Joncaire; but in the latter's absence, in the season of 1727, a man named Pommeroy — the documents speak of him merely as " Monsieur "— was in command at the fort. The change was scarcely made when an incident occurred which illustrates a condition no doubt arising often in those days. One Desjardin, a resident of Detroit, arrived at Niagara, " bound up " as the phrase is in modern lake traffic, with a canoe loaded with merchandise. When his pass was called for by Le Clerc, in charge of the trade at Niagara, he replied that a companion trader, Roquetaillade, who was a little ways behind with three more canoes, had the passes for all four. The next day Roquetaillade arrived with a permit for only three canoes. Desjardin, whose representations were seen to be fraudulent, had taken his goods across to the west side of the Niagara. Le Clerc deemed that the circumstances warranted him in seizing the cargo. With the younger Joncaire (Chabert junior) and other soldiers he crossed the river and confiscated the goods in the name of the King. The contents of the canoe would have stocked a country store in more modern times, and indicates the needs and whims of the far-off post of Detroit at this early day. There were goods for the Indians and goods for the French settlers and their wives: four packages of biscuit, six sacks of flour, a sack of gun-flints, numerous guns, a bundle of leather, a large covered kettle and seven small kettles, 322 pounds of lead in five sacks, and other things, all of which were taken to the storehouse at Niagara. When the packages were opened there they revealed men's clothing, four pairs of children's shoes, a pair of women's slippers, boys' and men's shoes, fifteen small hatchets, a barrel of prunes and another of salt, a white blanket and two red ones, two pieces of the woolen fabric called *calmande*, with rolls of other weaves indicated as *estamine au dauphine*, and *indienne* or cotton print. Still another package contained wax, cotton wicks for candles, French thread ("*fil de Rennes* "), cotton cloth, shoemaker's thread, and blue cotton stockings for women — perhaps the earliest indication we have of the *bas bleues* in the Lake region. The confiscation of such a cargo of frontier necessities was a serious loss to the unlucky Desjardin. His large bark canoe ("*canoe d'ecorse de huit places* ") was also confiscated. Such was the penalty for failure to comply with the prescribed regulations of trade.

Perhaps worthy of note, in these minor annals of the frontier, are the names of the soldiers which with those of Le Clerc and Joncaire, Jr., are signed to the report of the seizure, under date August 21, 1727. Here we meet, as it were, St. Maurice de la Gauchetière, La Jeunesse de Budmond, L'Esperance de Port Neuf, Sans Peur de Deganne, St. Antoine de Dechaillon, St. Jean de Lignery, and Bon Courage de Deganne. Surely, with Youth, Hope, Fearlessness and Good Courage for comrades in the wilderness, to say nothing of the saints, life at Fort Niagara in the gray old days could not have been wholly forlorn.

On a day in the spring of 1735 two canoes, deeply laden, came skirting the northern shore of Lake Erie to the discharge; took the good channel through the little rapids, and were speeded along at a pace of some six to eight miles an hour, past the low shores over which Buffalo now extends. In the wider reaches of the river at the head of Grand Island, where the current slackens to some two miles, the red voyageurs plied again the paddles, and soon made the ancient landing at the margin of the river above the great cataract. Here, as they stepped ashore, the party was seen to consist of eight Indians and their employer, a half-breed trader, who though well-nigh as dark-skinned as his followers, spoke the French of Quebec with fluency. There was a quick agreement with the resident Senecas, who carried his packs and his canoes over the old portage path, down to the lower river, receiving for their labors one hundred beaver-skins. Reëmbarking, the little flotilla hastened out of the Niagara and on along the Ontario shore to Oswego fort, where the suspicious trader stayed on the strand with his canoes, sending the Indians into the fort to dispose of his furs. The sale accomplished, he made his way westward, once more stole his way past Fort Niagara, and after gaining again the upper river, hastened on, weary league on league, until he finally came again to his abiding-place at Missilimackinac.

This was Joseph La France. His father was a French Canadian, his mother of the nation of Sauteurs, living at the falls of St. Mary, between Lakes Superior and Huron. Here he was born about 1707. His mother died when he was five years old, and his father took him to Quebec, where he spent six months and learned French. Quebec had then, according to the subsequent testimony of La France, "4 or 5,000 men in garrison, it being about the time of the Peace of Utrecht." Returning to his people at St. Mary's, he resided there until the death of his father in 1723, when the son, then sixteen, embarked upon the career of an independent trader. He took what furs and skins his father had left him, went down to Montreal by the Ottawa-river route, disposed of his goods and returned to acquire a new stock for barter. For the next ten years or so he seems to have taken his furs regularly to the French. In 1734 he adventured in new fields, going down the Wisconsin to the Mississippi, and down that stream to the mouth of the Missouri, returning by the same route.

In 1735, stealing by night past the French settlement at Detroit, for fear of being stopped, he came down Lake Erie, on his way to try the English at Oswego. As on the Detroit, so on the Niagara, he appears to have avoided the French, whom he subsequently reported to have "a fort on the north side of the Fall of Niagara, between the Lakes Errie and Frontenac, about 3 Leagues within the Woods from the Fall, in which they keep 30 Soldiers, and have about as many more with them as Servants and Assistants; these," he added, "have a small trade with the Indians for Meat, Ammunition and Arms."[1] Probably his dealings with the English became known to the French; for later, when he went again to Montreal with a cargo of furs, although he gave the Governor a present of marten-skins and 1000 crowns, for a license to trade the following year, the Governor would neither give the license nor restore the money, charging La France with having sold brandy to the Indians, and threatening him with imprisonment. La France escaped from Montreal, and toilfully made his way up the Ottawa, reaching Lake Nipissing, after forty days of paddling and portaging. At Mackinac he gathered another stock of furs and set out once more to try his fortunes with the French; but on the way to Montreal, in the Nipissing [French] River, he suddenly met the Governor's brother-in-law with nine canoes and thirty soldiers. They took all he had and arrested him as a runaway without a passport; but he made his escape through the woods at night, and after

[1] La France was the first man of whom we have record, to cross from Lake Winnipeg to Hudson's Bay. The account of his presence on the Niagara is found in Vol. II of the "Report from the Committee appointed to enquire into the State and Condition of the Countries adjoining to Hudson's Bay, and of the Trade carried on there," etc., London, 1749.

ANNALS OF THE WILDERNESS 281

weeks of hardship returned to St. Mary's, resolved to be done for ever with the French. Having lost all, he determined to go to the English at Hudson's Bay. His subsequent adventures belong to the history of the fur trade of the far north and west. His testimony, given in an enquiry regarding the operation of the Hudson's Bay Company, affords many useful glimpses of the conditions of the time.

La France was the type of a class of men who at this period were a source of great trouble alike to the French and the English. The French especially, at Frontenac, at Niagara and Detroit, were exasperated by their disregard of the *congé*, their unlicensed brandy-selling to the Indians, and their journeys to the upstart British post at Oswego. As La France made his way past Fort Niagara, with canoes loaded to the gunwale with winter furs, the French of that little garrison, if not indeed Joncaire himself, may have noted the passing, standing impotent to prevent it, or perchance enraged by the yells and derisive cries of the defiant freebooters, no longer at pains to conceal themselves when once safely past the fort.

There developed in England at this time a considerable outcry against the monopoly enjoyed by the Hudson's Bay Company; and an ingenious advocacy of free trade in North American fur-gathering. The experiences of Joseph La France provided a fruitful text for those who, like the author of " An Account of the Countries Adjoining to Hudson's Bay," etc., undertook to show their countrymen and their king how British trade might be extended in the Lake Erie region, and the French at the Lake Erie and Niagara posts utterly routed. Arthur Dobbs, who combined with the long-existant British hostility to the French, a bitterly critical attitude towards the Hudson's Bay Company, set forth at length in his book views which no doubt met the approval of many of the British public of his day. Curiously enough, one of his strongest arguments was based on a map-maker's blunder. On the large map which accompanies his work, the Great Lakes are shown, with " the great fall of Niagara " properly indicated at the outlet of " Conti or Errie Lake." The whole region of the Lakes is shown, as accurately on the whole as on many another map, up to that time; but running into Lake Erie, a few miles south of the present site of Buffalo, the unknown geographer has borrowed, from a dubious source of 40 years before, a stream of considerable size, and named it "Condé River." The Condé River originated with La Hontan, on whose map of 1703 it first appears. Its reappearance, in Dobbs's book is curious, inasmuch as the best maps, from La Hontan to 1744, show nothing of the sort. On Coronelli's "*Partie orientale du Canada*," etc., 1689, a small unnamed stream is shown entering Lake Erie at this point. De l'Isle's map of 1703 shows no stream at that point, nor do most others. La Hontan names it and gives its source in a small lake farther east than the eastern end of Lake Ontario. In the minutes of the Provincial Council of Pennsylvania, January 25, 1747, is an allusion to the Indians at "Canayahaga, a place on or near the river Condé, which runs into the Lake Erie." Its real prototype, in the annals of earlier explorers, may have been the Cattaraugus or Eighteen-Mile Creek; but here we have it, shown unduly large, as the only stream entering Lake Erie, its headwaters coming from vague mountains to the southeast.

Contemplating this stream, and the exigencies of the fur trade in the region, Mr. Dobbs saw a great opportunity for the British, "by forming a Settlement on the River Condé, which is navigable into the Lake Errie, which is within a small Distance of our Colonies of Pennsylvania and Maryland, and being above the great Fall of Niagara, and in the Neighborhood of the Iroquese, who are at present a Barrier against the French, and a sufficient Protection to our Fort and trading House at Oswega, in their Country upon the Lake Frontenac, who by that Trade have secured the Friendship of all the Nations around the Lakes of Huron and Errie. We should from thence, in a little Time, secure the Navigation of these great and fine Lakes, and passing to the southward, at the same time, from Hudson's Bay to the Upper Lake, and Lake of Hurons, we should cut off the Communication betwixt their Colonies of Canada and Mississippi, and secure the Inland Trade of all that vast Continent."

Further on we have more details of the geography, real and

imagined, of our region: " The Streight above Niagara at the Lake is about a League wide. From this to the River Condé is 20 Leagues South-west; this River runs from the S. E. and is navigable for 60 Leagues without any Cataracts or Falls; and the Natives say, that from it to a River which falls into the Ocean, is a Land Carriage of only one League. This must be either the Susquehanna or Powtomack, which fall into the Bay of Chisapeak." He further argues the wisdom of making a settlement on this wonderful river Condé, of building proper vessels there to navigate these lakes, so that " we might gain the whole Navigation and Inland Trade of Furs, etc., from the French, the Fall of Niagara being a sufficient Barrier betwixt us and the French of Canada," etc. It was alleged that the British Government might readily induce colonists from Switzerland and Germany " to strengthen our settlements upon this River and Lake Erie." Another suggestion was that disbanded British troops be sent on half pay to Lake Erie, where they would " make good our possessions, which would be a fine retreat to our Soldiers, who can't so easily, after being disbanded, bring themselves again to hard Labour, after being so long disused to it." The more Mr. Dobbs dwelt upon it the more important this particular project appeared. The French were to be cut off from communication with the Mississippi; Canada was to be " made insignificant for the French." The entire fur trade of North America was to fall into the hands of the English. And finally, with a burst of sentiment which recalls the devout aspirations of the French missionaries, but is an anomaly in the plans of British traders, he exclaims: " How glorious would it be for us at the same time to civilize so many Nations, and improve so large and spacious a country! by communicating our Constitution and Liberties, both civil and religious, to such immense Numbers, whose Happiness and Pleasure would increase, at the same Time that an Increase of Wealth and Power would be added to Britain." [2]

[2] See " An Account of the Countries adjoining to Hudson's Bay," etc., by Arthur Dobbs, London, 1744. Dobbs became Governor of North Carolina, and died about 1765.

Life at Fort Niagara never ceased to be dependant on the King's provision ships. If the annual shipment came early in the season, the garrison abated its chronic discontent in reasonable assurance that it could endure until spring on the inevitable flour and pork. But often the ships reached Quebec so late that the annual cargo of food and other necessaries could not be sent through to Niagara until the following spring. In 1732 the *Ruby*, bringing subsistence for the forest garrisons, reached Quebec late in September. The utmost dispatch was made, but the supplies designed for Niagara got no further that fall than Frontenac. The winter of 1732-33 was a most severe one, the meager harvests of the colony had been even smaller than usual, and there were privation and distress in the towns as well as at the lake posts. At Niagara they felt the additional burden of the smallpox, which this winter ran through the Iroquois villages, interfering with the usual hunting and trapping. In the summer of 1733, stimulated by the urgent tone of the official reports, the King's ship anchored off Quebec on July 9th. Even with this early arrival, it was September before the barrels of flour which she brought were safe in the storehouse at Niagara. In 1734, the *Ruby* arrived, August 16th; but in 1735 there was another failure to receive anything; the Niagara provisions indeed reached Frontenac, and were loaded on a bateau; but when the lumbering, laden craft essayed the autumnal lake, a gale drove her ashore and the trip was abandoned — with what result at the waiting garrison, may be imagined. There, short rations and bad more than once bore fruit in mutiny and desertion. Again the Government sought to atone for the costly delays of one season, with excess of zeal in the next; so that in 1736 the King's ship was at Quebec on August 7th, and in the next summer the *Jason* arrived August 8th. And so it went, with varying uncertainty, the efficiency and well nigh the existence of Niagara depending largely on the modicum of attention it might receive from the Minister and his agents in France.

Although the two barques which had been constructed at Frontenac in the winter of 1725 were only eight years old in 1733, one of them had then become unfit for service, so that

ANNALS OF THE WILDERNESS

there remained but one sailing vessel on Lake Ontario that season. The Intendant, Hocquart, sent four ship-carpenters to Frontenac to repair the other, but they found it so far gone that the best they could do was to take the iron-work from it and build a new vessel. This they did, at an expense of some 5,000 livres. The second boat, says a report of that summer, was greatly needed to carry goods to Niagara.

At Detroit, after the first few bitter years, conditions for self-mainenance were far better than they ever were at Niagara. The latter post never had the thrifty class of settlers about it, which very early began to provide flour and other produce not only for Detroit but for Mackinac and other upper-lake posts as well.

So productive were those early grain fields about Detroit that in 1730 a memorialist of the Crown — possibly de Noyan, though this particular memorial [3] is not signed — seeking certain privileges in the western trade, unfolded a plan for supplying Niagara with flour. To further this project, the Government was asked to build one or two light-draught vessels ("*barques plates*") to navigate between the Niagara, Detroit and the Upper Lakes. The advantage of such vessels, in case of Indian troubles, was pointed out: soldiers could be quickly transported. But the opportunities of trade loomed large in the eye of this speculator. At present, he wrote, it costs the *voyageurs* twenty livres freight per packet of furs, from Detroit to Montreal. With the desired sailing vessels the furs could be carried for ten or twelve livres per packet. Detroit would gather from its tributary country annually 1,000 to 1,200 packets; Mackinac and the upper posts could be counted on for 2,000 more. The petitioner knew well the conditions of the fur trade. The *voyageurs* — canoe freighters — reached market by the Ottawa route. By the Niagara route he proposed to carry them at fifteen livres each. Thus on 1,000 packets from Mackinac he counted on 15,000 livres, and on 1,000 from Detroit, 10,000 more; and 25,000 livres freight receipts in one season should have appealed to a Ministry ac-

[3] "*Mémoires concernant l'état-present du Canada en l'an 1730*," MS. copy in the Archives Office, Ottawa.

customed to know only of outlay in connection with the lake posts.

True, some expense must be incurred, to start the business. This plan contemplated the construction of a palisaded warehouse above the Niagara fall, at a point where the barques could make easy and safe harbor. The portage road was to be extended and improved. There would have to be a clerk at the warehouse above the falls, and carts for carrying the peltries down to the lower river — the landing of the old *Magazin Royal* — where two flat-boats would be needed to convey them on down to the mouth of the river each summer in July or early in August. The desired barques, it was urged, could make at least three voyages, Niagara to Mackinac, between June and mid-August. On their first down trip they could bring away the furs collected in the neighborhood of Mackinac; on the second and third trips, they would take the packets which by that time would have been brought in from the Lake Superior and more distant posts. The author of this memoir foresaw the prejudice which he would have to overcome among the traders; but if even half of them were afraid to risk Niagara, and chose to forward by canoe down the Ottawa route, he figured that even then the profit with the barques would be considerable. Each packet paid in freight twenty-five livres, Mackinac to Montreal, by the Niagara, where the Ontario barques would receive them. It was recommended that the Lake Erie craft be built " five or six leagues above the Niagara portage," and the promoter thought that with a master and four sailors for each vessel, business could begin, especially if soldiers from Fort Niagara and other posts could be called on for service when required.

This was probably the first project for trade by sailing vessels from the Niagara to the Upper Lakes, since the disastrous voyage of La Salle's *Griffon*, fifty years before. The Government did not lend its aid, and the plausible and elaborate memoir bore no immediate fruit.[4]

[4] The Intendant Hocquart wrote to the Minister, Oct. 23, 1730, in behalf of one Fleury who had " particularly at heart the building of a barque on Lake Erie for the fur trade." Hocquart approved the under-

With the growth of trade and settlement at Detroit, and, from about 1730, the increasing substitution of the Niagara route over that of the Ottawa — the *grande rivière* of the toilful old days — traffic adjusted itself to a recognized tariff; so that, in the latter days of the period we are studying, if not indeed to the very end of the French dominion on the Lakes, transportation by the Niagara route was to be counted on for its fixed charges as much as any inland transportation by boat or rail is to-day; but how different the items! The Detroit merchant of say 1730, returning homeward from Montreal with goods, brought them by canoes or flat-boats to Fort Frontenac, there transferred them to the little barque that took its chances with all the winds of heaven, on the long traverse to Fort Niagara, some seventy leagues, as the old sailing-masters made it. Reloaded on bateaux, the freight was poled and pulled up the Niagara, to the foot of the portage. There, in the earlier years, each packet and cask was hoisted to the shoulders of an Indian or Canadian *engagé*, for the hard climb up the levels and through the forest, some seven miles to the point of reëmbarking above the cataract. Just when horses or oxen were first used on the portage road is uncertain. We know that the English had proposed to use them there, in 1720, and that the French did use them for a number of years. All this transportation was paid for by a percentage on the weight. The cost of outfit, too, was considerable. If the merchant owned his own canoe — a *canot de maître*, of six or eight places — it cost him at least 500 francs. For the journey, he paid his six *engagés*, who not only paddled the canoe but helped make the portage, 250 francs each. The needed food for the journey would include at least 100 pounds of biscuit and twenty-five pounds of pork or bacon, per man. These with other necessaries brought the cost of equipment and maintenance to 2,260 francs. Such are the actual figures of one "voyage."

taking but the Minister did not. Forty years before (1690) one Sieur Charron had advocated a system of "barges" to be used as freighters from Fort Frontenac "and at the fort that would be established for navagating the Lakes above the Fall of Niagara," but nothing came of it.

It has been noted that the winter's supplies occasionally failed to reach the Niagara garrison. Sometimes the supplies which were there were bad. There was a serious state of affairs in 1738, owing to the wretched quality of flour furnished by the Government for the subsistence of the garrison. The supply was eked out by Canadian flour, of which there was great scarcity. The commandant, to head off, if possible, the desertions to which the soldiers at Niagara were always prone, if not indeed a mutiny of the whole garrison, sent several officers as an express to Montreal. They reported that the soldiers were absolutely unable to live on their short rations of bad bread and salt meat, and begged that better supplies be sent. Some relief was gained from the Canadian harvest, and the spoiled French flour was shipped back from the lake posts to Montreal.

In the summer of 1729, life at the little garrison had been disturbed by a mutiny among the soldiers, due probably to bad food and not enough of it. Whatever the cause, it made a most crucial season for Rigauville, commandant at the time. The prime mover in the uprising was one Charles Panis, and with him in rebellion were Laignille, La Joye, one Bernard — "called Dupont," — and so many others that the maintenance of any discipline at all was in jeopardy. The especial enmity of the mutineers was directed against the commandant and Ensign Ferrière. A Government secretary, Bernard, who was at Niagara at the time auditing the accounts of the storekeeper, was sent off post-haste to Montreal with a report of the affair. Beauharnois promptly sent back Captain Gauchetière and Ensign Céloron, with a detachment of twenty trusty men to replace the rebels. The latter were taken to Montreal, where they were held under arrest, in irons. An affair followed which made more of a stir than the original mutiny. The uprising at Niagara had occurred on July 26th. It was not until after a long and dangerous delay that the offenders were brought to trial before a council of war, which in due time, pronounced sentence. Laignille and La Joye were condemned to be hanged and broken ["*pendus et rompus*"]; while Dupont, a deserter, was merely to be hanged. Early in the morning of October 18th, before the executions were to take place, one of the condemned men cried out for help for his comrade, who feigned to be sick. The jailor's daughter ran to them, but scarcely had she opened the door of their dungeon, than the three criminals, who had broken off their irons, threw themselves upon her, overcame the sentry, climbed over the palisades and ran away. The gallows and platform, which had been made ready for the executions, were surreptitiously taken down and carried off, by whom the authorities could not learn. As it was deemed necessary to make an example of some one, the jailor was removed from his post, though it was not shown that he was in any wise responsible for the escape. There is no record found that any of the seditious soldiers were punished.

The official reports became very fretful over the matter. It was complained that the priests and women had meddled with the affair, creating sympathy for the prisoners. The whole system of procedure was criticised; there had been shown a complete ignorance of the laws and ordinances. "There is scarcely an officer in the country, and especially at Montreal, who knows how to conduct a procedure of this sort." "If the officers who composed the council of war had been instructed in the ordinance of July 26, 1668, the execution of the criminals need not have been delayed more than twenty-four hours," etc. The Governor and Intendant took the occasion to renew with great urgency their frequent request that more troops be sent to the colony.

As for "Charles Panis," the instigator of the Niagara mutiny, he was put aboard the French vessel *St. Antoine*, and sent to Martinique in banishment. The Governor there was requested to hold him forever as a slave, forbidding him ever to return to Canada or to go even to the English colonies. This culprit, whose name is written in the documents as Charles Panis, may not unlikely have been Charles, a Panis or Pani, the name by which the French designated the Naudowasses or slave Indians. These people occupy a strange position in the history of North American tribes. In Joncaire's time, they are frequently found as slaves and menials not only among the Senecas and other warlike tribes, but among the French. Nor is it wholly improbable that such an Indian should have been the instigator of a mutiny among French soldiers, for more than once in the records may be found mention of Panis who served with the French troops. Several of them, in Péan's following, were killed at Fort Necessity in July, 1754. In 1747 a runaway Panis was shipped from Montreal to Martinique, there to be sold for the benefit of his owner. Facts like these, and the further fact that "Panis" is an unlikely French name, pretty clearly point out the character of the instigator of the mutiny at Fort Niagara.[5]

As for Laignille and his lawless associates, they no doubt soon found their way into the ranks of *coureurs de bois* and unlicensed traffickers with the Indians, not improbably allying themselves with some remote tribe, where they forever merged their identity with that of their savage associates. The wilderness lodges were harbingers of many a white outlaw in those days.

To the period we are considering, belongs — if it belongs to history at all — the Niagara visit of one Claude Le Beau, "*avocat en parlement*," romancer and adventurer at large. According to his own testimony, this young man, a native of Rochelle, went to Paris in 1729, and in the same year was drawn from his legal studies into a voyage to Canada. Shipwrecked in the St. Lawrence, he arrived at Quebec, in sad plight, June 18, 1729. He found employment as a clerk in the fur business ("*bureau du castor*"), where he continued, making his home with the Recollect Fathers, for more than a year. He ran away from sober pursuits, in March, 1731, and took to the woods with two Indians. His many adventures are too numerous, and of too little consequence, to make even a summary of them worth while here. His narrative puts the time of his arrival at Niagara in June, 1731, and under sufficiently fantastic conditions. He was accompanied, with other Indians, by his mistress, an Abenaki maiden, with whom he had

---

[5] Details of the Fort Niagara mutiny are given in a report of Beauharnois and Hocquart to the Minister, Oct. 23, 1730, and in other documents of the time.

exchanged clothes. He had resorted to this and other disguise to avoid arrest by the French as a deserter. A long story is made of his encounter with soldiers from Fort Niagara, and of his final sanctuary in Seneca villages. He says that letters were received from Montreal, by the commandant at Fort Niagara, ordering his arrest, if he appeared in the neighborhood.

Needless to say, no mention of Le Beau is found in the official correspondence. His book has for the most part the air of truth; he is precise with his dates, and in his account of Indian customs shows much accurate knowledge. Among the things that tell against him are his allusions to a Jesuit priest, Father Cirene, among the Mohawks; but this name is not found in all the Relations of the order; although there was a Father Jacques Sirême. Le Beau's account of Niagara Falls is dubious; he says they are 600 feet high. This is La Hontan's figure of many years before. Le Beau has much to say of La Hontan and his misrepresentations, but the indications are that he accepted one of that gay officer's wildest exaggerations, and that he may never have seen Niagara at all. He probably came to Canada and had some experience among the Indians; and when he wrote his book, chose to so enlarge upon what he had really seen and experienced, still holding to a thread of fact, that the result has little interest as fiction, and no value whatever as history.[6]

From the time of the establishment of Fort Niagara, Chabert Joncaire the elder was more and more an object of jealousy and hatred for the English. It was not without reason that they ascribed to him the success of the French on the Niagara. Now rumors began to fly. It was reported to the French

---

[6] See the "*Avantures du Sr. C. Le Beau, avocat en parlement, ou Voyage curieux et nouveau, parmi les Sauvages de l'Amerique Septentrionale*," etc., Amsterdam, 1738. So far as I am aware, this curious book has never been published in English. While the cause of history would scarcely be promoted by such a publication, yet it is singular in these days of reprinting anything that is old and curious, that no publisher has given us a new edition —" with notes "— of Le Beau. There is a German edition. Le Beau's American adventures are discussed in J. Edmond Roy's paper, "*Des Fils et Famille envoyés au Canada*," Memoirs, Roy. Soc. Canada, Vol. VII.

King, on the word of Sieur de La Corne, that an Indian had promised the English that the house at Niagara should be razed, and that the Iroquois had been bribed by the Albany people to get rid of Joncaire. Louis approved the order to send word to Joncaire himself of all this, and instructed him to learn the truth of these reports, and to prevent the accomplishment of English designs. As the English at this time were making lavish presents to the Indians, Joncaire's task was no light one. They even sent wampum peace belts to remote tribes — to the Indians of Sault St. Louis, the Lake of the Two Mountains, to the Algonkins and Nepissings, inviting them all to remain quiet while the Iroquois were tearing down Fort Niagara. When the English overtures took any other form than substantial gifts, the Indians tired of them. As we have seen, to the English demand that the Iroquois should allow them to build a fort on the west side of the Niagara, opposite the French establishment, the savages replied that they did not wish to be troubled further about it; that they did not regret having given their consent to the French; and if the English wished to build on the Niagara, they must settle it with "Onontio"; as for them, they would not interfere;[7] which, after all, was not bad diplomacy on the part of the savage.

For the next few years Joncaire's chief employment was to inform his superior officers of English intrigues among the Iroquois, and to thwart them by his experience and influence. He was among the Senecas on such a mission in 1730, the Sieur de Rigauville being then in command at Fort Niagara.

It was at this time (1730) that he appears to have essayed to repeat, at Irondequoit Bay, his achievements on the Niagara, but without a like success. I find no record of the enterprise in the French documents; the English report of it puts Joncaire in a ridiculous rôle. It was Lawrence Claessen who carried the news to Albany in the autumn of this year, that Joncaire with a following of French soldiers, had gone among the Senecas and told them "that he having disobliged his governor was Duck'd whip'd and banished as a malefac-

[7] Marquis de Beauharnois to the Minister, Sept. 25, 1726.

tor, and said, that as he had been a prisoner among that Nation, and that then his life was in their hands, and as they then saved his life, he therefore deemed himself to be a coherent brother to that Nation, and therefore prayed that they might grant him toleration to build a trading house at a place called Tiederontequatt, at the side of the Kadarachqua lake about ten Leagues from the Sinnekes Country, and is about middle way Oswego and Yagero [Niagara] . . . and that he the said Jean Ceure entreated and beg'd the Sinnekes that they would grant him liberty to build the aforesaid Trading house at that place, in order that he might get his livelyhood by trading there and that he might keep some Soldiers to work for him there whom he promised should not molest or use any hostility to his Brethren the Sinnekes," and much more to like purport. He was further said to be an emissary of the Foxes.

Some correspondence ensued, on this extraordinary report by Claessen. The commissioners for Indian affairs at Albany made it the subject of a long letter to representatives of English interests among the Senecas, but even they saw the absurdity of Joncaire having a following of French soldiers if he had been banished from Canada. The part assigned to him in this affair by the Dutch interpreter is at utter variance with what we know of Joncaire's character and employment at this time.

The more one studies the old records, with the purpose of gaining therefrom a true conception of Joncaire's character —of discovering just what manner of man he was, and what is his true position among the men who made the history of his times — the less does he appear as a half-wild sojourner among the savages, the more is he seen to be a man of character, of marked ability to control others, and of some social standing and culture, as those qualities went at the time. His own letters, written in a day when many, even men of affairs, knew not how to hold a pen, testify to the excellent quality of his mind. He had the reputation among his brother officers of being a braggart; but even those who charged him with it, admitted that his achievements, especially in handling the Senecas, gave good warrant for boasting.

For forty years his relations with the missionaries, especially of the Order of Jesuits, were intimate. His association in his early years with Fathers Milet, Bruyas and Vaillant has been noted in the narrative. For Charlevoix he became host on the banks of the Niagara, and no doubt gave the priest many useful suggestions for his famous journey up the Lakes in 1721. It was Joncaire who told Charlevoix of the famous oil spring at Ganos,[8] now near Cuba, N. Y. "The place where we meet with it," wrote Charlevoix, "is called Ganos; where an officer worthy of credit [Joncaire] assured me that he had seen a fountain, the water of which is like oil and has the taste of iron. He said also that a little further there is another fountain exactly like it, and that the savages make use of its waters to appease all manner of pains." Joncaire may have been the first white man to visit these or other oil springs in the region, and so, possibly, to become the discoverer of petroleum. But others had heard of them, whether they visited them or not, long before Joncaire's day. The "Relation" of the Jesuits for 1656–57, edited by Le Jeune, says, in its description of the Iroquois country: "As one approaches nearer to the country of the Cats [*i. e.*, the Eries], one finds heavy and thick water, which ignites like brandy, and boils up in bubbles of flame when fire is applied to it. It is moreover so oily that all our savages use it to anoint and grease their heads and their bodies." Father Chaumonot was among the Senecas in 1656, as were, at various times, Fathers Fremin, Menart and Vaillant. These or still other missionaries may have been led to the oil springs more than half a century before Joncaire; to whom none the less belongs some credit for making them known.

One of the few students of our history who have discovered in Joncaire anything more than a rough soldier and interpreter, erroneously calls him a "chevalier," and pictures him as especially zealous in behalf of the Roman Catholic religion. "To extend the dominion of France," says William Dunlap,

[8] *Ganos* is derived from *Genie* or *Gaienna*, which in the Iroquois signifies oil or liquid grease (Bruyas). This oil spring is in the town of Cuba, Allegany Co., N. Y. The other referred to is in Venango Co., Pa.

" and of the Roman religion, this accomplished French gentleman bade adieu to civilized life, and by long residence among the Senecas, adopting their mode of life, and gaining their confidence, he procured himself to be adopted into the tribe, and to be considered as a leader in their councils. His influence with the Onondagas was about as great as with his own tribe. By introducing and supporting the priests, and other missionaries, employed by the Jesuits and instructed by the Governor; by sending intelligence to Montreal or Quebec, by these spies; by appearing at all treaty councils, and exerting his natural and acquired eloquence — it is necessary to say, he was master of their language — he incessantly thwarted in a great measure the wishes of the English, and particularly set himself in opposition to the Government of New York. But the views of Burnet, in regard to the direct trade, backed by the presents displayed to the savages, met their approbation in despite of Joncaire and the Jesuits." Dunlap adds that the conduct of Joncaire is only paralleled by that of the Jesuit Ralle (Rasle). "It is not improbable," he continues, "that Joncaire as well as Ralle, was of the Society of Jesuits, for it is the policy of this insidious combination that its members shall appear as laymen, in many instances, rather than as ecclesiastics." [9] He elsewhere speaks of the influence of "the Jesuits, Longueil and Jonceau." In references like this to Joncaire, he may naturally have been confused with his priest brother, François.

Obviously hostile, with the old-time prejudice of his kind, to the work of the Catholic missionaries, Dunlap nevertheless does a certain justice to Joncaire, in bringing out this phase of his activities. There is no warrant found in the documents for the supposition that Joncaire was a member of the Society of Jesus; many things indicate that he was not. Nor was he, probably, above the average standard of morality among the French soldiers of his day — a type, as we well know, not conspicuous either for piety or purity. But it remains true that Joncaire's services among the Senecas were calculated to

[9] "History of the New Netherlands," etc., by William Dunlap (N. Y., 1839), Vol. I, pp. 286, 287.

help on the efforts of the missionaries, who found him an invaluable ally against the ungodly English.

There exists, of date 1725, a memoir "by a member of the Congregation of St. Lazare," in which various measures are urged to prevent the English from working injury to the colony of Canada and the cause of true religion among the Indians. The author suggests that the Recollects (who were Franciscans), should be allowed to remain at any posts where they then were, in capacity of missionaries or chaplains; and that in these capacities they be sent to posts which should thereafter be established, where regular parochial organization could not be effected; but that the Jesuits, who preferred to be missionaries among the Indians rather than chaplains at the French posts, might nevertheless be established at Niagara, "in order that from this post they may carry on their mission among the Iroquois. It is highly important to the Colony to establish and to maintain these missions in the interests of France. To the end that the Jesuits may find means to hold the Iroquois nations it is desirable to give to them a tract of land near Niagara where they may build a house and make an establishment."

This plea for a Jesuit establishment at Niagara, which, plausibly, was made with the knowledge and endorsal of Joncaire, was not granted; but when the new post was garrisoned, it is probable that the first priest who as chaplain accompanied troops thither, was a Jesuit. The traditions of the post already associated it with that order. At least three Jesuits had been at the short-lived Fort Denonville on the same spot — Fathers Enjalran, Lamberville and Milet. No priest is mentioned among the soldiers who brought new life and stir to the old plateau in 1726. The first clergyman of whom we find record at Fort Niagara was Father Emmanuel Crespel, also a Jesuit. He was stationed there for about three years from 1729, interrupting his ministrations there with a short sojourn at Detroit where a mission of his order had been established.

Of Fort Niagara at this time he says: "I found the place very agreeable; hunting and fishing were very productive; the woods in their greatest beauty, and full of walnut and chestnut trees, oaks, elms and some others, far superior to any we see in France. The fever," he continues, " soon destroyed the pleasures we began to find, and much incommoded us, until the beginning of autumn, which season dispelled the unwholesome air. We passed the winter very quietly, and would have passed it very agreeably, if the vessel which was to have brought us refreshments had not encountered a storm on the lake, and been obliged to put back to Frontenac, which laid us under the necessity of drinking nothing but water. As the winter advanced she dared not proceed, and we did not receive our stores until May." Father Crespel records that while at Niagara he learned the Iroquois — probably the Seneca — and Ottawa languages well enough to converse with the Indians. " This enabled me," he writes, " to enjoy their company when I took a walk in the environs of the post." [10] The ability to talk with Indians afterward saved his life. When his three years of residence at Niagara expired, he was relieved, according to the custom of his order, and he passed a season in the convent at Quebec. While he was, no doubt, succeeded at Niagara by another chaplain, it is not until some years later that we find in the archives any mention of a priest at that post.

In 1731 Joncaire entered upon a new service, which, apparently, was to be his chief employment for the few remaining years of his life. He was now past sixty years. Grown gray in the King's service, seasoned by a lifetime of exposure and arduous wilderness experience, wise in the ways of the Indian, and understanding the intrigues and ambitions of the English, he was preëminently a man to be entrusted with an important mission. It is not to be inferred, however, that his lifetime of service on the outposts had cut him off from the official, the military or the domestic associations of Quebec and Montreal. The latter town, then of not above 5,000 inhabitants, was his

[10] " *Voiages du R. P. Emmanuel Crespel, dans le Canada et son naufrage en revenant en France. Mis au jour par le Sr. Louis Crespel, son Frére. A Francfort sur le Meyn,* 1742." There are numerous editions: 1st German, Frankfort and Leipsig, 1751; 2d French, Frankfort, 1752; Amsterdam, 1757; an English edition, 1797, etc., with numerous variations in title. The rare first edition was reprinted at Quebec in 1884.

home; and there, from 1707 to 1723, Madame de Joncaire bore to him, as we have already noted, ten children, the eldest of whom, Philippe Thomas, and his younger brother Daniel, known respectively as Joncaire the younger and Chabert, are both to bear a part in the history of the Niagara. In 1731, Joncaire, Jr., then about twenty-four years old, accompanied his father to the Senecas' villages, and probably to Niagara. He had even then " resided a long time among those Indians " and was " thoroughly conversant with their language." But now he was to be intrusted with new responsibilities; he was to assume the rôle which his father had filled for so many years among these vacillating and uncertain people. Reporting on these arrangements to the French Minister, de Maurepas, in October, 1731, Beauharnois wrote: " There is reason to believe that Sieur de Joncaire's presence among the Iroquois has been a check on them as regards the English, and that by keeping a person of some influence constantly among them, we shall succeed in entirely breaking up the secret intrigues they have together. On the other hand, the Iroquois will be more circumspect in their proceedings, and less liable to fall into the snares of the English, when they have some one convenient to consult with, and in whom they will have confidence. Sieur de Joncaire's son is well adapted for that mission."

The story of this son, and his share in Niagara history, belong for the most part to a later period than we are now considering. It may be noted here, however, that it was the brother Chabert who, in the winter of 1734, came from Montreal to Fort Niagara on snowshoes, bringing letters from the Governor. He returned through the heart of New York State, visiting the Iroquois villages *en route*. He was then in his twenty-seventh year; active, hardy, speaking the Seneca and probably other dialects of the Iroquois as well as his native French, " wise and full of ardor for the service." Later in this year he was serving in the company commanded by Desnoyelles, and from this time on his career becomes more and more a part of Niagara history.

It is plain that no credence was given by Beauharnois to the reports reflecting on the integrity of the elder Joncaire's character. That he was thoroughly loyal to the French might also be inferred from the responsibility of his new mission. He was entrusted with the removal to a new place of residence of the Chaouanons.

These people are better known as the Shawanese. To enter fully into their history here would be to travel afar from our especial theme. It will suffice to state that they were of southern origin. About 1698, three or four score families of them, with the consent of the Governor of Pennsylvania, removed from Carolina and established themselves on the Susquehanna, at Conestoga. Others followed, so that by 1732, when the number of Indian fighting men in Pennsylvania was estimated at about 700, one half of them were Shawanese immigrants. About the year 1724 the Delaware Indians, in quest of better hunting-grounds, removed from their old seats on the Delaware and Susquehanna rivers, to the lower Allegheny, upper Ohio, and its branches, and from 1728 the Shawanese gradually followed them.

The friendship of these Ohio Delawares and Shawanese became an object of rivalry for the British and French; the interests of the latter among them were now confided to Joncaire. The vanguard of the Shawanese migrants appears to have gained the upper Ohio as early as 1724, for in that year we find that Vaudreuil had taken measures to weld them to the French. An interpreter, Cavelier, had been sent among them, and had even induced four of their chiefs to go with him to Montreal, where they received the customary assurances of French friendship. At this date, the Ohio Shawanese numbered over 700, but their attachment to the English appears to have been even greater than to the French. They evidently paid some respect to the authority of the French in the Ohio Valley, for on this Montreal visit they asked if the French Governor "would receive them, and where he would wish to locate them." Beauharnois replied that he would "leave them entirely at liberty to select, themselves, a country where they might live conveniently and within the sound of their Father's voice"— i. e., within French influence; "that they might report, the next year, the place they will have chosen, and he should see if it were suitable for them."

In the spring of 1732 Joncaire reported to the Governor that these Indians were settled in villages ("*en village*") " on the other side of the beautiful river of Oyo, six leagues below the river Atigué. The " Beautiful river," or Ohio, at that time designated the present Ohio and the Allegheny to its source. The Atigué [11] was the Rivière au Bœuf, now known as Le Bœuf Creek or Venango River. This seat of the Shawanese, therefore, was a few miles below the present city of Franklin, Pa. To them Joncaire was remanded with gifts and instructions to keep English traders away, and to do all possible to cement their friendship with the French.

In this connection may be noted a curious statement made by an old Seneca chief, whose name is written by the French as Oninquoinonte. Being with Joncaire at Montreal in 1732, the Seneca made a speech to the Governor in which he said: " You know, my father, it is I who made it easy to build the stone house at Niagara, my abode having always been there. Since I cannot conquer my love for strong drink, I surrender that place and establish myself in another place, at the portage of the Le Bœuf River, which was and is the rendezvous of the Chaouanons." He added with unwonted ardor, that the French were masters of all this region, and he would die sooner than not sustain them in their work of settling the Shawanese.

A fair degree of success appears to have rewarded Joncaire's efforts. He is hereafter spoken of as commandant among the Shawanese, and his residence for a considerable part of each year was in the beautiful valley that stretches between long-sloping hills below the junction of the Venango and the Allegheny. Already a historic region, it was destined in a few years to be the scene of important events which should link its story yet more closely with that of the Niagara. Here at the junction of the rivers, Washington is to camp on his way to demand that the French withdraw from the region. Here France is soon to stretch her chain of forest-buried forts, that rope of sand on which she vainly relied for the control of a continent.

[11] See Bellin's "*Carte de la Louisiana.*"

The disposition to migrate further west, shown by several of the Indian tribes at this period, gave a remarkable turn to the policies of the rival white nations on the continent. It was an early wave in the movement of an inevitable flood; though there is little in the old records to indicate that either the English or French saw very far into the future, or gave much heed to anything save relations of immediate profit and advantage. The migrations of the Shawanese covered many years, and included many removes. In 1736 Joncaire found his villages on the Allegheny restless with the prospect of a new settlement in the vicinity of Detroit, on lands ranged over by their friends the Hurons. The next year, the sale by the Senecas and Cayugas of certain lands on the Susquehanna, near where some of the Shawanese had continued to live, started a new migration, and fostered bitterness towards the English. From this time on for many years — for many years indeed after the fall of New France — we find traces of the Shawanese at many points in the Ohio and Mississippi Valleys; and not until the French were finally forced out did the rivalry cease for the friendship of these shifty and uncertain savages; not, obviously, for the sake of that friendship, but because the rival Powers deemed it essential for their control of the inland highways and of the fur trade.

Regarding the proposed settlement at Detroit, the Shawanese pledged themselves to Joncaire to go to Montreal in the spring of 1737, " to hear the Marquis de Beauharnois discourse on their migration." Louis XV, whose phrase has just been quoted,[12] thought that the proposed settlement " is very desirable, so as to protect the fidelity of these Indians against the insinuations of the English. But the delay they interpose to that movement induces His Majesty to apprehend that the Marquis de Beauharnois will meet with more difficulties than he had anticipated, and that the English, with whom His Majesty is informed they trade, had made sufficient progress among them to dissuade them therefrom."

And the main instrument on whom both Governor and King relied was the veteran Joncaire. But the time of his achieve-

[12] Dispatches, Versailles, May 10, 1737.

ments was at an end. On June 29, 1739, he died at Niagara. A band of Shawanese, conducted by Douville de la Saussaye, reached Montreal on July 21st following, and carried the news of the death of the veteran. As the dispatches speak of the receipt at Montreal of news of his death, and do not state that his body was carried there, the conclusion is at least plausible that he was buried somewhere at Niagara.

On September 12, 1740, the Five Nations sent a deputation to Montreal, where they addressed M. de Beaucourt, the Governor, with much ceremony and the presentation of many wampum belts. "Father," said their spokesman, extending a large belt, "you see our ceremony; we come to bewail your dead, our deceased son, Monsieur de Joncaire; with this belt we cover his body so that nothing may damage it. . . . The misfortune which has overtaken us has deprived us of light; by this belt [giving a small white one] I put the clouds aside to the right and to the left, and replace the sun in its meridian. Father," the orator continued, holding out another string of wampum, "by this belt I again kindle the fire which had gone out through our son's death"; then, by way of condolence, with still another belt: "We know that pain and sorrow disturb the heart, and cause bile; by this belt, we give you a medicine which will cleanse your heart, and cheer you up." Eight days later, the Governor, who had been detained at Quebec, sent reply to the warriors: "You had cause to mourn for your son Joncaire, and to cover his body; you have experienced a great loss, for he loved you much. I regret him like you." The marquis promised to send back with them Joncaire's son, already well known to them. "He will fill, near you, the same place as your late son. Listen attentively to whatever he will say to you from me." And thenceforth, in the affections of the Senecas of Western New York, the son is to reign in his father's stead. The story of Chabert de Joncaire the elder is ended.

NOTE.— Much of the data in the foregoing chapters, especially chapters XIV and XV, is drawn from the unprinted "*Correspondance Générale,*" and accompanying *mémoires,* special reports and letters preserved in the Archives at Paris, and in part, by means of copies, in the Archives at Ottawa.

CHAPTER XVI

SONS OF THE ELDER JONCAIRE

THE VARIED SERVICES OF PHILIPPE THOMAS, DANIEL AND FRANÇOIS DE JONCAIRE — THE VALUABLE MEMOIR OF DANIEL — THE EXPEDITION OF 1739 AND DISCOVERY OF LAKE CHAUTAUQUA — A NIAGARA INCIDENT.

IF any ambitious student of French-American history would have problems to solve, he may find what he seeks by attempting to set forth clearly the records of the sons of Louis Thomas de Joncaire. The part they played in New York State, in Canada and the Ohio Valley during the last 20 years of French dominion, makes it worth while to record all that can be verified about them. The father and two of the sons were the most influential agents the French ever sent among the Iroquois. For many years, their influence was the greatest force opposed to Colonel (later Sir) William Johnson and the English Governors of New York Province.

The father's achievements are comparatively clear, and have been set forth with sufficient fullness in preceding pages. But from the time of his death to the downfall of France in America, although the activities of his sons brought them into frequent notice, there is nothing but confusion and contradiction among all writers who speak of them at all.[1]

[1] Much of the confusion that exists in references to Joncaire and his sons is due to the fact that writers have not noted the death of the elder Joncaire in 1739; although it is matter of precise record in the French documents, and of approximate accuracy in English records. It was known to the New York Indian Commissioners at Albany at least as early as March 19, 1740 (N. S.), when an Onondaga Indian went to them "with 7 hands of wampum to acquaint them that the Sachems of their Castle intend as soon as the Waters are open to go to Canada to condole the Death of Jean Cœur, and to invite the other Sachems of the 5 Nations to join them in this Ceremony." (McIlwain's "Wraxall," 216.) The English may naturally have rejoiced at his death, but they also professed to be angry with the Indians who would show respect to his memory. They sent Lawrence Claessen to the Mohawk and Onondaga towns to notify the tribes that the Lieutenant Governor of New York "would take it ex-

If one turns to the documents, he finds the name in many forms; and the English, especially Sir William Johnson, who rarely wrote a French name correctly, gave it many strange spellings, so that the student finds it as Joncaire, Joncœur, Jonkeur, Jonquaire, Joan Cœur, Jean Ceur, Jean Ceure, and in other forms. This variety leads to no particular difficulty. Confusion sets in when use is made, not of the name, but of the seigneurial title. The elder Joncaire, who died at Niagara in 1739, was the Sieur de Chabert, an official interpreter and lieutenant, and is often spoken of as Chabert, or Joncaire-Chabert.

He had a large family. Four of his sons were in the army, colonial troops or the Indian service. Two of them were killed early in life, and may be eliminated from the problem. One became a priest and resided in France. Two others lived for

treamly ill to have them absent in Canada condoling the Death of a Man who had ever been an inveterate Enemy to this Colony." (*Ib.*)

In his Life of Washington, published (vol. I) in 1855, Washington Irving falls into the error of confusing the Joncaire who met Washington at Venango in 1754 with his deceased father. On Washington's arrival at Venango, says Irving, he "inquired of three French officers whom he saw there, where the commandant resided. One of them promptly replied that 'he had command of the Ohio.' It was in fact, the redoubtable Captain Joncaire, the veteran intriguer of the frontier." The "veteran" Joncaire had been dead 15 years, and would have been 84 years old had he still lived — rather aged for strenuous frontier service.

We have no more trustworthy historian of the French in America than Francis Parkman. His scope is continental, and his thoroughness and accuracy beyond question. Only one who has in some measure traversed the same documents that he studied, can realize how unassailable his statements usually are. It is therefore in no spirit of pettiness that we note that in his "Half Century of Conflict" the senior Joncaire and one of his sons are spoken of as the same person, and no distinction is made between them in the index.

Franklin B. Hough's translation of Pouchot's "Memoir" goes further in error. It indexes "Jean Cœur" as one person, and "Joncaire (or Jonquière)" as another; an amazing blunder, for Jonquière was an admiral of the French Navy, and a Governor of Canada, but in no wise connected with the family of Joncaire.

These are but sample errors. Less capable writers and editors have increased them a thousand fold. One modern instance occurs in Augustus C. Buell's "Sir William Johnson," in which some of the deeds of Daniel de Joncaire are ascribed to one "Jean François Joncaire," and many statements are made utterly at variance with the testimony of contemporary documents.

SONS OF THE ELDER JONCAIRE

many years, and the story of Western New York from 1740 to 1759 cannot be told without frequent mention of them.

The eldest son, Philippe Thomas de Joncaire, in 1739, on the death of his father, became " Sieur de Joncaire et Chabert." He was occasionally called Hardi, from the name of his paternal grandmother. In his later years he was oftenest spoken of as Captain Joncaire, and we will so refer to him, to distinguish him from his father and brothers.

Daniel de Joncaire, Philippe's junior by at least seven years,[2] was the " Sieur de Chabert et de Clausonne." He is designated in the documents and reports of his own time, now as Chabert, now as Joncaire-Chabert, again as Chabert de Joncaire, and sometimes as Clausonne or Clauzon. In these pages he will be called Chabert.

The service in which the two brothers were engaged was at some periods the same, and they went and came throughout the same region. Many a reference to them as " Joncaire " or " Chabert " it is impossible to refer with certainty to Philippe Thomas, or to Daniel.[3]

A third brother enters slightly into our story. This was François, born at Montreal, June 20, 1723. He was ordained priest, and signed his name " François de Joncaire." He early removed to France, where he became Vicar of Grasse. Further note of his activities will be made in due place.

The eldest son, Philippe Thomas, born 1707, was taken by his father when a little boy of ten, to live with the Indians. Thomas Wildman, an Indian who had been sent to the Onondagas to spy on the French, reported to the Indian Commissioners at Albany, January 11, 1717 (N. S.), that " Jean Cœur the French interpreter had introduced a little son of his to the Indians in the Senecas' country and desired their pro-

[2] Nine, according to Tanguay.
[3] In the " Documents relating to the Colonial History of the State of New York," very ably edited many years ago by Dr. O'Callaghan, many documents appear, as copied from the originals in London or Paris. The very full index to these volumes contains more than a page of entries relating to the Messrs. Joncaire. The present writer has been unable to reconcile some of these statements with the facts which he has from other sources.

tection and favor for him, that after his death this his son might be received amongst them in the same friendly manner as he himself had ever been; upon which he gave them a belt of wampum and they readily assented." [4] Wildman further reported that " Jean Cœur had a little trading house in the Senecas' country by the side of the lake where he kept goods and traded with them, also a smith to work for them." This was in the vicinity of old Kanadasaga, near the present Geneva, N. Y.

Ten years later we find Philippe Thomas with his father at Fort Niagara; from which post, in 1727, he was sent to the Senecas to get news of a council which had been held at Albany. In Montreal, July 23, 1731, he married Madeleine Renoud du Buisson; she died about 1746. In an official list of 1732 [5] he is mentioned as an ensign, aged 24. In April, 1736, the King granted him promotion to *ensign en pied*, a rank which carried pay. In 1744 he was made lieutenant, and in 1751 promoted to a captaincy, by reason of seniority in service; and because of the requirement that he reside most of the time among the Iroquois, he was given the rank and pay of captain, without a company.[6] For the next few years he was sometimes at Niagara, but oftener among the tribes of Central and Western New York, and the Allegheny Valley. On his father's death in 1739, Philippe was looked to as his natural successor as chief agent for the French among the Iroquois. In September, 1740, these people sent a great delegation to Montreal to ask that he be so appointed. The Governor granted their request, and Philippe truly enough " reigned in his father's stead."

Captain Joncaire — to use the title of his later years — became associated with the Abbé Picquet, who in 1749 founded the famous mission of La Présentation on the site of the present city of Ogdensburg. It is stated by a careful student,[7] that it was Captain Joncaire who built the fort at La Présentation, " aided by Picquet," and that a little later he built another

[4] Wraxall's N. Y. Indian Records (McIlwain, ed.), 117.
[5] Canadian Archives, Ottawa.
[6] Navy Board to La Jonquière, June 6, 1751.
[7] The Abbé Daniel, in his Life of the Chevalier Benoist, p. 49.

on Lake Ontario. This last is uncertain; but certain it is that the militant priest and the adroit and experienced Indian agent and interpreter were long and closely associated; so intimately indeed that by early English writers Captain Joncaire was sometimes termed a priest. On the other hand, the Abbé Picquet, in 1751, mentions Captain Joncaire's Indian wife.

Naturally, the death of the father brought forward both of the sons. Daniel in that year served as interpreter at Niagara and elsewhere, and in official reports was commended for his zeal and efficiency. He shared in the Chicasaw campaign of 1739, as *cadet à l'aiguillette* — the lowest grade of officer. On his return he was made *ensign en second*. At the time of his marriage, January 11, 1751, he was a lieutenant, beyond which rank he did not advance.

Chabert's part in our frontier history is more important than his brother's, and much more may be definitely told about him. After the conquest of Canada, and on his part, a series of vicissitudes and misfortunes which will presently be narrated, Chabert settled at Detroit. From that day to this his family has been numerously represented in Detroit and vicinity, though now the generations are much scattered. From the parish records of St. Anne's Church, Detroit, and from a manuscript genealogy [8] of the family of Daniel, prepared largely from those parish records by the Rev. Father Denissen, some of the facts in the following pages are gathered. It may be noted here that Daniel, whom we are to speak of as Chabert, had a large family. One of his sons was Colonel Francis Chabert; and it is matter of record in the family that of about 100 descendants of Colonel Francis only two bear the name Chabert. Descent has been in the female lines. So far as the present writer has carried his inquiries, he has found no member of the family using the old name Joncaire. In America at least it seems to have been wholly superceded by Chabert, and this in turn is nearly lost, later generations bearing other names gained in marriage.[9]

Many writers refer to the sons of the first Joncaire in Amer-

[8] Preserved in the Burton Library, Detroit.
[9] For further genealogical notes, see Appendix.

ica as having an Indian mother. Captain Pouchot, who personally knew both Captain Joncaire and Chabert, wrote of the former:

"This colonial captain was a half Indian Canadian living among that nation, and possessing much influence. He and his brother Chabert had more than sixty relatives and children which they or their father had among them." [10] This matter has been touched on, in sketching the father's career. It may suffice here to refer to the genealogy as given by Tanguay, which not only does not recognize any admixture of Indian strain, but gives the birth dates of the sons, among other children of the French woman Madelaine le Guay, who was Madame de Joncaire. The obvious explanation is, that Chabert had two families, one in Montreal, the other, a Seneca wife and numerous half-breed children, who lived either at the Niagara portage or in one of the Western New York villages, probably Kanadasaga. This is clearly indicated by several allusions, even more definite than Pouchot's. When Sir William Johnson came to the Niagara in 1761 he learned that the Senecas had sent messengers to Detroit, to hold council with the Hurons, Ottawas and other tribes, more or less hostile to the English. An Onondaga told him that the message "was chiefly spoken in Shabear Jean Cœur's name, who, before [being] taken, advised that step to be taken, in case the French should fall." Sir William noted in his private diary that "Shabear's son, who went with the war belt to Detroit, was named *Tahaijdoris*"; he and another Seneca had undertaken to stir up the Western Indians against the English. Years after, the memory of this no doubt influenced Sir William, for he made strong objections to Chabert's request for a permit to trade at Niagara and Detroit.

Chabert himself said, truly enough, that his relationship with the Senecas was that of adoption, according to the ancient custom of the tribes with whom his father, brother and himself spent a large part of their lives.[11]

[10] Pouchot. "*Mémoires.*" II, 33, note.
[11] The Abbé Auguste Gosselin, in his study of the Abbé Picquet (Proc. Roy. Soc. Can. 1894) says of Daniel de Joncaire: "He was a Frenchman

The most important and trustworthy source of information about Chabert is the memoir which he wrote, or his lawyers wrote for him, when after the loss of Canada, he and others were prosecuted by the French Government for alleged complicity in frauds. The memoir forms part of the voluminous report of the commission established for what was known as "the Canada Affair." One volume is largely made up of the "Memoir of Daniel de Joncaire-Chabert, late commander of the Little Fort Niagara." Printed by Government in Paris in 1763, it has never been put into English, and has long been — probably has always been — excessively rare. One of the most valuable of sources for our regional history in the period under consideration, it is here freely used to picture life on the Lakes and the Niagara in the last two decades of French power.

Whoever would sketch, be it ever so faintly, the conditions of native life in Western New York and the region of the Lower Lakes, as seen by the soldiers and traders of France, and as intimately shared in by a few men of the type of the Joncaires, must give due recognition to the known phases of existence among the Senecas, at this period.

We habitually speak of them as savages, and as the foe of the white man. It is true, they were savage, but the Iroquois federation of which they were a part had passed very far beyond a state of primitive savagery. At the time of the first coming of white men among them, they had reached a degree of enlightenment, of social and economic order, far in advance of anything known elsewhere on the continent. What ultimate form it would have taken, if the evolution could have gone on, uncorrupted by European influence, is a suggestive theme for speculation. They were no longer nomads, but lived in fixed villages. If removal to new sites was more frequent than among Europeans, it was because made necessary by conditions and way of life.

We conceive of the Indian as the natural enemy of the white; an unjust conception, as applied to the aborigines in Western New York at this period. As a white man's town contains

married to an Indian woman, who enjoyed great credit among the Indians." This wholly ignores his French-Canadian wife.

honest men and thieves, old men who are guided by reason and young men who yield to passion, so in Seneca communities existed like diversity. Many times, in the documents, do we find the old men of a nation or a village trying to condone some rash act of their young men. The war parties were made up of young men, partly because they were physically vigorous, partly because their savagery was more in evidence than in maturer years. In time of peace the Seneca was a hospitable host. Even a Frenchman, intruding into their villages, unless suspected of crafty and treacherous purpose, would find a welcome, food and shelter, and an escort on his way. There are many instances of warm personal friendships between red men and white.

When Chabert, for instance, made his long sojourns among the Senecas, he resided, as they did, in a well-built cabin of bark. There was no regularity of streets in a Seneca town, but the houses were scattered, like the trees of the forest that sheltered them. The community or "long house," in which many families lodged under one roof, which was the earlier custom of these people, gradually gave way to the separate hut. The village life however always centered around one principal point, where was the council house, place of meeting, of ceremonies, and of trade. The ancient custom of surrounding their villages with stockades was no longer observed.

The Senecas had no wells, and so fixed their abodes convenient to springs and streams. In the years under notice — one may fairly say, throughout the Eighteenth century — they relied for subsistence quite as much on agriculture as on hunting and fishing. We rate them as poor farmers; yet the first whites who came among them found great fields of corn, pumpkins and squashes. They had orchards of apples and plums. They raised hogs; and before the middle of the century they kept cattle, and had acquired some horses. They were expert at pottery-making and basketry, and showed taste in decoration.

The great spur of modern communities, traffic for the sake of individual gain, had no place among the Senecas. They had no money. Before the advent of the white, wampum was a medium of exchange, but it was ceremonial. It was more in the nature of a message, a proclamation, a defiance, a condolence, than for the payment of debt. It symbolized a great deal for which the civilization of the white had no counterpart. The Indian valued trinkets and liquor as the white man valued furs. While the exchange of these commodities constituted a true trading system, for many decades, it never presented to the Indian the opportunity of profit. He might satisfy his immediate needs and wants; but the accumulation of property formed no part of his scheme of life.

When Chabert was sent by the Governor to winter among the Senecas, what did he find?

He traveled over paths as well established as any modern highway. Save for a few swamps and treeless bottom-lands in river valleys, Western New York was a forest through which ran many footpaths. We have no roads to-day as old as the trails that Chabert knew. They were immemorial in his time and presented the same features they had borne for centuries: here worn deep through forest loam, winding and turning about great roots and boulders; there skirting some bog or pond; or, scarcely perceptible to an untrained eye, following some rocky ridge; yet as a whole making a direct and advantageous route between important points. One great trail, from Lake Erie to the Hudson, is to-day, for much of the way, the course of the New York Central Railroad. The Indian trails served so well the purpose of early settlement that the first white men's roads followed the old highways of travel — of the beginning of which no man knoweth. Trees were cut and tracks were widened. Came the horse, sometimes the train of an army; then the surveyors, the pioneer's wagon, the stage coach, the railway, the motor car; but the world of business and of pleasure to-day merely rolls in luxury where the trader and the Indian, with pack or deer on their shoulders, plodded with moccasined feet. Nature for the most part decreed where paths should go — until in these latter days engineering sometimes defies nature.

The Indians were great travelers. Year after year bands of them gathered at Montreal, some of them coming from the region west of Lake Superior or in the Mississippi Valley. As early as 1677 Indians from the Niagara went to Albany to meet the New York Commissioners and " renew the chain of friendship." To come a thousand miles with furs to Fort Niagara was a common thing. This aptitude for great journeys was perhaps but a survival of the nomadic habits of not very remote ancestors, and is many times illustrated by the Indian's habit of bringing his family and camping for weeks in the neighborhood of the fort, to which he looked for sustenance.

One must keep in mind the conditions that still prevailed, even in the old settled parts of the country. Wild animals were a pest, in New York and New England, long after the Indians ceased to be a terror. In the journal of the New York General Assembly are numerous Acts offering reward for the destruction of wolves and panthers — these last especially in Dutchess and Orange counties. Even in Albany County, wolves and wildcats annoyed the settlements until long after the period we are studying. In the region of the Lakes and the Niagara, the dangerous or obnoxious animals had constantly to be guarded against, but with many species the value of their pelt made their presence not unwelcome. Deer and other useful game abounded, and the Niagara gorge was famous for its rattlesnakes.

Western New York was full of trails, a network of footpaths between important points; and many of them were familiar to Chabert, whose life was largely spent in coming and going through the forests. Canoes sometimes served him; but the records contain no mention of the use of horses, until the latter part of our story. For the most part, he traveled on foot, as did his friends the Senecas.

Emerging from the forest path, pausing at the door of the council house, he found first of all, a greeting, for he was an adoptive member of the tribe, as his father had been before him. Seneca friendship, when the trust is once given, is staunch. The obligations incurred in the ceremony of adoption were sacred and not to be lightly treated. Living as he did, for long periods, year after year, with the Senecas, Chabert, however certain his own French parentage, had a Seneca family, as his father had. The records, naturally enough, are silent on this aspect of his life, but Pouchot knew the ways of the time. It was the rule, rather than the exception, for the French traders and *coureurs de bois* to take Indian wives, even as Sir William Johnson did at his " castle " on the Mohawk.

When Chabert went to his Senecas, he dwelt in intimacy, in a bark cabin among the trees near fresh water, by some clear stream or on the margin of one of Western New York's fair lakes. His coming, after a term of service elsewhere, or attendance at Montreal or Quebec, was none the less welcome because he always brought a store of presents. More and more the Seneca came to rely on the whites — either French or British, as best served — for the necessities of life. Gradually the deerskin garments of their own make, trimmed with dyed porcupine quills, gave way to the blankets and broadcloths, the beads and galloon which came out of the stores at Niagara and Oswego. Grease and vermilion, beads, silver bracelets, knives, mirrors, tomahawks, powder and flints, guns, flour and liquor, came from the same source, and through the generous and friendly hands of Chabert. Sometimes he brought a smith with him, who set up his forge in the forest, repaired the guns and supplied the iron work which the Seneca could not make for himself.

The routine of life in a Seneca village was by no means monotonous. It varied with the seasons, but there was always much for the women to do. They planted, hoed and gathered the crops. When the hunter returned with game, the women prepared it. There were removals, for weeks at a time, to favorable fishing places; and the Seneca village of the Little Rapid — or as it sometimes is written, the Little Seneca Rapid — meaning a Seneca settlement at the outlet of Lake Erie, where is now the city of Buffalo — was such a temporary lodgment of a band whose other home was on the banks of the Genesee or the shore of Seneca Lake. In early spring, when the sap began to flow, the making of maple sugar engrossed the village, perhaps taking the people miles from home. More exciting yet were the raids on the pigeon roosts, when thousands of birds were slaughtered.

These were some of the avocations of peace. The hunting season occupied the men. There was much leisure for the playing of games, gambling, the telling of tales, and for dancing. The Iroquois dances were an elaborate evolution, and some of them, combining song and recitative, fitted every mood; now medium of devotion and thanksgiving, again serving as a stimulus to passion, preliminary to the warpath.

With all these aspects of Seneca village life, and many more, Chabert was as familiar as with the streets of the little French town of Montreal, or the steep highways and official quarters of Quebec. In after years, when a prisoner in the Bastille, he wrote his memoirs, recalling his youth in the forests of Western New York.

My father, [he says] prisoner of war with the Iroquois, had the good fortune of escaping the flames through the protection of an Indian woman who adopted him. This privilege, hereditary with these people, made us pass, my brothers and I, as children of the nation. This adoption caused us to be chosen by the Baron de Longueuil, then Commander-General of Canada, to be sent as hostages among the Five Iroquois nations. . . . I lived, then, with them and with several other neighboring tribes (Ottawas, Chippewas, Shawanese),[12] from 1725 to 1735. Thus I have had the honor of using well for the service of my King several years which in ordinary service slide away in pure loss to the country. This military and Indian education was little likely to fit me for the shady schemes of fraudulent finance.

That even at this early period in his career Chabert had won the approval and confidence of the highest officials in Canada, is indicated by a letter from the Intendant, Hocquart, to the Minister, October 25, 1734, in which we read:

Pardon the liberty I take, Monseigneur, in writing to you in favor of a young cadet of the troops, who is both prudent and full of zeal for the service — the Sieur Chabert Joncaire, the younger son of the Sr. Joncaire, lieutenant and Iroquois interpreter. This young man, who is 21 or 22 years of age, is full of honor and [good] feelings, and is always ready to proceed as soon as any duty is in question. Last winter he made a journey on snowshoes as far as Ni-

[12] Chabert gives them as: "*Outaouacs, Sauteux, Chaonasnons.*"

agara and returned by the country of the Iroquois, whose language he understands perfectly. He is now in the expedition under the command of M. Desnoyelles, and I am sure he will distinguish himself if there is an opportunity to do so. I could not, Monseigneur, say too much in his favor. He deserves to be promoted. The Marquis de Beauharnois, who values him, will bear quite as favorable testimony about him.

The many words of praise for him, found in official reports, clearly show that he was a young man of exceptional force of character and devotion to the service, and largely endorse his own estimate of his achievements.

The reader may be reminded that the memoir from which we draw these details of Chabert's service was written to win royal favor. No opportunity is lost in it to assert his honesty and uprightness. It must be conceded, that Chabert and his lawyers made a very strong case of it; but for the present we pass over that phase of the story, seeking merely to show what were his employments during the years now under study.

My brother [Captain Joncaire] having been assigned to the chiefs of the Five Nations by the Governor in 1735, I found myself alone among these peoples. I learned that the English, in order to avenge some particular wrong, were getting ready to fall upon our villages. I was 18 years old [13] and I had to be my own adviser. I saw nothing better to do than to make alliance [14] with the Indians, to get the start of the enemy. Discovered and forestalled, the English made overtures; they were listened to; peace was concluded.

Chabert was convinced that the English, could they have taken him at this time, " would have done me a bad turn "; but, he adds, " this was only a feeble prelude of dangers without number which I have since run, in laboring without relaxation among so many barbarous nations for the good of the Colony." He continues:

In 1736 I was ordered to go among the Five Nations, to the Fort of Niagara, there to await the chiefs from the nations of the Sault

[13] This date agrees with Tanguay (III, 283), but not with the Detroit records, which give Daniel's birth as in 1714.
[14] Does this mean marriage?

S. Louis and from the Lake of the Two Mountains, and to escort them to the Missisagués, in order to make a good peace between these allies of France. The negotiation succeeded; I returned to the fort, from which I repaired twice to the Five Nations, in order to keep them always peaceably disposed.

The tribes on the Ohio were suspected of being prevailed upon by the English to stir up the neighboring nations against the French. The suspicion was well founded. I was sent there in company with chiefs of the Five Nations. I broke up the conspiracy, and remained all summer [1737] in that country, from which I came back to winter, partly at the Fort, partly among the Five Nations.

In the spring [1738] I was again charged with visiting different villages, in order to keep informed on what happened, and to assemble the councils, of which I sent a report to the Governor.

As a general thing, when I was not on some military expedition, my ordinary employment, winter and summer, without let up, was to travel over this vast continent; in summer by canoe,[15] in winter on foot, across the ice and snow; to cultivate friendship, check imprudence, dispel plots, or break off the treaties of these people with the enemy. Also may I add that there is no warrior in his Majesty's service who has known less than I the [comforts of] winter quarters. I do not say in time of war (that would be all the year in this country), but even in time of peace; for these perpetual negotiations offer dangers as manifold and more formidable than those of battle, for they are concealed under the false appearance of peace [16] and of friendship; and that it may not be thought that the allurement of profit led me to engage in enterprises so perilous, it is well to remark that I was only fed by the King [when] in the French posts. When I set out, they gave me provisions for ten days, such as would be given to a soldier in France. The rest of the journey, and my stay in the villages, was entirely at my own expense.

I had thus made more than forty journeys, up to 1738, without

[15] Chabert adds this note: "As these rivers are often dry in several places, one has to transport overland the provisions and goods to a place more navigable, with what excess of fatigue in a country where the heat as well as the cold are much more than here. In winter, one absolutely must walk with snowshoes, which, by compressing a larger surface of snow prevents one from sinking; this foot-gear doubles the fatigue."

[16] "When the Indians break with any one they have no other way of showing it than by the tomahawk and the gun; if one comes among them under these circumstances, a deputy is no more than an enemy in their eyes."— *Note in original.*

receiving any recompense, and indeed, for a still longer time, without being promoted.

After having wintered, as I have said, as much at Niagara as with the Five Nations, I was ordered to set out for Fort la Reine.[17] It was said that the English thought of making an establishment in the neighborhood. I perceived the falsity of this report. I thereupon descended the Ohio with the troops commanded by M. de Longueuil. We entered Louisiana, and I was deputed, along with the chiefs who accompanied us, to treat with the Illinois, whose warriors I led to the general meeting-place, which was at Fort de l'Assomption.[18]

Chabert continues with some account of the campaign. The war waged by the French in 1739-40 against the Chicasaws in what is now Western Tennessee is obviously a theme remote from our subject; but it was the occasion of an expedition through Lake Ontario, the Niagara, and Lake Chautauqua, which appears to have escaped the notice of those who have written of the region. Chabert's own memoir and other corroborative documents, establish the fact that white men were on Lake Chautauqua ten years before the expedition led by Céloron, which has been regarded as the original exploration of that region.

From the 16th to the 30th June, 1739, 442 men left Montreal under command of the Baron de Longueuil, Major of Montreal, to go to serve under Bienville of Louisiana, in his campaign against the Chicasaws. That this Canadian force passed through Lake Ontario, up the Niagara, along the south shore of Lake Erie, and through Chautauqua Lake into the Ohio, is proved by existing documents.

Among the officers who accompanied de Longueuil in 1739, were several whose early military training had been had in the organization known as the Company of Gentlemen Cadets of the Colonies — *La Compagnie des Cadets-Gentilhommes des Colonies*. It was created under the War Department of

[17] Fort Lorraine.
[18] Near the mouth of the Margot or Wolf River, Tennessee, according to Monette. ("Valley of the Mississippi," I, 290.) Bancroft locates it on the bluff of Memphis. ("United States," III, 363.) Louisiana, as the name was used in those days, was virtually the Valley of the Mississippi.

France in 1730, to provide under-officers suitably trained for service in India and America. The cadets appear to have been drawn from families of good social standing, their military training was thorough and judicious, and the Company not only gained a high repute for the efficiency of the young men it supplied for colonial service, but it also, and naturally enough, developed something of zealous pride and exclusiveness — a true *esprit de corps*. In the earlier years of the existence of this Company, the number of gentleman-cadets maintained in the establishment was 50; later it was reduced to 30. From 1730 to 1781, the Company furnished 72 officers for infantry and artillery regiments in colonial service. From them were appointed ensigns for the infantry regiments, corporals, sergeants, and *anspessades*. In 1781, apparently for reasons of economy, the Company of Gentlemen-Cadets was consolidated in an "auxiliary battalion," which proved, according to one seemingly well-informed critic,[19] against the good of the service.

There is a list of 28 cadets appointed by the Court in 1731, signed at Quebec by Beauharnois, whose pay in the same service began January 1, 1732. In it appear the names of De Lignery, Portneuf the elder, Contrecœur, Chabert and Belestre, all of whom figure in our story. Another list (*cadets à l' eguillette*), 1739–42, briefly characterizes the officers, many of whom were to become history-makers, during the next two decades, in the region here under study.

Of Duplessis Fabert it is noted: "Of little capacity." De la Chauvignerie is vouched for as "good officer, zealous for the service, an Iroquois interpreter." De Léry, "good officer." Chevalier de Repentigny, "of *esprit*, still young but promising." De Belestre, "good officer, zealous for the service." Céloron, "young man, discreet and very promising"— an interesting note in view of his prominent part in the region a few years later.

The following are named as having served against the Chica-

[19] Author of an unsigned memoir on the Company of Gentleman Cadets, in the Paris Archives; a copy at Ottawa.

SONS OF THE ELDER JONCAIRE

saws, which implies that they shared in the expedition through the Niagara and Chautauqua Lake in 1739:

Hertel de la Fresniere; Hertel de Beaubassin; Langly the elder — of whom it is noted: " Zealous in the service; was sent with the detachment against the Chicasaws, but was obliged to remain at Niagara because of an accident; impossible to speak too well of him." Langly de Fontenelle; Rigauville ("promising youth"); Marin ("zealous, capable and of good conduct," etc.); Joncaire de Clauzonne ("interpreter at Niagara, zealous," etc.); Joncaire Leguay [20] ("detached to the Senecas, zealous and exemplary, he was in the Chicasaw campaign"); and several others, of less importance in our annals.

Still another document [21] shows that among the officers of the expedition were Lieutenants de Sabrevois, de Vassan, and Le Gardeur de St. Pierre; Portneuf, who ranked as second ensign; and de Lignery, ensign and major of the detachment. It names four cadets: Michel Hertel de Rouville, Chaussegros de Léry, Joncaire de Closonne, and La Gai [Le Guay] de Joncaire.

A Recollect priest, Father Vernet, was attendant chaplain; and the expedition was accompanied, at least to Lake Erie, by the Jesuit missionary La Bretonnière, " of the Iroquois of the Sault," and by M. Queret, an ecclesiastic from the mission of the Lake of the Two Mountains. There was also a surgeon, whose name is not given.

With 24 soldiers —" one drummer " being especially mentioned — 45 Canadian *habitants* to manage the canoes, and 319 savages, de Longueuil and his staff, in the early summer of 1739, arrived at Fort Niagara, made the long portage and skirted the Lake Erie shore to the westward. Many a traveler to-day notes with pleasure the gradual rise of those Chautauqua hills, rich with grain fields, orchards and vineyards; but to the men who marched with de Longueuil they could have meant little save toil and danger. Just what their route was,

---

[20] " Le Guay " was the mother's family name. Only in this instance have I found it used for one of the sons.

[21] Paris archives; copy at Ottawa.

from Lake Erie, cannot be stated; but that it approximated the route of Céloron in 1749, is probable. De Léry's journal of 1754 indicates a point on Lake Chautauqua "where our camp was in 1739"—proof that the expedition passed that way.[22]

On this expedition Chabert had hard experiences. Of one episode he records: "We had 18 days of marching and provisions for six days. Moreover, charged to observe and not to fight, we could not even fire a musket. When our provisions were consumed we lived on acorns roasted in hot ashes."

A little later in this year, he says, "I again set out with a war party. . . . We brought back several prisoners to the fort." In 1740 his service was largely among the Chicasaws — full of incident and adventure but not essential for the present narrative. "I served as interpreter," he says; "an understanding was reached, and I led the chiefs of the Tehicachas (Chicasaws) to the Fort de l'Assomption, there to ratify the treaty; after which the Governor sent me back to Niagara; whence I had to go, all winter long, from village to village, with as much of risk as of fatigue, to hold or regain several nations which the English had drawn to their side." Chabert continues:

The necessity of treating with these and several other nations which came to Niagara for all sorts of provisions in the good season, kept me there nearly all summer [1741]. When I had negotiated with them, I resumed my ordinary journeys. Again, orders carried me among the Five Nations to make ratification of neutrality [1742] and to engage them to defend Forts Frontenac and Niagara, built on their lands, and which served as *entrepôt* for the trade which we were making with them; but they demanded on their side that Oswego, an English fort, should be spared, in the preservation of

[22] The Rev. Jacques Quintin de la Bretonnière, who passed through the Niagara and adjacent lakes with de Longueuil in 1739, had come to Canada in 1721 or earlier. He spent most of his life at the Sault St. Louis mission, not far from Montreal. The Jesuit, Nau, wrote, Oct. 2, 1739: "Father de la Bretonnière accompanied the 300 Iroquois from our village who take part in the war." A year later he wrote: "Father de la Bretonnière, who followed our savages . . . went back to France by way of the Mississippi." What a meager record of a great adventure! Of the missionary Queret, who went with him, I find no record.

Portion of Bellin's Map of 1745, Showing Lake Chautauqua and the Portage

which they had the same interest; this could not be refused to them, since the salvation of the colony depended on the tranquility of these savages, the most redoubtable warriors in all Canada.

This affair ended, I asked permission to join the King's troops; but the Governor wrote to me that the most brilliant exploits did not by any means equal the services which I rendered in a single day, in keeping the Five Nations pacifically disposed; that moreover he had no one who would be able to replace me among these peoples. So I continued, by his orders, to hold them in the way of duty. The good of the service called me three more times this year to Oswego, not to take them by surprise (this fort being comprised in the neutrality), but to keep an eye on the English, and discover if they were making any preparations against Niagara.

The second expedition of white men to the Ohio by way of the Niagara and Chautauqua route was in 1743. Reporting on the events of that year to the Minister, Maurepas, Beauharnois wrote from Quebec, October 13th, that he had instructed Joncaire to inform the Senecas of the proposed removal of the Shawanese, and adds: " I have, besides, enjoined on Sieur la Saussaye, who went up this summer to where they are collected together, not to neglect anything in regard to this migration," etc. No detailed account is found of La Saussaye's embassy; but when, in 1749, Céloron led his expedition by the Chautauqua portage to the Ohio, La Saussaye went with him. " The portage," wrote Céloron in his journal, speaking specifically of the path below the lake used because the water in the Outlet was low, " was shown to me by the Sieur de La Saussaye," who had passed that way six years before.

It was in 1743 that Chabert " got wind," as he says, of a serious plot against the French, involving Niagara and other posts. His account of it is too prolix for our present purpose. The Sauteux, in British interest, were active among all the tribes on the Ohio and even on the Illinois. According to Chabert, there was formed a far-reaching league against the French, achieved and cemented by English wampum-belts, " to induce them "— the tribes —" to lay violent hands on all the French scattered about in the different posts of this country.

I made haste to give notice to the commandant at Niagara. From there, setting out with four savages of the Five Nations, I was so expeditious that in five days I came up to the English agents, and ordered them to give the belts back to me. Fear made them docile. I sent them to the Governor (M. de Beauharnois) from whom I received as my only reward, great praise, with promise to make the most at Court of so essential a service. I doubt," Chabert caustically adds, " if he kept his word, for while he governed I received no promotion at all, nor other recompense for my labors, except the order to go through them all over again — a service as costly as it was barren for me."

His service in the year or so following was of the same character as already indicated, save that he was employed more in what is now New York State. "I continued to go and come, sometimes at the fort [Niagara], sometimes in the villages, sparing neither care nor attentions, efforts, blandishments, presents, to offset the advantage which their offers and their liberality tended to gain for the English." He complains that in the Indian villages there were always "busybodies" who on occasion were ready to murder, "which put me constantly in danger of being killed." Not even his relationship to the Senecas guaranteed him safety among other tribes where English influence was strong. And he came to be very much hated, and hunted, by the English. "Constantly," he writes, "when the English were at war with us, they did my brother and myself the honor of putting a price on our heads, testimony — as glorious as it was little intended — of the respect and fear which our influence and our talent for controling the savage mind, inspired in them."

It was at this period — Chabert does not give the date, but it was prior to 1747 — that the Senecas brought word to Fort Niagara that the English, from Oswego, were planning an attack. As soon as messages could be sent, Quebec was apprised. Word came back that Chabert should go to Oswego, to spy on the English. "I interrupted my negotiations with the natives," says the memoir, "to make three journeys to Oswego, to discover the purpose of the English, on whose part an expedition against Niagara was always feared. Indeed they were again making plans to possess themselves of this place." The plot included an attack on Niagara and a massacre of all the French by the Sauteux and other western tribes supposed to have been brought under English influence. Chabert learned of it all from friendly Senecas while absent from Fort Niagara. "On this information," he writes, "having taken with me twenty Iroquois, I hastened to notify the commandant of that place, that he might keep the soldiers from going out. I next went with a reinforcement of 15 Frenchmen from the garrison to overtake the Sauteux deputed for the English. I caught up with them in the second day's march, took them by surprise, and carried them all prisoners to the fort. They confessed the plot, after two days in prison. In order to manage their people carefully, they were set free, on their promise that they would turn against the English who had won them over. In fact, they killed several of them." The most exacting Frenchman could hardly have demanded a more striking proof of good faith.

The year 1747 brought to Fort Niagara new alarms, and in new guise. Now the cry was that the British had enlisted the Hurons and the Illinois with other tribes east and west, in a new plot to massacre the French. Here is Chabert's account of it:

The full moon of May was the day set for the general uprising. Some chiefs of the Five Nations, bought up with money, were the principal agents in this plot. On the other hand, Fort Niagara was to be surprised by the Loups des Montagnes, whose chief with a number of his warriors would ask for an audience with the commandant of the fort, massacre him with his officers even in the council, slaughter the garrison and burn the place.

The stroke was well planned and might have succeeded, but that an Indian woman, one of those called *dames de conseil* (since they have a voice in the councils, and know all the secrets of the tribe) revealed to me all the mystery of this conspiracy.

I went at once to the commandant at Niagara, and to the commandants of the other French posts, equally menaced; thence, without loss of time I quickly followed the savages sent by the English.

I found them in the woods after a march of fifty leagues. I bitterly reproached them for their treachery. They handed over to me, with a good grace, the English wampum belts, and assured me that they had undertaken the affair with regret because they saw that I would be included in the general massacre of the French.

I brought them back to Fort Niagara where they were well treated. M. de la Galissonière gave me thanks proportioned to the magnitude of the service which I had rendered to the colony in delivering it from one of the greatest dangers it had ever run.

The following year [1748], Chabert's services were recognized by a promotion at the hands of Government; he was commissioned " Commander of the Five Nations." In later and unhappy years, when the impoverished and imprisoned veteran was suing for clemency and justice, he could not refrain, in speaking of this promotion, from observing that it was " a mark of esteem and satisfaction for which I paid dear, although I had in fact already bought it." He continues:

We were holding these people [the Iroquois] only through their self-interest. With empty hands I would have lost all the credit and merit of my adoption; they were not however filled with the King's goods; my own supplied them. . . .

One day, as I was holding a great council to hear a message from the Governor-general, four savages bought up by the English entered the hall (or cabin) of the council, and approaching me as if to hear me better, one of them struck me with his dagger, and wounded me.

As he bent his head I swung on him, instantly, a heavy blow of my tomahawk, and laid him at my feet.

His three accomplices rushed up as if to pounce upon me, but the other warriors drove them out of the place, and compelled them the next day to beg my pardon. With this I had to be content. If these conspirators had been in larger number, I should have been lost. Behold to what a chief without a following finds himself exposed! At the mercy of the whims of these American barbarians, he must be prodigal of his goods and of his life, happy indeed if his obscure but useful services do not remain swallowed up in these vast wildernesses.

Chabert's statements regarding his varied services are well borne out by numerous documents, both French and English.

A few citations from them will not only shed some further light on the service in which the brothers Joncaire were engaged, but will also show how difficult it is to determine, oftentimes, which of the two is designated, each of them being called (in various spellings) the Sieur de Joncaire.

The employment of Philippe de Joncaire among the Iroquois began, as we have noted, several years before his father's death in 1739. In 1735 he was "assigned" to the chiefs of the Five Nations. From 1738 he and his brother had to confront a greater adversary than their father had known, for in that year William Johnson came among the Mohawks in English interest; was soon adopted into their tribe, made domestic alliances and long sustained as intimate and influential a place among them as the Joncaires did among the Senecas, besides having a far more absolute authority in his official capacity.

In an address to the Senecas, July 31, 1742, Beauharnois said: "I still leave you masters of your son, Joncaire, who came down with you. I send his brother with you to learn your language; you will not hold any councils except in the presence of the one or the other, so that I may be informed of what passes among you." The speech was followed by the gift of presents, "which," said the Governor, "I have instructed my son to distribute for me."

In April, 1744, the French Governor went up to Montreal to meet delegations from the tribes. On the 20th of that month he wrote to the Minister: "I have just this moment received a letter from Sieur de Joncaire, who is at the Seneca village, whereunto he annexes the message of the English sent to each of the villages of the Five Iroquois Nations." This message, which was said to have been sent throughout New York State the preceding December, with strings of wampum to command attention, was somewhat startling. "Brethren," it said, "I give you notice that Menade [New York] has been attacked, and that so many men have been killed on both sides, that nothing but blood is to be seen all around. I know not as yet what nation is attacking us; therefore, brethren, make haste and send one man from each village to Choueghen (Oswego) for the defense of the fort there, and you will go on the scout as far as Fort Frontenac." This and more seemed to Beauharnois so important that his letter conveying it to Maurepas was written, save for a few words, in cypher.[23] "One thing is certain," the Governor added: "according to what Sieur de Joncaire has written to me, that one Indian from each nation, except the Senecas, has remained at Choueguen since the close of December."

Another letter of the same year reports the desire of the Senecas to have the "Sieur de Joncaire" return to them, he having gone down to Montreal. In October a chief from the Sault St. Louis reports at Montreal that the Five Nations were under arms and that they were saying, "they saw clearly their Father was angry with them, since he did not send back their son Joncaire, as that alone could tranquilize them"; and he added that "a Mohawk squaw, his relative, had told him, should *Nitachinon* (that is, Sieur de Joncaire) return to the Senecas, all will be changed, and we shall be satisfied." And in the summer of 1745, when the Senecas heard that Joncaire was to be stationed elsewhere they begged of the Governor in characteristic language, that he might remain with them:

"Father, we have a child who heeds us not; he never ceases threatening us that he will leave our country; with that intention he has pulled down his house. Father, we pray that you reprimand him. When he is among us everything goes well, and when he talks of going away even the children are alarmed, all confiding in him for good times. Father, be assured that no insult will ever be offered him; we are all ready to place ourselves in front of him, and will defend him on all occasions."

To this characteristic expression the Governor responded: "You, it is, who reared the child of whom you now complain. He will remain with you as long as the good of the service will not require me to recall him. I am persuaded of your affection for him, and of the quietness he secures you when in your country."

There is no more doubt of Seneca affection for this man than there is of English hatred of him. Late in 1744 four

[23] N. Y. Col. Docs. IX, 1102.

Onondagas "came to Lake Ontario to warn Sieur de Joncaire not to pass by Choueghen [Oswego] except at night, as the English had issued orders to take him dead or alive." [24]

In 1745, writing to the Minister, the Count de Maurepas, Beauharnois observed: "At their [the Senecas'] request I have sent Sieur de Joncaire to their country; he is to preserve them in their apparent dispositions, and to render me an account of the smallest change that may be effected by the urgent solicitation of the English, and by the resolutions to be adopted at a great Council to be held in the course of this month at Orange, which the Five Nations are to attend." It was at this council in Albany, October 8, 1745, that Hendrick, a Mohawk sachem, looking for favors from the English, told a rambling tale of the plottings of one " Jean Ceur " who, it is explained in the English record, is " a French Indian who generally resides amongst the Sinnekes, one of our Six Nations, and does us much Mischief amongst them." [25] Two years later, a delegation of Cayugas and Onondagas told Governor Clinton that " some Cocknewaga [Caghnawaga] Indians were arrived at Yaugree [Niagara] with a large packet of letters, part of which were for John Ceur at the Seneca's Country, and part of which were opened at Yaugree, there being Indians present who say that when they went to read the letters, they locked the door on them, which made the Indians suspicious; so one of them, an Indian that understood French, stood and listened at the door, and found that they had or was about concluding to destroy the Five Nations, particularly the Cayugas. That three Nations of the Foreign Indians have agreed to destroy the Fort at Yaugree, for they say a sort of Witches about the said Fort always keep the Path foul and dirty, and for that reason they have resolved to make it clean." [26]

This interesting discovery was attributed to " the Missesagues, Wawehattecooks and Ockneharuse, who have eight big

[24] N. Y. Col. Docs. IX, 1111.
[25] N. Y. Col. Docs. VI, 293.
[26] Speech of Indians to Gov. Clinton, July 17, 1747. N. Y. Col. Docs. VI, 391.

Castles — the biggest of all the Nations, these people are 1500 or 2000."

The Mississagas we know as a tribe of Algonquin stock, with one or more villages on the west side of Niagara. The other tribes cannot with certainty be identified. First and last there was no lack of evil spirits — some of them fiends incarnate — at Fort Niagara; but the discovery of witches must be ascribed to the fondness of the aborigine for figurative speaking. " To keep the path clean " was one of the Indian's commonest and most expressive metaphors. While Governor Clinton and his council would have been well pleased to see the western tribes destroy Fort Niagara, they apparently paid little heed to the message, except as regarded " John Ceur." He was neither a figure of speech nor a thing of imagination, but an ever-active and able adversary.

Again, in an official report of the operations of the French in 1745, it is noted that "munitions and presents have been sent to Sieur Joncaire, to enable him to negotiate with the Iroquois . . . and to retain them neutral." Later (March 15, 1746) in a similar document, mention is made of " Ensign Joncaire of the troops, who was sent last fall to the Senecas, to retain the Iroquois of the Five Nations in a strict neutrality." In May, the " Sieur Joncaire, who resides among the Senecas, sends us, in a letter, of the 1st April, confirmation of the neutrality of the Five Nations; that the hatchet of the English, which had been accepted by some young Mohawks, had been returned to them by the chiefs of that nation, who have declared that they would remain quiet during the war." [27] In September, Joncaire writes that " no dependence is to be placed on the conduct of the Iroquois," etc., until they return from the Albany Council.[28] In a report of April 21, 1747, the Governor acknowledges letters from " Sieur de Joncaire, resident among the Senecas," who reports, among other things, that he has sent a spy to Albany, and " that there is a secret understanding between the Five Nations and our domiciliated Iroquois, to allow the whites to fight each other without interfer-

[27] N. Y. Col. Docs. X, 41.
[28] *Ib.*, 67.

ing with them on either side"; which would have been a most wise decision, could the Five Nations have stood by it.

It is interesting to compare the English records, at this point, with the French. At the Albany Conference of July, 1748, a Seneca orator declared: "We shall not suffer Jan Cœur nor any French to come and reside among us"; and again: "Jean Couer has been given up already by the Sinekes."[29] A French record of the same period, gives the news in different guise: "Sieur Joncaire, Resident at the Senecas, having demanded to be relieved, in consequence of his health, the General [La Galissonière] has appointed Sieur [Daniel] Joncaire Clauzonne, his brother, to succeed him."[30]

Citations regarding the employment of the two brothers might be greatly multiplied; but the foregoing sufficiently indicate the general character of their service. One or the other will reappear, often in connection with matters of great moment, as our narrative proceeds. It is clear that Joncaire *père*, who died in 1739, was succeeded as agent to the Iroquois by his eldest son, Philippe Thomas, otherwise Captain Joncaire. Most of the allusions in the above quotations are to him.

Daniel, otherwise Chabert, says he was sent to live among the Indians in 1725. Accepting 1717 as his birth-date, he was a little boy of nine when this service began. When his father died, Daniel was 22 years old, and in 1742, when Beauharnois sent him to the Senecas, he was 25. From that time on for some years, when both brothers are in like employment, and both usually referred to in the documents simply as "Joncaire," it would be pretense to assume to point out which one is sometimes meant.

In later years the confusion largely disappears. Philippe Thomas is a captain of the Marine troops; Daniel is a lieutenant of infantry in the regiment of Guienne, and as commandant of the fort at the upper end of the Niagara portage, tells his own story for us with graphic pen.

The commanding officers on the Niagara, during the earlier years of French control, have been indicated in the course of

[29] N. Y. Col. Docs. VI, 451, 444.
[30] *Ib.*, IX, 163.

our narrative. Whoever may have preceded La Salle in the region, whether priest or trader, had here no exercise of civil or military authority. La Salle had both, and properly heads the list. In his absence, La Motte for a brief time was in command at the mouth of the river, as was Tonty at the shipyard above the falls. Two officers commanded the short-lived Fort Denonville — the Sieur de Troyes, and after him, in 1688, Captain Desbergères. France neglected the region until 1708, when the Government agent, d'Aigremont, met with the elder Joncaire on the site of Fort Niagara and counseled how to thwart the plans of the English. Not again for 12 years is French authority in the region maintained by a representative on the Niagara. The building of Joncaire's trading house in 1720 made him the local commandant. In his absence his authority passed to the Sieur de La Corne. Six years later, with the building of Fort Niagara, began a succession of military commandants which continued until the French were driven from the river, in 1759.

The first commanding officer at the fort was the Chevalier de Longueuil, Jr.; after him, the elder Joncaire. In 1727 M. Pommeroy was at the head of the post; Joncaire again served; and in 1729 appeared the Sieur de Rigauville, whose advent was signaled by a mutiny, as already related. In spite of the disturbance, the dispatches of the time speak well of him. In a report to the Minister, more than two years after,[31] the Governor wrote that the Niagara mutiny would have been reported the year before, " had it originated from any other cause than the intoxication of some soldiers belonging to the garrison, on the day of the commotion, and perhaps the state of discipline which Sieur de Rigauville, the new commandant, had somewhat neglected." To counteract this accusation the Governor continued: " This officer comports himself very well at his post, where he causes the duty of the service to be performed with as much exactness as in a hostile country. We have none other than very favorable testimony to report to you, of his conduct." He is again commended, five years later,[32]

[31] Beauharnois and Hocquart to Count de Maurepas, Oct. 23, 1731.
[32] Letter to the Minister, Sept. 12, 1736.

View of Niagara Engraved to Illustrate Kalm's Narrative, 1751

At the Crest of the Fall, Extreme Right, "a," Indicates "Place Where a Piece of Rock was Broken from which while Standing Turn'd the Water Obliquely Across the Fall" (as in Hennepin's view); "b," "Two Men Passing Over the East Stream with Staves"; "c," "Indians Reascending Their Ladder"

for his care in keeping *voyageurs* from passing along the south shore of the lake, where they might fall into the toils of the English.

The officer commonly designated as de Rigauville, was Nicolas-Blaise des Bergères et de Rigauville. Born in 1682, he appears in official lists of 1695 as an ensign. At Quebec, April 4, 1712, he married Marie-Françoise, daughter of François Pachot. In 1727 he was seigneur of Bellechasse and lieutenant of a company; in 1736 he was made a captain. He appears to have commanded at Niagara from 1729 until about 1740. His death, which may have occurred at the old fort, is mentioned in a dispatch of May, of that year.

He was still in command, in 1738, when an incident occurred that broke the monotony of their isolated existence. Two of his Indian hunters had set out for Grand Island; on the way over the portage they had " tasted several times " some brandy, the result being that they were overcome in their canoe, and instead of paddling up to Grand Island they drifted towards the falls. By great effort they reached what is now known as Goat Island, but they could not get off. They made a ladder of basswood bark, let themselves down over the cliff between the two falls and in the lower river tried to swim ashore, but exhausted themselves in fighting the eddies and currents, which they could not get through. Worn out and wounded on the rocks, they climbed up their ladder, resigned to death by starvation. Nine days they were in this extremity. But other Indians on the eastern shore had seen their plight and carried the news to the fort. De Rigauville " caused poles to be made and pointed with iron; two Indians determined to walk to this island by the help of the poles, to save the other poor creatures, or perish themselves. They took leave of all their friends as if they were going to death. Each had two such poles in his hands, to set against the bottom of the stream, to keep them steady "— the river at the east side of the upper end of the island being shallow then as now. " So they went and got to the island, and having given poles to the two poor Indians there, they all returned safely to the main." A dozen years later, when Peter Kalm the Swedish botanist visited Niagara, the officers of the fort told him of the adventure, the first we have record of in a vicinity so prolific since of tragic mishaps. Kalm was so impressed that he wrote down the story, which was printed in the *Gentleman's Magazine,* January, 1751 — the first description by an eye-witness of Niagara Falls, to appear in English. An engraving, probably intended to accompany Kalm's letter, appeared in the February issue. It shows the ladder, which the Indians made and their rescuers, crossing with staves.

CHAPTER XVII

IRONDEQUOIT AND OSWEGO

CLAIMS AND CONTESTS FOR STRATEGIC HARBORS — PROJECTS OF GOVERNOR CLARKE AND HIS SUCCESSORS — FEATURES OF THE FUR TRADE AT OSWEGO — FORT NIAGARA THREATENED.

THE French had a practical acquaintance with the shores, bays, harbors, and islands of Lake Ontario while yet it was a hearsay region to the English. Though only the principal expeditions through its waters can be noted, one must remember that many traders whose names are not recorded, for many years skirted these shores, and from their many voyages carried back to Montreal and Quebec an intimate knowledge of every bay, bar and headland, which became familiar, though under a confusing variety of names, to all *voyageurs, coureurs de bois,* and even the less adventurous traders and officials of the towns.

We have seen how La Salle and de Casson followed the south shore in 1669. One of the earliest to know that route well, was the elder Joncaire, whose letter written from the Bay of the Cayugas, now Sodus Bay, in 1709, has been given. (P. 171.) Sodus received less attention from the early travelers than either the Oswego or Irondequoit. After Joncaire's visit of 1709 we find no mention of the place until 1725, when de Longueuil wrote that he was going there to " meet all the Iroquois, that being the most convenient rendezvous for all the tribes." After the establishment of the English post at Oswego, Beauharnois urged that the French build a trading establishment at present Sodus, and even went so far as to ask a grant of 38,047 livres for it;[1] but the Minister disapproved, and on submitting his views to Louis, was endorsed in the following unmistakable language:

The King will not have any establishment at Cayuga. That at Niagara has called forth that built by the English at Choueguen

[1] Dispatches of Beauharnois and d'Aigremont, Oct. 1, 1728.

(Oswego). If one were made at Cayugas Bay, the English would make one elsewhere. Besides, there are already too many posts.

In all the green circuit of the Lakes there is no fairer spot than Irondequoit Bay, on the south shore of Ontario some five miles east of the mouth of the Genesee. Shoal at the entrance, with a narrow channel, it is of good depth when once past the bar, and reaches inland five or six miles between picturesque banks, its resorts, camps and cottages populous in summer with pleasure-seekers and nature-lovers from the nearby city of Rochester. A sheltered and fruitful fishing-ground, it was a favorite abode of the Indian from days immemorial. Midway between Frontenac and Niagara, the French early visited it and longed to occupy it. La Salle stopped there, in 1669, and again in 1678, going by this route to the Seneca villages. In July, 1684, we find the priest Jean de Lamberville advising La Barre to make a friendly visit there — advice which the Governor would have done well to follow, but did not. Three years later the war-making Denonville made Irondequoit his rendezvous, and here came Tonty, from the west, to meet him and share in the inglorious destruction of Seneca villages and crops.

Irondequoit was reached by several Indian paths, and was the lakeside terminus of a much-traveled trail from the villages at the foot of Seneca Lake; but it had not the harbor facilities nor the strategic position of Niagara, gateway to the Ohio and the West; so that, save for an effort made by the elder Joncaire to establish himself there in 1730, the French for the most part passed by it. It early attracted the attention of the English. In 1700 Colonel Peter Schuyler, Robert Livingston and Hendrick Hanse, New York's commissioners to the Onondagas, gave credulous ear to Indian reports that the French were about to build five forts, one of which was to be on the Niagara, and another at Irondequoit, " where the path goes up to the Sinnekes Castle." The next year Lieutenant Governor Nanfan professed to believe that he had secured for the colony title from the Indians to lands " 800 miles long and 400 miles broad," a point on the boundary of this valuable grant being "Jarondigat," the Irondequoit of to-day.[2] Occasionally in the correspondence of Indian commissioners or governors Irondequoit is referred to as belonging to New York Colony because of this alleged Indian deed; but the groundless claim was presently abandoned, and New York sought to buy a site on the bay. Returning from Joncaire's house on the Niagara in June, 1720, Lawrence Claessen stopped at Irondequoit, where he found a French smith with forge set up, mending the guns of the Senecas; he was the first white resident of the region. The aggressiveness of the French caused much concern in New York Colony, especially at Albany, where, on September 14th, the mayor, recorder, and aldermen and justices of the peace made a formal "representation" on the unfavorable trend of events in what is now Western New York. In the view of Albany officialdom, the western frontiers were "in a deplorable condition"; the Five Nations were also "in a stagering condition," since "they dare not oppose the French in any of their designs, as is manifest by their suffering the French to settle above the Carrying place of Jagara at Ochsweegee, and also to suffer them to make another settlement below the great falls of Jagara this summer." "Jagara at Ochsweegee" means "Niagara at Lake Erie," and would indicate an attempt by the French to gain a permanent footing above the falls; but of this, at this time, there is no authentic record. The long document quoted from recites the dangers to the colony, should a war break out, "which Gord forbid"; claims that "the poor inhabitants of this City and County would have to flee," and "he that got away first was the happiest man"; and finally suggests the ousting of the French, "and the sooner the better by such ways and means as you shall think proper but that a fort be built in covenant place at Tierondequat about ten leagues from the Sinnekes Castle and one at Ochiagara [Niagara] and a sufficient number of brisk

[2] Some of the score or more of early spellings of the designation of this bay are formidable, as witness *Onyuidaondagwat*, *Kaniatarontagouat*, and *Ganniagatarontagouat*. The priest Jean de Lamberville used the latter form, and also *Paniaforontogouat;* all meaning "the lake turns aside."

young men posted there with proper officers and an intelligent sencible man reside there to defeat the intreagues of the French," etc.³ So strong a representation was not without effect. The next year New York voted £500, the use of which is best set forth in Governor Burnet's own language:

I have employed the five hundred pounds granted this year by the Assembly chiefly to the erecting and encouraging a Settlement at Tirandaquat, a creek on the Lake Ontario about sixty miles on this side Niagara whither there are now actually gone a company of ten persons with the approbation of our Indians and with the assurance of a sufficient number of themselves to live with them and be a guard to them against any surprize & because the late President of the Council Peter Schuylers son first offered his service to go at the head of this expedition I readily accepted him and have made him several presents to equip him and given him a handsome allowance for his own salary and a commission of captain over the rest that are or may be there with him & Agent to treat with the Indians from me for purchasing Land and other things which I the rather did that I might show that I had no personal dislike to the family.⁴

Into this western wilderness then came these Argonauts in English interest. There is nothing to show that they reached the Niagara, or tried to; but to Irondequoit Bay, probably on the east side near the head, the reputed site of the ancient Seneca village, these young Albany Dutchmen came in the fall of 1721. Peter Schuyler, Jr., was captain of the band; his lieutenant was Jacob Verplanck; and others were Gilleyn Verplanck, Johannis Visger, Jr., Harmanus Schuyler, Johannis Van der Bergh, Peter Groenendyck and David van der Heyden.⁵ There are said to have been ten in the company, but no other names appear in the records.

It was a fine adventure; and were the journal which Captain Schuyler was instructed to keep in known existence, it should afford material for an important and not unpicturesque chapter in the long strife between Great Britain and France

---

³ "Representation of the authorities of the city of Albany," Sept. 14, 1720.
⁴ Burnet to the Lords of Trade, New York, Oct. 16, 1721.
⁵ N. Y. Col. MSS. LXIV.

for control of the fur trade. In lack of it, we have no better source of information concerning the venture than Governor Burnet's letter of instructions; wherein it is set forth that these young men are to settle in the Senecas' country " to drive a trade with the far Indians that come from the upper Lakes." They were also allowed to trade with " Sundry French men called by the Dutch Bush Loopers and by the French Coureurs Dubois who have for several years abandoned the French Colony of Canada and live wholly among the Indians"; more important yet, they were to purchase land at Irondequoit (although the English already claimed title to it), and also " such lands above the falls of Iagara 50 miles to the southward of said falls" as the Senecas might be willing to sell. Governor Burnet wrote that " it is thought of great use to the British Interest to have a Settlement upon the nearest part of the Lake Erée near the falls of Iagara," [6] in other words, the present site of Buffalo. It was the first English attempt to gain a foothold in the region, and the second attempt to wrest from the French some part of the trade of the lakes. The earlier one, the disastrous expeditions of Rooseboom and MacGregorie in 1685–86, has been related. Nor was any better result to reward the present effort, for although Burnet was a man of insight and resolution, the monopoly enjoyed by the French at Niagara and Frontenac was not seriously disturbed. There was at this time no sale of lands on Lake Erie, nor at Irondequoit; after a year in the wilderness, the Albany Dutchmen returned home; Governor Burnet abandoned Irondequoit and a few years later fixed upon the mouth of the Oswego as a base for operations.

Irondequoit however continued a place of some importance in the affairs of the time; it was on the old highways and many a French trader turned his canoe between the headlands that guard the entrance to the bay, to find profitable traffic with the Indians, Iroquois or Western, who passed that way. The English never ceased to covet it. In 1724 the Commissioners for Indian Affairs urged that " forts be built and

[6] Burnet's Instructions to Capt. Peter Schuyler, Jr.; N. Y. Council Minutes, 1721, XII, 168–173.

men posted at Ochjagara or Therondequat or between these places." Nothing came of it; but seven years later we find Governor Clarke upbraiding the Senecas for giving the French leave to build at Irondequoit. In 1737, Lieutenant Governor Clarke sought to have the Senecas revoke the consent he heard they had given, that "John Cœur, a Frenchman from Canada," might build a house at Irondequoit. To the New York Assembly he argued that if the French occupied this point, they would intercept all the western fur on its way to Oswego. The chiefs protested that the French should not build there. The next year Clarke tried, but without success, to gain the coveted consent for the English. An Indian deed dated January 10, 1740, signed by several sachems and decorated with their crude clan symbols, acknowledges receipt of £500 and grants to the English a tract 20 by 30 miles, including Irondequoit Bay and the site of Rochester. For years after, the English alluded to this tract as a purchase, and from time to time made suggestions regarding it. In 1742 Governor Clarke wrote: "The present I fear is not the time to settle Tierondequat, the people's apprehensions of a French war deterring them from the thoughts of it."[7] In a subsequent letter[8] he pleaded earnestly for the occupation and defense of the region, though his plans were not confined to the Irondequoit grant, for Oswego was now well established. "I endeavored," he wrote, "all I could, to get people to settle at Tierondequat, but in vain. The apprehension of a rupture with France deters them, and makes it absolutely necessary to secure that important place before the rupture happens." He proposed that a detachment of 80 men from the four independent companies of New York Colony, with a captain and two lieutenants, be posted at Irondequoit, and that " a Proper Fort be built there, and some small Field Pieces with Ammunition, etc., sent thither both for their own defence and for that of the harbour." If he failed to kindle at Whitehall some glow of interest in these distant shores and waters, it was through no lack of enthusiasm on his part.

[7] Clarke to the Lords of Trade, Nov. 29, 1742.
[8] Same to same, June 19, 1743.

No historical narrative of Lake Ontario and Western New York at this period can ignore George Clarke. Could he have had his way, the French would have been driven summarily from the Lakes. In a long letter to the Duke of Newcastle, Clarke outlined the whole situation of lake control and traffic; told how the French had lately had three and now (1743) had two sailing vessels on Lake Ontario; how from their stone forts Frontenac and Niagara, they dispatched traders to all the tribes and down the Mississippi; to all of which the only opposition made by the English was the little garrison of 20 men at Oswego, sure to fall into the hands of the French as soon as war broke out. He wished vigorously to contest the control of the Lakes, and proposed that a regiment of 800 men be sent from England, or if only 400, as many more might be raised in the colony; these men, with engineers, artillery, ammunition and supplies, he proposed to place at various points on the Ontario shore "in the Sinecas' country, at a proper Harbour for building Vessels, there being more than one of sufficient depth of water. . . . That there be built two or three Vessells of superior Force to those of the French, on board whereof a few sailors, and a sufficient number of soldiers being put with the proper officers, we may take, sink or otherwise destroy the French Vessels, and then easily take their Forts on the Lake . . . and the Trade and Influence of our Enemy will be confined to the Cold Country of Canada, which will scarce be worth keeping."[9] But the south shore of Ontario was warm and fertile, and in the vision of this man, no sooner were the English in control of the lake, than farmers would flock to the lakeside garrisons, "being sure both of protection and of a market for what they raise." He even proposed that cattle be driven thither from Albany, "with as much ease as they now are to the garrison at Oswego."

Visionary, Clarke may be called; yet his vision was clear and far-sighted, and could his projects have received even a measure of support from the home government the development of Western New York under the English would have be-

[9] Lt. Gov. Clarke to the Duke of Newcastle, June 19, 1743.

gun half a century sooner than it did, and the control of lake trade and the Fall of Canada have been materially hastened. But to the Lords of Trade and Ministers in London, Lake Ontario, its shores and harbors, even the value of its trade control, were remote, vague propositions, on which money was not to be rashly wasted. Clarke's pleadings were pigeonholed and forgotten, and the French continued their domination for a decade and a half yet to come.

Of an old Somersetshire family, Clarke was a young barrister at Swainswick, near Bath, when in 1703 he was appointed secretary of the Province of New York. He was called to the Council in 1715 and became Lieutenant Governor in 1736. The suicide of the Governor, Sir Danvers Osborn, in that year, made Clarke the acting Governor. He administered the Government until 1743, when he was succeeded by George Clinton. Two years later he returned to England, taking with him, it is said, a fortune of £100,000 — a striking proof of the money-making opportunities in America, even at that early day, for public servants who chose to use them. Clarke died at an advanced age in 1759, the very year in which Great Britain practically carried out some of the measures against the French which he had urged twenty years before. He was a member of the New York Council four years before the elder Joncaire built his trading station at Lewiston, and ten years before the foundations of Fort Niagara were laid. For 30 years, as an official and administrator of the affairs of New York Province, he was a clear-sighted observer of all the French undertook on the Lakes.

In 1737, having heard that the French were to build a fort on Irondequoit Bay, Lieutenant Governor Clarke summoned the Six Nations to a conference. It was held at Albany, June 24th and days following.

"What is this I hear?" said Clarke to his "brethren"; "I am told you have given leave to the French to build a house at Tiorondequat; it is a thing so far beyond belief that I could give no credit to it on the first report, but it is now so confidently affirmed that I can no longer doubt of it." He spoke at length, and although there were the usual phrases about brightening the chain of friendship, renewing the covenant, and the like, his words were irritating to the red men.

"Brother Corlear," replied the spokesman of the Six Nations, "You spoke very fierce and roughly to us, and we hope you will give us the same liberty. We shall likewise tell you your faults." The Englishman was no match for the Indian in effective oratory, in courtesy, logic or accusation. "You tell us you commit your affairs to writing, which we do not, and so, when you look to your books you know what passed in former times, but we keep our treaties in our heads. . . . At the time when the French built a house at Iagara [Niagara] the Governor asked us in a public meeting why we suffered it and did not demolish it. We answered that we were not able to do it; but desired of the Governor to write to the King about it, which he promised to do; but we have never heard more about it."

From this telling thrust, to which Clarke could make no reply, the Indian orator passed to an assurance that the French should not be allowed to establish themselves at Irondequoit "on our lands."

In 1738, when the English wished to build a post on Lake Ontario, they were met by the same argument, and had to be content. The Indian had discovered that neither French nor English meant what they said, nor did what they promised, in regard to protecting him in his territorial rights.

Acting Governor Clarke's letters to the Lords of Trade, to the Duke of Newcastle, and others, especially towards the close of his administration, discuss, often at length, the measures which he thought should be taken against the French on the Lakes. To the Duke of Newcastle, April 22, 1741, he pointed out that the French were now somewhat crippled on Lake Ontario, one of their brigantines being "lately stranded and broke to pieces." They still had two others of about 50 tons each, which were kept busy transporting supplies and men to and from Frontenac and Niagara; each of these forts, he had learned, "garrisoned by a company of regular forces, consisting of about 30 or 35 men, which may presently be reinforced by the Indians. Both these forts," he added, "are built on the lands belonging to our Six Nations or Iroquois." In the case of Frontenac, at least, this was a fatuous claim. Clarke proposed that the British at once build two vessels on Lake Ontario, " of superior bigness and force to those of the French " at some point (which he could not specify) where there was a good harbor; and when this considerable achievement had been accomplished

being well manned and provided with gunns and ammunition we may easily take or destroy those of the French; and being masters on water, we may transport the troops that may be necessary to take their two Forts and hinder the Enemy from building any more on those shores; and no sooner will our conquests be known as it will immediately by the Indians now in the interest or under the influence of the power of the French, but they will shake off the yoke and submit themselves to His Majty's protection, whereby we shall of course be posest of all the Indian trade from Canada to Messasippi, which is now in the hands of the French, and cut off the communication between those two places, so long as those vessels are employed on the Lake, which they ought constantly to be, at least till we have taken Canada.

And more to the same effect. Governor Clarke wrote in a similar strain, and repeatedly, to the Lords of Trade, urging that control of the Lakes was essential in order to hold the Six Nations in allegiance. " I humbly think," he says, " that if there be a rupture with France it will be absolutely necessary to take from them their two forts on Cadaraqui Lake, *viz.*, Frontenac at the northeast end and Niagara at the southwest end, and to destroy the two brigantines that they have now on that lake which are employed in carrying their merchandize from one end to the other, and men, ammunition, and provisions to those forts."

Irondequoit Bay continued to be a coveted point. In 1744 Governor Clinton, who knew the region better than Clarke ever did, proposed a fort on Irondequoit, with a strong garrison; and in 1749 William Johnson, who knew it far better than even Clinton, wrote to the latter: " There is a place called Tierondequat in the Senecas' country which I believe was purchased in Mr. Clarke's time, that would be a very proper place to fortify and settle. The French I have been told are certainly trying to buy it." As late as 1754 we find Lieut.-Governor De Lancey repeating these same propositions. To the Lords of Trade he suggested a fort at Irondequoit, where, he professed to think, " the Indians would settle under its protection, become firm friends and join us when occasion offers to dislodge the French from Niagara." When the commissioners from the several colonies met at Albany in 1754 to consider a plan of union, it was voted expedient to build a fort at Irondequoit; but the New York Council, July 11th, raised objections, arguing that other forts were needed quite as much as this, and that the general union to be entered upon would make them unnecessary. These were not sound reasons, but unpatriotic subterfuges, mere excuses for not spending money. In October the Lords of Trade, goaded by the necessity of taking some decisive action, repeated parrot-like to the King the recommendation long since made to them, that a fort be built at Irondequoit, " that the harbor there should be fortified and that armed vessels, superior in strength and number to those the French may have upon the Lake, be forthwith built."

Governor Hardy of New York was not unmindful of the situation on Lake Ontario, though his concern was merely with the fur trade. It was less to contest the control of those waters, than to help trade conditions at Oswego that he proposed, early in 1756, he placing of a garrison on Irondequoit Bay. He heard that the soil there was good, and thought a " valuable settlement " might be made, under protection of a fort, " if the lands were granted out in small parcels, without fees, to persons that would reside on them, at first without rent for a term of years, and afterwards at a small quit rent to the Crown." [10] He asked the approval of the Lords of Trade on this exceedingly chimerical colonization project in the wilds of Western New York, urging that " by means of this fort and settlement we should soon be able to supply the garrison of Oswego at a cheap rate, and by the trade which would in consequence be carried on, with the Sennekas, so

[10] Hardy to the Lords of Trade, " Ft. George, N. York, 16 Jan., 1756."

near their own habitations, we might soon gain an ascendant over them, as numbers of them would draw near this fort for security by which means we might be able to fix the affections of these Indians, who are the most numerous of the Six Nations, to the British interest." [11]

There are still other recommendations in regard to the place, but no money was appropriated, nor were troops or builders, either of forts or vessels, sent to much-talked-of Irondequoit, which remained unfortified and unsettled, a rendezvous for traders and travelers over the old trails, until the end of the French régime, and Sir William Johnson's victory at Niagara gave the English for the first time a substantial hold on the region.

The operations of the French on the Lakes Ontario and Erie, in the earlier years of their activities, were of much the same character. Except for an occasional clash with savages there was little to be chronicled save the passing of expeditions. But during the last few years of French control, a very different train of events developed on the waters of Ontario, from any that Erie was to know. On the latter lake, with the exception of the portage landings of Chautauqua and Presqu' Isle, there were no French settlements to be defended, no fortified points to serve as base of operations; not even Detroit, which was 30 miles from the lake, became the occasion of any conflict or strategic movement on Lake Erie.

Sandusky Bay was a point of some importance for various early expeditions, but there was no French establishment there that demands our attention. In fact, the English, and not the French, first fortified it. As early as 1745 English traders from Virginia and Pennsylvania built a stockaded trading-post on the bay opposite the mouth of Sandusky River. This was the chief provocative of Céloron's expedition of 1749. It was the first English establishment on Lake Erie, and was made possible only by the enmity towards the French which was felt by the Indians who had their villages on or near Sandusky Bay. In 1751, when Céloron was commandant at Detroit, he built a trading-post on Sandusky Bay; and three years later the French built Fort Junundat on the east side of that bay.

[11] *Ib.*

IRONDEQUOIT AND OSWEGO

For the most part, the operations of the French in that vicinity pertain to the story of Detroit, or at least are so little associated with the movements which make up the history of the Niagara as to call for no further consideration in this connection.

The conditions on Lake Ontario were different. Here the French were well established at Frontenac on the northeast, Niagara to the southwest, and on a small scale at Toronto; while at Oswego were the English. Each of the rivals, in the later years, had some armed shipping, and by the time the war of 1756 was actually declared, was in condition to make an effort for the control of these waters.

The building of the first English post at the mouth of the Oswego River — occupied for trade as early as 1724, but first fortified in 1726, has been noted in a preceding chapter. Much to the irritation of the French the post was maintained, with a fluctuating but at times considerable trade drawn away from the French. In 1741 the Colonial Assembly granted £600 for building a stone wall around the trading house; but the next year Governor Clarke denounced the work as " a jobb calculated rather to put money in the Pockets of those who have the management of the business, than any real service to the publick," which has a singularly modern sound. Nominal peace between the Powers continued until 1744. During these first seventeen years of its existence its garrison rarely if ever exceeded 20 men, with a lieutenant sergeant and corporal; too feeble a force to have withstood any considerable body of the enemy, who were constantly passing between Frontenac and Niagara. An incident in the latter part of this period was the visit of John Bartram, the Philadelphia botanist, whose journey thither in July, 1743, and graphic description of conditions as he found them, need only be alluded to.[12]

A considerable settlement of traders and Indians grew up around the fort; but on the breaking out of King George's War in March, 1744, most of the whites retired to less exposed places. Lieutenant John Lindesay, founder of the settlement of Cherry Valley, was appointed commander at Oswego, and a

---

[12] See Bartram's "Observations," London, 1751.

reluctant Assembly authorized Governor Clinton in some small expenses for defense, the principal item being six cannon. A French attack was expected; now and again there were alarms. With their two sailing vessels and forts at either end of the lake, the wonder is the French did not seize Oswego. Beauharnois contemplated it, but decided the difficulties were too great. In an elaborate letter to the Minister,[13] he argued that, should he attack Oswego, " the inevitable loss of the post of Niagara " would follow; " and you know, My Lord," he added, " it is far from being in a condition to resist the force the English can dispatch against it." Niagara at this date had a garrison of 64 soldiers and six officers, commanded by Céloron. In the summer of 1744 de Léry and La Morandière had repaired and doubled the stockades, so that it was now in better state for defense than ever before; yet its armament was pitiably weak, consisting of five peteraros and four two-pounders — enough to deter Indians but of little avail against any English force determined enough to reach the place.

Beauharnois having reasoned that there were too many difficulties in the way, did not attack Oswego, but contented himself with gaining a pledge from the Six Nations that they would remain neutral. He thought it well, however, to order Joncaire, who was in Quebec at this time (October) to follow the north shore of Lake Ontario, in returning to Niagara. The Senecas were asking for their *Nitachinon*, by which name they designated Joncaire; who was warned by a delegation of four Onondagas not to pass by Oswego except at night, " as the English had issued orders to take him dead or alive."

Joncaire's younger brother, Chabert, was at this time among the Senecas. Returning to Niagara he reported to Céloron, the commandant, that two English messengers had come to the Seneca villages, with wampum belts, asking that a chief of each of the Six Nations be sent to Oswego to guard the fort. The English held that they were entitled to this, since the Senecas went so freely to Niagara. The Senecas replied, they had a chief on the Niagara " to settle any difficulties that liquor

[13] Beauharnois to the Count de Maurepas, Oct. 8, 1744.

IRONDEQUOIT AND OSWEGO

might occasion among the Indians in the work they had to do at the carrying-place," but they did not wish to participate in the war between the whites. It was a wise and well-kept neutrality.

As for the English at Oswego, they were as fearful of a French attack as were the French at Niagara, of an English one; so that the war came to an end, and the Treaty of Aix-la-Chapelle was signed, October 18, 1748, with no clash at arms having occurred between the rivals on Lake Ontario. The only effect of that war in the region was a mutual strengthening of all fortifications, and a disturbance of trade.

Note has been made in preceding pages, of the founding and early years of Oswego. The only English establishment in the region we here study, it was of marked effect on the policy and conduct of the French for more than a quarter century; not merely in a military way, but, even more vitally, in its rivalry for trade and for Indian allegiance. Many of the early provisions for its maintenance and regulation, are curious, and not without a bearing on our general theme.

An Act of the General Assembly, November 25, 1727, appropriated £1682, 7 s. 3½ d., to pay for and maintain " a convenient place called Oswego, a very good stone house of 2 storys high." This act was amended the following year, but continued in force. In 1729 it was enacted that " fines, penalties and forfeitures should be recovered from persons who have incurred the same by trading with the French during the time it was unlawfull so to doe, because most of them acquired great wealth by that means, whilst fair Traders did foregoe such advantages." These fines were to be applied to the Oswego debt.

A preamble to an Act of October 29, 1730, sets forth that the Government held it just and equitable that the traders should maintain Oswego, " because they reap the entire bennifit of the said house "; yet the General Assembly voted a tax of three shillings to be paid " by every Inhabitant Resident or Sojourner of and in this Colony young and old (except as is hereafter Excepted) as shall wear a whigg or Peruke made of Human or horse hair or mixt "— the exemptions to this tax — truly enough a poll-tax — being poor people receiving alms, and the King's soldiers and sailors. The revenue under this wig-tax law was to be applied, to the amount of £550, to victualling the troops at Oswego for one year from August 1, 1730.

It was ever a question with New York Colony, what to tax for the up-keep of this post. "An Act to support the troops at Oswego and to regulate the Indian trade there," passed September 30, 1731, laid a tax of a shilling a gallon on rum and ten shillings on every piece of strouds. This Act, a very long one, provided for the collection of the tax by commissioners, fixed their salaries, and aimed to meet every possible contingency. In 1729 Harmanus Wendel of Albany had entered into a three-years' contract to supply provisions for the troops at Oswego, but soon died; the new Act allowed his successors £406 yearly for the work, gave the doctor resident there £40, and appropriated £60 for shingling and repairing the trading-house. It also specified that huts for the traders should be at least 300 yards from the main tradinghouse; and further: "If any of the Traders shall upon the appearing of one or more Cannoes with Indians on the Lake goe with his or their Cannoe or other Vessell and shall either Trade with such Indians or take their Bevers or other skins into possession or hinder such Indians from carrying such Bevers or skins into their Owne Huts," they " shall forfeit the sume of £50."

Trade had become profitable and competition was keen. When a flotilla of canoes, gunwale-deep with furs, was seen approaching, enterprising merchants would hasten out in their own boats, greet the Indians on the lake and consummate a bargain before the savage vendors could set foot on shore. They would even seize the Indians' choicest peltries, and in the name of trade rob the red man at the threshold of the post. A hard, unscrupulous lot, these traders were. In 1733, complaint was made to the Governor, by 48 Indian traders, of the lawless state into which barter had fallen at Oswego. The Governor appointed David A. Schuyler, who knew trade conditions and Indian tongues, as commissary at Oswego.

Old Fort Oswego

From Smith's "History of the Province of New York," 1757

The bolder spirits held him in contempt. Finally the Colony took cognizance of their high-handed methods, and passed an Act (December 16, 1737) forbidding the traders thus to go out to meet the Indians on the lake, " or take their Beavors or other Skins into Possession or hinder such Indians from carrying such Beavors or Skins into their own Hutts." Disregard of this law, meant a fine of £20, if not a revocation of license; and the commandant was ordered to assign the visiting Indians a suitable place for their huts, and see " that they be at full Liberty to trade for, what & with whom they please."

The trading season was from April to August. The commissary for regulating the trade was required to reside at Oswego at least four months. Elaborate regulations were made for the trade and the sale of rum, with penalties for all infractions. A quaint view of Oswego, which forms the frontispiece of the first edition of William Smith's " History of New York " (London, 1757), shows a row of houses bordering the river, and to the west of them another row of huts, presumably used by traders and Indians. The soldiers at Oswego garrison, after the traders departed each season, had a playful fashion of burning or wrecking these huts. This " rudeness," as the old law styles it, was made the subject of legislation in 1732; for every such offense a fine of £6 was imposed, with further punishment in the discretion of the courts.

Another thing that gave worry to the General Assembly was the " pernitious Practice " that many traders had of putting water in the rum they supplied to the thirsty red man. To meet the difficulty, the commissary or commanding officer at Oswego was required, under an Act of 1735, " to Examine, Taste & Prove once every week or oftener all the Rum that is or shall be brought to Oswego." Provision was made for confiscating any liquor not " Really good and Merchantable," while the too thrifty trader was mulcted £30 for each offense. If he found adulterated rum, the commissary was required, " Immediately, and in the presence of the Traders & Indians, which shall then be present, to Pour out on the Ground, or into the River or Lake, all and every Drop of such Forfeited Rum, whether the same be in Cags or any other Vessell." Than such a scene as this, there could have been few more tragic moments in the history of the post.

More insidious were the attempts of numerous persons in the French interest to share clandestinely in the profits of the trade at Oswego. An Act of November 8, 1735, made it a matter of severe punishment for a trader to employ any foreigner in any way, even as interpreter; but negroes were excepted. It was also forbidden to employ Indians as interpreters, because persons thus engaging them " Engross a great part of the Trade which ought to be of equal benefit to all the Traders in General." These provisions were continued without material change, reënacted every two years in the Oswego supply bill, down to 1754. The Act of that year was in force when, in 1756, the place fell into the hands of the French.

In 1744, as soon as the English traders at Oswego learned that a state of war existed, they became singularly panic-stricken. Most of them left the place at the first alarm, selling such goods as they could to whoever stayed behind, and hurrying with the remainder back to Albany and New York. Their timidity excited the contempt of Governor Clinton. "You will judge," he observed, in a communication to the General Assembly,[14] " what a baulk and discouragement, this instance of pusilanimity has occasioned to those number of Indians, of the far Nations, who have rarely come to trade with us; but perhaps, finding the French had no goods to supply them at Niagara, resolved to proceed to Oswego, where some of them found the place was basely deserted by most of the people, and no goods to exchange for their furs; upon information whereof, many other Indian canoes were turned back before they reached that place. How mean an opinion must the savages entertain of us, when they find our people so easily frightened, as it were with a shadow."

Much debate resulted in an order, September 5th, that 50 men be sent from Albany to Oswego, to reinforce the garrison and stay during the winter.

[14] Aug. 20, 1744.

It was Walter Butler and Paul Combs who brought to Oswego the news of the declaration of war — and they charged the Colony £10 for making the journey. It was one of the first and one of the smallest expenses imposed on New York by the War of '44. Although in that war New York did not meet the French on Lake Ontario, she did go to extravagant lengths in the effort to gain, or hold, the several Iroquois tribes as allies. Ten years later, when the colony was on the eve of another war, a great part of its war debt incurred in 1744-48 was still unpaid.

In a strongly written " Representation," addressed to the Lords Commissioners for Trade and Plantations, the General Assembly, through David Jones, its Speaker, accused Governor Clinton of "applying great part of the money raised by this colony, to be laid out in presents for the Indians, during the late war, to his own use." They further accused him of appointing a colonel of militia who favored the French cause. It was no unusual thing for the New York Assembly to charge the Governor with wrong-doing; such was the habitual attitude towards many Governors; but this was not the ordinary spirit of fault-finding; nor was it a faltering hand that wrote, while protesting loyalty to the King, " yet we have ever looked upon the People of this Colony as Englishmen, and that as such they are entitled to the rights and privileges of English subjects." Expressions like this, cropping out with increasing frequency in the utterances of colonial assemblies, were the subdued thunder before the storm. The year 1754 marks, with scarcely less definiteness than does 1776, the rise of the spirit of American independence; nor can it be doubted that in the culmination of the conflict with France, there was in more than one quarter a dawning discernment of the fact that in winning the Lakes and the Ohio from the French, they were won not so much for a Power over seas, as for a nascent nation, destined to people and enjoy the regions contended for. Although Canada has remained a loyal colony, yet in the development and occupancy of what was *La Nouvelle France*, she has been practically as untrammeled and independent as her sister to the south of the Lakes.

Paschal Nelson, whose appointment as lieutenant in one of the New York companies was recommended in 1729, and who appears to have received it, was by his own account in command at Oswego, though the exact period of his service there cannot be stated. In commending him for promotion, Governor Montgomerie speaks of him as " a gentleman of this country." He was a nephew of Sir Thomas Temple, Governor of Nova Scotia. In 1745, Nelson wrote of his service as follows:

My duty as an Officer in one of his Majesty's Independent Companys at New York, has obliged me to be very much in the Inland Country amongst the Indians and practice their method of travelling. I have commanded a garrison on the great lake Ontario three years and a half, 250 miles from Albany, and have marched partys of men there by land and water six severall times, by which means everything relating to this Country and trade is familiar to me. I have had frequent intercourse with the French Officers of Canada and have kept a constant correspondence with Mons. Vaudreuele [sic], now Governor of Mississippi. By my advice and direction the Fort on that Lake has been enlarged and cannon sent to it. . . . Nigh seven years of the prime of my life has been spent in this sort of service, amongst the Indians, back of our Province, to whom I am well known, and as I was born in that part of the World, I have travelled thro' most of the Colonies both by the Sea shore and Inland. There is hardly a family of note with which I am not acquainted.[15]

In 1747 Oswego was somewhat strengthened, Lieutenant Visscher and a company being sent to augment Captain Lindesay's force. The war ended with no clash between France and England on the Lakes; the Treaty of Aix-la-Chapelle signed October 18, 1748, again proclaimed peace, and the warfare of trade, which had somewhat abated during the years of avowed hostility, once more resumed its paradoxical sway. Captain Lindesay resigned as commandant, but continued at Oswego as Indian agent and commissary until his death in 1751. In the next few years, Oswego was the seat not only of

[15] Paschal Nelson to Hon. George Lyttleton, July 23, 1745. The original MS. of which the above is an excerpt, was offered for sale at auction in London in 1915.

a growing trade with the Indians, and one of Sir William Johnson's important depots, but developed a considerable illicit trade with the French. In 1752 some building and repair-work was undertaken, Captain Stoddard and Lieutenant Holland being stationed there. In 1754 the New York Assembly voted the equivalent of $1300 for work on the fort; and the next year, which witnessed the coming of Shirley and his army, was further memorable because it saw the beginning of English shipping on the Great Lakes. On June 28, 1755, at Oswego was launched the schooner *Ontario*, the first English craft larger than a canoe to sail these waters. She had 40 feet of keel, mounted 14 swivel guns, and was made to row when necessary. This same season, at Oswego, were also fitted out a decked sloop of eight 4-pounders and 30 swivels, a decked schooner of eight 4-pounders and 28 swivels, an undecked schooner of 14 swivels and 14 oars, and another of 12 swivels and 14 oars. All of these were unrigged and laid up early in the fall.[16]

When Shirley withdrew, having relinquished the Niagara undertaking, Colonel Mercer was left in command with orders to build a new fort.

For many years the English maintained blacksmiths or gunsmiths among the Six Nations, who supplied to the Indians the metal-work they could not make or repair for themselves. Sometimes they were accompanied by traders, at other times they themselves were supplied by the Colony with goods, and carried on barter with the natives. Many of these men were Albany or Mohawk-Valley Dutchmen. Living thus apart from their own people at remote Indian villages, it was no doubt the rule rather than the exception that they took to wife Indian women and reared a family of half-breeds. That these people of mixed blood were numerous throughout what is now New York State, especially towards the close of the Colonial period and in years following, is attested by many records. As is the law with mixed strains, the half-breeds were usually more ignoble, more treacherous and less to be trusted than the worthier full-blood Indian.

[16] Mante, " History of the Late War," p. 30.

Although the forest from Onondaga to the Niagara — the mid-lake region where dwelt the Cayugas, and, from Seneca Lake westward, the habitat of the Senecas — was especially under French influence, yet even here the English contended for trade and the friendship of the aborigines. John Lansing " and company," for services as smiths " in the Seneka's country," from September 1, 1743, to September, 1744, presented a bill to the General Assembly, of £40.[17] In April, 1745, two traders with goods, a servant and a blacksmith, were sent to the Senecas; the traders were to receive £100 each, the smith £30 for remaining a year among the Senecas. Tobias TenEyck and John Van Sise were thus sent out, in 1749; William Printup in 1751; and many another. The smith most frequently mentioned was Myndert Wemp or Wemple — both forms appearing in official records — who in 1753 was sent to the Senecas " at Seneseo [?Geneseo], lying near Tirondequat or Niagara," at a yearly wage of £70, with an allowance of £50 for gifts to the Indians.[18]

The particular point of this service is, not merely that New York Colony was not neglectful even of the remotest of the Six Nations; but that Chabert, his brother Joncaire and other agents of the French, found their special field disputed and contended for. Wemple resided for some years between the Genesee and the Niagara, and it is no flight of fancy to suppose that there was more than one clash between him and Chabert as to their respective rights in the villages by the lakes and streams of Western New York. Here surely is suggestive material for the romancer, with a basis of fact none can dispute.

In 1756, Wemple was sent into the Seneca country, but the natives were so short of food that in April they sent him back to Fort Johnson, where he reported to Sir William that as they passed eastward some Cayugas, lately at Niagara, told

[17] This and other instances cited are drawn from the Journal of the N. Y. General Assembly.
[18] In 1747 the Commissioners of Massachusetts, New York and Connecticut agreed to send gunsmiths to the Six Nations, two men with each smith, to spend the winter; £360 N. Y. currency was appropriated to buy goods, which were to go, to the Senecas, £120; and £60 each to the Oneidas, Onondagas, Cayugas and Tuscaroras.

him there were but 100 soldiers at that fort, but that the French were repairing it, making it very strong, and had plenty of provisions. It does not appear that Wemple ever reached the Niagara. He complained much of the rum-selling carried on by John O'Bail, a famous half-breed, who boasted that he did not care for Sir William or his regulations, since " for every quart of rum he sold he got a Spanish dollar "; but according to Wemple, even the Senecas themselves protested against the mischief he worked among them.

English enmity towards the Joncaires finds expression many times over, in New York colonial documents. At a Council meeting held at Governor Clinton's house in Greenwich, April 25, 1746, a letter was read from the Commissioners of Indian Affairs, " signifying that certain persons will undertake upon proper encouragement to bring Jean Cœur, a French priest, to Albany, who is settled among the Sinnecas. And they are of opinion his removal from the Indians will be of very great service to the British interest." This proposition, which probably refers to Chabert's elder brother, was referred to a committee, but no Joncaire was carried prisoner to Albany. The next year a number of Iroquois chiefs assured Colonel Johnson they would not let " Jan Cour " live any more among the Senecas, and even promised to go and destroy Fort Niagara, if the English would supply the guns and ammunition. Johnson thought seriously enough of it to refer the matter to Governor Clinton, with the suggestion that munitions for the Indians could be had from Philadelphia; and pledged himself to bring into the field a thousand warriors in six weeks if the Colony would clothe and arm them —" or forfeit 1000 pounds." [19] In the New York Council minutes of that summer occurs this entry: " That of the new levies now in this Province . . . 6 or 700, together with 200 Indians, be employed against the French fort at Ongiara, at the same time as an attempt against Crown Point." An estimate of the cost of the two expeditions was £13,560.

Affairs were at a low ebb, this summer, at the feeble little fort which was supposed to guard the mouth of the Niagara.

[19] Johnson MSS.: Johnson to Clinton, July 25, 1747.

De Contrecœur and his uneasy garrison had ample reason to be apprehensive, for Chabert and his brother kept them informed regarding the smoldering hostility which the English were doing their best to fan into a blaze. The western tribes also, dissatisfied with the frugal offerings of the French in trade at Niagara, were reported ready to destroy the place. Johnson gave eager ear to these reports, and passed them on with his own suggestions to the Governor. August 4th he wrote:

Ottrawana, the great Cayuga Indian, and others of the Five Nations, since they were at Albany with your Excellency, informed me at a private meeting at my house, but in the most formal manner, with belts of wampum, that the foreign nations, *viz.* the Chonondedeys,[20] etc., were resolved to destroy Niagara as being an impediment in their way to Oswego, where they are sensible they have been always well treated, and much imposed on at Niagara, having been stopt there this Spring by their artifice, and obliged to pay 20 Beavers for a Stroud blanket. They have applied to the Six Nations privately for liberty to destroy Niagara, which they are likely to obtain, having the consent of some of the chiefs of each nation, though I am rather of opinion that a proper number of the King's troops against it in conjunction with the Indians who are so hearty, would make it more practicable; besides it seems to me, there would be a necessity of keeping large garrisons both here and at Oswego, for the French would not quietly brook the loss of it, being of the greatest consequence, next to the reduction of the whole country.

A few days later [21] Johnson again wrote to the Governor that the "Foreign Nations"— meaning western tribes, usually hostile to the Iroquois — had sent six large belts of wampum to the Six Nations "desiring their liberty to destroy Niagara, and that it should be done very shortly, meaning in a month or so." He added that the Six Nations had sent to these western tribes, to come and join them in the proposed attack.

That it did not take place was due to several causes. The French, forewarned, sent up reinforcements. More effective yet, were the better bargains which they granted in trade. Most effective of all, were the constant labors of Chabert and

[20] I do not identify this tribe.
[21] Johnson MSS.: Johnson to Clinton, Aug. 19, 1747.

his brother. It may be doubted if an Indian uprising against Niagara was as imminent as Colonel Johnson's letters made it appear. The Six Nations, at least, would have looked to the English for substantial backing, and would have been slow, without such aid, to cast in their lot with traditional enemies of the west, whose wrath towards the French was liable to change, like an eddy of a summer breeze, at the first offer that took their fickle fancy.

The brothers Joncaire continued to be thorns in the flesh to Johnson, and he wrote often of them to the Governor. " I am very sensible," replied Clinton,[22] " of what service it will be to win Jancour from among the Indians if he can by any means be brought over to leave the French and settle with us." This had evidently been Johnson's suggestion. In a former letter the Governor had authorized Johnson to win him by promises, " but if that cannot be done you are to endeavor by all means to have him removed from among the Indians, and if possible brought a prisoner hither and you shall be paid whatever expenses shall be necessary for this service. It is left to your judgment from the Intelligence you shall receive and take what method you shall think most likely to succeed, either by promises to bring him over, or to remove him by force. Perhaps the hints from Jeancour of leaving ye French may be only to prepare something wherein he may value himself among his Countrymen."

This allusion is probably to the elder brother, Joncaire, for at this period Chabert was chiefly occupied with the duties of the Niagara portage, and the Indians of the Allegheny and upper Ohio.

[22] Johnson MSS.: Clinton to Johnson, March, 1749. The letter to which this is a reply has not been noted.

CHAPTER XVIII

THE NIAGARA-OHIO ROUTE

INSEPARABLE IN TRACING THE STORY OF TRADE AND WAR — TRAGIC EPISODES IN THE DEVELOPMENT OF THE GREAT CONTEST — THE BROTHERS JONCAIRE ON THE OHIO — THE NIAGARA PORTAGE FORT.

FROM 1739, when the elder Joncaire died, for 20 years, the activities of his sons covered the country from the Mohawk to the present State of Ohio. Often they were associated, and shared in the same expeditions. The elder brother, Philippe Thomas, succeeded his father as special agent among the Iroquois of New York State, but he also was sent on important missions to the Shawanese and other tribes of the Ohio with whom his father had been especially concerned in his last years. In the latter years of his life the elder son was withdrawn from this field, being succeeded there by his brother Chabert, master of the Niagara portage; but each, on occasion, appears in the other's territory, and both made frequent journeys to Montreal and Quebec, often with delegations from the tribes. Returning from the councils, with new instructions and stocks of goods, each would set out from the Niagara to the villages or tribes he was directed to visit.

It was a curious system of physical and political control; it was also a costly and wasteful system, nor was it always successful, for the English more and more pushed into the territory. In spite of their close relations with the Indians, in spite of their skill, energy and devotion to the cause of France, the sons of Joncaire met many a rebuff, ran many a risk, and on the whole played a losing game, but they played gamely and with spirit to the very end.

In the last years of his life, as we have related, the elder Joncaire — Louis Thomas — was instrumental in relocating the wandering Shawanese in the upper Ohio Valley. Both of the sons shared with their father in duties relating to them, and in the years following the father's death were often sent to scattered villages in the wide wild district designated merely as "the Ohio." As the years passed, it was more often the younger son, "Sieur de Chabert et Clauzonne," whom we speak of as Chabert, than the older brother Philippe Thomas, who was sent to this field. In 1747 the health of this Joncaire, broke down and Chabert succeeded him as resident agent of the French among the Senecas [1]— whose villages, it will be borne in mind, were not merely in Western New York, but throughout the valley of the Allegheny. Chabert was made a second ensign on full pay in 1748; [2] ensign *en pied*, 1751; and lieutenant, 1757. In 1756 he replaced his elder brother among the Six Nations, who with ceremony pledged fidelity to him and agreed to send their chiefs with him to Montreal the ensuing spring.

The elder brother Joncaire having recovered his health was again in active service in 1750, in which year he was sent on one of the most important missions of his whole career. He set out from Montreal with a staff of *cadets à l'eguillette*, and four soldiers. Two loaded canoes belonging to the trader Guilhot, were taken along, for Indian barter. Two Cayuga chiefs who had been promised a share in the expedition, were sent for, and the little company proceeded by way of Fort Frontenac, the Niagara and Chautauqua portages, down the Allegheny to the old Indian town of Chinangué or Chininqué, where Joncaire was directed to establish a trading-house; it was to be two stories high, battlemented (*crénelé*) for defense. So run the instructions of the Governor,[3] but one may be skeptical about the battlements. The word "loop-holes," better than "battlements," indicates the probable construction. It suffices that it was to be a house capable of defense. Joncaire was directed to explore the region, to learn all he could of

[1] "Sieur Joncaire, resident at the Senecas, having demanded to be relieved, in consequence of his health, the General has appointed Sieur Joncaire Clauzonne, his brother, to succeed him."—*Journal of occurrences in Canada*, 1747-8, in N. Y. Col. Docs. X, 163. The same statement occurs in numerous French documents.

[2] President of Navy Board to La Galissonière, Feb. 28, 1748.

[3] La Jonquière to Joncaire, June 22, 1750.

the Yenangu8kran (Monongahela), and to find a new route by way of the River Blanche, into Lake Erie. He was to go down the Ohio as far as the Scioto, discover new routes, make friends with the tribes, and finally, report to Céloron at Detroit. He was also instructed to keep a journal — a treasure to the student to-day could it be brought to light.

Such were the missions on which Joncaire and his brother Chabert were sent, year after year. Makers of history in a vast region, their names are scarcely mentioned, their identity and services confused or unmentioned in most narrative histories dealing with their time.

The next year Lieutenant Joncaire made his presence on the Ohio known to Governor Hamilton of Pennsylvania by the following letter:

DE CHININQUE,[4] June 6, 1751

Sir: Monsieur the Marquis de La Jonquière, Governor of the whole of New France, having honored me with his orders to watch that the English should make no treaty in the country of the Ohio, I have directed the traders of your government to withdraw. You cannot be ignorant, sir, that all the lands of this region have always belonged to the King of France, and that the English have no right to come there to trade. My superior has commanded me to apprise you of what I have done, in order that you might not affect ignorance of the reasons of it, and he has given me this order with so much the greater reason because it is now two years since Monsieur Céloron, by order of Monsieur de La Galissonière, then Commandant General, warned many English who were trading with the Indians along the Ohio, against doing so, and they promised him not to return to trade on the lands, as Monsieur Céloron wrote to you.

I have the honor to be, with great respect, Sir,
Your very humble and obedient servant
JONCAIRE
Lieutenant of a detachment of the Marine.

This letter was written from the old Shawanese town on the Ohio below Pittsburg which later became Logstown, and later still, the approximate site of Economy, Pa. This historic name is now no longer used, the place being a sub-station of Ambridge.

The French by no means had things their own way in the

[4] Shenango.

valley. In 1752 Chabert de Joncaire, on the Ohio, was assured by an English trader that the Governor of Virginia was coming in September, with many men and 800 horses, to hold a council at Chiningué; and Chabert as in duty bound, sent the report to Canada.[5] It was a false alarm; but the winter that followed — a desperate time for every one on the Ohio, with both famine and smallpox to contend against — so wrought up the tribes that in the spring of 1753 they sent a deputation of chiefs to Niagara. At the old fort, in April, a council was held at which, in formal but we may believe impassioned speeches, the French were warned to keep out of the Ohio country. The Indians had heard of the great army that was coming; but neither protests nor threats, nor the picture which they drew of famine and death, stayed the undertaking, one of the most dramatic in the history of our region.

Increasingly, as the years passed, the French endeavored to control the Ohio Valley — to make it a recognized possession of France, to open communication with Louisiana, to hold the allegiance of the resident tribes, and to keep out the traders from Pennsylvania and Virginia. Quebec was obsessed with this idea — the Ohio must belong to France; and instead of concentrating her forces and promoting the peaceful development of the St. Lawrence Valley, she frittered away her strength and exhausted not only the colonial exchequer but the Royal patience in sending expeditions and great wealth of presents to the shifty and unfaithful tribes of the Allegheny and Ohio.

The gateway to the region was the Niagara. The story of this frontier, always a chronicle of coming and going, is never more so than for the years on which our narrative now enters. Nor can that story be told without paying some attention, however slight, to the region to the southward.

If we leave aside the alleged discovery of the Ohio, by La Salle, it is an open question which people, French or English, had precedence in the region. English traders were on the

[5] A memorandum of Oct. 1, 1753, records: "To Sieur de Joncaire, Commandant Belle Rivière, annuity falling due in June, 1752, payable to Sieurs Morin and Penissaut, 3000 livres."

river as early as 1700, but made no claim for their Government. In 1715 the French were complaining because traders from Carolina had appeared on the Wabash. For some years the situation continued practically unchanged. The English did the trading, the French did the complaining— and nothing came of it. A French officer, one of the Messrs. de Longueuil, was sent thither in 1719, but no narrative of his going or coming is found in the communications of the time. The Niagara was the only way, even though he went on to Detroit before turning south. No mention of a French expedition into the Ohio country is found until about the time when Fort Niagara was built. It was in 1724 that the Marquis de Vaudreuil began his efforts to establish the Shawanese "nearer to the colony." His theory was that by assisting them to settle nearer Detroit, or other French posts, they would be further removed from British influence and through the agency at Detroit be kept in French interest.

In 1739 Céloron and St. Laurent had passed up the Niagara with a force of French from Montreal and Quebec, which has been described as a "company of cadets, composed of select youths, all of gentle birth, and the sons of officers." After a short apprenticeship, they were entitled to be, in their turn, commissioned as officers.[6] With these, and a considerable force of Northern Indians, Céloron apparently made his way through Lake Erie and into the Illinois country, whence, in November, he joined forces with other leaders from Western posts and from Louisiana, in a campaign against the Chicasaws and Natchez. In March, 1740, a treaty was made, by which a number of the Natchez were turned over to Céloron, who according to the writer just cited, returned with them to Canada, " after having razed to the ground Fort Assumption." Céloron, it is stated, was the only officer who won any honors in the Chicasaw campaign.

The undertaking scarcely concerns us, except that it proves the passage of an armed force through the Niagara and adjacent lakes in 1739, and its return with captives in the spring of 1740. That this passage was also through the Chautauqua

[6] Gayarré, "History of Louisiana," N. Y. ed. 1867, p. 507.

THE NIAGARA-OHIO ROUTE 363

route is established by records which appear later in our narrative. Pouchot, describing the Lake Erie region, said: " The River Chatacoin is the first that communicates from Lake Erie to the Ohio, and it was by this that they went in early times that they made a journey in that part." This could hardly refer to anything so recent in Pouchot's day, as the expedition of 1749.[7]

After a decade, more or less, during which the British grew ever bolder in their trading incursions west of the Alleghanies, and the French more and more indifferent and expostulatory, irritation reached the point where the existing peace between the rival Powers was ignored, and the French commandants at western posts with the aid of friendly Indians, captured any traders in English interest whom they could lay hands on. Some of these captives presently made a great din at the British Court; it was in fact the beginning of skirmish fire preliminary to an inevitable conflict. The story of several of the traders thus seized comes into the Niagara region and should be noted. Earliest of all, perhaps, of this category, are the adventures of John Peter Salling.

This worthy was a weaver of Williamsburg, Va., of whose remarkable captivity conflicting accounts exist. The data which are beyond doubt are to effect that about the year 1738 Salling and one Thomas Morlin, a peddler, trading from Williamsburg to Winchester, Va., set out on a tour of exploration into the country to the westward. They traveled up the Shenandoah, crossing the James and some of its branches and had reached the Roanoke, when Salling was taken captive by a party of Cherokees. His companion, Morlin the peddler, eluded them, and made out to reach Winchester, where he told what had happened. There is somewhat less certainty about what befell Salling. The most detailed and apparently most

[7] Reuben Gold Thwaites, a usually careful writer, says that "in 1746 De Léry went with a detachment of troops from Lake Erie to Chautauqua Lake and proceeded thence by Conewango Creek and Alleghany River to the Ohio, which he carefully surveyed down to the mouth of the Great Miami. ("Afloat on the Ohio," Chicago, 1897; p. 304.) He refers to no authority. De Léry passed through Chautauqua with the expedition of 1739.

trustworthy account — Withers' precious "Chronicles of Border Warfare"— says that he was carried to what is now Tennessee, where he remained some years. While with a party of Cherokees on a buffalo hunt, a band of Illinois Indians surprised them, captured Salling from the Cherokees and carried him to Kaskaskia, where he was adopted into the family of a squaw whose son had been killed. Salling made excursions with his new captors below the mouth of the Arkansas, going once to the Gulf of Mexico. One account says he returned; but Withers says that Salling, on the lower Mississippi, fell in with a party of Spaniards who needed an interpreter and bought Salling from his Indian mother "for three strands of beads and a calumet." He attended them to the post at Crevecœur, on the Illinois, "from which place he was conveyed to Fort Frontignac." The route, at this period, would have been by Fort Niagara, which he reached, apparently about 1743 or 1744; for at Frontenac he "was redeemed by the Governor of Canada, who sent him to the Dutch settlement in New York, whence he made his way home after an absence of six years."

Some time in 1750, Ralph Kilgore and Morris Turner, two men in the employ of John Fraser, a Lancaster County, Pennsylvania, trader, who had bought more skins from Miami Indians than their horses could carry, were returning from Logstown for a second load, when seven Indians came into their camp one evening a little after sunset. They asked for victuals, and when meat was given them, dressed and ate it in friendly fashion. After their appetites were satisfied they began examining the traders' guns, apparently from curiosity; one picked up a tomahawk, and others asked for knives to cut their tobacco. Suddenly the two traders were seized and securely tied. The Indians hurried their prisoners off toward Detroit, which at that time contained about 150 houses, securely stockaded. The prisoners were delivered to the commandant, Sabrevois, who gave to the Indians as reward a 10-gallon keg of brandy and 100 pounds of tobacco. Kilgore and Turner were put to work with a farmer, hoeing his corn and cutting his wheat. The Indians frequently came to see them and exult over them, taunting them and calling them dogs, and declaring that they were going down to the Wabash after more traders. After three months of this servitude, on the arrival of a new commandant, apparently Céloron, who assumed command at Detroit, February 15, 1751, our traders were sent down Lake Erie to Fort Niagara, where they met Joncaire, who they styled "the chief interpreter," and who was just setting out on one of his countless journeys to carry a present to the Indians of the Ohio country. The prisoners saw his goods spread out on the river bank, and estimated them worth £1,500. Here too they learned that a reward of £1,000 was offered for the scalps of George Croghan and James Lowry, whom the French justly regarded as the most influential of the Pennsylvania traders. When the French at Niagara undertook to transfer Kilgore and Turner to Montreal, while following the shore of Lake Ontario, the prisoners made their escape.[8]

It was in reference to these fugitives that Colonel Johnson wrote to Governor Clinton, in September, 1750, saying that two Englishmen had come to him "in a miserable naked condition." He states the circumstances of their capture and escape, substantially as above given; and adds: "They say the French are making all preparation possible against the Spring to destroy some nations of Indians, very steadfast in our interest. . . . They met in the lake 10 or 12 large battoes, laden with stores and ammunition for said purpose, with whom were several officers, in particular two sons of one of their Governors, whom I suppose to be Monsr. Longquile's sons." He was indignant at hearing the French had offered prizes to any Indians who would "take or destroy" Croghan and Lawrie, and says of Joncaire — probably Philippe Thomas —" I wish he may meet his proper desert." Joncaire this summer had had the temerity to appear at Oswego, in the vicinity of which post he had distributed valuable goods to the Indians.[9] His brother

[8] Summarized from the depositions of Kilgore and Turner. *See* Walton's "Conrad Weiser and the Indian Policy of Colonial Pennsylvania," pp. 241–242.

[9] "Arent Stephens the interpreter, who came lately from Oswego, saw

Chabert was at this time similarly occupied on the Ohio, where he sought to impress upon the none too credulous red men that the French wished to establish trading posts in the region for the convenience of the tribes, " to supply what goods they needed, so they would not have to go so far to market "— in other words, to Oswego.

When Johnson heard of this he reminded the Indians that they could get goods cheaper from Philadelphia, than from the French.

Late in 1750 Chabert loaded five canoes with Indian goods, at Fort Niagara, and started for the Allegheny Valley. The need of a protected storehouse and depot of supplies above the Falls was much felt, and as we shall presently see, was soon to be supplied. He crossed the eastern end of Lake Erie and made his way by Chautauqua and the Conewango, into the beautiful valley which to the French of that day was always " *la belle rivière*," and, to the English, by an absurd adaptation, the " Bell " River.[10] From the junction of the Conewango to the junction of Le Bœuf Creek — from Warren to Franklin — it wound between heavily forested hills, with shallows and riffles, and many a willow-grown island, but with ever-deepening channel. As the valley widened and the hills receded, the flat bottom-lands, thick with rank growth, made lurking-places for many possible foes. The river was a natural highway, but it was never a secure road. No flotilla of canoes could pass without detection and the risk of a volley at a hundred points. Wilderness travel presented problems which would overwhelm the average modern; but they also developed character, and Chabert, who knew the wilderness and its signs even as the red man himself, was as thoroughly at home in these journeys as the wild denizens of the woods themselves. The wildcat and lynx that lay crouched and watchful on the boughs beneath which his canoe glided, were not more wary than he.

and spoke with Jean Ceur, who made no Scruple to tell the Intent of his Journey."— *Gov. Clinton to Gov. Hamilton, Sept. 3, 1750.*

[10] One of the Colonial newspapers reported the taking of Fort Duquesne as " Fort Du Guerne on the Fine River."

It was a populous valley, and at its many wigwam or bark hut villages, he beached his canoes, held palavers with the chiefs, and dispensed his goods. Further down the river, at old Logstown, an Iroquois war party reported to Andrew Montour and George Croghan that they had seen "John Cœur [Joncaire] about 150 miles up the river at an Indian town, where he intends to build a fort, if he can get liberty from the Ohio Indians." [11] Chabert sent two messengers to Logstown, desiring the Indians to "clear the road for him," that is, grant him a favorable reception; "but," wrote Croghan, "they have had so little respect for his message that they have not thought it worth while to send him an answer as yet." [12]

It was not all smooth sailing for Chabert, and more than once his life was in danger. The next year he tried again, but it was like running into a hornets' nest. With a small Indian escort and one Frenchman he appeared at Logstown where Croghan and other representatives of Pennsylvania were in council with the Indians. It was a large gathering attended by head men of the Six Nations, whose jurisdiction included the Upper Ohio Valley, and large numbers from the subservient tribes, the Delawares, Shawanese, Wyandots and Twightwees, these last a branch of the Miamis. Croghan, with the English goods, was cordially received. With great temerity, knowing that all sentiment was against him, Chabert called a council and asked his "children" to reply to the speech Céloron [13] had made to them when he went down the river two years before, and asked them to turn away the English traders.

One of the Six Nations' chiefs immediately replied to Chabert, with a good deal of heat; refusing to call the French Governor "Father," or themselves his "children," which was a great affront. Chabert was told that the English were the brothers of the Six Nations, and that they should stay in the Ohio Valley; and they threw back at him the wampum belt he had given them; which was the greatest insult they could offer, short of personal violence.

[11] Croghan to Gov. Jas. Hamilton, Dec. 16, 1750.
[12] *Ib.*
[13] Croghan's journal has it "Monsieur Shularone."

This was on May 21st. On the 25th, Chabert had a conference with Croghan in which — according to the latter's version — he begged Croghan to excuse him " and not think hard of him for the speeches he made to the Indians, requesting them to turn the English traders away; for it was the Governor of Canada ordered him and he was obliged to obey him, although he was very sensible which way the Indians would receive them, for he was sure the French could not accomplish their design with the Six Nations, without it could be done by force; which, he said, he believed they would find to be as difficult as the method they had just tried, and would meet with the like success." For one who had shown Chabert's resolution, this was a surprisingly indiscreet admission; but it will be kept in mind that his adversary was the reporter.

The end of the episode was not yet. On May 28th, a treaty with all these tribes was held at Logstown. There were present ten English traders, with their loads of goods; Andrew Montour, interpreter for the English, and George Croghan, chief spokesman for the Province of Pennsylvania. Chabert was also present. After much speech-making, and a fulsome exchange of compliments between Indians and English, one of the Six Nations' chiefs singled out Chabert, and speaking " very quick and sharp, with the air of a warrior," harangued him (according to a version preserved in the Pennsylvania records) as follows:

How comes it that you have broken the general peace? Is it not three years since you, as well as our brothers the English, told us that there was peace between the English and the French? And how comes it that you have taken our brothers as prisoners on our lands? Is it not our land? (stamping on the ground and putting his finger to Chabert-Joncaire's nose.) What right has Onontio to our lands? I desire you may go home directly, off from our lands, and tell Onontio to send us word immediately, what was his reason for using our brothers so; or what he means by such proceedings, that we may know what to do, for I can assure Onontio that we, the Six Nations, will not take such usage. You hear what I say? These are the sentiments of our nations. Tell it to Onontio, that that is what the Six Nations said to you.

And as if this scolding were not enough, they gave Chabert four strings of black wampum, which meant deadly enmity. Chabert retraced his way to the Niagara. For the moment, he was checkmated; but that he had no thought of giving up the game, subsequent events will show.

In 1750 there assumed command at Fort Niagara a young man of marked ability and distinguished lineage — Daniel Hyacinth Mary Liénard de Beaujeu, scion of a family which figures in French history from the Eleventh century, and which has left its name to the Beaujolois, one of the divisions of the ancient province of Dauphiné. Living members of this line point with warrantable pride to Guichard, Sire de Beaujeu, who in 1210 was sent by Philip Augustus as his ambassador to Pope Innocent III; to Humbert V, Sire de Beaujeu, Constable of France, who attended the coronation of Baudouin II as Emperor at Constantinople, and to William de Beaujeu, Grand Master of the Templars in 1288, killed at the siege of Antioch in 1290. One of the name fought under St. Louis in Egypt; another fell at the siege of Montbart in 1590; another, Paul Anthony Quiqueran de Beaujeu, is famous for his daring escape from prison in Constantinople in the Seventeenth century.

About the close of the Seventeenth century one of the family, Louis Liénard de Beaujeu, is found serving his king in Canada, where he received the Cross of St. Louis, married, was Mayor of Quebec in 1733, and held grants of land on Chambly River. His second son, Daniel Hyacinth Mary, born at Montreal, August 19, 1711, entered early upon military life. In 1748, at the age of 37, he was a captain of the Marine, and in this capacity attended the great conference at the Castle of St. Louis, in Quebec, between the Marquis de La Galissonière and deputies from the Six Nations. It was not the least notable of the many conferences held in the grand council chamber of the castle, between the cultured and court-wise officers of France and the painted and befeathered sons of the forest.

On this second of November the council chamber was thronged. Besides the Commander, and Bigot the Intendant General, de Vaudreuil, lieutenant-governor of the town and

castle of Quebec, Gaspard Chaussegros de Léry, the royal chief
engineer, Captain de Beaujeu and "a great number of persons of distinction," were some eighty chiefs and warriors of
the Six Nations; while fraternizing alike with their brother
officers in the royal service and with the red lords of the wilderness were Captain de la Corne and others who could serve as
interpreters, notably Philippe Thomas de Joncaire, in cordial
if not domestic relations with his friends the Senecas from the
Genesee and the Niagara. As for the conference, thus held
with much formal speaking, it was the same old strife for Iroquois allegiance with which the reader has already become familiar, if not weary. La Galissonière asked if the "cantons"
had become subjects of the English; read to the chiefs letters
of Governors Clinton and Shirley, claiming that the Six Nations were "vassals of the Crown of England, and that you
are bound to go to war for the English, whenever they order you
so to do." It was impossible that these Iroquois should ad-
mit that they were vassals to anybody; and they made the customary reply, "That they had not ceded to any one their
lands, which they hold only of Heaven," and that they desired
to remain at peace with both French and English. With this
equivocal assurance La Galissonière had to rest content. He
had the speeches and answer formally transcribed into an *acte*,
signed by all his officers present, among the others Captain de
Beaujeu, and by the uncouth totem marks of the Six Nations.[14]

Very soon after this conference de Beaujeu appears to have
been assigned to the command at Detroit;[15] but we next find
him at Niagara, where the service called for a man able to
cope with the English in holding on both to the friendship of
the Iroquois and the fur trade.

An anecdote is preserved which illustrates his uprightness
and strength of character in dealing with the aborigines.

While he was in command at Niagara serious thefts were
made from the canoes of the sieurs Gaucher-Gamelin and Godefroy. The thief, a Seneca, was detected, seized and locked up

[14] N. Y. Col. Docs. X, 186–188.
[15] Documents of Hon. M. Saveuse de Beaujeu, cited by John Gilmary
Shea, *Pa. Mag. Hist.*, vol VIII, p. 123.

in the dungeon of the fort. In great anger, a company of Seneca chiefs came to the fort, demanding instant release of the culprit, and menacing de Beaujeu with all the " vengeances of their nation." The sturdy officer replied to their howls and threats:

" I am surprised, my children, at the language you use. I think that you ought to ask pardon for Theou8ayane, obliging you to make him atone for his fault, or, in his failure, to atone for it yourselves. As it is late, and the gates of the fort must be closed, I give you the night to think over what you will do. As for me, I shall do only what I ought to do. As for your threats, I do not fear them. I wait for you and your followers."

The next day the Seneca deputies came again to the fort, in changed mood. They admitted that they had not shown good sense, but declared that their incarcerated brother was unable to make restitution, and that they themselves could not do it for him. De Beaujeu replied:

" My children, in punishing your brother I have wished to keep him from other follies, and to prevent others from imitating him. This house is a house of peace, and I am resolved that it continues to be. The canoes of Gaucher-Gamelin and Godefroy have been stolen. They must be returned, or paid for. That is just and reasonable. Until this affair is settled, do not expect any further favors from me."

Whether impressed by the high justice of de Beaujeu's position, as the old record has it, or whether just making the best of the situation, the " great chief " Annechoteka promised to make reparation, and presumably did, for the incident concludes: " Then M. de Beaujeu, satisfied, had refreshments served to all the Indians and sent them back to their cabins, well pleased."

De Beaujeu had been especially instructed to pursue a liberal and vigorous policy in his traffic with the Indians who came down with furs from the westward. Report of this reached the alert Colonel William Johnson, at Mount Johnson on the Mohawk, who lost no time in writing to Governor Clinton, under date of September 14, 1750:

"Mr. Kalm, a Swedish gentleman (who was lately at my house in his return from Niagara) said he assured me he read a letter from the Lord Intendant of Quebec to the commanding officer at Niagara, dated some time this last summer, wherein he desires him to supply all Indians (who pass in their way to Oswego) with goods, at such a Price as may induce them to trade there to gain which point at the time, he says, the Lord Intendant in his letter says, he will not regard the loss of 20 or 30,000 Livres a year to the Crown. He also allows said officer to supply said Indians with what quantity of brandy or rum they may want, which never was allowed before, for their Preists [sic] were always against selling them liquor, but finding liquor to be one of the principal articles, they trade for, they are determined to let them have it as they would otherwise go to Oswego for it. I take it their view in this, is as much if not more, for preventing any communication between us and said Indians, as for engrossing the trade, and in my opinion they could not have fallen upon a better scheme to accomplish. Said Mr. Kalm told me he heard the officers at Niagara say that by their letters from Canada, they had an account that Oswego would be given up to them as an equivalent for the island Tobago."

Colonel Johnson's guest and informant was Peter Kalm, a Swedish botanist of distinction. His three-volume narrative of his travels in America, at least in the English translation, contain, singularly enough, no account of his journey to Niagara Falls; but a most interesting record of that visit, is afforded in a letter which Mr. Kalm wrote from Albany, September 2, 1750, to a friend in Philadelphia — undoubtedly Bartram the botanist. In this letter Mr. Kalm makes no mention of his visit at Johnson Hall, nor does he tell how he came to be aware of instructions to the commandant at Niagara who had recently been his host. Whether those facts, which as we have seen, he ungenerously disclosed so soon to the enemy, were surreptitiously acquired by his scientific mind, in some unwatched nook of the old mess house at Niagara, or whether de Beaujeu himself showed the letter, in an after-dinner hour of good feeling and boastfulness, is not now essential.

Daniel Hyacinth Mary Liènard de Beaujeu
By Permission, from the Pennsylvania Magazine, Vol. VIII

Available documents are silent regarding the rest of de Beaujeu's service at Niagara. That it was acceptable may be inferred from the fact that before entering upon the next sphere of activity in which we know him, he received that coveted reward of the French soldier in America, the Cross of St. Louis. In 1755 he was sent to Fort Duquesne, where he succeeded M. de Contrecœur, and where, on that memorable 9th of July, in the defeat of Braddock's army, he won glory and a grave — a grave now unknown and unmarked. That he was in chief command of the French forces which defeated Braddock, and that to him belongs the credit for that victory, has been a subject of some contention. Dr. John Gilmary Shea, apparently resting his case chiefly on the " *Registre du Fort Duquesne*," bestows all the laurels for this defeat of Braddock and Washington upon de Beaujeu, of whom he enthusiastically writes that " not one even of his gallant race ever achieved so great a success, or turned a desperate cause into a triumphant defeat of so superior a force." The French official reports of the battle are of different tenor, speaking of Contrecœur as commandant of Fort Duquesne, and as making the arrangements for the engagement; and of Captain Dumas as having saved the day, after the death of Beaujeu.[16] The latter was carried back into the fort and on July 12th was buried in the garrison cemetery, all traces of which long since disappeared.

A further word should perhaps be devoted to Peter Kalm. Although he had fortified himself with passes and permits, he was never quite free from French suspicion. Cadwallader Colden introduced him to Colonel Johnson as " a Sweedish Gent'n . . . travilling in order to make discoveries in Botany and Astronomy." He was recommended to La Jonquière, somewhat more accurately, as desiring to visit Canada and the Niagara, " to make botanical researches." The King directed his officers to aid him, but at the same time to see that he did nothing to interfere with trade. Kalm, however, diligently

[16] " Such a victory, so entirely unexpected, seeing the inequality of the forces, is the fruit of Mons. Dumas' experience, and of the activity and valor of the officers under his command."— N. Y. Col. Docs. X, 304. *See also* X, 338, 382, 410, 528, 914.

gathered information regarding the fur trade at Niagara, which he published at his earliest opportunity.[17]

The need of a fortified trading post on the Niagara River above the falls, at the head of the portage, was more and more felt as travel increased and expeditions multiplied. The great convoy of 1748, and the still greater one of 1749, with the added labor, confusion and loss incident to the passing of Céloron's force, hastened decisive action; but when, in the spring and early summer of 1750, 220 western canoes, laden with a thousand packets of furs, swept down the river, ignored Fort Niagara, and hastened on to make their trade at Oswego, it was recognized by high and low that if France was to hold this trade at all, she must strengthen herself on the Niagara.

As usual with achievements in which many are concerned, several claim credit for this accomplishment, none more justly than Chabert. It was from representations made by him, and by de Beaujeu, commandant at Fort Niagara, that the Governor, La Jonquière, and Bigot the Intendant, in their official communications to the Minister, told of its need, and then of its construction, as though achieved through their own foresight and zeal.

The year 1750 was an important one in Chabert's career. From this time on the part he plays in the drama of the Niagara grows in importance; nor can we better show the conditions of the time than by giving him, for a little, the center of the stage.

In the year named, he was charged with a delicate mission — the escort of a party of chiefs from the Iroquois tribes, to Montreal, " to make satisfaction to the Abenakquis, of whom it was said they had killed three men." Chabert gives it to be

[17] A French translation of his Journal is contained in the *Mémoires de la Société Historique de Montreal,* 1880. Nothing about his Niagara visit is to be found in his well-known "Travels," of which a 3-vol. English translation by Forster appeared 1770–71. It was Kalm's purpose to include Niagara in a continuation of the "Travels," which never appeared. The account of his Niagara visit was published with John Bartram's "Observations," in London, 1751, and has been reprinted. An English translation of the Dedication and Preface to his "Travels" (Stockholm, 1753), by Adam J. Strohm, is in the *Penn. Mag. of History and Biography,* vol. XXXVI (1912).

understood that the desired end was accomplished, though very difficult " for proud, fierce men whom a single threat threw into a rage."

It was during this visit to Montreal that the new establishment above the falls was determined upon, and Chabert was commissioned to build and command it. It was characteristic that in returning to Niagara, he should come by way of Oswego, and in the stronghold of his adversaries boast of what was to be done.

All, however, was not left to the exuberant Chabert. De Beaujeu, the distinguished young officer in command that season at Niagara, was supreme in authority on this frontier. He it was who selected the site for the new post, which La Jonquière, although he persisted in writing of it as " below the portage," assured the Minister was " very advantageous." " I gave orders," he wrote, " that no time be lost to put it in good condition, feeling sure that the English, angered by the harm which it will do to their Oswego trade, would stir up the Five Nations to oppose it." [18]

De Beaujeu, who soon departed for Detroit, left his mark on the Niagara. He opened a new and shorter road on the portage, easier for the carts, and, according to La Jonquière, " enabling the carters to avoid the drunkards commonly found in the old road." He explains that de Beaujeu had done a good deal more than was ordered; but this officer departing for Detroit, " I reiterated my intentions to the officer who commanded at Niagara in his absence; that is to say, that all that was needed was a trading house where the clerk could lodge, a room for ten soldiers who would serve as guard, and a little room for the commandant, the whole surrounded with a palisade, somewhat flanked. I charged above all things that care be taken to avoid large expense, and to hasten the work.

" I confided its care to the Sieur Joncaire de Clauzon, ensign of infantry, chief interpreter in the Iroquois tongue."

This is one of the few instances in the official communica-

[18] La Jonquière to the Minister, Quebec, Oct. 6, 1751. In this letter he cites correspondence of the year before, and reviews what had been done.

tions in which the " Sieur de Chabert et de Clausonne " is designated by the second of his seigneurial titles.

Before undertaking actual construction, Chabert addressed himself to the more difficult task of gaining consent of the Iroquois. The Five Nations, he says, were opposed to it, " nevertheless the undertaking was confided to me in the hope that I would have the credit of making them approve of it, even as my father had had the credit of building Fort Niagara on their land, notwithstanding their unwillingness and the lively opposition of the English."

Although self-interest inclined the Senecas to consent, they held off. A greater depot of goods at so convenient and much frequented a spot, meant much to them. Nevertheless, intimate as were his relations with them, Chabert had to use his most persuasive phrases to gain their consent. " Children," he said, " your father (the French Governor), having out of a tender regard for you, considered the great difficulties you labor under, by carrying your goods, canoes, etc., over the great carrying-place of Niagara, has desired me to acquaint you that in order to ease you all of so much trouble for the future, he is resolved to build a house at the other end of the carrying-place, which he will furnish with all the necessaries for your use." The speech was followed by gifts. The Indians accepted the gifts, but said they would consider the request. The Onondagas, supreme in influence, were also reluctant.

La Jonquière ordered further overtures to be made. Three strings of wampum were sent to the principal villages of the Five Nations, and a summons to a " little feast," at which resort was had to the usually effective argument. " Several pots of wine " having been consumed, " the savages replied that they consented with pleasure to this establishment." [19]

Chabert promptly began work. Plank and joists were sent by de Vassan, from Fort Frontenac, but the plank giving out, bark was used for roofing. Construction occupied three months, and the cost was 15,000 livres. There was no com-

[19] La Jonquière to the Minister, Oct. 6, 1751.

plaint of waste or extravagance in connection with it. A year or so later the President of the Navy Board wrote to La Jonquière's successor: " The establishments of Toronto and the Portage of Niagara . . . were approved last year. . . . I approve what has been done for the execution." [20]

This new post, the building of which made well nigh as much stir, among both English and Indians, as had the building of Fort Niagara 24 years before, was officially designated Fort Little Niagara. It was also styled Fort du Portage, and the Little Fort.[21]

As soon as navigation opened in the spring of 1751, two canoe-loads of trading goods were sent to it, on the King's account; and on May 3d the first barter with Indians was held within the enclosure. It is a date of some note in the commercial history of America, for, though the transactions were trifling, it marks a definite step in the strife for trade control, which underlies the whole course of the history we here seek to trace.

" The Sieur de Joncaire," the Governor reported, " has employed all his talents with the savages, to stop their canoes at this establishment; he would have succeeded well if he had not lacked brandy." One band of Western Indians lingered a whole month at the Little Fort, awaiting the arrival at Fort Niagara of the barque bringing goods for trade. This affair was finished July 31st, with a satisfactory accumulation of furs for the French.

Fort Little Niagara, as built at this time, stood about a mile and a half above the Falls, nearly midway between Grass Island and the mouth of Gill Creek. Fort Schlosser, subsequently built by the British, was placed somewhat further down the river. The old French landing, the earliest known to have been used, was still nearer the Falls; in fact, just above the head of the rapids, below the lower end of Grass Island. Here the earliest portage road came to the river. At the period we now write of, the increase of traffic made it advisable to

[20] Navy Board to Duquesne, June 16, 1752.
[21] Lewis Evans' map of 1755 marks it " Fishers Battery."

have the point of embarkation further up stream, the portage road being continued along the river bank to the new location. Later this point was reached by the new portage road direct from the north.[22]

Governor La Jonquière habitually referred to it as "below the portage," obviously meaning that it was at the south end; but he confused the officials of the Navy Board in Paris, who wrote that it should be " at the head of the Niagara portage " — where indeed it was — adding: "By letter of La Jonquière, October 6th, it appears they have put it below the portage, a mistake for many reasons." [23]

The head of the portage was a populous vicinity. In the year that Little Niagara was built Peter Kalm the Swedish naturalist visited it and reported that some 200 Senecas then lived " at the carrying-place, who were employed in carrying on their backs over the portage, packs of bear and deer skins " at 20 pence a pack. It was at the portage that the Indian of the region first learned to labor for pay. The ascent of the escarpment above the Lewiston level was so arduous that the Senecas called it *Duh'-jih-heh-oh,* meaning to walk on all fours, that being the attitude of one climbing the steep path with a pack on his back.[24]

Chabert in his memoir has a reference to " the cables " used at the foot of the portage, thus establishing the fact that the French used some labor-saving contrivance, probably a hoist worked by a windlass, to raise packages to the heights above Lewiston. After the English were in possession, Captain John

[22] "The French built a sawmill at the Falls, and cleared a few acres of land about the forts and landing places, and on the high river bank opposite Goat Island."—*Albert H. Porter,* "Niagara," 1875. Mr. Porter gives neither time nor place of construction, nor any authority for his statement. It is however, entitled to credence for several reasons. The writer was a son of Judge Augustus Porter, who personally knew the vicinity as early as 1796, when remains of French constructions were still to be seen. Another sawmill was evidently set up by the French not far from the mouth of Chippewa Creek, for in 1761 Sir William Johnson found there a quantity of sawn lumber. Our narrative shows that the French carried a sawmill to Presqu' Isle, to cut plank for bateaux.

[23] Navy Board to Duquesne, June 16, 1752.

[24] Albert H. Porter's "Historical Sketch of Niagara," published anonymously about 1876.

THE NIAGARA-OHIO ROUTE 379

Montresor, in 1764, erected a more efficient device for this work.[25]

Fort Little Niagara, as we learn from a description written the month after trade began there, was a trading house (and no doubt minor buildings) surrounded by a triangular palisade, "badly made," "with two kinds of bastions at the two angles of the side towards the roads which lead to [Fort] Niagara." A gate formed the third angle, on the upper side, "the whole contrary to rules of fortification."[26]

Very promptly Governor Clinton had word of it; and just as promptly he complained to the Governor General of Canada: "I have repeated information that some persons, pretending to act by commission from your Excellency, are erecting a fortified House on the River of Oniagara, between Lake Erie and Cadarchin Lake," a blundering designation of the Niagara-Chautauqua route; but it was Fort Little Niagara the Governor had heard of. He registered his protest on the old familiar ground of the Treaty of Utrecht, and in the same letter protested against the actions of the French who "detained in Prison in Irons near Oniagara," "six Englishmen, subjects of the King my Master, who were peacefully pursuing a Lawful Trade with the Indians.[27]

In December, when Chabert's fort had been put in state of defense, the Cayuga sachem Scanaghtradeya appeared at Mount Johnson and told what Chabert had done, above the Falls. Colonel Johnson with great show of earnestness, warned his informant against the French and their plans. "The only way," he said, "is to turn Jean Cour away at once from the Ohio and tell him the French shall neither build there,

[25] See "The Achievements of Captain John Montresor," a narrative based on his journal, in Buffalo Historical Society Publications, Vol. V.

[26] This none too clear description is the Abbé Picquet's, incidents of whose visits at Fort Little Niagara will presently be given. No more authentic description of the place is known to the present writer. Albert H. Porter, a resident of Niagara Falls, wrote in 1876: "It was a wooden work surrounded with palisades, with ditches and angles in the usual form." According to the Abbé, it was an unusual form. Mr. Porter adds: "The outlines are still distinct." In the 40 years since elapsed, all trace of them has been obliterated.

[27] Clinton to the Marquis de la Jonquière, June 12, 1751.

nor at the carrying place of Niagara, nor have a foot of land more from you." [28] But already Chabert's establishment was capable of defense and the Indians were profiting by his favors.

Four English traders were brought to Niagara in the spring of 1751 to whose seizure, as much as to any single act, may be ascribed the ultimate conflict between France and Great Britain in America. That war was the outcome of a rivalry which had many centers of activity, but no cause was more far-reaching than the strife for the fur-trade; nowhere did the interests of the two Powers clash more sharply than in the region between the Lakes and the Ohio; and no incident of that competition did more to bring matters to a climax than the seizure of these four men.

One of them was Thomas Bourke, 23 years old, who had left his native town of Cork to try fortune in the new land, and who called Lancaster, Pa., his home. Another young Irishman was Luke Irwin of Philadelphia, 28 years old. With him were John Patton and Joseph Fortiner, the last-named a servant. Irwin described himself as a "traveling merchant." These young men, of an age and temperament which laughed at danger and were keen to take risks for the sake of profit, were typical of a class which followed a highly adventurous and picturesque calling. Armed with a license from Governor Hamilton of Pennsylvania, they loaded their pack-horses with goods, substantial or tawdry, which the Indians might fancy, and following the Indian trails made their way to the villages on the Allegheny, the Ohio and its tributaries. When the French at their feeble posts ordered them out of the country, it amused these cunning Pennsylvanians and Virginians to pretend to comply, only to push their adventurous travels still farther, for the more remote the Indian village the greater the harvest of furs which they could gather for their wares. Céloron's futile expedition of 1749 had been little but a threat against invaders of this class; but when John Patton boldly came with his train to the very gate of the fort of the Miamis, now Vincennes, Indiana, the French commandant, de Villiers, under orders from

[28] Conference between Col. Johnson and a Cayuga sachem, Mt. Johnson, Dec. 4, 1750.

Céloron at Detroit, promptly arrested him. A like fate befell Bourke and his companions "near the little lake of Otsanderket," *i. e.*, Sandusky. The four worthies were brought down Lake Erie and after a brief detention at Fort Niagara, were sent on to Montreal, where with other prisoners, June 19th, they underwent an examination by the Marquis de La Jonquière. Three of them at least, Bourke, Irwin and Patton, were sent to France as prisoners, and were still held in confinement at Rochelle, the following year, when the Earl of Albemarle, British Ambassador to France, interested himself in their behalf, and they were set free.[29]

There had been many English traders in the Ohio country before Bourke and Patton, and some of them had been roughly dealt with; but until now no case had really stirred the British public. Now, however, the press made much of it, both in America and in England; and from this time on until the war is declared the statesman and the pamphleteer — especially the latter — have much to say regarding French encroachment on the Ohio.

At this period Governor de Longueuil and other officials were much concerned over the loss of reports and dispatches from Céloron, commanding at Detroit, and from other posts as well. These dispatches were addressed to de Lavalterie at Niagara, and were duly received by him. He assigned a soldier from the fort to take them to Fort Rouillé, now Toronto, whence they would be sent down to Quebec. The soldier set out from Niagara with the precious documents, and was never seen nor heard of afterwards. A Mississaga Indian from Toronto, soon after coming in at Niagara, was closely ques-

[29] Albemarle to Holdernesse, Paris, Mar. 1, 1752. There was also correspondence between Governor George Clinton and the Canadian Governor, La Jonquière, regarding these prisoners. "The Mystery Revealed"(London, 1759), an excessively rare book, contains an account of their capture and examination at Montreal; but in this and some other accounts the names are misspelled well nigh beyond recognition, Irwin becoming "Arowin," Bourke, "Broke," and John Patton, "George Pathon." The *Boston Gazette*, June 5, 1753, reports their return to Philadelphia "with Capt. Budden, by the solicitation of the British Ambassador, who was so good as to clothe them and send them to England, the French having stript them naked and used them hardly."

tioned but knew nothing of the missing messenger. Search was made, but to no purpose. The one thought was that he had either deserted or, more likely, been killed by Indians who made off with the dispatches to the English. The loss of the soldier may have been regretted, but the official correspondence laments only the loss of the dispatches.

The story of John Trotter illustrates the conditions of the time. One night in the summer of 1752 he and a companion, James McLaughlen, were brought into Fort Niagara, in irons; and after a few hours, were put on board a bateau and sent across to Fort Frontenac, thence to Montreal and Quebec. It was not until mid-March, 1754, that Trotter's captivity and wanderings ceased at Philadelphia: where, March 22d, he told his tale before Chief Justice William Allen, and swore to it, and, as he could not write, signed the statement with his mark.

Trotter was an Indian trader of Paxtang in the county of Lancaster, Pennsylvania, and in the year 1752 was 28 years old. That summer, with Timothy Reerdon as partner and £400 worth of Indian goods, they made their way to the Ohio country. They traded at Atigué, at Logstown and Weningo [Venango]; near which place, August 15th, "as he was about to pass the river opposite to Weningo, in company with James McLaughlen, a hired servant of his, a party of Frenchmen, 110, came and seized them and their horses, took away the goods and bound this deponent and the said McLaughlen with Indian hopples, made of wild hemp, in their arms and legs." They were "drove" through the woods, part of the time tied together, and three days from "Weningo" they came to Presqu' Isle. Trotter's deposition says he "saw the French had cut a road — and were hawling great guns to a place where they were going to erect another fort." At Presqu' Isle the two traders were put in irons and confined under guard in an out-house for four days. They were then put on a bateau and brought down Lake Erie to the "small wooden fort," at the head of the Niagara portage. "From thence they were put into a cart, and set out about noon, and came to a large stone fort at night." From old Niagara, as above stated, the unlucky traders were sent forward on the long water route which hundreds of other prisoners, French, English and American, were to pass over in captivity in the troublous years to come. Trotter was kept in irons during the whole voyage; was held in "Jayl" at Montreal four days, and at Quebec 30 days; then with other English prisoners was put on board a French man-of-war. Arriving at Rochelle, he was again locked up in prison for a month, on bread and water; then was set free, a pauper in a strange land. Trotter and McLaughlen and one Jacob Evans, a fellow exile, begged their way from town to town, finally reaching Bordeaux, where Trotter fell in with Captain Snead of the ship *Betty and Sally*, who took pity on him and gave him passage to Philadelphia. Such were the fortunes and misfortunes of the Indian trade in the Ohio country in the year of peace, 1752.

In the winter of 1752, the French on the Niagara were threatened. "The savage allies of the English prowled in multitudes around Fort Niagara, and filled them there with fear," says Chabert, who was ordered to raise a war-party in behalf of the French. "I set out over the ice in the month of January," he says, "to gather my recruits." Troops appear to have been sent up from Montreal at this time. Later in this year we find Chabert, with an attendant band of chiefs, paying his respects in Montreal to M. de Longueuil, who administered the colony *ad interim*, from the death of La Jonquière until the appointment of Duquesne. For the next year or so he was employed in various expeditions, from Quebec to the Ohio, but with his home at the Little Niagara fort. In the winter of 1753 he was sent into Central New York to notify the Five Nations, "in the Governor's name, that he was going to the Ohio, to take possession of it, and to build forts on its banks, adding to this announcement the most terrible menaces for any one who would have the audacity to oppose him in this matter. . . . The savage ear will not listen to this sort of talk; it was received with bitter and insulting laughter. They declared to me that nobody but a child of the nation could have spoken it with impunity."

In the winter of 1753 the command and control of the Niagara portage were given to Chabert in addition to his other and seemingly conflicting duties of commandant at the upper fort, on the Niagara, and frequent emissary to distant points. Years after, summing up his services for the King, he wrote as follows, of Niagara and the portage:

Canadian history makes mention of this famous fall which the eye of the traveler never sees except with awe and admiration. Lake Erie, constantly augmented by the waters of the upper lakes, Huron, Michigan, etc., contracted by two chains of mountains, pours its flood into this strait with the impetuosity of a torrent and in the river Niagara hurls itself down 130 feet with a terrible noise, which can be heard more than twelve leagues round about. Such is the invincible obstacle encountered by navigators going to Presqu' Isle, to the Ohio, to the Straits [Detroit] and other French forts built above the Niagara.

The trader and the officer are there obliged to put down, below the falls, the goods, merchandise, supplies for war and for food destined for the different forts. Men must carry the canoes and the goods by the narrow and stumbling paths over three steep hills. As for the very heavy bales they can be transported only by the aid of cables, and by force of arm.

Before I was appointed Commandant of the Little Fort, there was no one for this Portage, since the natives would not undertake it except at very great expense; thus it came about that the service suffered further on, and that the Governors were unable to carry out expeditiously movements ordered, which were urgent and necessary. They encountered there a further inconvenience, still more vexatious. The Indians entrusted with the transport of goods, and naturally inclined to pilfer, would quit the open path, open the bales, steal whatever pleased them, without fear of punishment or restitution, since they acknowledged no master; still one was obliged to treat them with consideration, often indeed because their thievery has not been discovered until too late to lay a claim against them.

The colony fairly echoed [30] with the clamor and complaints of the merchants and officers. The Governors-General, badly informed, gave orders which were of no effect. They established regulations, but without success. Their shrewdness employed all the resources of the politician, their wisdom spent itself in systems; and the abuses always continued. Every measure was useless, because the untractable savage knew only his own caprice, and the most equita-

---

[30] "*Retentissoit sans cesse des cris,*" etc.

ble law could make no impression on barbarian minds, without sincerity or discipline. Finally, after a hundred years of effort and consideration, and the trial of all possible resources, no more effective means was found for remedying so many inconveniences, than to put me in charge of the establishment of the Little Fort of Niagara, and of the business of the portage.

Chabert was reluctant, he says, to assume responsibility for the Portage, but could not have failed to see the opportunity for making a fortune, which it afforded. However, he assures us, " I silenced the voice of interest in order to hear only that of honor, of duty and of public service." Chabert's service as Master of the Portage and the Fort Little Niagara continued for five and a half years, until the end of French control in the region. The advent of the British was not the only disaster that overtook him; for as soon as France could lay hands on him, and others who were charged with having plundered the King, he was called to account for his stewardship. In his defense he set forth, with a skill that reflects credit either on him or his legal adviser, the circumstances which induced him to take charge of the Portage.

He entered into the agreement with the King, he tells us, because his Majesty " formally pledged himself to return at the expiration of the lease, the horses, cattle, harness, yokes, conveyances and implements necessary for the said Portage." The Governor (Jonquière), Chabert says, forced him into the undertaking, and when the lease — apparently for the season 1753–54 — expired, he wished to give it up, because he was losing on the contract, and because Government had not furnished the promised help; but M. Duquesne (Jonquière's successor) induced him to renew the contract, promising, in the King's name, " that the iron, the steel, the repairing of the iron-work for the carts, and the cost of shoeing the horses, would be at the King's expense." Again the promises were not kept, and again Chabert sought " to quit absolutely, but M. de Vaudreuil would not consent to it, and ordered me always to keep the command of the Little Fort, and to take charge of the King's food-supplies and stores. Behold," he exclaims, " the source of all my misfortunes!"

CHAPTER XIX

THE FUR TRADE IN THE '40'S

PERPLEXITIES OF A CONTRACTOR — EFFECT OF THE WAR OF 1744 — FOUNDING OF TORONTO — THE CONVOY SYSTEM — CÉLORON'S EXPEDITION OF 1748.

IN the last chapter we traced the development of the Niagara-Ohio route, and the varied services of the brothers Joncaire. We must now return to a somewhat earlier period, for a review of other phases of the history of the region.

In no period of its Eighteenth century history has so little been recorded of the Niagara region as in the years immediately following the death of the elder Joncaire. This is in part due to the fact that the regional events of that period relate less to expeditions and military plans than to the development and prosecution of trade. Far from being barren or even meager, the unpublished documents of the time afford much from which to sketch conditions on the Niagara and neighboring lakes.

At this period — the decade of the '40's — Fort Niagara, as a garrison, was pitiably weak. In 1744, when Céloron was sent to command there, the post had but 34 men. In that year 34 men were added, and there were six officers. The cannon in all Canada were so few that Beauharnois, writing to the Count de Maurepas, October 8th, regretted that he could not send any more to Niagara, where there then were five peteraros and four 2-pounders. In this summer de Léry and La Morandière came up to make such improvements for defense as the feeble exchequer permitted. They repaired and doubled the old stockade, and apparently did some work on the stone house. Two years later (October, 1746) when Captain Duplessis was holding the place with 41 men — officers and soldiers all told — Beauharnois promised that Niagara should be reinforced " on the first movement of the enemy."

These notes sufficiently indicate the strength — weakness,

rather — of the old fort at the period we are now to consider. Until near the close of the decade of the '40's, when the control of the Ohio region dominated all else in the Government policy, Niagara was valued chiefly as a base of operations in the fur trade, and a depot of supplies for the Indians. It has been related [Chap. XIV] how, in order to make that trade more profitable, the post had been put under the lease system. It is interesting to note how that system worked at this later period.

In 1742 an agreement was reached with the French Company of the Indies, by which they undertook to carry on the trade at Forts Frontenac and Niagara, beginning January 1, 1743, for a period of six years. Under the company, the active "farmer of the posts," or lessee of trade privileges, was one whose name appears in the records as Charles, Chasles, Chales, Chabet, and — most often and probably correctly — as the Sieur Chalet. One document styles him "Inspector for the India Company." The Intendant, Hocquart, wrote that he had known Chalet a long time, and would vouch for his "activity and intelligence." In the same letter [1] the Intendant urged greater economy at the Lake Ontario posts; he thought that 20 soldiers at Niagara, and 15 at Frontenac, with two officers in each post, would be garrison enough to stand off any Indian attack likely to be made.

There was much correspondence before the articles of the lease were agreed upon and approved by the King. Chalet was to transport goods, and material for warehouses, at his own expense; but he was given the use of the two sailing vessels on the lake, to carry his merchandise to Niagara. In the autumn of 1743 one of them was stranded, near Niagara, with considerable loss to Chalet. Apparently as partial offset to this, the next year he was allowed 300 livres for canoes, though in general, during the period of his lease, he was required to furnish his own canoes. He was also relieved of the cost of transporting his supplies from Montreal to Lachine.

The payment required of Chalet to the Government, under his lease, was, at the outset, 4,000 livres per year for each post.

[1] Hocquart to the Minister, Quebec, Oct. 15, 1742.

In 1745, because of losses arising from the war, it was reduced to 2,000 livres.

Under the monopoly of the French India Company, only its agents could buy or sell beaver skins in Canada; but trade in other furs was open to all. Whoever wished to engage in the Indian trade procured a license from the Governor General, paying therefor a sum proportionate to the advantages offered by the locality in which he proposed to operate. The trader who stocked a bateau and sent it up the Lakes with four or five men, paid for his license some 500 or 600 livres; some posts were so profitable that a license to trade at them cost 1,000 livres. All trade permits for certain posts were occasionally withheld, which gave rise to the charge that they were reserved for favored relatives or friends. The money paid for trade licenses was received by the Governor General, who was understood to use half of it for the poor, and who did use a part of it for the relief of widows of officers.

But the forest traffic fluctuated as much as modern stocks. There were times when traders' licenses were sold very cheaply, and other times when the Government could not induce men to undertake the business.

In the summer of 1743 Chalet made the round of Lake Ontario, visiting Forts Frontenac and Niagara, to learn the requirements and conditions of the trade. Except for an occasional visit of inspection, he appears to have conducted the business, during the period of his lease, at Quebec, relying on agents resident at the posts to look after the actual buying and selling. There was no establishment at Toronto, but Chalet sent thither, this summer, several *voyageurs* who camped at the mouth of the Humber and carried on a considerable trade with passing Indians, most of whom, had they not found the French here, would have gone with their furs to Oswego. One of the principal lieutenants was one Chicot, spoken of as a carpenter and smith, " of very moderate ability for trade, but absolutely necessary for the maintenance of buildings at Frontenac and Niagara." Chalet paid part of his wages.

On his return to Quebec, from Niagara, Chalet made vigorous

protest against what he styled as abuses, but which were by no means peculiar to Niagara.

At all of the posts, for years, the officers had been accustomed to engage in the fur trade on their own account. Not only the officers, but soldiers, clerks, workmen, could exchange a blanket or a gun with a friendly Indian who had a desirable peltry to give in exchange. It was an irregularity, long tolerated because not easily checked, but the lax system had given rise to many abuses. Certain posts were in favor among the officers because of the opportunities for profit which they afforded. When the posts were leased or — to keep close to the French phrase, " farmed " out, to a " *fermier* " such as Chalet — the officers, finding their opportunities thus curtailed, did what they could to hamper and embarrass the usurper of their privileges; with resultant bickerings and complaints which perplexed and angered all who had a hand in the administration.

Nowhere did the situation become more difficult than at Niagara, as soon as Chalet undertook to assert his rights. Here the commandant, Céloron, following the custom of his predecessors, had engaged in the Indian trade on his own account. When he could no longer do so, he made things as difficult as possible for Chalet; and each, in letters to their superiors, complained of the other.

Chalet's first year or so as farmer of the Lake Ontario posts, although fairly profitable, resulted in vigorous demands for better terms of the lease. In 1744 there were gathered furs valued at more than 94,000 livres. The barque which was stranded in the autumn of 1743 was not floated until the following spring; but she was condemned and Chalet replaced her by another of the same burden. This once more gave Lake Ontario two sailing vessels. In September, 1745, four carpenters were sent to Frontenac to build another, which was ready in the spring, when it replaced one of the old boats. Hence, although the French at this period operated four vessels on the lake, not more than two were in commission at the same time, and often, only one. In 1747 an inventory refers to the two "barques" then in commission as the *St. Charles* and *St. François*.

Many Western Indians who took their wares to Oswego, in the summer of 1745, not being satisfied with what was offered in trade, returned with their furs to Detroit, where, obviously as a last resort, they were disposed of. An official dispatch which relates the occurrence, observes that this " of a truth was to the prejudice of the Sieur de Chalet, but the commerce of the Colony lost nothing." That the company's stores at Niagara should be thus ignored by savages who had brought a wealth of furs so far, and for nothing, gave new cause of complaint to Chalet; while the scornful Céloron improved the occasion to remind the Governor that the trade at Niagara was ruined through the incompetence of Chalet; and that troubled contractor complained to the Intendant that if the Niagara establishment was for a time not supplied with goods it was because of the stranding of the vessel which was carrying them thither; and besides, he could not be expected to foresee that Indians going to the English at Oswego would bring their untraded furs back to Niagara. In any case, continues the report,[2] if Céloron had been less prejudiced against the farm system, " it would not have been difficult to make with Chalet proper arrangements, to prevent the complaints of the savages; but I cannot overlook that this officer, as well as most of those at the other posts, are little pleased at the arrangements which have been made for carrying on trade, seeking only to hamper the lessees instead of assisting them as you ordered them to do." Céloron not only thwarted the lessee, but refused to come to an understanding with Hocquart or with Michel, the commissioner of the Marine, and Beauharnois threatened to recall every officer who opposed the lessees. In April, 1745, the President of the Navy Board, with royal sanction, wrote as follows to Céloron:

I am informed, sir, that since you have filled the command accorded you, of the fort Niagara, the lessee of the trade of that post, far from receiving from you the assistance and aid which you should

[2] President of the Navy Board to Beauharnois, May 5, 1745.

give him for the good of his undertaking, has found at your hands only difficulties and obstructions.

I am likewise informed, although neither M. Hocquart nor M. Michel have written of it, that since you have been in this post, you have not deemed it incumbent to take council with either in regard to the improvement of the trade, nor details concerning the fort and garrison.... I warn you, that if you give further occasion for complaint, I shall not be able to prevent His Majesty from making you feel the effects of his displeasure.

Céloron was soon after recalled from the command at Niagara, being succeeded by Captain Duplessis. He had persisted in his traffic with the Indians, much to the disgust of Chalet, whose complaints could not be ignored; but the Governor General, in writing of the affair, did not disguise his admiration of certain qualities which distingushed the solder: "I can only attribute such stubbornness to the inflexible character of this officer who has moreover all the essential qualities of a man of war. He has, however, felt the blow which has been given him; I know that he has seriously reflected," and he begged Monseigneur to "forget this affair," promising to report later how Céloron comported himself.[3] When a removal for disobedience of orders was coupled with such praise, it was hardly to be viewed as a disgrace; the conditions in the service were well known, and the following year we find him reinstated as commandant at Niagara.

Disgusted, and pleading ruin, Chalet sought to have his lease canceled. His troubles were not confined to quarrels with Céloron. Trade, which in the first year of his lease, had been encouraging, soon fell off. The Indians who came down the river with canoes full of furs, were not satisfied with the goods which the French offered, nor with the rate of exchange. After prolonged but unfruitful dickering, they would resume their paddles and make their way to Oswego, where the English were better stocked and more liberal in exchange. Not merely at Frontenac and Niagara, but at all the western posts, the Indian trade lapsed into a precarious and unprofitable state.

In 1744, war was declared between France and England,

[3] Beauharnois to the Minister, Oct. 18, 1746.

and there was a great falling off in the amount of goods taken up for trade at the posts, in comparison with recent previous years. The merchants who furnished outfits had but a small quantity of goods on their hands, and the Indian traders grew discouraged. Beauharnois complained that although he offered licenses for nothing, especially for Detroit, in order that there should be abundance of goods at that post, only ten traders went up this year. " I was obliged," he wrote, " to give seven of these licenses gratis, in return for conveying the effects of the commandant and of the garrison which could not otherwise be carried up without great expense to his Majesty." It required, he continues, " considerable solicitation " to induce nine canoes to go to Mackinac, so slight was the prospect of profit. " The same reasons apply equally to all the other leased posts; also to those of Niagara and Fort Frontenac, which are hardly better provided with goods necessary for the Indian trade there, and will be much less so next year, no supplies of any description having reached us this year."

The despondent Governor was writing at Quebec, October 28th. The season of gales was at hand, no ships were likely to arrive for more than half a year; and even were supplies abundant at Quebec, relief of the Lake and Western posts during the winter was out of the question. The Governor realized that with no goods for trade at the posts, the general trade of the Colony would fall off, and the Indians, no longer finding their necessaries at the French posts, would turn to the English, where their wants would be satisfied, but on conditions entirely opposed to the interests of the French.

After the recall of Céloron, Beauharnois wrote to the Minister in sanguine mood: " There has been no more quarreling since the new order was established in the trade at Niagara and Frontenac. Nothing has happened contrary to the good of the trade, at least nothing has come to my knowledge." An effort had been made, before the war of 1744, to reduce the garrisons to the lowest possible point, in the interest of economy; but since that date, increases were deemed necessary.

It was not a happy time at these feeble forts. Duplessis

THE FUR TRADE IN THE '40'S 393

in command at Niagara, fell sick "of fatigue, conjoined to bad diet," [4] and asked leave to go down to Quebec to recruit his health. The real trouble was that the Senecas refused to supply the post with fresh meat. Joncaire, living amongst them, was also dangerously ill at this time. The Niagara garrison was but a feeble handful. Besides Duplessis there were Lieutenant de Contrecœur; two ensigns, de Boulascry and Chevalier de Garner; one 2d ensign, a son of Duplessis; four sergeants and 33 soldiers, two of them gunners.

And the trouble really grew out of the trade situation. Dissatisfied with what they received at the fort, and the withholding of brandy, the Senecas refused their customary help as hunters. It was the first boycott on the Niagara, and it nearly ruined the post.

Duplessis was allowed to leave, with appreciative mention in the dispatches: "He is a good officer, who has well acquitted himself among these people [the Senecas] in very critical times." The command passed to de Contrecœur.

A memoir written by Chalet [5] sheds some light on the conditions of the trade at the lake posts.

On the basis of the business of 1743 and '44, Chalet declared that he was being ruined, and must relinquish the lease. The agreed amount payable to the King for the trade privilege at Frontenac and Niagara, was 8,000 livres, yearly. The cost of transporting goods to these posts was 10,000 livres; for use of bateaux, 1,500 livres were paid; wages of sailors and bateau-men exclusive of their food, 1,800 livres; wages of employes and workmen at the posts, 4,000; and gratuities to the officers, 2,400 livres. This last item is frequently mentioned. It was customary, so long as the French were in control of the lake posts, to allow to the principal officers a substantial "*gratification,*" perhaps as solace for the lost privilege of barter on their own account.

The above items made a total expense account of 27,700 livres; to which were to be added the cost of rigging, etc., for the barques, tools, and supplies for boatmen and for employes

[4] Boisherbert on Indian Affairs, Nov., 1747.
[5] Dated Quebec, Oct. 20, 1744.

at the posts. The other side of the ledger showed as follows: 50,000 livres worth of merchandise sold at Frontenac and Niagara at 15 per cent. profit, netted the lessee 7,500 livres. Profit on food supplies was figured at 2,500 livres and on brandy, sold at 100 per cent. above cost, at 8,000; a total of 19,000 livres, against expenses of 27,700 livres. It is hardly necessary to observe that the profit on Indian goods which were paid for in furs, undoubtedly, at least ultimately, far exceeded the 15 per cent. allowed by Chalet; but by his own figures the terms of the lease were ruinous. His pleas resulted in a reduction of the annual rent; but the depressed and disturbed state of trade which followed the declaration of war led to the abandonment of the contract before the six-year term had expired.

The war raised the price of goods in France. After the risk and difficulty of transport to Quebec, the price was still further raised; so that, when finally laid down in the storehouse at Niagara, the guns and knives, blankets and trinkets represented a far greater value than under more favorable conditions. But these far-reaching causes meant nothing to savages who had paddled a thousand miles with their canoes gunwale-deep with beaver, mink, marten and fox. They only knew what had been given for these furs on other visits at Niagara. When Chalet's clerks valued his wares on a basis 60 per cent. higher than their cost in France — as was the case in 1744 — the Indians refused to trade, and went on to Oswego.

It was estimated in 1744 that all of the posts under company control produced 200,000 livres' worth of beaver. If this fur could have reached the manufacturers in France in good season, the market would have been well sustained; but with shipments from Quebec few and uncertain, values fell off, and the basis of barter at the posts was still further demoralized. "I am convinced," wrote the Intendant to the Controller-General, in October, 1744, "that an increase in the price of beaver will induce all of the Indians who are now going on to the English, to stop at Niagara." Accounts of the time show that both

French and English allowed from three to four francs for green beaver pelts and 30 for the dry.

In 1746 Chalet relinquished his lease of the Lake Ontario posts. Efforts were made to induce him to continue, for there was a scarcity in the colony of men able and honest enough to assume such duties. He appears indeed to have yielded in some measure to the call for his continued services; for in 1747 we find him supervising a new arrangement of the convoys, of the correspondence with the store-keepers at Frontenac and Niagara, and in general, working for an economical administration at those posts. He is also mentioned as having been very useful during the war (1744–48) because of his knowledge of English and his ability to learn from prisoners the state of things with the enemy. He died prior to July, 1748, at which time his brother-in-law, Gobert de St. Martin, petitioned for a copy of his will and an inventory of his property.

It is worthy of note, that during this four years of war, the French abode at Frontenac and Niagara, the English at Oswego, and neither attacked the other. Each party contemplated such an attack, and both gave it up through mistrust of the Iroquois, without whose help they dared not hope for success. In April, 1745, John Lydius reported that the French with 600 Indians under Belestre, were coming to attack Oswego. The matter was considered by the Council at New York, and by the Mohawks at their castles, but there was no attack. The French had given it up because the Senecas and other tribes would not pledge support.[6] The English on their part, also considered an expedition against Fort Niagara, but abandoned it for the same reason — the refusal of their Indian allies to aid them. For once, Iroquois neutrality was respected by both belligerents, though neither would have respected it, had he felt strong enough to ignore the Indians.

In the summer of 1745, fearing an English attack on Niagara and the portage, and that the convoys to that post and

[6] Memo. of the King in instructions to the Marquis Duquesne, Versailles, May 15, 1752. See abstract in Can. Arch. Rept, 1905, L, 165.

to Detroit would be intercepted and pillaged, Beauharnois had sent to the Niagara the Sieur de St. Pierre, with 60 Nipissings and Algonquins. With them came also the Sieur Demuy, the elder, with a force under orders to proceed to Detroit. At the same time de Longueuil gathered a horde of friendly savages and came to the aid of Niagara. It is not clear that the English even contemplated an attack on Niagara at this period. At any rate, none was made; but Beauharnois justified his elaborate steps for defense by the fact that the English were deterred, and that his precautions had induced many traders, coming down from the upper country, to tarry with profit at Niagara. The scare also resulted in a strengthening of the fortifications; but the rapid caving in of the lake banks near the fort led the Governor General to advise moving the fort to the other side of the river, "where I am assured it would be on a rock foundation."[7] A year later, perhaps as a result of protective work, he writes that "the lake, which was undermining the place where the fort stands, has made no further progress for a year."[8] He was now disposed to strengthen the fortifications and enlarge the garrison; "it is certain," he assured the Minister, "that this place is one of the keys of the country, and must be made proof against both savages and the English." He urged the necessity of taking possession of Oswego; but before his plans could take shape, the Peace of Aix-la-Chapelle, October 7, 1748, brought armed strife on the lake to an end. "Only a true" at best, that treaty did not in the least check the strife for control of the Indian trade.

A serious loss to the French, at this time — the late season of 1748 — was the wreck of the vessel relied on for transport between Frontenac and Niagara. Bigot was instructed[9] to take necessary steps to replace "the Niagara barque," without which the lake posts, Niagara most of all, were seriously handicapped in their efforts to hold the Indian trade.

The strength of the Niagara garrison, as stated by Indians or English soldiers, carried there captive, can seldom be ac-

[7] La Galissonière to the Minister, Oct. 19, 1747.
[8] Ib., Oct. 5, 1748.
[9] Navy Board to Bigot, Apr. 11, 1749.

THE FUR TRADE IN THE '40'S

cepted as trustworthy. Deserters from the post were better informed. One such wanderer, who reached New York and was examined in February, 1745, reported that there were 100 men at Niagara, with four cannon.[10] Obviously, the size of the garrison varied with each new arrival or departure of troops; and there was much coming and going of small parties. In 1744 the garrison varied from 30 to 64 soldiers, with six officers.

Not a season passed without some effort at repairs and protective work at Fort Niagara. In the summer of 1744, De Léry and Morandière rebuilt the walls. Duplessis, in 1745, strengthened the fortifications and was commended for his precautions.[11] He also tried to stay the constant caving off of the high lake bank north of the fort. A year later we find the Navy Board writing about it; "It is vexatious that the timber revetment on Lake Ontario to prevent the water from reaching the base of Fort Niagara [12] has not been kept up, and the earth continues to cave in. Some way must be found to prevent it, as soon as possible." [13] Many letters were written on the subject. Replying to a proposal by La Galissonière, to abandon the place, and rebuild on the west side of the Niagara, the President of the Navy Board admitted that a bad choice had been made in the site of Fort Niagara, and complained of the endless expense incurred in trying to stop the wearing away of the banks. However, he added, "before submitting to the King the proposition you have made, of moving it to the other side of the river, you must show the advantages to follow, both as to substantial location, and in regard to the Indian trade.[14] A great point was, whether such removal would further the efforts of the French to prevent Western Indians from carrying their furs to Oswego. The scheme did not receive royal sanction, and was dropped.

Contrecœur's request to be relieved was granted. June 15, 1748, when the convoy reached Fort Niagara, it brought a new

[10] N. Y. Council Minutes.
[11] Letter from Pres. of the Navy Board, Mar. 7, 1746.
[12] "*Jusqu' au pié du fort de Niagara.*"
[13] Navy Board to La Jonquière and Hocquart, Mar. 13, 1747.
[14] Pres. of the Navy board to La Galissonière, "Marly, Jan. 23, 1748."

commandant in the person of Captain de Raymond, who had already commanded there in 1743. His full name has not been noted in the correspondence of the time, and but little concerning his military service. In July, 1746, he had conducted, from Montreal to Quebec, a party of English prisoners, who had been taken captive by Indians. He had been at Niagara but a few weeks when he wrote a long letter,[15] in which he dwelt on the importance of the post and the great danger of an attack by Indians in English interest. It was because it was so exposed, he boasted, that the Governor, Galissonière, had called him to its command. " It is in the way of all the savage nations of the upper country who are continually going and coming for trade with the English at Oswego, Albany and Boston. It is moreover, one of the most important keys of the country. . . . With Niagara in the hands of our enemies, the Lakes Ontario and Erie would be closed to us." He enlarges on this point, and concludes by calling attention to his 26 years of zealous service for France in America, and begs for appointment to one of the vacant majorities. He was transferred from Niagara apparently in 1749; was made a captain and commended for his gallantry at Ticonderoga in 1758, but does not again come within the field of our narrative.

Out of the trade conditions and rivalries of the time came the establishment which grew into the present city of Toronto. An official communication of October 9, 1749, signed by both La Jonquière and Bigot, advises that a more substantial establishment be made on the north shore of Lake Ontario near the mouth of the Humber — a natural harbor and portage terminal which had long been called Toronto. As has been noted, traders were sent there some years before; now it was proposed to send " an officer, 15 soldiers and some workmen to build there a little palisaded fort," to intercept the Indians from the West, on their way to Oswego. We shall presently see how this suggestion was acted upon. For a period, both Frontenac and Toronto were " King's posts," where trade was

[15] Raymond to Monseigneur ———, dated " Fort de Niagara, 8 7bre [Sept.] 1748." Can. Arch., ser. F., vol. 92, pp. 163–4.

conducted on Government account. Furs received there, by barter with Indians, were afterwards sold at public auction, and the proceeds were supposed to be turned into the treasury.

It is not until April 15, 1750, that official record appears of a new lease of trade privileges at Forts Frontenac and Niagara. The lessee is only mentioned as "the Sieur Roger," and one of his first troubles was the "trade limits" which were drawn between Niagara and the new post of Toronto; traders from the latter place were warned not to encroach on territory tributary to Niagara.

La Jonquière would have established trading posts on Lake Erie, and still others on Lake Ontario, but had to be satisfied with the new Toronto. "The forts of Niagara and Detroit," wrote the President of the Navy Board, "will always suffice to assure the communication of these lakes. More posts would mean merely more expense and a scattering of the forces of the Colony. The King has not approved your views in this regard, and his will is that these posts be not made." He did however look with favor on a new post for the Ohio country, to ensure communication with Louisiana; and later, as related, a post on the Niagara at the upper end of the portage, was established, subsidiary to Fort Niagara. It became, in the few years of its existence, of very great importance. Its controlling spirit, Chabert, received elaborate instructions regarding that part of his duties relating to trade. In 1756, de Vaudreuil authorized him to establish a storehouse for the Indian goods, and sent out a blacksmith who should be stationed where most needed among the tribes. "We anticipate," wrote de Vaudreuil, "that the Five Nations will make their trade at Niagara," and he admonished Chabert to give them all possible attention: "We have sent to Niagara provisions and goods needed for the trade. The Sieur de Chabert knows how important it is to us that the Five Nations have no occasion to regret the English. The clerks put in charge of the King's trade shall give the goods to them on as favorable terms as possible." [16]

[16] Instructions of the Marquise de Vaudreuil, given to the Sieur de Joncaire-Chabert, Oct. 19, 1756.

There had been, in fact, two objects in establishing the lease or farm system wherever practicable. One was to increase the revenue of the King, and, by means of the fur trade, offset as far as possible, the cost of the posts, which was ever becoming more and more burdensome. A second object was, to keep the officers and employees at the posts from being interested in trade profits, and put an end to the constant complaining of both traders and Indians.

As late as 1752, the admission was made in official correspondence, that the system had not proved satisfactory. In some cases, the lessees of a post, instead of fighting the issue to a finish, as Chalet did with Céloron at Niagara, with less integrity connived with the officer in command, sharing both privileges and profits. There were so many "deals" of one sort and another, that in June, 1752, the President of the Navy Board asked the Governor, Duquesne, to consider if it might not be better to abolish the farm system, and make the trade free at the posts, merely imposing certain conditions on the traders, either in the form of licenses (*congés*) to be paid for, or by requiring them to transport provisions and supplies for the King's storehouses. In 1749 an order had been issued to the commandants at Frontenac, Niagara and Detroit to see that the traders or storekeepers of those posts put on their goods the same prices that the English were charging at Oswego. It was hoped in this way to check the swelling tide of trade at Oswego; but it was not materially checked until, in 1756, the fortunes of war took Oswego itself away from the English. The Indians of the Lake region then had no alternative, except by the long journey to Albany; and so for a time, even in these years of war, the French posts enjoyed a revival of trade. A report of October 30, 1757, observes, that the trade of Frontenac, Niagara and on the Ohio would have been considerable, the past season, if the posts had been sufficiently stocked with goods; but they were left unprovided at a time when the upper country Indians had abundance of peltry. "Most of them have left their peltries in the King's storehouses, and content themselves with a receipt from the storekeeper, who pledges himself to satisfy their demands next spring." Vaudreuil, who is here quoted, foresaw that the lack of supplies would occasion serious want, and did what he could to meet the needs of the service. "It is certain," he wrote, "that in peace the King's posts will yield large profit, for the quantity of furs which come from everywhere have no other market since they have lost Oswego." But there was to be no more peace; and in the closing years of French domination, legitimate trade at the lake and river posts was to be swallowed up in the general deluge of fraud and waste.

In the summer of 1747, after the Hurons of Sandusky Lake had murdered five Frenchmen, and all the Lake posts felt uneasy, unusual care was exercised in making up and dispatching the Convoy. All the trading canoes bound for Detroit and other western posts were ordered to leave Montreal with the Convoy carrying the Government shipment of post supplies. As this large and picturesque flotilla was paddling its way through Lake Ontario, it came upon a large canoe full of white men, women and children. Instead of attempting a defense or an escape, they rested on the quiet lake until the canoes of the French overtook and surrounded them, then informed their amazed and voluble captors that they were refugees from Oswego. One of the men, who spoke French, said he was a deserter from the English troops quartered there, and explained to Commander Dubuisson that his party were all Irish, who had become dissatisfied with the state of things at the English post, and had decided to seek their fortunes among the French. It developed later that this Oswego refugee was one "Kollin," as Dubuisson reported it; being Irish, his name was no doubt Collins. He and his family were subsequently sent down to Quebec where, on examination, he stated that "he had fled from Choueguen [Oswego] through apprehension of being prosecuted for having infringed some prohibitory regulations," which is vague enough. One or more soldiers had followed him. The Governor concludes: "They have remained at Quebec and profess the Catholic religion." Among other bits of news which the refugees told the French was the information that the Governor of Menade — that is,

New York — wishing to corrupt Joncaire Chabert, had offered him a captain's commission in the British service. Joncaire refusing to be thus corrupted, the Governor had turned his attention to the Senecas, some of whom had gone over to him.

The uncertainty of Seneca friendship at this time made Dubuisson cautious. At Fort Niagara he landed 20 men to cut wood for the garrison; then hastened up to the Heights. " The portage was passed very promptly and quietly," wrote Duplessis, the commandant at Niagara, " except the last night, when some drunken fellows of the guard gravely illtreated the Grand Chief of the Senecas, who is very much dissatisfied in consequence." Duplessis sent Chabert to the village of the Little Rapid, " with something to restore the temper of that chief." What the " something " was, the records fail to state, but Chabert, as expert as he was diplomatic, unquestionably knew what palliatives would soothe this ruffled lord of the village of the Little Rapid — the Buffalo of 1747.

These troubles adjusted, Dubuisson and his laden canoes paddled off into the mists of Lake Erie; but when Detroit was reached, de Longueuil, there commanding, announced that he had authority to detain at his post all the people of the convoy, even the voyageurs and employees, if any treachery were apprehended from Indian sources.

Neither travel nor traffic were ever free from great hazard at this period; but in September, so large a deputation of Senecas and other Iroquois visited Quebec, that the Administration again " breathed easy "; for so long as their head men were guests of the French, no war parties were likely to molest French posts or settlements. Profiting by this situation, the garrisons at Frontenac and Niagara were reinforced and newly stocked with food and goods for trade.

The needs of the Detroit colony, and the growing number of traders in the West, greatly increased the traffic through the Niagara and over the portage. For many years before the end of French dominion on the Lakes, for the sake of economy, convenience and protection, the transport of goods from the East to the West was somewhat systematized. Although there was much coming and going, during the season of navigation, the main shipment was made in late summer, and because the boats were dispatched under armed protection, it came to be known as the Convoy. Many boats were loaded at Montreal, by the Government, with goods for the settlers, still more goods for the Indian trade, building material, arms and ammunition. Even money, and some articles of luxury, were sent by the Convoy. An adequate armed force of the King's troops, or of Canadian militia, accompanied. Because of the protection thus afforded, the merchants of Quebec, Three Rivers and Montreal, who had agents or representatives anywhere to the westward, sent out their supplies and recruits at the same time. Thus the Convoy was swelled to a large fleet of laden canoes and bateaux, against which no roving band of ill-disposed savages was likely to do harm. The departure from Montreal was in August. The toil of the rapids and the portages was lightened with jest and song. The force was so great that the night encampments felt secure. Together the laden craft threaded the channels of the Thousand Isles, and insolent in their strength, swept past the impotent post of Oswego, to taunt and challenge the handful of helpless British. The arrival of the Convoy at the mouth of the Niagara was the great event of the year for the lonely garrison at the fort. Then followed busy and stirring days, with profit for the Indians of the portage, who with incredible loads toiled up the steeps and through the forest to the landing above the Falls — after 1750, Fort Little Niagara. If one would conceive of the labor of the portage, let him even to-day pass over the improved road, which does not wholly coincide with the old portage path, and try to imagine the means and effort required to transport, not the light bark canoes, but the heavy plank bateaux, up the heights and through the forest, eight miles to the point of reëmbarkation. Although bateaux were kept in reserve, at either end of the portage, there were times when these heavy boats had to be transported in numbers, up and down the hills. Oxen and horses were used in the later years; but many a loaded train passed that way with no motive power but human muscle.

Small wonder if, after the greater tasks were over, before the boats paddled off up the river to Lake Erie, there were hours of idleness and drunkenness. The old portage road was always a place of theft from the goods in transit, and of exasperating and demoralizing debauch, especially by the Indians who served as carriers, and profited by the needs of all who went that way.

The story of the portage, here touched on only as incidental to the general course of our narrative, rivals in incident and importance the story of Fort Niagara itself. In some respects it is more significant, for the portage is a part of the great story of the West. For half a century, Detroit, largely dependent on the East for means of subsistence, watched with apprehension and deep concern, the successful passing of the Niagara portage, not only by the annual Convoy, but by her high officials, her soldiers and her traders, with their families and possessions. One random record from the old days may serve to vivify the conditions of the times. It was at the Niagara portage that the baby Nicolas Campeau, son of Etienne and Jeanne Cecile (Catin) Campeau, was dropped in the river by a *voyageur;* but instead of meeting the fate of countless unfortunates since, the lusty youngster was rescued and lived to be known for many years as " Niagara " Campeau. In the records of the Huron Mission near Detroit (1733–56) are many references to this " Niagara." In 1751 he was farmer for the mission and appears to have lived on Bois Blanc Island. The reader of the old mission records will discover that among " Niagara " Campeau's live stock was a valued cow named " La Niagara "; but whether she too had adventures at the portage is not stated; and perhaps we are carrying our regional researches further than is edifying or essential.

The shipment of goods to Western trading posts was well systematized. To Detroit and posts east of it, on the Lakes, 90 canoes were sent out annually, of which 10 were apportioned to Niagara. As the average value of a laden canoe was 7,000 livres, the wealth represented by a great flotilla of them is apparent. These capacious canoes were of three, six,

12 and even 24 places, and the larger ones could carry 3000 pounds weight.

In 1748, the Convoy was commanded by an experienced officer, already alluded to, Pierre Joseph Céloron.[17] He was a veteran in Canadian service and had received knighthood in the Military Order of St. Louis. Prior to 1739 he had been in command at Mackinac and had shared in the Chicasaw campaign. In 1740 he was again in command at Mackinac and passed back and forth through the Niagara, as he probably had in earlier years. As already noted, he was in command at Fort Niagara for about two years from the fall of 1744, and was transferred from the Niagara to Fort St. Fréderic on Lake Champlain where he served in 1746-47. At the time of his recall from that post, in November, 1747, Boisherbert wrote of him: " He has acquired the esteem of everybody "; " deserves promotion, being one of the best officers we have, and even one of the oldest captains."

The Convoy which this experienced and trusted officer commanded, in the summer of 1748, was a notable one. The second in command was M. de La Naudiere, and the escort consisted of more than 100 Frenchmen, with 10 or 12 of " the most reliable Nepissing Indians of the Lake," *i.e.*, Lake of the Two Mountains, above Montreal, and a great number of *voyageurs*, who were going up to trade. This imposing flotilla, " while passing Fort Frontenac, made a strong impression on the Iroquois and other nations it met." So wrote the Governor to the Minister;[18] and, he adds, " the news of its approach, I think, determined more than anything else, the principal chiefs of Detroit to come to Montreal."

Up the Niagara and through Lake Erie the great Con-

[17] He was the Sieur de Blainville, but has been inaccurately designated by writers as Bienville, and even Bienville de Céloron.
[18] Galissonière to Count de Maurepas, Quebec, 23d Oct., 1748. In the Canadian Archives I have noted the following in reference to Céloron: He was appointed Fort Major ("*commandant sédentaire*") at Detroit, May 23, 1749, being the first to fill that post. He received 12 livres a year, and a gratuity of 3000 livres to be taken from the *congés* funds. Long instructions were given for his conduct. A town on Chautauqua Lake and an island in the Detroit River, bear his name. For a sketch of his career, by C. M. Burton, *see* Mich. Pioneer & Hist. Colls., XXXIV.

voy was successfully guided. Speedily, too, for Céloron arrived back at Quebec September 5th. The down journey, especially if the canoes were not burdened with fur packs, was often made with incredible celerity.

CHAPTER XX

TWO FAMOUS EXPEDITIONS

CÉLORON'S UNDERTAKING OF 1749 — ADVENTURES OF THE BROTHERS JONCAIRE — THE CHAUTAUQUA PORTAGE — GREAT BRITAIN WARNED FROM THE OHIO — THE ABBÉ PICQUET COMES TO NIAGARA.

LESS than two months after Céloron's discharge of this duty, the war between France and England was ended by the Treaty of Aix-la-Chapelle, signed October 1, 1748. Ostensibly, this treaty established peace between the two Powers; but not for an hour did it lessen the strife for the control of trade at Niagara and the Lake posts. Of even greater moment was the utter failure of the treaty to establish boundaries between French and British possessions south of the Lakes. France had long claimed the region south of Lake Erie, having no more substantial support for the claim than the shadowy adventuring of La Salle nearly 80 years before. Now the British, regardless of French assertions, were insolently taking possession. The Ohio Company, a Virginia association with a royal grant, was sending its traders into the great valley west of the Alleghenies. If they gained the Indian trade, more or less certain tribal allegiance would follow.

The energetic Galissonière, at Quebec, realized that the hour for aggressive action had come. Sustained by King and Court, he fitted out an expedition. Its object was, to show both to British and to Indians, that the region of the " Beautiful River " belonged to France. No attempt was to be made to build forts or establish garrisons; but British intruders were to be warned off, and the resident tribes were to be pledged anew in fealty to France. The two Powers being now at peace, warlike methods might not be used; the most impudent of traders from Virginia or Pennsylvania might not be captured or killed; he could just be told to get out;

and the whole vast watershed of the Ohio was to be claimed anew for France by the singularly peaceful method of burying, at convenient spots, leaden plates inscribed with the proclamation that France, by means of this expedition and bits of buried lead, had repossessed herself of her own.

Impotent as such a procedure may seem, it was not without precedent, though perhaps it had never been relied on under such discouraging conditions. The Indian was too shrewd, the frontier trader too insolent or indifferent, to be impressed by archaic mummery.

Ineffective as the methods to be used may seem, they were the main reliance of France for assertion of authority in this inland empire. It was her first show of force in the region, where heretofore she had sent only a few emissaries of the type of Joncaire the elder. The gateway to the region was the Niagara; and the chosen leader was Céloron.

The force gathered under his command left La Chine on the afternoon of June 15, 1749. There were 23 canoes, carrying 250 men, French and Indians. There were eight subaltern officers, six cadets, an armorer, 20 French soldiers, 180 Canadians, 30 Iroquois and 25 Abenakis. The reader will note that in this expedition, which historically is of such extraordinary import, the trained soldiers of France were but a handful. It was the Canadian — the *habitant* — on whom the Governor relied for strength, endurance and knowledge of waterways and woodcraft. But the main reliance, the principal influence which at the outset seemed to insure success, and kept the men from degenerating into a mere rabble of wilderness wanderers, was Céloron and the officers under him. They were a picked lot of fine fellows, experienced in frontier service and in the control of men, white and Indian. One of them was de Contrecœur, whose part in our regional history deserves attention. His full name is written Pierre Claude de Pecaudy (or Pecaudry), Sieur de Contrecœur. His father, an officer in the regiment of Carignan, had been ennobled, by Letters Patent, January, 1661, and in 1672 secured the Seigniory of Contrecœur, which in due course passed to Pierre, who is thereafter known as De Contrecœur. He spent a long life as a soldier for France in Canada. As early as 1710 we find him an ensign in Acadia. He first came to the Niagara as a lieutenant under Captain Duplessis, and in 1747 succeeded that officer in command of Fort Niagara. Later in that year, at his own request, he was relieved, being succeeded by Captain de Raymond. In later years he is to bear a conspicuous part in the war which was the natural sequence of the expedition in which we now find him engaged.[1]

Still more notable is another of Céloron's company: Joseph Coulon de Villiers, whose name appears in the documents sometimes as "Captain Coulon," sometimes as De Villiers, but most often as De Jumonville. He was one of seven brothers, six of whom served in the Canadian wars and four of whom are more or less identified with the Niagara frontier. A younger brother, François, was also in Céloron's following. A few years later it was to be the fate of Jumonville to fall by an English bullet, for which a young Colonial officer in British service, by name George Washington, was held responsible; and it was to still another brother of this same family De Villiers that Washington surrendered, July 4, 1754. Some further note of this remarkable family will be made in due course.

Philippe Thomas de Joncaire (the second Sieur de Chabert), and his brother Daniel were both in the expedition. Years after, Daniel wrote of it:

In the spring [1749] I went down the Ohio with M. de Céloron and Father Bonneau,[2] royal professor of hydrography at Quebec, to take possession in the King's name with the accustomed formalities. We were escorted by a detachment of 250 men.

The second object of the expedition was to drive out the English established on the banks of this river, and to punish a tribe which had killed several Frenchmen. My commission did not extend to all that, for I was ordered by M. de La Galissonière to go down to Montreal; but the commandant, who thought my presence necessary,

[1] In February, 1748, Contrecœur, then commandant at Fort Niagara, was promoted from lieutenant to captain, and given a company. De Vassan, Legardeur de St. Pierre and Marin at the same time received a like promotion.

[2] So printed in the Joncaire *Mémoire*. Obviously an inadvertence for Bonnecamps.

kept me, and took upon himself to have the Governor approve this counter order.

We thought we should perish several times in this journey, encountering enemies greatly superior in number; my brother would have been burned if he had not called out his own name, and awed these people by the fear of having the arms of the Five Nations turned against them. These savages have said since, that but for my brother and myself, not a Frenchman would have escaped.[3]

Among others who accompanied Céloron were his son; and the Sieur de Niverville, who was of the Boucher family — probably Joseph, eldest son of Jean Baptiste Boucher. Joseph was an ensign when serving with Céloron; later he is mentioned as lieutenant.

In some respects, the most important member of the party, next to Céloron himself, was the Rev. Jean de Bonnecamps, "professor of hydrography" in the Jesuit College at Quebec; a singular-enough chair of learning for the time and place, but one that was maintained from 1671 until the Conquest. Father Bonnecamps styles himself "*Jesuitte Mathématicien.*" He had mastered astronomical reckoning, and on the march he made frequent record of latitude and longitude. His journal, and that of Céloron, are the principal sources of information regarding the expedition.[4]

The expedition set out in high spirits, June 15th. Two days later, at the Cedars, the canoe of "Monsieur de Joncaire"— Father Bonnecamps' journal does not say which Joncaire — was lost, and one of the four men in it "perished before our eyes, without our being able to give him the slightest

[3] From the "*Mémoire de Daniel de Joncaire-Chabert,*" etc., being a part of the report of the "*Commission établie pour l'affaire du Canada,*" Paris, 1763. For the use of a copy of this excessively rare volume, acknowledgment is herewith made to Mrs. John P. Bronson, of Monroe, Mich., whose great-grandfather was Francis, son of Daniel de Joncaire-Chabert.

[4] Both documents were discovered, in Paris depositories, by the late O. H. Marshall of Buffalo; to whose researches all subsequent students of this episode are indebted.

The Pére Bonnecamps returned to France in 1757. On his representation that he had received 800 livres per annum in Canada, he was given a gratuity of 600 livres and sent to live in Touraine "where all the officers from Canada are stopping."— *Orders of the King, and Minutes*, Oct. 9, 1762.

aid. This," adds the reverend chronicler, "was the only man we lost during the expedition." Eight days later they reached the mouth of the Oswegatchie, now Ogdensburg, where the Sulpitian missionary, the Abbé Picquet, had just begun his establishment. They found him "lodged under a shelter of bark, in the midst of a clearing of nearly 40 *arpents*." Close by was the palisaded fort, 70 feet square, which he had built. His purpose was to gather at this place as many Indians as he could bring under the influence of France and Christianity. He is destined to win a marked success and to play an extraordinary part in colonial history; but when Céloron and his people paused there, "his whole village consisted of two men, who followed us into the Beautiful River," *i.e.* the Ohio.

The season was propitious, the lake was calm, and on July 6th, the expedition entered the mouth of the Niagara. No Convoy ever caused such excitement, for here was an extraordinary errand. This large force were to cross to the south shore of Lake Erie, climb through the forest over the watershed, and by waterways which the red man knew but which had seldom been used by white men, were to enter that delectable but debated land of the Beautiful River.

Father Bonnecamps' journal holds some observations which should have place in these pages.

Of Lake Ontario he notes that the waters "are very clear and transparent; at 17 and 18 feet, the bottom can be seen as distinctly as if one saw it through a polished glass. They have still another property, very pleasant to travelers — that of retaining great coolness in the midst of the suffocating heat which one is sometimes obliged to endure in passing this lake."

The condition of Fort Niagara during its first decade has already been shown. In 1736 its armament was six small cannon. In 1745 there were but four efficient cannon, though the fluctuating garrison reached 100 men. Now, four years later, Father Bonnecamps, though he does not tell the strength of armament or garrison, draws a good picture of the place:

The Fort of Niagara is a square made of palisades, faced on the outside of oak timbers, which bind and strengthen the whole work. A large stone barrack forms the curtain-wall, which overlooks the lake; its size is almost the same as that of Fort Frontenac. It is situated on the eastern bank of the channel by which the waters of Lake Erie discharge themselves. It will soon be necessary to remove it elsewhere, because the bank, being continually undermined by the waves which break against it, is gradually caving in, and the water gains noticeably on the fort. It would be advantageously placed above the waterfall, on a fine plateau where all canoes are obliged to land to make the portage. Thus the savages, people who are naturally lazy, would be spared the trouble of making three leagues by land; and if the excessive price of merchandise could be diminished, that would insensibly disgust the English, and we could see the trade which is almost entirely ruined, again flourishing.

An artillery return for Fort Niagara in 1749 shows that it had four iron guns throwing 2-pound balls, four others for 1½-pound balls, a 6-inch iron mortar, one mortar for grenades, five swivels, and 13 iron shells (*boîtes à pierriers*).

Our "Jesuit-Mathematician" was not the first to suggest that the fort would have been better placed above the falls; nor was he to be the last, as we shall see, to comment on the encroachment of Lake Ontario.

On July 6th and 7th he "observed the western amplitude of the sun, when it sets in the lake." It gave him 6° 30′ northwest for the variation of the compass; he found the latitude of the fort to be 43° 28′. We know it to-day as 43° 15′.

Céloron, who crossed Lake Ontario by a different route than that taken by his Indians, at Quintè fell in with La Naudiere, his lieutenant of the year before, who assured him that the nations around Detroit, having learned of his proposed march, were ready to join him at the first invitation. He did "not give much" (*Je ne donnai pas beaucoup*, etc.), he says, for Indian promises, but none the less he hastened on to Niagara, where he overtook Jacques Charles de Sabrevois, on his way to his command at Detroit. They conferred together; Sabrevois passed on up the portage, as did Contrecœur with the canoes that had arrived. Meanwhile Céloron, waiting at Fort

Niagara for the Indian contingent, wrote to Chevalier de Longueuil, stating what he had learned from La Naudiere and begging that, if the Detroit Indians were still of a mind to join him, their setting-out be hastened, so that they could meet him at the Scioto between August 9th and 12th; but if they had changed their minds, he wished to be informed of that as well.

By the 8th, the entire army had passed up the portage, and four days later were " encamped at the little rapid at the entrance of Lake Erie," that is, within or opposite the present site of Buffalo. Oddly enough, no mention is made by any of the four men who were in the company, and wrote of the expedition — Céloron, Bonnecamps, de Léry or Daniel de Joncaire — of Buffalo Creek, though they all, probably, became more or less familiar with it. Father Bonnecamps gives us a little description of the portage and the cataract:

> The channel which furnishes communication between the two lakes is about nine leagues in length.[5] Two leagues above the fort the portage begins. There are three hills to climb, almost in succession. The third is extraordinarily high and steep; it is, at its summit, at least 300 feet above the level of the water. If I had my graphometer, I could have ascertained its exact height; but I had left that instrument at the fort, for fear that some accident might happen to it during the rest of the journey. When the top of this last hill is reached, there is a level road to the other end of the portage; the road is broad, fine and smooth.
>
> The famous waterfall of Niagara is very nearly equidistant from the two lakes. It is formed by a rock cleft vertically, and is 133 feet, according to my measurement, which I believe to be exact. Its figure is a half-ellipse, divided near the middle by a little island. The width of the fall is perhaps three-eighths of a league. The water falls in foam over the length of the rock, and is received in a large basin, over which hangs a continual mist.

The Indians for whom Céloron waited at Fort Niagara, had again to be tarried for at the Lake Erie end of the river. " We remained in our camp at the Little Rapid," wrote Fa-

[5] The French league is usually reckoned as two and a half miles. The actual length of the Niagara River is 37 miles.

ther Bonnecamps on the 13th, " to await our Indians who were amusing themselves with drinking rum at the portage, with a band of their comrades who were returning from Oswego." Later, when a similar delay occurred, he notes in his journal that the savages are " a class of men created in order to exercise the patience of those who have the misfortune to travel with them." On the 14th the fleet entered Lake Erie, but a heavy head wind drove them to an early camp, " some leagues above the Little Rapid," says Céloron. They were on the south shore, with which Céloron was not familiar. The first camp, probably in the little bay, not far beyond the southwestern limits of Buffalo or its steel-making suburb of Lackawanna, was made under guard of 40 men.

On the 15th, an early start was had, in the hope of reaching the place of portage, but Céloron's own canoe struck a rock ledge which came near the surface, some distance from shore. " But for quick help," he records, " I and all my crew would have drowned." This mishap, probably in the vicinity of Stony Point, sent them ashore to mend their broken boat and delayed them so that it was noon of the 16th before the place of portage was reached. This was the mouth of the stream which the French called *Rivière aux pommes* — Apple River — but which, since permanent settlement in the region, has been known as Chautauqua Creek. The lake shore at this point was but an open roadstead, beset with rocks and unsheltered. The place had however long been used by the Indians in passing from Lake Erie to the Ohio Valley. By this route, too, six years before, Douville de la Saussaye had probably passed on his mission to the Shawanese. In the present expedition he is a guide for Céloron through the Chautauqua region.

The boats were beached and toil began. While 50 men, under de Villiers and Le Borgne, began to clear a road, Céloron studied the landing place " in case it should be desired, hereafter, to make a settlement." He saw no advantages and many obstacles. " The lake is so shallow, on the south side, that barques can come only within half a league of the portage. There is no isle or harbor which offers shelter; they would have to anchor and unload by means of bateaux. Gusts of wind are frequent, and I think they would be in danger. Moreover, there is no native village at this place."

The opening of the portage road was excessively hard work. Some eight miles to the southward was "Chatakoin," on which they planned to launch their canoes and float easily down by the Outlet and connecting streams, into the Ohio. But the lake lay 730 feet above Lake Erie, and to reach it an elevation of at least 1000 feet had to be overcome. The way, broad enough and clear enough for the carrying of canoes, was to be made for much of the distance up the long steep slope of the divide, through a heavy forest growth of oak, maple, beech and other native hard woods, mingled with pine and hemlock. The route cut out was nearly ten miles in length and for the most part may still be traced. The modern road coincides with the original path for some distance.[6]

On the 17th, about two and a half miles were opened; on the 18th, scarce half as much. Besides the fatigue which the men experienced, in cutting and climbing on the steep slopes, heavy rain fell; but Céloron philosophically reflected that if it delayed progress, it would also raise the streams, by which he hoped to float southward. Half a league was the record for the 19th. Two more days they crawled on; and on the 22d stood on the Chautauqua strand, with a "passably good" road behind them, over which all the impedimenta were brought. One day they rested on the shore of Lake Yjadakoin, as Bonnecamps writes it; and at noon of the 23d the flotilla paddled swiftly past the pleasant shores where in modern days of ease countless thousands resort for intellectual uplift, or such renewal of physical vigor as green woods and pure waters give.

Céloron and his army had advanced to the Chautauqua portage, before news of their proceedings was published in New York. On July 17th, the *New York Gazette* had intelligence from Thomas Maddox, "an Englishman who is the King's interpreter," that a thousand French and Indians were going to a place "called La Belle river, about 300 leagues from Can-

[6] *See* "The Old Portage Road," by H. C. Taylor, M. D., Fredonia, N. Y., 1891.

ada, on a branch of Mississippi River, in order to destroy some Indians that were under the allegiance of the Crown of England, and to drive off the English who were building a fort there." When the Mayor of Albany heard of it, he remarked that the place was supported by the Pennsylvania Government! New York was not concerned in the matter. A few years later it found itself very much concerned.

Just prior to Céloron's invasion, the Governor of Pennsylvania had sent 12 barrels of gunpowder to the Indians of the Ohio. Naturally, they looked to Pennsylvania for backing, in their resistance to the French.

At the Outlet, Céloron found, not the swollen stream he had hoped for, but "barely two or three inches of water." The boats were unloaded and the goods sent across a portage which La Saussaye knew. Days of many difficulties followed, but on the 29th their canoes floated in the deep water of the Allegheny at the mouth of the Conewango. The way of the Beautiful River was clear before them.[7]

Céloron made his way down the Conewango, the Allegheny and the Ohio as far as the mouth of the Great Miami, which he reached August 28th. Six of the lead plates were buried:

[7] The author made inquiry regarding this portage, of the Hon. Obed Edson, a resident of the region and close student of its history. Mr. Edson replied: "The short portage made by Céloron, of three-fourths of a league, I suppose was made before he entered the real rapids that he describes. These rapids began where the traction line crosses the Chadokoin at Jamestown. Above these rapids is a smoother, slow water, as far up as the foot of the lake. Late in the season (this was July 25th) the water is often low in some — not all — places, so that loaded boats could not well pass over them. In the rapids below Jamestown, the swift running of the same stream in the same direction would aid the passage of the boats and thus obviate the necessity for a portage. Céloron writes: '*Before* entering the place [i. e., the rapids] the *greater part* of the baggage was unloaded, with people to carry it to the rendezvous.' Where the rendezvous was is obscure, but I believe it was at or near the hills of Jamestown, and at the head of the rapids. This short portage along the Outlet to the real rapids seems to have occurred on the 24th, for on the morning of the 25th a consultation was had which resulted in Joncaire being sent upon a mission with some savages to *Paille Coupée*. The canoes were repaired and probably the 26th was occupied in passing the many rapids between their commencement at the trolley bridge at Jamestown, and their ending at Levant, a distance of three leagues (7½ miles), where, on the morning of the 27th, they first found the still waters of the Cassadaga."

One on the south bank of the Allegheny (which in Céloron's time was regarded as the Ohio), opposite the mouth of the Conewango, near present Warren, Pa.; one about nine miles below the mouth of French Creek, under a great rock engraved with strange hieroglyphics;[8] a third at a point not clearly indicated, but probably at the junction of the Ohio and Wheeling Creek, on the north bank of the latter stream; a fourth, on the right bank of the Muskingum, at its junction with the Ohio; a fifth, at the confluence of the Kanawha; and a sixth at the mouth of what Céloron calls Rock River (*Rivière à la Roche*), now known as the Great Miami.

Two of the plates have been found. In 1798, boys bathing at the mouth of the Muskingum found a plate of lead in the river bank, inscribed in a strange tongue. If they knew nothing of French, or of the ancient claims of France, they did know the value of lead. The plate was taken home and a part of it used for bullets. Many years later, the rest of it, with its mutilated inscription, came to the knowledge of Caleb Atwater, a historian. He sent it to Governor De Witt Clinton, who gave it to the American Antiquarian Society, in whose building at Worcester, Mass., it is now preserved.

In 1846 a boy playing on the margin of the Kanawha, found the plate which Céloron buried there 97 years before. This plate is now in the keeping of the Virginia Historical Society. So far as known, the others have not been recovered, though in some cases considerable search has been made.

The plates were 11 inches long, 7½ inches wide and ⅛ inch thick. The inscriptions were identical, except as to the place and date of burial. The name of the engraver, Paul de Brosse, appeared on the reverse. They were evidently prepared in France, or possibly at Quebec, and were a most precious part of Céloron's luggage. As it happened, one of them was stolen, on the Niagara, or between the Niagara portage and the Chautauqua outlet. This we learn, not from the French journals, but from the correspondence of Colonel

---

[8] The rock, long famous in Western Pennsylvania history, is pictured, and the inscription given in facsimile, in Schoolcraft's "Indian Tribes in the U. S.," vol. VI, p. 172.

William Johnson, to whom a sachem of the Cayugas carried a lead plate, saying that the Senecas " got it by some artifice from Jean Cœur (Joncaire)." Johnson referred it to Governor Clinton, who in reporting the matter to the Lords of Trade wrote that he " would send to their Lordships in two or three weeks a plate of lead, full of writings, which some of the upper nations of Indians stole from Jean Ceur, the French interpreter, at Niagara, on his way to the river Ohio." [9] Its mysterious character aroused in the Indian mind an uneasiness which Johnson did not fail to stimulate, dwelling in harangues to them on the dire evils sure to follow if the sinister designs of the French went unchecked. Even Governor Clinton's letters to the Lords of Trade expressed uncommon concern at the land-grabbing activity of the French, which contravened the treaties between friendly Powers.

In reality, Céloron's expedition accomplished nothing substantial. At the burial of each plate, the officers and men were mustered with all possible show of power — and finery, the Arms of Louis XV were nailed to a tree, the plate was impressively buried, and a formal *Procès Verbal*, or decree of taking possession, was drawn up and signed by the officers, those who could not write meanwhile contributing to the occasion with shouts of *"Vive le Roi,"* and more or less discreet consultation of the commissariat. The on-looking savages, more entertained than edified, refused to be impressed; it was not the sort of show of force for which they had respect. And as for the British traders in the region, they paid very little attention to the warnings and threats of Céloron, knowing that the resident tribes were friendly to them. Even councils conducted by the adroit Joncaire failed to win from the Indians any satisfactory pledges, and by the time the Great Miami was reached Céloron was aware that his arduous mission was a failure. He was amazed at the number of English traders in the region. At the village of Chiningué — later known as Logstown, near the site of the modern town of

[9] It cannot be stated what became of the stolen plate. No further mention of it is found in the correspondence of Gov. Clinton and the Lords of Trade.

L'AN 1749 DV REGNE DE LOVIS XV ROY DE
FRANCE NOVS CELORON COMMANDANT DVN DE-
TACHEMENT ENVOIE PAR MONSIEVR LE M.... DE LA
GALISSONIERE COMMANDANT GENERAL DE LA
NOVVELLE FRANCE POVR RETABLIR LA TRANQVILLITE
DANS QVELQVES VILLAGES SAVVAGES DE CES CANTONS
AVONS ENTERRE CETTE PLATVE ....

PRIS DE LA RIVIERE OYO AVTREMENT BELLE
RIVIERE POVR MONVMENT DV RENOVVELLEMENT DE
POSSESSION QVE NOVS AVONS PRIS DE LA DITTE
RIVIERE OYO ET DE TOVTES CELLES QVI Y TOM-
BE DE TOVTES LES TERRES DES DEVX COTES JVSQVE
AVX SOVRCES DES DITTES RIVIES AINSI QV'EN ONT
JOVY OV DV JOVIR LES PRECEDENTS ROYS DE FRANCE
ET QV'ILS S'I SONT MAINTENVS PAR LES ARMES ET
PAR LES TRAITTES SPECIALEMENT PAR GEVX DE
RISVICK DVTRCHT ET DAIX LA CHAPELLE

One of Céloron's Lead Plates, Found 1846, at the Mouth of the Great Kanawha

Economy, Pa.— he encountered 10 traders from the English colonies; even the British flag was flying there, the first, apparently, to be shown west of the Alleghenies. Céloron ordered the intruders out of this " French territory." The English leader, " who saw us ready to depart," says Bonnecamps, " acquiesced in all that was exacted from him, firmly resolved, no doubt, to do nothing of the kind as soon as our backs were turned." No one was in the least deceived. Several other Englishmen were encountered, with like result.

Céloron's main reliance, for controlling the Indians, was on Joncaire and his brother Chabert. There was no one among all the French in America of greater influence among the tribes; yet even they not only found themselves powerless, but in danger. On one occasion, when the two Joncaires and Niverville were sent in advance to announce the coming of Céloron, the savages fired on them, the musket-balls piercing the French flags; and when Joncaire began to harangue them, one of the savages cried out that the French were coming to destroy them; the excited horde seized the three envoys and were about to burn them when a friendly Iroquois appeased the others, who were Shawanese, " by assuring them that we had no evil designs." This recalls the occasion referred to by Chabert in a passage already quoted.[10]

The English had been kept well informed. It was the sachem Hendrick who carried news of the expedition to Colonel William Johnson, and through him to Governor Clinton; and it was Céloron himself who wrote, August 10th, from his camp on the Ohio to Governor Hamilton at Philadelphia, that he had expelled the English traders from that region.

Turning northward, Céloron hastened into a safer neighborhood. In 37 days the expedition made its way from the mouth of the Great Miami to Detroit, reaching that post October 7th. They traveled up the Great Miami to Loramie Creek; occupied five and a half days in the long portage to the Maumee, which they made with the help of horses supplied by Captain Raymond, in command at Kiskakon, now Fort Wayne, Indiana. Thence, in Indian pirogues — not canoes,

[10] See page 316.

but dug-outs — they descended the Maumee to Lake Erie, some of them going overland to Detroit. The journey was not without its hardships and adventures, upon which we need not here dwell. October 8th the party again set out by canoe, skirted the north shore of Lake Erie and on the 19th arrived at Fort Niagara. After three days for rest and repairs, in which, we may be sure, many tales of the Ohio wilderness were told, the party set out once more along the south shore of Ontario. It was a hard and hazardous traverse, for the gales of autumn overtook them. On November 10th, Montreal was reached and on November 18th Céloron and Father Bonnecamps arrived at Quebec, five months and 18 days after having left it. By the priest's computation they had traveled 1200 leagues; and with the exception of Joncaire's boatman, accidentally drowned at the outset, not a life had been lost.

Mention has been made of the officers named Coulon de Villiers. Of no one, whose history pertains to the Niagara region, not excepting even the Messrs. Joncaire, has there been more error and confusion in printed allusions than of the family Coulon de Villiers, several of whose members were on the Lakes and the Niagara. A few facts regarding them, mostly gleaned from documentary sources, may be here submitted, but, let it be added, with no assumption of infallibility.

Nicolas Antoine Coulon de Villiers, who came to Canada near the close of the Seventeenth century, in 1705 or 1706 married Angelique Jarret de Verchères, a sister of the young Madeleine de Verchères whose splendid defense against an Iroquois attack in 1696 made her one of the best-beloved heroines in Canadian history. Antoine and Angelique gave to the colony a typical family of that day, not unworthy to be remembered with the Le Moynes. Of their twelve or thirteen children, at least four shared in history-making on this old frontier of France.

Nicolas Antoine the father, about 1725, replaced M. de Villedonné as commander at Fort St. Joseph of the Illinois. With the Jesuit priest Charles Michel Mesaiger, he landed at the mouth of the Niagara before Fort Niagara was built, and passed over the portage while the elder Joncaire yet maintained his *Magazin Royal* under the heights of Lewiston. With him, or soon joining him in the West, was his eldest son, also named Nicolas Antoine. This youth again passed over the Niagara portage in the fall of 1730, bearing messages from his father's post to Quebec.

In 1731 the elder Coulon de Villiers was at Fort Niagara *en route* to Quebec. A little later he was made commandant at Green Bay, with the rank of captain; and at that post he was killed in 1733.[11]

It is recorded that he had with him at Green Bay, six sons and two sons-in-law. The latter were Duplessis-Faber and Dagneau Douville. One of the sons, François, afterwards the Chevalier de Villiers, was wounded; and with his brother-in-law, Douville, carried to Quebec the news of what had happened at Green Bay. They probably journeyed by the Niagara route, as did the elder brother Nicolas Antoine, who signed himself "Coulon de Villiers," and is referred to in documents as "M. Coulon." He was made lieutenant in 1734, and succeeded his father in command at Green Bay, and later at St. Joseph of the Illinois. In 1742, or early in 1743, we find him again at Fort Niagara, on his way to Quebec, where he soon after married under the name and title of Captain Antoine Coulon, Sieur de Villiers. His later service was in eastern Canada, and he died at Montreal in 1750, having won the coveted Cross of St. Louis.[12]

A younger and more famous brother was Joseph Coulon de Villiers, called de Jumonville. Born at Verchères in 1718, he was a lad of 15 when he first came to the Niagara in 1733, on his way to Green Bay, where he served under his father. He came again in 1739, as did also his brother François, with that fine company of young soldiers who made the Chica-

[11] Ferland, II, 440.
[12] Numerous writers, Parkman among them, have credited to this Coulon de Villiers the defeat of Washington at Fort Necessity in 1754; but if he died in 1750, as the Abbé Amédée Gosselin asserts in his painstaking study ("*Notes sur la Famille Coulon de Villiers*," Lévis, 1906), the hero of 1754 was obviously not Nicolas Antoine. The Abbé Gosselin's monograph rests on records found in parish registers, the official correspondence of Governors, and other original sources.

saw campaign.[13] In succeeding years he saw hard service in Acadia, and in the Mohawk Valley, where in 1748 he led an expedition against the English, killing 14 or 15.[14] He served with Céloron in 1749,[15] as did his brother François; and was again on the Niagara in 1754, a few weeks before his death. Of his last coming into the region we here study, further note will be made in due place.

Jumonville's death left but two brothers, Louis and François, both older than himself. It was the former who was to be the avenger of Jumonville; and it was François — afterwards styled the Chevalier de Villiers — who was to share in the last French defense of the Niagara, and there become a prisoner of the English.

An episode of some significance, in the summer of 1751, was the tour around Lake Ontario and up the Niagara made by the Sulpitian missionary, François Picquet. No other man of his time, save possibly Chabert de Joncaire, exerted a greater influence over the Indians of the mid-lake region.

Born at Bourg in Bresse, France, December 4, 1708, we find him at the age of 27, arrived in Montreal a member of the Company of St. Sulpice. In the five or six years following, while fulfilling his priestly duties he devoted himself to the study of native dialects. Capable and exceptionally zealous, it is said of him that by 1740 he " made known the sovereignty of France among the Algonquins, Nipissings, Iroquois and Hurons." At the mission of Lac des Deux Montagnes — now Oka, near Montreal — he gained such mastery of the Algonquin and Iroquois tongues that, says Fournet, " he surpassed the ablest orators of those tribes." [16] The mission became populous, a Catholic center in the midst of pagan tribes. Visitors at Oka to-day are shown the Calvary erected by Father

[13] MSS., *Collection Moreau St. Méry* (*Arch. de la Marine;* copies in the Archives at Ottawa), vol. 44. In these papers one finds the names of " M. de Villiers " and of the " Chevalier de Villiers." The latter was François.

[14] N. Y. Col. Docs. X, 168.

[15] This service of Jumonville is not mentioned by the Abbé Amédée Gosselin, but is indicated by the official correspondence of the time.

[16] Article " Picquet " in the Catholic Encyclopædia.

Picquet, with its well-built stations stretching along the mountain side facing the lake.

The Abbé Picquet's influence over the tribes was for many years combated by the English. During the inter-colonial strife of 1743-48, it was Picquet who held the Five Nations in virtual neutrality, while the tribes which were open allies of the French harried New England with their bloody raids, or served as scouts and aides of the French troops.

In June, 1749, the Abbé founded his famous mission of La Présentation, now the city of Ogdensburg. To gather recruits for this establishment he set out, early in the summer of 1751, on a tour around Lake Ontario. The record of this interesting journey is preserved in a memoir by one from whom we would little expect a chronicle of missionary labors. It was written by Joseph Jérôme de Lalande, the eminent astronomer, famed alike for his scientific attainments and for his lack of Christian faith. The atheist is the biographer of the missionary. Born in 1732, in Picquet's native town of Bourg, Lalande was but 28 when the Abbé returned to France, and but 20 when, in 1753, Picquet visited France. It was then that he first gave Lalande an account of his adventures. " A missionary," wrote the younger man of the elder, " praiseworthy for his zeal and for the services which he has rendered to Church and State, born in the same town as I, and with whom I have been intimate, has put it in my power to set forth his labors. I have thought this account worthy of place in the *Lettres édifiantes* . . . and have been pleased to be able to offer honorable testimony to the memory of a compatriot and friend as estimable as the Abbé Picquet." [17]

It is not, however, from Lalande, but from the Abbé Picquet's own journal,[18] that we draw an account of his tour around Lake Ontario.

[17] "*Lettres édifiantes et curieuses (Mémoires des Indes),*" Paris, 1783, vol. XXVI. André Chagny's recent work, "*Un defenseur de la Nouvelle France, François Piçquet 'Le Canadien,'*" (Paris, 1913), draws largely on Lalande's memoir. See also: "*Le Fondateur de la Présentation,*" by the Abbé Auguste Gosselin. Trans. Roy. Soc. Canada, 1894.

[18] MS. copies are preserved in the Canadian Archives, and in the library of the Buffalo Historical Society.

Setting out June 10th, from his mission at the mouth of the Oswegatchie, the little flotilla, consisting of a "king's bateau," in which were the missionary, the Chevalier Le Borgne, and six Canadians, and a bark canoe paddled by "five faithful savages," made its way through the islands, reaching Fort Frontenac on the 12th. The abbé was struck by the weak and half-abandoned aspect of the place, where thirty soldiers "with a handful of militia" constituted the garrison. The missionary laments that the bread and the milk were bad and there was "not brandy enough to dress a wound."

At Kaoi (Coui), a few hours to the west of Frontenac, the missionary was amazed to encounter a negro, a fugitive from Virginia, who informed him that it would not be difficult to draw to his mission "most of the negroes and negresses of New England"—evidently meaning the English colonies—since they would be well received in Canada if they could be given assistance during the first year, and granted lands like the *habitants*. "The Indians," said the Virginia refugee, "would gladly serve them as guides; the negroes would be the most terrible enemies of the English, realizing that they could never hope for pardon, if the English should become masters of Canada; and they would contribute greatly to the development of the colony by their labor." He added that there were also Hollanders, Lorrains and Swiss who would follow the example of the blacks, "since they were uncomfortable with the English and did not love them."

Considerable might be gathered regarding the negro in the Lakes region in Colonial times. So many negro slaves ran away to the French in Canada, from New York and Albany, that in 1745 the New York Assembly passed an Act to prevent it. There were negroes among the Indians of the Lakes region at an early date but they were never numerous. In 1736 Louis Campau had two negro slaves at Detroit, the presumption being that they had gone thither by way of the Niagara. New York was a slave-holding colony, from which some negroes made their way into the Iroquois country and even Canada. In January, 1753, four English traders, Alexander McGenty, Jabez Evans, David Hendricks and William

Powell, were taken on "Kantucqui" River near the Ohio, by a band of Caghnawagas, who plundered them and brought them to Fort Niagara, whence they were later sent to Montreal. Their captors valued each man at 400 livres ($80 to $100), and wanted negro boys —" little slaves "— in exchange. The proposition and basis of exchange, roused the indignation of the *Pennsylvania Gazette*. " By this insulting letter," it said,[19] " we may see the contempt in which we are held by these savages." A letter in French, purporting to come from the chief Ononraquiete, had reached Colonel Schuyler, saying these Indians would return no more prisoners alive unless paid for. " If they are suffered to go on in this manner," continued the *Gazette*, " and to make a trade of catching our people and selling them to us again for 400 livres a head, it may in time cost us more to satisfy the demands of that handful of barbarians than would serve to defend the Province against all its enemies."

The memoir does not state whether these propositions found favor with the abbé. Zealous as he was for building up his mission, we find no mention of negro or other recruits there, save his beloved Indians.

Making his way through the winding passages of the Bay of Quinté, the Abbé Picquet next visited the scene of the early Sulpitian mission where, as early as 1668, two young priests, the Abbé Trouvé and François de Salignac-Fénelon — a relative of the renowned author of " *Télémaque* "— had labored among fugitive Cayugas. Here, too, were associations of Dollier de Casson, of the Abbé d'Urfé and other Sulpitian missionaries whose presence here more than eighty years before, may well have made this part of his journey seem to the Abbé Picquet a veritable pilgrimage.

Skirting the shore to the westward, he arrived at the fort of Toronto, June 24th. The new establishment there had been officially named Fort Rouillé, for the Count de Jouy, Antoine Louis Rouillé, who in 1749 had succeeded Count Maurepas as Colonial Minister of France. The Count was eminent, escially as a patron of letters; was the head of the Royal Li-

[19] Aug. 15, 1754.

brary and the friend of authors; but his name found slight hold in the Lake Ontario region, and the Abbé Picquet, like most of the men of his time, always spoke of Fort Rouillé as the fort of Toronto.

At the date of his visit, it was but a year old. The bay and river of Toronto — now the Humber — from days immemorial had been part of a traveled highway to Lake Simcoe and the Georgian Bay. The mouth of the river had long been a place of trade; but no substantial buildings were erected here until the spring of 1750, when La Galissonière, spurred on by the increasing trade of his rivals across the lake at Oswego, accomplished here the erection of a storehouse, protected by a stockade. Fifteen soldiers and a few workmen constituted the garrison. In fact, during its first winter, there were only a clerk or trader's agent, two or three *engagés*, and a few Indians. The Abbé Picquet does not describe the buildings, though he says he found good bread and wine there and everything requisite for trade, " which they lack at all the other posts." Captain Pouchot, who saw Fort Rouillé a little later, found it a palisaded square of about 30 *toises* (180 feet), with flanks of 15 feet. The curtains formed the buildings of the fort. He thought it better built for trade than for defense. A plan of Captain Gother Mann, many years later, shows five buildings within the French stockade.[20]

The Mississagas gathered in numbers about the missionary within the stockade, where there was neither church nor chapel, and in behalf of their wives and children begged for as good treatment as the Iroquois had had. " They complained that instead of building a church for them, there had only been provided a brandy shop " (" *qu'un cabaret d'eau-de-vie* "). Picquet checked them in their fault-finding, told them that they had been treated according to their taste, that they had never shown the least zeal for religion, that their conduct had been opposed to it, but that the Iroquois, on the contrary, had shown their love for Christianity. So it seemed, no doubt, to

[20] " Plan of the proposed Toronto Harbour," etc., Quebec, 6th Dec., 1788. The group of old French buildings is marked on the map, " Ruins of a trading fort, Toronto."

the good priest; though from the general trend of historical testimony one may be permitted some reservation of judgment. The missionary bethought himself in time, that his leave to gather recruits for his mission did not include the Mississagas; and so, although they indicated a readiness to follow him, he could not bid them do so, and hastened on his way.

On June 27th, the abbé landed at Fort Niagara. It was the fête of the holy apostles Peter and Paul, and the missionary's first act was to celebrate Mass in the chapel of the fort. He makes no mention of the resident chaplain. After dinner, in company with the commandant, M. de Becancour, he looked over the fort, " there being no savages with whom he might speak."

Triangular in form, the fort presented only one face open to land attack. That was 300 feet long, looking out upon a wood from which it was separated by an open plain. On this side, approach was easy. On the other sides, it commanded at once both lake and river, to the north and to the southwest, where its walls rose above natural slopes sufficiently steep to make scaling difficult. The visitor commented on the wide view enjoyed from the fort, which made it easy to see all canoes and barques which came to land there; " but the high banks," he wrote, " little by little are washed away by the rain, notwithstanding the great expense the King has been to, to maintain them." This encroachment of the lake continued for more than a century. There were originally several rods of ground to the north of the stone mess-house or " castle," so that the garrison garden was there. Gradually it crumbled into the lake, until, in the latter part of the last century, the United States Government put in protective work which appears to have stayed the invasion of the lake, the banks of which, at this point, are some 25 feet high.

Much had been said, even in Picquet's day, of the insecurity of Fort Niagara from this cause. He was familiar with the complaint current at Versailles, that the site was an unfortunate one, involving constant cost to maintain; and he no doubt was aware that La Galissonière had but recently, in all seriousness, proposed to move the fort to the other side of the river, now the site of Niagara-on-the-Lake. "It is evident to me," wrote Maurepas to La Galissonière, "that by the bad choice of a site for Fort Niagara, this fort is exposed to continued wearing away [of the earth banks], and the expenses for repairs, since it was built prove only too well the truth of it. However, before the King shall approve the proposition which you make, of transporting the fort to the other side of the river, it is well that you should consider more fully the advantages to follow this change, not only as regards the solidity of the fort, but in its effect on the Indian trade, for it has been urged that this change would tend to stay most of those who go to Oswego." [21]

The abbé, though not an engineer, came to the conclusion that the present site was not so bad as had been represented; and recorded the opinion that the space between the high land and the wharf might be filled in so as to support it and make a glacis there.

He was disappointed not to find at the fort the Indians whom he was told came there to trade; and set out for the portage fort above the falls in the hope of finding them there. On his way he turned aside to view the great cataract, of which he wrote:

This cascade is as marvelous for its height and the volume of water which descends as for the diversity of its falls, of which there are six principal ones, separated by a little island, which puts three to the north and three to the south. They are, together, of a singular symmetry and an astonishing effect. It is one of the mightiest cataracts which there may be in all the world. We heard it, far off. Near, one is well compensated for the deafening noise which the waters make in seeing the whirlpools and the jets which shoot from the clear and limpid depths, bedecked with the brilliant colors of the rainbow. The falls are nearly always covered with mist.

The description is not conspicuously accurate. The Abbé Picquet measured the height of the fall on the south side — doubtless at Prospect Point — reporting it as 140 feet, *i.e.*,

[21] *Archives du Ministère des Colonies,* series B. vol. 87, p. 7.

French measure, equivalent to 149.2 English feet; an approximately accurate measurement.

On June 29th the missionary and his companions passed up the portage and sought lodging at the new fort. "I was received by M. Chabert Joncaire," he wrote in his journal, "with every sort of politeness and with much joy by the savages." His description of Fort Little Niagara has already been given (p. 379). On July 1st, M. de Rigauville, fort major at Niagara, and three of Abbé Picquet's Indians went up to the Little Rapid — the outlet of Lake Erie — and exacted a promise from the chief residing there, that he would come to meet the missionary.

At the Little Fort, and on the river in general, the abbé found trade depressed, for the same reason that he had noted at Frontenac and Niagara. "The savages, who come there in great number," he wrote of the Portage, "had every disposition to carry on trade; but not finding what they want, they go on to Oswego." He deplored the carelessness or incompetence of the functionaries of the Intendant, the more when he counted on occasion as many as fifty canoes on the strand under the palisades of the Little Fort. He adds the conviction that "several hundred" of them would have landed their peltries if the storehouse had been better provided with goods for exchange.

He was, however, gratified to meet here large numbers of the Indians. He gathered many of the Senecas about him, talked to them like a father, counseled them to beware of brandy, and pledged them to join his establishment of La Présentation. They seem to have taken the summons with great seriousness, for as a guarantee that they would keep their word they gave him twelve young boys. "Parents," they assured him, "have nothing dearer than their children. Behold, we give you twelve as hostages, and as proof that we will soon follow you." The chief of the Little Rapid, whom Picquet's christianized Indians had exhorted "like veritable apostles," assured the missionary that he would join his train with all his family.

The incident introduces, all too vaguely, the first aborigine of influence and authority who is associated with the present site of Buffalo. We do not know his name. No permanent Seneca village existed hereabouts at that period. But the "Little Rapid" was the outlet of Lake Erie, and the chief who took his name from it evidently brought his people to the vicinity for fishing and a temporary camp. He antedated by a generation the Indians who are the first we know by name as residents of the region; and appears as the First Citizen, if not the first "Boss" of the site over which now spreads the city of Buffalo.

The Abbé Picquet was pleased by the obvious success of his mission to the Portage, and grateful to Daniel de Joncaire, who, he says, "has forgotten nothing that would help me accomplish my purpose, and comports himself like a good servant of God and the King."

One day when the missionary was reading his breviary in the neighboring forest, all the Indians who were in the habit of resorting to the portage fort, met there in secret council. The reason of this mysterious confab proved to be that, fearing for the life of the missionary, they wished to persuade him, in returning to La Présentation, not to go by way of Oswego. They begged Chabert to use his influence; whereupon the commandant, perhaps taking the thing seriously, sought his guest at the edge of the woods. "Your Indians and the Senecas," he said, "know your firmness of decision. Learning of your purpose to return by way of Oswego, they have urgently begged me to pledge you not to do it. They are aware of the designs of the English, who regard you as their most redoubtable enemy, the one who can do them most injury. They would sooner be cut in pieces than that you should come to any harm. But," added Chabert, "all that amounts to nothing, and the Indians, your 'children,' will lose you forever through the devices of that nation which hates you. On my own account, I beg you not to pass that way."

Touched by this solicitude, the abbé thanked the officer. He was loth to change his plans, but in order not to grieve his dear

Indians, he acquiesced with their desires in the vague formula: "It shall be as you wish, my children." [22]

When, on July 3d, the abbé set out to return to Fort Niagara, he was escorted by Chabert, the commandant, M. Rigauville, interpreter, and an imposing train of savages. The missionary led off with his own Indians; Chabert and Rigauville followed with the recruits. The return, down the old portage road took on an aspect somewhat remarkable: "Everywhere as we passed," wrote the abbé, "at every place where there were camps, cabins, storehouses, the Indians saluted us with a discharge of firearms. That happened so often that I thought all the trees along the way were loaded with powder."

This return to Niagara, along the old portage path through the woods and down the green hills, presents a cheerful picture to the imagination. Nor is it wholly a matter of imagination, for we have his friend Lalande's word for it that the priest, in spite of the dignity of his calling, was the embodiment of high spirits and good humor. "Of an imposing commanding figure, he had an open and engaging countenance. He was of a gay disposition. Notwithstanding the exactions of his office, he exhaled only gayety. He made conversions to the music of instruments; he was theologian, orator, poet. He sang and composed canticles, now in French, now in Iroquois, with which he amused and interested the savages. He was indeed a child to some, a hero to others. His mechanical ingenuity often won the admiration of the Indians. In short, he knew how to use all proper means for drawing proselytes and attaching them to him. As a result, he had all the success that could reward his industry, his talents and zeal."

Such a portrait, drawn by an intimate and friendly hand, warrants a touch of lightness and of color in the present sketch. It was evidently with a robust school-boy's exuberant overflow of animal spirits that the abbé led his train of yelling and powder-wasting savages down the slopes. He might well

[22] Lalande gravely records the formidable vocable supposed to embody this idea: "*Ethonciaouin*"!

exult. He had won a goodly following of the primitive folk he came to seek. His missionary tour prospered. He had perhaps done something to check the enemy. It was not the hour for austerity, and so in high spirits, with song and noisy banter and salvos of muskets, he led the gay and volatile retinue to the Lewiston plateau, where he took leave of his hosts of the Portage and with 39 Indians [23] embarked for Fort Niagara.

He was received at the fort with ceremony and a salvo of cannon. The next day, for the first time, he gathered all his Seneca recruits in the chapel of the fort where he preached to them, made them say some prayers, and gave them presents. The Niagara, more than any other place visited in his tour, had yielded the recruits he sought.

It was on July 6th that he finally embarked, having waited for the chief of the Little Rapid, followed by a numerous flotilla of canoes, and coasted the lake shore to the eastward. Entering the Genesee River on the 12th, the priest " encountered a mass of rattlesnakes; the young Indians leaped into their midst and killed 42, without being bitten." After viewing the lower falls of the Genesee the journey was resumed. On the 14th they reached Sodus Bay, which Father Picquet thought a good place for the French to fortify; " but," he adds, " it will be still better to destroy Oswego, and never let the English rebuild it." On the 16th, he arrived opposite this post; and to keep the pledge given to Chabert, did not stop there, but viewed the post in passing, drawing as near to shore in his boats as seemed discreet. He judged the place would be easy of capture: " Two batteries, each of three 12-pounders, would be more than enough to reduce it to ashes." He passed thence across the lake to Frontenac, where he was received with ceremony, half military and half religious. By July 20th he was again at his beloved mission on the Oswegatchie. The tour around Ontario had been far from fruitless. It is reported that in the next year 392 Indian families went there to live, and that on one occasion 132 converts were baptised by Mgr. de Pontbriand, the last French Bishop of

[23] So says Picquet's own memoir: " *Nous s'embarqua avec 39 sauvages, dans mon grand canot.*"

Quebec. A banner, still preserved at the Oka mission, perpetuates the memory of this event. The conditions of trade at the lake posts and on the Niagara had greatly interested Picquet, whose comments thereon give color to the report that his tour was made not merely in the capacity of a missionary, but as a secret agent of the French Government. He noted that the great menace of Oswego lay not in its military strength, but in the fact that it gave to the English an easy means of communication with the Indian tribes to the north and west. He learned too that the storehouse at Oswego was stocked, not only with goods for the Indian trade, but with articles which only the French would care for. This pointed to an illicit trade. If the orders of the Minister had been followed, he wrote, " the Oswego trade, at least with the Indians of Upper Canada, would be almost ruined; but it was necessary to supply Niagara, and especially the Portage, rather than Toronto. The difference between the first two of these posts and the last is, that 300 or 400 canoes could come to the Niagara Portage, loaded with peltries; while there could only come by way of Toronto such canoes as could not pass by Niagara and on to Frontenac, such as the Otaois (Ottawas) from the head of the lake and the Mississagas; so that Toronto could not but lessen the trade of these two old posts, which would have been more than sufficient to stop all the Indians, if the storehouses had been supplied with goods to their taste. The English should have been imitated in the matter of trinkets which they sell to the Indians, such as silver bracelets, etc. The storekeeper at Niagara assured me that they compared and weighed them, and found that the bracelets from Oswego, which were as heavy, of as pure silver and more elegant, cost only two beaver-skins, as against ten, asked for them at the King's posts; so that we are discredited and this silver-work remains a dead loss in the store-houses."

The Indians relished French brandy better than English rum; but the abbé noticed that this did not keep the thirsty from going to Oswego for their liquor. " To destroy this trade, the King's posts should be supplied with the same goods as Oswego, and at the same price."

Note has been made (Chap. XIV) of difficulties occasioned by the liquor traffic in the earlier years of Fort Niagara. Those difficulties never ceased; but whereas in the earlier years it was the administrators of the Colony who sought to regulate it, or the priests who grieved at the harm it did, in later years it was the Indians themselves who asked to be saved from this great temptation. Over and over again in the reports of councils and conferences, this touching appeal is made. At a general meeting of the Six Nations held at Onondaga, September 10, 1753, being the conclusion of a long confab between Sir William Johnson and the Mohawks, the savages begged that the sale of rum at Oswego be stopped; to which Sir William replied that it would greatly please the French, to see the sale of liquor stopped at Oswego, if they could still sell " what they thought fitt " at Niagara. " I expected they [the Indians] would first hinder the French selling liquor there, before they proposed having it stopped at Oswego." It never was stopped at either place.

In the summer of 1751, Lieutenant Benjamin Stoddart, stationed at Oswego, reported the passing of a French expedition, bound for the chief town of the Miamis, where the English were trading and were said to have built a stone house. For a good many years Stoddart — usually referred to as Captain — gave useful service to New York Colony, at Oswego and elsewhere, in gathering information about the French. On more than one occasion he was sent to Quebec to negotiate the exchange of prisoners, and by reason of these visits, was better informed than most of the English as to conditions in Canada. That the General Assembly was slow in his case, as in some others, to reimburse expenditures made in the public service, is indicated in one of Stoddart's outspoken letters: " I shall be obliged to depend on the D—d Assembly for what is due to me. Shall expect very little for my trouble, as you are sensible they are such D—d S——d—ls." [24]

For many years the Oswego Supply Act named the Commissioner, who was sometimes the Commandant. In 1744, Lieutenant John Lindesay, in a letter to the General Assembly,

[24] Stoddart to Col. Wm. Johnson, Mch. 7, 1748–9.

recommended himself for Commissary. He was a Scotchman of good family, a man of repute in the Colony, whose memory is especially cherished to this day at Cherry Valley, of which once thriving community he was the founder. He was given the desired appointment,[25] and continued the most able and active representative of English interests in the Lake region, until his death in 1751. His name usually appears in the documents as " Lindsay," " Lindsy " or otherwise misspelled. He was so efficient in gathering the frontier news, and reporting to his Government the movements and plans of the French, that they presently came to refer to him in their correspondence as " Lindsay the Spy."

He had his troubles, at Oswego. In his zeal to strengthen the place, he made repairs which the Council of the General Assembly were discouragingly slow to pay for, although he had submitted estimates, and was diligent in dunning. In 1745, he paid out for repairs more than £193; but was allowed only £140. His financial necessities, incurred for the good of the Colony, are the burden of many letters.

On an April day in 1750 there appeared at Lieutenant Lindesay's headquarters none other than Chabert de Joncaire himself. Although the war between the rival Powers was over, one cannot believe that great cordiality had sprung up between French and English on Lake Ontario. Even in times of professed peace, French visitors at Oswego were few. It was the more remarkable, that the most notorious ⌐d mischievous of them all should favor Lindesay with a visit. Chabert was on his way to Niagara from Montreal where, as has been related, he had just been commissioned to build and command a fort above the Falls, and it is characteristic that he should cross his rival's threshold and with complacent audacity tell of his new commission. " He said," Lindesay reported to the Governor, " he was going to command the new fort on the carrying place above Niagara." The report [26] speaks of Cha-

[25] A sketch of his career (N. Y. Col. Docs., VI, 707, *note*) says he was Commandant at Oswego until Feb., 1749, and thereafter Indian Commissary and agent. In a letter to the Lords of Trade, June 13, 1751, Gov. Clinton speaks of him as " Commandant and Commissary."
[26] N. Y. Col. Docs. VI, 706.

bert as " Joncaire's brother," and tells of " Joncaire " as active on the Ohio. Lindesay was not likely to confuse the two, and his statement is entitled to weight as showing that both brothers shared in service on the Ohio.

Lindesay kept well informed regarding Chabert's operations to the westward. May 30th, he wrote to Governor Clinton that " the French are building a fortified house on the river Oniagara between the Lakes Erie and Cadaraqui." In July there came in on him a band of savages led by the Bunt and the Black Prince's son. These singular names designate two chiefs who were familiar figures on the Niagara at this period, but regarding whom little that is definite appears in the records. They told Lindesay that the French had not only built at the Niagara carrying-place, but also on the Ohio; that they had landed a large expedition at Niagara, were going to drive all the English traders from the Ohio, and compel the Miamis, who were most addicted to English trade, to remove from their old towns and live where the French should order them.

Lindesay entertained the Bunt, for his friendship was worth cultivating; and sent on his reports, true and false, for the edification of the Council and Assembly. In this same month of July Lindesay had yet more news from the Cayuga chief Attrowaney, who had been at Fort Frontenac, " where they were building a large ship, which was to have three masts." He had seen there six cannon three yards long with a wide bore, and was told the French were going to cross the lake and take Oswego. Lindesay reported it to Colonel Johnson; and probably also to others; it was perhaps his last report, for he died that year. His services at Oswego were varied and valuable; and the reports here noted well illustrate the method by which intelligence of the enemy was gathered on these frontiers.

END OF VOL. I

www.ingramcontent.com/pod-product-compliance
Lightning Source LLC
Chambersburg PA
CBHW050245230426
43664CB00012B/1834